Invitation to Social Theory

An Invitation to Social Theory

DAVID INGLIS
with CHRISTOPHER THORPE

polity

First published in 2012 by Polity Press

Reprinted 2012 (twice), 2013

Polity Press
65 Bridge Street
Cambridge CB2 1UR, UK

Polity Press
350 Main Street
Malden, MA 02148, USA

ISBN-13: 978-0-7456-4208-6 (hardback)
ISBN-13: 978-0-7456-4209-3 (paperback)

A catalogue record for this book is available from the British Library.

Typeset in 11.25 on 13 pt Monotype Dante
by Toppan Best-set Premedia Limited
Printed and bound in Great Britain by MPG Books Group Limited, Bodmin, Cornwall

The publisher has used its best endeavours to ensure that the URLs for external websites referred to in this book are correct and active at the time of going to press. However, the publisher has no responsibility for the websites and can make no guarantee that a site will remain live or that the content is or will remain appropriate.

Every effort has been made to trace all copyright holders, but if any have been inadvertently overlooked the publisher will be pleased to include any necessary credits in any subsequent reprint or edition.

For further information on Polity, visit our website: www.politybooks.com

Contents

Figures and Tables

Figures

Tables

Introduction: Extending an Invitation

My friend, all theory is grey, but life – life is green

– The Devil to Faust

Theory is Grey?

Faust is a story about a man who sells his soul to the Devil in return for love, riches and power. Explaining to him why his current life is deadening and pointless, the Devil says that he has spent far too much of it cooped up in his study, poring over the theories of dead philosophers, when he should have been outside, in the 'real world', enjoying all that life has to offer. 'Theory is grey', argues the Devil, a mere shadow of real life, an exercise engaged in by those too timid or too dull to grasp all the opportunities that the outside world affords.

This may well be your own feeling as you open this book. It is a sad fact, but many students before they begin a social theory course – especially if they have never taken one before – feel a sense of gloom descending upon them. The thought of taking a theory class can fill you with trepidation. Thoughts that might be going through your head can include:

> *Isn't theory impossible to understand?*
> *Isn't theory really difficult?*
> *Isn't theory boring?*
> *Isn't theory completely unrelated to the rest of my studies?*
> *Isn't theory not for me?*

The answer to these questions is: *no*.

It *is* the case that social theory can be difficult to understand – but only at first. Yes, it is often written in ways you have to work hard at to understand. A lot of it is not immediately comprehensible. Yes, theory will be boring and tedious – if you are absolutely convinced it will be boring and tedious. Yes, theory can seem disconnected from the rest of your studies. It is sometimes not immediately obvious how it relates to other, more empirical courses, or those dealing with research methods. Yes, it can seem to stand in isolation, not just from other parts of your degree, but the 'real world' more generally. Yes, it can seem like eavesdropping on a conversation involving people whom you don't know, whom you can't understand and therefore whom you don't like much. Yes, it can seem like something that has little or no relevance to your own life.

But all of that is just one side of social theory, its downside. But that is just one part of the story, and not a very large part. On the upside, there are a number of very important pluses.

In the first case, you have to draw a crucial distinction: between ideas and the words they are expressed in. Let's take the words first. Often it is the case that people who write social theory express themselves in what, for the newcomer, seem like excessively difficult ways. Learning about theory is like learning a new language. You wouldn't expect to go to a country you had never been to before, had little prior knowledge of, and couldn't speak the language of, and expect to understand everything going on there straight away. You have to put some effort in initially in order to work out what is going on. Then once you have started to have some idea of what people are like and what they are doing, you have to work some more to get a basic grasp of the language. Entering the world of social theory is like going to such a country. You are going to have to put in some effort to work out what is going on initially. You will have to start to understand the language that is being used. There's no avoiding the fact that you are going to have to put in some effort to understand what the people are saying, and why they are saying it.

But you have an advantage. You understand English, and the social theory you will be reading is in English. Translators have put a great deal of effort into putting the ideas of social theorists whose first language is not English into that language. Now, it may seem at first that all social theorists, even the native English speakers, are hardly writing in English at all, so unfamiliar does their use of it seem. Bear in mind some reasons for that. It is true that some of them do write rather badly, with clumsy expressions and needless complication. Some of them should have gone on creative writing courses to make their writing better!

However, it is also the case that social theory does need to be written in particular ways. You would not expect to read a book about theoretical physics, and expect to understand it all if you had little or no background in physics. Physicists and other natural scientists have to speak to each other in their own special language. They need to write in what outsiders regard as a cryptic way, because they have to assume that the people they are writing for already have a pretty good knowledge of the issues being discussed. If these scientists had constantly to explain everything about what they are saying, then what currently takes a book to say would take a hundred books to say. Scientists necessarily have to write in a kind of short-hand, so that they can get their messages across in an efficient way. Writing in a kind of code means that you don't have to keep laying bare all of the assumptions and taken-for-granted ideas that you assume the people you are writing for already know. Expressing yourself in the accepted code that is known by other people like you, means you can quickly and efficiently say new things, without constantly having to explain yourself. *All* languages work like that, including the one that you use every day.

Exactly the same is true of social theory authors. They have to write in a kind of code that other social theorists can understand. If they didn't, they would constantly have to be explaining *everything* – and that would take up a vast amount of time, space and energy. So just as people like physicists express themselves in their own particular code, so too do social theorists, and this is unavoidable. So to understand social theory, you have to 'crack' that code. Once you have cracked it, you'll be in the inside of the social theory world, understanding what goes on and why, rather than being stuck on the outside looking in, as you may be feeling at the moment.

This book is intended to help you crack the code of social theory. More precisely, it is meant to help you crack the various different sorts of codes used in social theory. The book gives you a sense of major social theories and theorists. Each of these uses a distinctive type of code. This book is going to help you understand each of them – both in terms of *what* they are saying and *how* they are saying it.

Let's return to the distinction you should make – between ideas and the words they are expressed in. The book will help you crack the codes of each main type of social theory and the works of the major social theorists who have worked within each type. In so doing, it will help you understand their main ideas and concepts – what these are, how they fit together to make up a coherent 'theory', how they differ from and also overlap with the ideas and concepts of other sorts of theory, and what their significance is, both for social theory, for people in the 'real world', and, crucially, *for you*.

A really important thing to realize is that *even if the language of social theory is difficult, the ideas which that language expresses are not really very difficult at all.* Social theory is a lot easier to understand than it first looks. You will see that once you have cracked some of the codes. Looking back at some point in the future, you will see that what at first may have intimidated you was actually not really all that difficult. Social theorists are generally intelligent and talented people. But what they are saying is not somehow radically different from the thoughts of 'mere mortals'. Social theories are in many ways just worked-up versions of what we all know anyway, if often in semi-conscious ways.

This is because what social theorists are trying to understand is the nature of human life, both in general and in terms of the specific forms it has taken in the past and which it takes today. All they are doing is trying to express certain thoughts about things *you already know a lot about.* These include why people act in certain ways, how human beings interact with each other, and how what we do is influenced by other people and the things around us. As you read through the book there should be regular flashes of recognition, where you think 'so that's what they are saying!', because the things social theorists are talking about are in many ways things that you already know a lot about and which happen to you and around you all the time. Once you have cracked the code used by a particular thinker or school of thought to express their ideas, you will see that the things they are referring to are things that are in many respects recognizable to you.

In addition to that, though, social theory can *reveal* things to you. Sometimes these are things that you sort of knew about or were dimly aware of, but which by understanding what social theorists have said about them, you can see these things and their significance much more clearly. At other times, you will discover things that you were not at all aware of before. These might well include the historical reasons, created over centuries, lying behind how we think and interact with each other today (see especially Chapters 1 and 7 in this regard). Social theories of various types do not just get us to see our present-day activities in a new light, they also want to show us how these were constructed over time by people in the past.

So cracking the codes of social theory can allow you to see things you weren't aware of before. But a lot of the time social theory is just putting into a slightly new form, and into new words, things already familiar to you. In that sense social theory is not something completely alien to you. Because it draws upon things you already know, or things that you were partly aware of, social theory *is already part of you* – it's just that you don't know that fully yet. This book will help you see how this is the case.

Structure of the Book

If you read the whole book through, and think carefully about what is being said in each chapter, then by the end of it, you will have cracked the various codes of social theory. In so doing, you will go a long way along the path that has to be travelled in order to learn anything. You start off from a point where social theory seems to be both alien and unfamiliar. But as you go along the path, it will seem more and more familiar, until you get to a point that you start to feel comfortable with it, and you no longer feel intimidated by it. After that point has been reached, the journey becomes easier, because the terrain you are travelling through seems ever more recognizable.

This is in large part because you will start to see recurrent things (themes and ideas) turning up again and again. This raises an important point about the world of social theory as a whole. In order to make sense of it, the book has been divided up into different chapters, each covering a major 'school of thought' or 'paradigm' in social theory. Simply what we mean by this is that in each chapter we have presented the ideas of particular theorists who have a lot in common with each other, often writing explicitly in light of each other's ideas, engaged in a dialogue of like-minded thinkers.

But just because we have arranged the book into chapters dealing with different paradigms does not mean to say that there is not a great deal of overlap between different paradigms. Different thinkers and schools of thought often borrow, take up or criticize the same sorts of ideas and themes. The paradigms we present are not self-enclosed and isolated from each other. Instead, they should be seen as often quite loose assemblages of ideas that often have a lot more in common with other paradigms than it may at first seem. One of the less appealing aspects of some social theorists is their tendency to present their ideas as if they were wholly unique, and completely different from other people's ideas. But generally this is not the case, because 'different' paradigms often take ideas from the same sources, and although they use them in different ways, certain resemblances and similarities remain between apparently very different theories and approaches.

Another less-than-admirable tendency of some authors is to present their ideas as if they were totally unprecedented and that no one had ever thought them up before. But social theory as it has developed over the last one hundred years or so – which is the focus of this book – is basically a patchwork of ideas of earlier thinkers being borrowed by later thinkers, and then being transformed for new (or sometimes not-so-new) purposes. Sometimes the debts to earlier thinkers are clear, sometimes they are hidden, even sometimes deliberately covered up. What the book gives you is a map of the main tendencies in social theory over the last century and a half. Wherever appropriate, it will be highlighted where particular later thinkers have taken up and used the ideas of earlier ones.

This is why we start the book with a depiction of the ideas of the so-called 'classical theorists', those who lived and wrote in the nineteenth and early twentieth centuries. In many ways what is called 'modern' or 'contemporary' social theory involves playing around with and transforming the ideas of the classical social theorists. Some new elements that are purely twentieth century in origin – notably the ideas of Sigmund Freud, Ferdinand de Saussure and Ludwig Wittgenstein – get added into the mix as time goes on. But in very important ways, theory nowadays is still a response to, and involves diverse uses and transformations of, the ideas first created in the nineteenth century by the classical authors, such as Marx, Weber, Durkheim and Simmel.

But as we make clear in Chapter 1, these classical thinkers also had their sources that they took inspiration from. At the very heart of almost all social theory are the concepts of the German philosophers Immanuel Kant and Georg Hegel. Their work had a huge influence on the classical social theorists, in all sorts of diverse ways. You can't really understand 'classical social theory' unless you understand the basic aspects of Kant's and Hegel's thinking. Although their philosophies are complex, luckily the essential issues that inform social theory are easy enough to understand if explained clearly – which is what Chapter 1 is concerned with.

The shadows of Kant and Hegel continued to fall over more modern social theory, sometimes mediated through the appropriation of their ideas by the classical theorists, sometimes more directly and sometimes in hidden and unacknowledged fashions. Kant and Hegel are not just two boring old dead men. Their ideas continue to inform what theorists do today. The recurring theme of the 'social construction of reality' that you will find turns up throughout this book again and again, is basically derived from Kant. Subsequent thinkers in many different paradigms twisted his ideas about this theme in ever new directions. Likewise, issues to do with the relationships that might exist between 'social structure' and individuals, which many different thinkers and paradigms have grappled with, are all variations on themes originally thought about by Hegel. For that reason, you can't really understand 'modern' social theory unless you understand its 'classical' ancestors, and you can't really understand the latter without a basic knowledge of what Kant and Hegel were talking about. So we recommend that whatever chapters you look at, and however you read the book – from start to finish, or jumping around from chapter to chapter – that you read Chapter 1 first, because it contains the seeds of everything that comes later in social theory, right up to the present time. The tradition of Kant and Hegel is a *living* tradition, absolutely still relevant for today and still put to use, though sometimes in disguised ways.

Recurring Themes

Almost all social theories have to deal, in one way or another, with three key themes. In each chapter we will lay out what the main schools of thought, and thinkers within them, have said about these themes. They are:

(1) Knowledge

Obviously every type of social theory makes claims about what it understands as the 'real world'. So the first key theme that any theory must involve is to do with 'knowledge'. In social theory, knowledge has two central dimensions. The first is what philosophers refer to as 'ontology'. Ontological claims that a particular theory makes involve the assumptions it holds about what the 'real world' is like, what is in it and what makes it up. For example, one 'ontological' position – which we can roughly call social 'structuralism' – claims that the primary elements of the human social world are 'social structures'. These are 'real' and have a strong influence on how individual persons think and act. So structuralism presents 'structures' as the basic and most fundamental aspects of human social life. Examples here would include functionalism (Chapter 2) and some kinds of Marxism (Chapters 1, 3 and 9).

By contrast, the ontological position we can call 'individualism' claims that the 'real' things in human life are individual people. From this viewpoint, social structures either do not exist, or are merely the products of individuals acting and interacting in particular ways. The ontology of a particular theory involves its central assumptions about what is 'real' and therefore what should be the focus of study.

The second central dimension of knowledge for each social theory is the 'epistemological' dimension. This involves how the theory intends to study what it thinks of as the 'real world'. A particular division between different types of social theory involves what they want to model their 'epistemology' on. For some paradigms (e.g. phenomenology, symbolic interactionism and streams within feminism – see Chapters 4, 5 and 11), social theory, and the social science that it guides, should be modelled on the techniques to be found in humanities disciplines, like literary criticism. The means by which we should understand social life is by 'interpreting' the meanings to be found in the heads of individuals as they go about acting and interacting with each other. A related but rather different viewpoint is to be found in Rational Choice and Exchange theories (see Chapter 6).

An alternative epistemological position is that of 'positivism', which holds that social theory and the social sciences should be modelled on the natural sciences, which search for general 'laws' (e.g. the laws of thermodynamics), which collect 'facts' that are uncontestable if collected properly, these facts often being found in statistics. Both 'interpretivism' and 'positivism' are explained more in Chapter 1.

The point here is that the epistemology of a theory is intimately connected to its ontology, the one leading to the other and vice versa. For example, the epistemology of positivism is based on a particular ontology – the claim that there are facts 'out there' to be captured, and they exist 'outside' of any particular person's consciousness. The epistemology of interpretivism involves a very different ontology – that the most important things in the world are the meanings to be found in people's heads, which are shaped by particular cultural systems or forms. The heart of any theory is what it says about its own ontology and epistemology. This fundamentally underpins any theory's views of what the world is like and how it is to be studied.

(2) Structure and action (or agency)

The second key theme that most social theories deal with has to do with their views on the relative importance of 'social structure' or individuals'

hat is the real promise of social theory. At its best, it holds
romise of you transforming yourself by engaging with it,
you in all sorts of possible ways, including for the better.
1 come to 'get' social theory, you may well come to 'get'
nd the people around you in new ways too. That, ultimately,
cial theory is neither boring nor a chore, but something poten-
y valuable. Its value starts to become apparent once you crack
is codes. So let's begin.

'actions' in their analysis of how the social world works. (More recent social theory often replaces the term 'action' with 'agency'.) This relates to the ontological issues just mentioned, as to whether structures or individuals are the most important, and powerful, aspects of human social existence.

It should be noted, however, that some theories assume there is a fundamental, ontological distinction between 'structures' and 'actions', while others reject this divide, trying to create a terminology which goes beyond thinking in terms of a stark divide between the two. These issues will be seen particularly acutely in Chapter 7, where we encounter 'process sociology', and Chapter 10, where we examine structurationist thinking, both of which reject the division between structure and action, society and individual. All we have to note at the moment is that some theories put more emphasis on the power of individuals to shape their own lives, while others put far more emphasis on the capacity of social structures to influence what people do.

One other thing to add is that not all forms of social theory explicitly formulate 'structure' and 'action' as their focus of concern – these tend to be theories that come from sources most distant from the discipline of sociology, certain brands of structuralism being the obvious case in point, as they are more centrally derived from the discipline of linguistics (see Chapters 8 and 9). These theories are much more centrally concerned with thinking about the nature of 'subjectivity' (the ways in which a person's mind is shaped by social and cultural factors) and 'identity' (the ways in which a person thinks about themselves and their place in the world). Some more sociologically oriented theories deal explicitly with these matters too, so we will highlight instances of thinking about subjectivity and identity where these arise.

(3) Modernity

The third and final key theme that social theories deal with concerns what they say about contemporary society, how it developed, what it is made up of, how it operates and how it is changing. Social theory generally uses the term 'modernity' to describe what it is centrally about. This term was in large part invented and elaborated by the classical theorists. It is generally taken to refer to the kind of society which arose from about the sixteenth century onwards in Western Europe, which replaced the previous type of social organization (medieval 'feudalism') in that part of the world, and which then spread, in all sorts of complicated and uneven ways, to other parts of the world over the next several centuries. The various classical theorists produced ideas about modernity that in some ways shared similar assumptions and in other ways were quite different from each other, especially in terms of how enthusiastic or not they were about the new kind of society they saw as having relatively recently arisen (see Chapter 1). Theorists ever since then have drawn upon these classical ideas in a diverse range of ways, altering them in the process.

Since the late 1960s, there has been a widespread sense among many social theorists, reflecting perceptions in wider society, that the version of modernity we have today is in important ways different – perhaps exceptionally different – from the version of modernity the classical theorists tried to understand. A major part of social theory over the last thirty years or so has involved trying to determine what this 'new modernity' looks like and what it should be called. Terms that have been coined in this regard include post-modernity (Chapter 9), late modernity (Chapter 10), risk society (Chapter 12), the network society (Chapter 12) and globalized modernity (Chapter 12). All of these terms reflect the broader epistemological and ontological commitments of the people who have coined them, as well as their senses of what structure, action, agency, subjectivity and identity look like in the present day.

Some Advice Before Embarking . . .

Social theorists of all varieties, even the most eminent and highly regarded ones, are not that much different from you or me. But they are sometimes presented as if they are. This is especially so, it seems, in Britain and places influenced by its academic culture, where certain social theorists are particularly set up on pedestals and treated as if they were wholly unique human beings (Outhwaite, 2009).

Some social theorists are indeed intellectually first-class, as is evidenced in the fact that after reading their writings, you may never look at the world in the same ways again. The very best social theory is worth getting to know and understand because it will help you see the world in new, more sophisticated ways – but ways you often already had some awareness of. Some of the best social theorists have the knack of putting into words things you only dimly perceived before.

Ultimately that is why social theory is not a drag or a chore. It is worth persevering with, even if it is an uphill struggle at first, as it is almost

inevitably going to be. This book has b gle to understand social theory very beginning to read social theory for the intriguing and appealing, and other aspe can be said with a lot of confidence is: THE EFFORT IN THE LONG RUN.

The problem with putting some peop as 'great thinkers', is that they start to s pletely unlike the rest of us. Paradoxicall reading their work, as it starts to seem understandable by, an intellectual elite. Bu to reach out to their audience, to commu wider public and also (perhaps especially) t the capacity to understand what they are productive, even *exciting*, meeting of minds

At its best, that meeting of minds will – on circumstances – allow you to understa around you better, or at least in different way social theory is really doing its job properly, it horizons, making them see *themselves* in new ened, and your understanding deepened, of and how the world works. That is no small th

A curious but very important ramificatic *knowing* through understanding social theory is stand social theory, the more you will understa it, and why you find some theories appealing vincing. You will be able to use what you hav yourself, and the *social* (not just purely 'individ ticular relationship(s) you have both to social t particular types of it. The social reasons why yc (liking some aspects, disliking others) in the spec do, are only fully discernible once you have grasp of finding and explaining those very reasons. This 'reflexive' powers and capacities of social theory understand yourself better, *including your own rela*

Maybe some social theories will tell you what already-held beliefs. Or maybe some theories will c or perhaps even more dramatically, attitudes that y now. Either way, once you have got to the state the general gist of any specific theory, you will b

yourself. out the changing Once yo yourself is why sc tially ver its vario

1

Classical Paradigms

'Classics' and 'Moderns'

The legacy of the 'classical' social theorists looms large in modern social theory. Despite being long dead, the works of the 'classics' continue very much to inform present-day theorists and theorizing. Even when contemporary thinkers are unaware of the legacy of the classics on their own thinking, that legacy continues to be important.

No writer of the eighteenth, nineteenth and early twentieth centuries saw themselves as a 'classical theorist' – that was a label put onto them later, by particular people for specific reasons. The people we now conventionally define as classical theorists were engaged in debates about specific issues that very much reflected their own periods and social contexts. There is a danger of lifting ideas out of their original social contexts, presenting them as if they were context-free intellectual products, rather than ideas put to use by particular people for particular purposes at particular times (Skinner, 1969). The original uses of those ideas might have been very different from how we use the same ideas today – if in fact they are the 'same' ideas, because how we use them now may transform them fundamentally from what they used to mean. Thus any use of classical authors inevitably involves *interpretation*, and the work of interpretation never ceases (Alexander, 1987). Disputes over the interpretation of the nature of particular authors and their works constitutes one of the distinctive features of social theory. Through debating who our intellectual ancestors were and what they said, we come to new understandings of ourselves as theorists. And as these disputes go on constantly, our senses of what social theory is, and of what it can achieve, change too.

You cannot really understand modern social theory if you do not understand what is defined as 'classical' social theory. The very term 'modern' only makes sense in contrast to what it is seen to be not i.e. 'classical'. Conventionally, classical theory is thought to have ended, and modern theory to have begun, in the 1920s and 1930s. This is because those thinkers defined as the last of the classics, most notably Émile Durkheim and Max Weber, died around the time of the First World War. Their mental universe was one shared with their predecessors of the nineteenth century, whereas the intellectual landscape of the generation after them seemed in certain ways to be very different, involving funda-mental breaks with what went before. One important break is that both Durkheim and Weber did not live long enough to engage with the revo-lutionary ideas of Sigmund Freud, which started to be significant from the 1920s onwards (Elliott, 2004). Classical theorists inhabited a pre-Freudian intellectual universe, whereas those thinkers definable as 'modern' theorists came to exist within a world where the ideas of Freud could not be ignored.

So there are some fundamental differences between 'classical' and 'modern' social theory. The difference was marked by some of the earliest of those we now call 'modern' theorists, because they reflected back on their predecessors and defined them *as* classics. In so doing, these thinkers drew a dividing line between 'classics' and 'moderns', but also argued that the moderns had a lot to learn from the classics. The most major work to do this was Talcott Parsons' (1937) *The Structure of Social Action*, pub-lished in the late 1930s. Parsons was one of the first to claim explicitly that there was indeed a 'classical tradition' in social thought, thus implying that there was now a post-classical (i.e. modern) field that was distinctive of, but could take inspiration from, the ideas of the classics, re-working them for new purposes. Parsons included Weber and Durkheim among his clas-sics, but not Georg Simmel and Karl Marx. This shows that what counts as 'classical social theory' shifts and changes over time, and varies from place to place. Who and what gets to count as a true 'classic' varies accord-ing to circumstances, especially as regards which people have the power to define what a classic is or who counts as one.

Really to understand modern social theory, you have to know about what modern theorists have done with classical theories. Classical theories provide many (but not all) of the building-blocks from which modern theories have been assembled. Each modern theoretical position can be under-stood as – at least in part – a particular combination of specific bits of classical theory, put together in certain ways for distinctive purposes. Modern theorists take certain bits of classical theory, while rejecting, criticizing and ignoring others. They must actively re-interpret the bits that they take, and work out how they have to be transformed in order to make them useful for present-day purposes. Sometimes the selection of bits is done self-consciously and in full awareness of the borrowing from classical theorists, other times semi-consciously or unconsciously. Classical theory very much informs modern theory, but this is not a crushing domination by the old over the new. It is about how the new is constantly using and reconfiguring the old for its own purposes, and this is a creative process. To understand what follows in the rest of the book, one must know the central ideas drawn from the classical theorists that have been taken up and used again and again, by different modern theorists in different ways.

A Foundational Thinker: Kant

Just as modern theorists have constantly drawn upon the ideas of the classics, so too did the classical theorists draw upon and transform earlier ideas. Both classical and modern social theory can be seen as responses to, and transformations of, the ideas of two foundational thinkers: the German philosophers Immanuel Kant [1724–1804] and G. W. F. Hegel [1770–1831]. Both have supplied many (perhaps most) of the central ideas of social theory over the last 200 years. Some familiarity with their ideas is crucial for understanding subsequent theoretical developments.

Kant's contribution is primarily about the nature of knowledge (*epistemology*) and reality (*ontology*). Kant's philosophy was an attempt to avoid the extremism of two earlier, opposed philosophical positions: *realism* (the idea that world exists wholly independently of my mind's perception of it) and *idealism* (the world is merely a projection of what my mind imagines it to be). Kant's (1999 [1787]) middle way between these polarized positions involved claiming that each object in the world has two sides. On the one hand, there is its *noumenal* side, which is its essence and which exists beyond human perception. Human perception is inevitably limited because it cannot grasp the noumenal aspect of things, 'things in themselves'. On the other hand, each object has its *phenomenal* side, which is the object as it appears in human perception. So the world is 'real', and exists beyond human perceptions, but we never gain direct access to that world (the world of *noumena*). This is because the mind plays an active role in organizing the world that the human being sees presented before it. The mind shapes the *phenomenal* (visible) aspect of things, and so constitutes (or creates) the world as we perceive it. So we only ever have access to the phenomenal world, the world shaped for us by our minds, while the noumenal world – the world of objects 'in themselves' – is always out of our grasp. A person only ever experiences the world as their mind constructs it for them. The noumenal world has no form or structure, and so is meaningless. It is the human mind that projects form and structure onto the world, so making sense of the world and rendering it meaningful for us (Bennett, 1966).

Kant argues that all human minds are alike, and so the world as perceived by me is the same world as perceived by you – or by anyone else – because everyone's mind is identical and processes the world in the same ways (Korner, 1955). The history of post-Kantian thinking, especially in the social sciences, broke down this view, tending towards the denial of the existence of *noumena* at all, and seeing the world primarily, or only, as a series of *phenomena*. Here is the root of the central social theoretical idea that the world and everything in it are 'socially constructed'. Social theory has kept the Kantian idea that the world is constructed for us by our minds, but adds that how the human brain works varies from one social or cultural context to another. Different groups of people are seen as possessing 'their own' unique cultures. Each culture has its own distinctive ways of shaping the minds of the people living within it. Different societies and cultures shape the world differently. It is through culture that the world not only is *perceived* by people in that cultural context, but is in fact *constituted*. In other words, *different societies create different realities* for the people that live within them (Lizardo, 2011).

Classical social theory developed these ideas in multiple directions. Early nineteenth-century thinkers associated with the intellectual movement called 'Romanticism' stressed that each particular culture is unique. Thus the experiences of people living in different cultural contexts are so radically different, it is difficult or impossible to argue that there is one single 'human nature', only a multiplicity of different ways of thinking and acting, all totally divergent from each other (Berlin, 2000). Social theory in France, beginning at the time of Montesquieu [1689–1755], argued that different societies involved different 'mental structures', each of these producing radically different experiences of the world. This view was developed much later – just before the First World War – in Émile Durkheim's [1858–1917] last major work, *The Elementary Forms of the Religious Life*, which is a sociological reinvention of Kant (Durkheim, 2001 [1912]). Durkheim understands the perception of phenomena as rooted not in the individual mind (as Kant argued), but in the classifying structures of particular social groups. These systems of 'collective classifications' specify what is perceivable and not perceivable, thinkable and not thinkable, by all members of the group (Durkheim and Mauss, 1969 [1903]).

In Germany, similar claims were developed, but whereas the French tended to talk about how 'societies' created systems of 'classification', the Germans tended to conceive of 'cultures' which were seen to shape human sensory experience. The German classical theoretical tradition reaches its most developed expression in the work of Max Weber [1864–1920], where the culture of a particular group is understood as projecting 'meaning and significance' onto the 'meaningless infinity' of the noumenal world (Turner, 1996: 5). Culture makes the world meaningful for the people in it, by selecting from a potentially infinite number of objects and concerns in the noumenal world a finite set of things, and directing people's attention towards them and not to others. This is how the world comes to have meaning for us, and how we come to feel 'ontologically secure', that is, feel reality is patterned and orderly, and not going to erupt into chaos and meaninglessness at any moment (Giddens, 1991). These ideas have been taken up in a very wide variety of ways in modern social theory, such as in structuralism (see Chapter 8), which derives from primarily French classical sources, and in phenomenology (see Chapter 4), which makes more use of German classical ideas. These various theoretical positions all endeavour to elaborate on the central post-Kantian idea that all forms of 'reality' are social (or cultural) fabrications, and that anything that seems to be 'objective' is only so from the cultural perspective of a particular social group (Berger and Luckmann, 1991 [1966]).

As the original Kantian ideas were taken in the direction of claims as to society and culture shaping reality, they also had conceptions of *social power* added to them. The social and cultural forms which shape a particular group's world for them, are seen themselves to be shaped by power relations. Particularly important here were two innovations: the account of *ideologies* put forward by Karl Marx [1818–1883], and the philosophy of power created by Friedrich Nietzsche [1844–1900]. Both Marx and Nietzsche – although in different fashions – argued that the ways each group looks at the world are shaped by the power relations that exist both within that group and in its relations with other groups. For Marx, cultural forms are shaped by *ideologies*, which express the ideas of ruling classes, the groups which control and dominate particular societies. For Nietzsche, cultural forms embody the *will to power* – the desire for individuals and groups to have control over other people.

Through Marx and Nietzsche, many later theorists came to regard all cultural forms as being thoroughly shot through with power relations, even though the people who lived within the terms set by those forms were often unaware of this fact. While later Marxists have obviously sought to use and transform the ideas of Marx (see Chapter 3), those who have drawn upon the ideas of Max Weber have implicitly also utilized certain themes from Nietzsche, which were taken up by Weber. One of the main tasks of the 'critical' wings of social theory, whether Marxist or non-Marxist (e.g. the work of Foucault – see Chapter 8), has been to identify the ways in which power works in and through cultural forms, and how this comes profoundly to affect how people think and how social life is constructed, maintained and altered.

Another Foundational Thinker: Hegel

Just as Kantian ideas were important for the development of subsequent social theory, so too has been the philosophy of Hegel. One could plausibly claim that Hegel is *the* most influential and important source of subsequent social theorizing, sometimes his ideas being taken up explicitly by later thinkers (most famously, by Marx), but more often his notions having more hidden influences. Hegel's (1979 [1807]) philosophy comprises an extensive and often difficult body of work, which we will only give brief outlines of. The most important element later thinkers have taken up is the notion of 'dialectics'. This is itself an idea with various meanings, but at its most elementary it refers to *processes of movement and change*. It particularly refers to situations where opposing forces clash with each other. The clash transforms both forces, each being reconfigured by the other, such that they come to have new natures, comprising elements of each other. The clash also creates a new situation, which takes elements from each of the opposing forces, but which goes beyond each of them to create something novel. So the clash of opposing forces is 'dialectical', and the clash creates new forces and situations that are also themselves dialectical in nature.

Marx concretized these abstract notions by using them to understand how human history changed through the antagonism of opposing social classes (Arthur, 1986). Ruling and subordinate classes come into conflict, and the conflict changes each of them. The conflict produces a new situation where the previously most powerful class is weakened and disappears, the previously subordinate class becomes the dominant one, and a new class appears which then enters into conflict with the new powerful one – at which point the dialectical movement of conflict and change occurs once again. Hegel believed that dialectical processes in human history would eventually reach an end-point, a final situation where all conflicts had been resolved. Marx extrapolated from this to argue that the final class conflict would occur in modernity between the capitalist class and the revolutionary working class, and when the latter triumphed and the former was defeated and disappeared, this would bring about a new society (communism). This would be a society where there would no longer be any class conflicts, because all people would be in the working class and therefore there would be no class to oppose it. The dialectical irony, as Marx saw it, was that the capitalist class had created a society which produced an enemy class, the working class, which then destroyed that very society.

Beyond Marx's use of Hegel's dialectics, many subsequent theorists have argued that social order involves dialectical processes, i.e. processes where certain forces produce effects that come to rebound on those forces themselves, changing them as a result. Social theory built on dialectical thinking has a strong sense of irony: human history involves groups of people engaged in activities which have consequences that no one could foresee or control. On this view, human beings tend to do things that have 'unintended consequences' that they did not aim for and that they could not have guessed would happen.

Many thinkers have also stressed the dialectical relationships that pertain between the actions of individuals on the one side, and social structures and institutions on the other. Classical thinkers otherwise as diverse as Marx, Weber and Simmel were all of the (Hegelian) view that the actions of various individuals can over time cohere into fixed patterns of action and interaction – these are what are called 'social structures' and 'institutions'. These then come to seem to the people living within them to be simply 'real' and to have an objective existence of their own, even though all they are in fact are routinized patterns of action and interaction that have become habitual and taken-for-granted. The structures and institutions thus come to shape individuals' further actions and interactions. In this way, a particular social order based around these structures and institutions is reproduced and maintained over time. However, if for whatever reason individuals were to start acting differently, then the structures and institutions would be altered, or even transformed altogether.

On such a view, 'social structures' and the 'actions' of individuals are *dialectically intertwined*: each has effects on the other, each could not exist without the other, each makes the other. So once structures and institutions have come to exist, they both constrain *and* make possible individuals' actions. This is because they generate, and are centred around, cultural forms which shape the view of the world that people have (here we return to the Kantian ideas above). However, particular structures and institutions may not rigidly dictate what individuals think and do; they may allow space for individual choices, in that the cultural forms may be ambiguous, open to interpretation, allowing individuals more than one course of action. So individuals may engage in actions and interactions which either maintain the current patterns of the structures and institutions, or which transform them. And, thinking dialectically, structures and institutions may produce forces (ways of thinking and acting) which unintentionally come to change or even destroy them. All of these ideas, found throughout this book (see especially Chapter 10), derive ultimately from Hegel.

For most versions of social theory, the division philosophy makes between pure individual free will (the capacity to do anything you want) and complete determinism (the power of circumstances to force you to do certain things and not others) is too abstract to grasp what actually goes on in human society. Marx (2000 [1852]) famously phrased the social theoretical view: people 'make history but not in conditions of their own choosing'. The thoughts and actions of individuals (and groups) make and remake structures and institutions; these in turn make and remake thoughts and actions; thoughts and actions remake structures and institutions, and all of this goes on in never-ending processes (Abrams, 1982). People are neither wholly constrained by social order (if they were, nothing would ever change), nor are they totally free to do as they choose (for then there would be no social order, no relatively stable patterns of thought, action and interaction).

This notion is nowadays called 'structuration' (see Chapter 10) – how structure relates to action (or agency, as it is more often called now). The key social theoretical task becomes to find words which more specifically describe this situation. Marx, Weber, Durkheim, Simmel and other classical theorists all endeavoured to do this. All their attempts have subsequently been regarded as flawed in one way or another. If the aim is to provide an account that gives equal due to both 'structure' and 'action', then different thinkers can be criticized as having given more weight to one side of the equation than the others: Marx and Durkheim are often said to overemphasize 'structure' at the expense of 'action', whereas Weber is said to have been stronger on understanding action and correspondingly weaker on explaining structure. But the work of the classical theorists is always open to interpretation and creative rethinking. As we will see in Chapter 10, in present-day theory Pierre Bourdieu's analysis owes a lot to Marx, Weber and Durkheim, whereas Anthony Giddens'

Kant: *noumena* **and** *phenomena*
The human mind shapes the world of perceptions (phenomena)

Hegel: dialectical processes and alienation
People unconsciously create enduring social structures and institutions,
which then come to impact on those people

Figure 1.1 Summary of Kant and Hegel.

views are closer to those of Simmel, as are those of Norbert Elias (see
Chapter 7).

Modern Society and Alienation

Another of Hegel's ideas, 'alienation', has also been very influential in
social theory. We have seen that when over time the actions of various
individuals cohere into fixed patterns, then social structures and institutions are formed. These then come to seem to those living within them
to have an 'objective' existence of their own. The implication of Hegel's
thinking – later to be taken up by Marx – is that such a situation is an
alienated condition, where people create things that then seem to them to
be 'real' and to have great power over them. Just as Baron Frankenstein
created a monster he could not control, so too does human life involve
the creation of things (structures, institutions, ideas, cultural forms) that
come to control, even enslave, the very people who have made them, and
then later on their descendants too. Once a product of human activity is
thought to have its own objective reality, and is thought not to be a
product of human actions, then the people who made it are alienated
from their own product, which comes to stand over and above them.

Marx (1981 [1844]) applied these Hegelian ideas to religion: the idea
of God has been invented by people, but this has been forgotten, such
that God seems to have a life of His own and the power to control
people. For Marx, the only way to get out of this sort of situation into
a non-alienated one is for people to realize that what controls them
was in fact made by them themselves. Once they realize that, they can
regain control, taming that thing and putting it to their own uses. For
Marx, the revolutionary working class would in the near future realize
that the institutions and ideologies of capitalist society which oppressed

them were not objective, natural or inevitable, but in fact were merely human products that could be altered and done away with. Hegel's notion of alienation was particularly influential in later German social theory, although it has made an impact in all theory influenced by Marx (Liebersohn, 1988).

Most classical theory asked this question: what is unique and specifically 'modern' about 'modern society'? All classical social theorists agreed that there were huge differences between modernity in Europe (and North America) and the social order it had replaced, namely medieval feudalism. Feudalism was primarily rural, had small-scale communities, was based around an agricultural economy, and had an aristocratic ruling class and a subordinate class of peasants (agricultural labourers). Modernity was based around huge cities, had a capitalist economy, its ruling class were the class of capitalists, those who owned the big industrial companies, and this class dominated the majority of the population, the working class ('proletariat'), who mostly worked in factories. As Figure 1.2 shows, the classical theorists invented different binary oppositions to identify more specifically the peculiar nature of modernity, comparing it to the pre-modern society it was seen to have destroyed and replaced (Bendix, 1967).

Some diagnoses of the pre-modern/modern division were more optimistic about the nature and future of modernity, playing up the positives (e.g. Durkheim, Herbert Spencer), others were more pessimistic, playing up the negatives (Weber, Tönnies), while others were dialectical, seeing modernity as a mixture of good and bad elements (hence Marx deploring capitalism as an exploitative social order, but praising it for the way it would destroy itself and create the better society called communism).

Ideas as to whether modernity was a good or bad thing were based in different general understandings of social change. Both Spencer and Durkheim regarded modern society as the result of a long period of social evolution, which involved a transition over thousands of years from small, simple social orders to modernity's large-scale complexity (Sztompka, 1993) (see Chapter 2). Marx was also an evolutionary thinker of sorts, but one who followed Hegel's dialectical conception of social change (see above), involving clashing social forces producing ever new, more sophisticated stages of human development. By contrast, Weber rejected evolutionary thought, regarding human history as much more disordered and contingent than evolutionists thought. However, his own criticisms of evolutionary theory were rather contradicted by his emphasis on how over many centuries, the Western world had become more and more highly rationalized, dominated both by rational forms of thought

	Pre-Modern society	Modernity
Karl Marx	**Feudalism** Economy centred around exploitation of peasants by aristocratic lords	**Capitalism** Economy centred around exploitation of industrial workers by capitalists
Ferdinand Tönnies	*Gemeinschaft* Social order centred around tightly knit communities	*Gesellschaft* Social order centred around self-seeking individuals with little or no community sense
Herbert Spencer	**Military Society** Violent conflicts within and between states; forced regulation of the population by elites	**Industrial Society** Peace and social harmony; voluntary associations of individuals
Émile Durkheim	**Mechanical Solidarity** Simple division of labour; individual members of a group all alike	**Organic Solidarity** Complex division of labour; individuals very different from each other; different occupational groups all reliant on each other
Max Weber	**Society Based on Substantive Rationality** Individuals' actions motivated by values and ideals e.g. religious beliefs	**Society Based on Instrumental Rationality** Individuals' actions motivated by purely 'instrumental' concerns e.g. making profit; highly bureaucratized social life

Figure 1.2 Ideas of Various Classical Theorists – The Nature of Pre-Modern and Modern Society.

(particularly exemplified in natural science) and by rational forms of social control (particularly exemplified in bureaucracies). This seemed like an evolutionary story smuggled in by the back door (for the complexities of Weber's ideas, see Collins (1986)).

These various views of social change in general, and the transition to modernity in particular, were rooted in broader ideas as to what social science was, as we will see below. Almost all the classical thinkers (the main exception being Herbert Spencer, who was not influenced by German philosophy) thought modernity had very alienating aspects to it, and many of them had taken such views from Hegel. So another key question most classical theorists wanted answers to was: why is it that modern society is *particularly* alienating in comparison to others, including the one that came before it?

Many intellectuals in the nineteenth century, of both left-wing and right-wing political viewpoints, regarded modern society ('modernity') as highly problematic, especially as it seemed to be so alienating. The very large cities it had created seemed to be lonely places, bereft of any real sense of community (a theme pursued by both Tönnies and Simmel). The factories that working people laboured in involved very poor conditions and had taken all creativity and enjoyment out of work (a theme pursued by Marx). Capitalism seemed to have replaced any sense of morality and compassion, with a monomaniacal focus on money and profits (a theme pursued by Marx, Tönnies and Simmel). All previously held values and ways of thinking, including religion, were seen to be extinguished by the kinds of rational thinking promoted by a society increasingly centred around money on the one hand, and scientific knowledge on the other (a theme pursued by Weber and Simmel). So in multiple ways, modern people were alienated by ideas and institutions that they and their ancestors had created. Modernity seemed like a huge machine, that swept up everyone, rich and poor alike, into its workings. To use Weber's terms, modern people had created a dispiriting, mechanical form of social order, which had become wholly routinized and from which they apparently could not escape.

Hegel had already anticipated such ideas at the start of the nineteenth century, applying his general notions about alienation to the analysis of modern society, describing it as 'a vast system of commonality and mutual interdependence, a moving life of the dead. This system moves . . . in a blind and elementary way . . . like a wild animal' (cited in Marcuse, 1999: 40). Hegel had in mind the emergent capitalist system, which is seen to be both completely irrational in its operations, and 'dead' in the sense that its mechanisms (the market, stocks and shares, factory production) have been made by human beings, but have come to weigh oppressively upon them. These are social structures created by living human beings but now running mechanically, devoid of any human spirit.

These ideas were developed later by Marx's (1988 [1865]) analysis of the 'commodity fetishism' created by capitalism. Workers make things in factories. These are then sold by capitalists (factory owners) for profit. The workers are thus alienated from their work, and from the things they make. They are in fact alienated from their human nature, because that involves people working freely and creatively, for their own benefit, and for that of people in their community. But human nature becomes alienated when work is organized so that none of this is possible, and when the only consideration is the capitalists' profits, regardless of the negative effect on the workers. When the objects the workers make are sold for money, they become 'commodities' in the capitalist market. Transactions in the capitalist market *look like* they involve relationships only between things (commodities, money). In actual fact, the capitalist market is made up of human relationships involving making goods and selling them. So a human product (the market) comes to seem as if it has a life and mind of its own, as if it has not been made by human beings, when actually it has. Marx's point was that if people took back full control over their social relationships, then they would no longer be enslaved to alienated and alienating products like the capitalist market.

Marx's use of Hegel's ideas about alienation in modern society is only the most famous instance of later theorists' use of Hegel. Weber's idea of modern society being like an over-rationalized, highly bureaucratized cage owes a lot to it. The original Hegelian idea was that humans ('subjects'), who are full of life and creativity, create 'objects' that come to control them, threatening to snuff out all their life and creativity. But subjects can realize this is happening and bring the objects under control again – through social revolution, Marx claimed. By contrast, Georg Simmel [1858–1918] believed human life is more *tragic* than Hegel or Marx would admit: the divide between the human subject and the objects it makes can never be fully transcended, with objects made by subjects always coming to shape profoundly what those subjects subsequently do (Simmel, 1997).

Simmel argued that modern society particularly accentuates this situation. In modernity, social relations are profoundly centred around the use of money. Money has certain characteristics which come profoundly to shape the ways in which the people who use it think and feel (Simmel, 1990 [1907]). Money is above all *impersonal*. It is not tied to any particular group of people, so potentially anyone at all, from the highest to the lowest, can use it. Money is also *universalising*: it brings more and more people, regardless of their social position, under its sway (an idea taken up by Norbert Elias – see Chapter 7). A money economy is based not on sentiments, customs, morals or values, but always comes down to the 'bottom-line': how much money one makes or loses. Money creates a culture based around purely rational calculations. Things and people become evaluated not in terms of their *qualities*, but in terms of their monetary value and rational usefulness. Social relationships become less based around qualitative matters (e.g. family ties, religious beliefs) and much more centred around the economic needs of the individuals involved. When I deal with the supermarket cashier, we have no personal relationship: our interaction is based solely on a monetary transaction. My only social connection with the cashier is enacted through the money I hand over. Our relationship is like money itself: impersonal, formal and transient. Thus money is a mechanism that alienates people from each other, and from themselves.

Modernity for Simmel is also particularly alienating because it *mass produces* objects on a scale unheard-of before, so that for the typical individual there is inescapably:

> . . . the feeling of being surrounded by an immense number of cultural elements [objects], which are not meaningless, but not profoundly meaningful . . . either; elements which have a certain crushing quality as a mass, because an individual cannot inwardly assimilate every individual thing, but cannot simply reject it either, since it belongs potentially . . . to the sphere of his or her cultural development. (Simmel, 1997: 73)

Simmel has in mind the proliferation of mass-produced cultural objects of his time, like paperback books, popular magazines, and mass circulation newspapers. All of these things ('objective culture') threaten to smother the individual's mind ('subjective culture') with too much information, which, however the individual feels, cannot just be ignored. Unable to cope with all of these objects, and also the vast amount of sensory stimuli thrown at them by living in a big city, individuals retreat into themselves, presenting a face to the world that looks outwardly bland and unconcerned, but which actually masks inner anguish and discontent, problems that the individual does not realize spring from the alienating qualities of modern society itself. It is from these ideas that certain symbolic interactionists, most notably Erving Goffman, have developed their notions of how social interaction, especially of typically 'modern' types, involves the masking of inner states and the presentation of public faces, to the extent that the latter can start to colonize and control the former – a condition of interactional alienation (see Chapter 5).

It should be noted that not all classical theory regards modern society as an inescapable trap. For Marx, modernity is above all dynamic and constantly changing:

> Constant revolutionizing of production, uninterrupted disturbance of all
> social relations, everlasting uncertainty and agitation . . . All fixed, fast-
> frozen relationships . . . are swept away, all new-formed ones become
> obsolete before they can ossify. All that is solid melts into air, all that is
> holy is profaned. (Marx and Engels, 1968 [1848]): 207)

So just as some thinkers – especially in Germany – could regard modern
society as one which crushed traditional activities and individual freedom
through mechanisms of domination, so too could others imagine it as a
realm that prepared the ground for a liberation of humanity from the
shackles of tradition (Liebersohn, 1988). Modernity is viewed in classical
theory variously as both promise and curse, a theme that continues into
modern theory too.

Although not really a classical social theorist as such, Sigmund Freud
[1856–1939] has also been highly significant in subsequent social theory,
both that claiming explicitly to be Freudian and that which just draws on
some of his ideas (Elliott, 2004). He is worth mentioning here because,
although his revolutionary ideas as to the 'unconscious' elements of the
human mind were unknown to most of those we count as classical theorists, the idea that the human mind was not a coherent or stable entity
would not have surprised thinkers such as Marx, Nietzsche and Durkheim.
They all contributed in their own ways to the general idea, which
nineteenth-century thought points towards and Freud radicalizes,
that the individual human mind ('subjectivity') is created by social and
cultural forces that operate beneath the level of conscious awareness.

Given the German intellectual context in which he lived, Freud's theory
of how society works can be seen as a variant of post-Hegel theories of
alienation. For Freud (2002), in its natural state the human being has
unruly instinctual drives – towards violence and sexual gratification –
which produce desires for gratifying them that are contained in the part
of the mind called the 'id'. The conscious human being – the part of the
mind called the 'ego' – is torn between gratifying the desires of the 'id'
and suppressing them. What demands their suppression is the third and
final part of the mind, the 'superego', which is the internalization of the
morality and demands of surrounding society, inculcated through childhood socialization. Id and superego are constantly at war within the ego
and the unconscious. For social order to exist at all, and for chaos to be
avoided, the superego must tame the id, bringing it into line with social
expectations, such as how to regulate sexual desires. But if the superego
tames the id too much, this causes psychic turbulence in the unconscious.

If an individual's sexual drives are too repressed by the superego, which is the internal mental representative of society, then the person becomes neurotic. A healthy society creates a balance in the ego and the unconscious between id and superego. Freud's (2002) critique of modern Western society is that it is based around a culture that has created overly repressive superegos, with often devastating effects on the psychic health of individuals. This too is a condition of alienation fostered by modern society. Such ideas were later taken up by Marxist-Freudians such as Erich Fromm and Herbert Marcuse (Chapter 3). Freudian notions were also radicalized by later disciples such as Lacan (Chapter 8), adapted to fit functionalist theory by Parsons (Chapter 2), and used as a springboard for Elias' account of the 'civilizing process' (Chapter 7).

Varieties of Social Analysis

The classical theorists were concerned not just with the nature of modern society but also how it should be studied. This involved controversies about what counted as 'science' when applied to social matters. Classical theory can be seen as being structured by a division between more 'Enlightenment' and more 'Romantic' ways of thinking (Berlin, 2000). Some thinkers, like Marx, have elements of both strains of thought in their work. However, generally speaking, French authors were more oriented to Enlightenment thinking, while German thinkers were more attuned to Romantic ideas.

Enlightenment thinking came to prominence, particularly in France, in the later eighteenth century (Hawthorn, 1976). The themes pursued by Enlightenment philosophers such as Voltaire and Diderot included an emphasis on scientific thinking as being superior to other types of thought, especially the more imaginative and poetic types. Enlightenment thought also put a strong emphasis on the power of rational thought to *expose* how social relations and cultural phenomena are formed by powerful groups, especially those of the aristocracy and Church. By exposing the hidden nature of power, rational thought wanted to create a more liberated and democratic social order. Enlightenment thought regarded the past and tradition as its enemies, and had a faith in a better future society, that would be guided by scientific thinking rather than outdated religious dogmas. Enlightenment believes in 'progress', a movement away from simpler social orders towards more complex ones, and away from more despotic and exploitative political and economic systems towards more egalitarian ones (Eagleton, 1991).

'Romanticism' arose in the early nineteenth century as a critical response to Enlightenment ways of thinking. While Enlightenment thought glorified science and scientists as the embodiments of human reason, Romantic ideas were primarily produced by artists and poets. Romanticism defended against the scientific mentality of Enlightenment such values as poetic expression and artistic imagination. It often glorified the past, regarding tradition in positive ways, and rejecting Enlightenment ideas about social progress. Romantic thinking often, but not always, looked to the future with trepidation, seeing an emerging capitalist and industrial social order that was marked by the destruction of all that was good in traditional ways of life, replacing them with materialist values and a social order devoid of any sense of community. While Enlightenment thought praised science, Romanticism instead saw scientific rationality as a threat to other values like beauty and religious ideals (Williams, 1958).

Enlightenment and Romantic thinking very much disagreed about the nature both of modernity and of the social science that was to study it (Dawe, 1970). Enlightenment thought argued that the analysis of social issues should be a project based on the model of the natural sciences. Auguste Comte [1798–1857] and other early thinkers in the (primarily French) 'positivist' tradition, later developed by Durkheim, argued for the study of 'laws' of social life, based on 'hard' scientific evidence about them. Just as there were laws of physics and biology, so too were there laws of society, and the study of society (sociology) could therefore be modelled on the procedures of the natural sciences, including their commitment to being wholly objective and unbiased. An assumption here was that human nature is uniform everywhere, so the same scientific procedures can be used to study people in any context.

Conversely, Romanticism argued that there was vast cultural variance among different groups of people: there was no one single 'human nature', only multiple different societies and cultures, each with their own unique ways of experiencing the world. (Romanticism was very much responsible for the post-Kantian understandings of multiple ways of making sense of the world described above.) If 'human nature' varied radically from one cultural context to another, then that called not for an Enlightenment-inspired positivist approach to social analysis, but rather necessitated more interpretative and imagination-driven methods, deriving not from the natural sciences but from the humanities disciplines like literary criticism (see Chapter 4).

While French Enlightenment thinking regarded its object of analysis as primarily *social* factors (structures and institutions), German Romantic-inspired thought took *cultural* phenomena (ideas, values, experiences) as its main focus. The philosopher Wilhelm Dilthey [1833–1911] formulated a distinction which subsequently came to be very influential in German social theory (Makkreel, 1975). He argued that the natural sciences (*Naturwissenschaften*) and the human (or cultural) sciences (*Geisteswissenschaften*) are wholly different, whereas Enlightenment thinking had urged that the latter should be modelled on the former. They were different in terms of the objects they studied and their methods of study. The natural sciences study natural objects, which are either life-less (e.g. geological formations) or sub-human (plants and animals). By contrast, the objects of the human sciences are living human beings, invested with mental capacities (*Geist* or 'spirit' – hence the **Geisteswissenschaften**) making them conscious and full of creative potential. German Romantic-inspired thinking thus makes a strong distinction between 'nature' and 'culture', the former being wholly non-human in character, and the latter the realm of the distinctively human, namely thoughtful consciousness, which non-human life lacks. Enlightenment thought regarded social and cultural phenomena as part of nature, or at least as being like them enough to mean that the study of these could be done in the same way as natural science studied nature.

Enlightenment thought believed that humans were endowed with reason, but regarded that reason as equally shared among all people, leading to predictable outcomes of action that generated social patterns, which could be measured and studied objectively. Romanticism, however, regarded human mental capacities as being a mixture of more rational and more imaginative and emotional characteristics. A person's 'spiritual' life is thoroughly shaped by the culture of the community in which they live. So the *Geisteswissenschaften* are literally the study of the human 'spirit', both of groups (cultures) and of individuals (especially the non-rational aspects of their mentalities). As each culture is different from every other, and as individuals can act in relatively unpredictable and unique ways, then we cannot use the methods of natural science, which assume uniformity of behaviour by individuals across contexts, to study them. Instead, we must engage in acts of creative *interpretation* (*Verstehen*) of the values and forms of consciousness of groups and individuals, understanding the specific mental motivations and intentions that give rise to particular actions (Rickman, 1988). In the early twentieth century, Max Weber attempted to codify these widely held German views, defining sociology as 'the interpretive understanding of social action' (Alexander, 1983: 30). The aim was to reconstruct why a person acted as they did, and this is achieved by reconstructing the values and ideas that motivated their actions, which in turn are seen to be rooted in the surrounding cultural context.

The German tradition of social theory is therefore very much about *hermeneutics* – the interpretation of meanings, especially the meanings that motivate people to do what they do (see Chapter 4). Enlightenment-derived positivism, however, is much less interested in the meanings in people's heads, and more focused on observable patterns of interaction between people, which form institutions and are formed by them. Where hermeneutics wants to investigate mental states leading to actions, positivism emphasizes the existence of 'social facts' – institutions and the norms embodied in them – which are seen to compel people to think and act in certain ways (Durkheim, 1982 [1895]). Hermeneutics is about how *cultures* implant *values* that are drawn upon by people in their *actions*, while positivism is about how *norms*, rooted in *institutions* and *social structures*, exist outside of individual minds but are *internalized* by individuals, thus guiding their actions in *patterned* ways.

There are some overlaps between positivism and hermeneutics: both want to know why people act as they do; both insist it is to do with mental functioning; both want to know why actions and interactions are patterned, leading to social order. But the differences rest in how these issues are formulated. Hermeneutics *starts with individuals* and sees how culturally derived values can lead multiple individuals to do the same sorts of things over time, thus creating social institutions that guide further action. But positivism *starts with institutions* and the norms they create, seeing how these compel or motivate individuals to act in ways that reproduce those institutions over time. In terms of the structuration issues mentioned above, a positivist like the earlier Durkheim tends to assume the existence of social structures, then examines how individuals' actions reproduce them. But a hermeneutic scholar like Weber starts with actions, and examines how cultural values can shape repeated actions that then *may* stabilize into structures, although this is not guaranteed. While for Durkheim structures have their own independent existence, being more than the sum of their individual parts, for Weber structures are never anything more than the actions of individuals repeated over time. Whether one starts with structures or with individuals' actions makes a great difference as to how you understand social life more generally (see Chapter 10).

Enlightenment Thought/Positivism	Romantic Thought/Interpretivism
France	Germany
Natural science	Literature and art
Search for laws and facts	Search for meaning in individual's mind and in groups ('culture')
Constant human nature everywhere	Variable cultural dispositions, no single human nature
Criticism of tradition; positive view of modernity	Nostalgia for tradition; ambivalent or negative view of modernity

Figure 1.3 The Enlightenment/Romanticism and Positivism/Interpretivism Divides.

Connected to the positivism/interpretivism (hermeneutics) division is the dispute between 'materialism' and 'idealism'. This involves controversies as to whether social order is driven more by 'material' factors (economy, technology, production of goods, etc.) or by more 'ideal' phenomena (culture, ideas, values). Obviously hermeneutics agrees with the latter view. Materialism however can be adopted by either positivists (e.g. the early Durkheim) or by certain kinds of anti-positivist, like Marx and certain kinds of Marxists. While Marx was indebted to Hegel for his dialectical methods (and it was these that made Marx an anti-positivist, despite later attempts to define him as one), Marx rejected Hegel's idealist position that it was ideas and values that structured social order. Marx famously 'turned Hegel on his head', arguing that it was the other way round: 'It is not the consciousness of men that determines their existence, but their social existence that determines their consciousness' (1977 [1859]: 21).

Marx's method of *historical materialism* sees material conditions – the natural world around us – as the primary factor in human life. But Marx retains an idea from Hegel: human beings act upon nature to produce objects that keep them alive (e.g. food, clothing, shelter), and in so doing, they not only transform nature but also transform themselves in the process. This is why Marx sees human nature as being both fixed (it is primarily about making things) and changing (how things are made, and what this means for human mental development, changes over time). The economic element of human life is about humans transforming the natural environment to make goods for their own use. The economy is the most important dimension of any society, as without it nothing else could exist. Marx tried to explain the economically driven nature of human life using the famous metaphor of 'base' and 'superstructure':

> In the social relations of their existence, men inevitably enter into definite relations, which are independent of their will, namely relations of production . . . The totality of these relations of production constitutes the economic structure of society, the real foundation, on which arises a legal and political superstructure, and to which correspond definite forms of social consciousness. The mode of production of material life conditions the general process of social, political and intellectual life. (1977 [1859]: 21)

The ways in which the production of goods is organized in a given society involves the social relations that pertain between different groups of people. In particular, the organization of production concerns *property* relations: which groups own which things. The key factors which can be owned are (a) *raw materials* (e.g. wood, coal) which are turned into goods, (b) the *means* (e.g. tools and other technologies) by which those raw materials are made into useful objects, and (c) the *finished objects* themselves. The group which owns all of these factors will be the *ruling class* in that society. This class controls the class of people which actually makes the products. In modern, capitalist society, this division pertains between the class of capitalists (primarily factory-owners) and the working class (the proletariat, primarily factory workers).

The class that controls the economy will control every other sector of society. All other dimensions of storeys – law, government, culture (i.e. ways of thinking), education, family and kinship – are placed by Marx in the social 'superstructure'. Social order is like a house – the foundations are the economy, and the upper storeys all the other sectors of society. The economic base generates, shapes and over time controls the sectors in the superstructure. This is why cultural forms and ways of thinking are 'ideological' – they not only express the views and interests of the ruling class (or classes), they also *disguise* this fact. Post-Kantian theory posits that culture shapes how people experience the world. For Marx, culture is always ideological, tacitly supporting and promoting ruling class interests and working against the interests of the classes they control. The aim of analysis is to reveal this situation, make the dominated classes aware of it, and thus to foment revolutionary social change.

The base and superstructure metaphor was intended by Marx to clarify his views. But it has created so much controversy and confusion over the

---

Social superstructure
- government, law, education, family, culture, ideologies

Economic base:
- production of material objects
- control by a ruling class over a class that makes those objects

---

Figure 1.4 Marx on 'Base' and 'Superstructure'.

years because it actually makes Marx's position seem cruder than it is. It suggests a simple causal chain from base to superstructure, with the latter simply a product of the former, and unable to have any effects on it. As we will see in Chapter 3, many subsequent Marxists have thought the metaphor so misleading it has had to be replaced by more supple ways of presenting Marxian theory. In his later life, Marx's collaborator Friedrich Engels (1968 [1890]: 692) endeavoured to present a more nuanced version of Marx's historical materialist method:

> ... the *ultimately* determining element in history is the production and reproduction of real life ... if somebody twists this into saying that the economic element is the *only* determining one, he transforms that proposition into a meaningless, abstract, senseless phrase. The economic situation is the basis, but the various elements of the superstructure ... also exercise their influence upon the course of the historical struggles and in many cases preponderate in determining their *form*. There is an interaction of all these elements in which ... the economic movement finally asserts itself as necessary.

So the elements of society hitherto relegated to the superstructure are seen to be more active than had been inadvertently implied by Marx, for they are able to influence the economic sector just as it influences them. The conflicts between classes may be very much shaped by factors such as ideas and values, e.g. disputes over religious doctrines. But *ultimately* economic factors – the production of goods, and conflicts between ruling and dominated classes – are the most important aspects of social order and social change. How convincing this view is continues to be a point of much controversy among Marxists and non-Marxists alike.

As a thinker operating within the German hermeneutic tradition, one would expect Max Weber to reject the Marxist emphasis on material factors, and to argue in favour of how 'ideal' phenomena are much more important in shaping human activities. This is in fact only partly the case.

Weber (1982) insisted that Marx had over-emphasized classes as the main social groupings. Cutting across classes were status-groups, organized in a hierarchy of prestige. Although people might *objectively* be part of a class (e.g. because of the type of job they had), *subjectively* they might see themselves as part of a status-group (e.g. a particular profession) and regard class membership as less important, or in fact be unaware of being a member of a class altogether. It is how cultural forms allow people to perceive themselves in certain ways that is more important than material factors like class membership.

Yet Weber's work also represents an attempt to go beyond the materialist/idealist divide, drawing on elements of both. As he put it, it is 'not my aim to substitute for a one-sided materialistic an equally one-sided spiritualistic . . . interpretation' of social life (1930: 183). Weber rejected *mono-causal* explanations – those which privilege only one set of factors – in favour of *poly-causal* ones – those which try to combine more materialist and more idealist factors, and which show that each informs the other (Alexander, 1983). For Weber, Marx went wrong because he over-emphasized 'economic' issues; but his focus on such matters is still valuable, as long as it is combined with examining more 'ideal' factors as well. Particular phenomena have intertwined material and ideal elements, each influencing the other in complicated ways. This is the notion of 'elective affinity' (*Wahlverwandtschaft*). Weber used it to describe the subtle forms of connection that pertain between a group's material lifestyle and economic interests on the one side, and their cultural preferences and tastes on the other.

It is in part through the ideas of Weber that the philosophy of Nietzsche made its way into classical theory. One of Nietzsche's (1977) central notions was the 'will to power' – the natural drive by stronger individuals and groups to dominate weaker ones. Nietzsche's most famous aphorism is 'God is dead'. This does not just refer to the fact that modern society is seen to have killed off Christian (and other) religious beliefs, a common attitude among classical theorists. It also means that there is no

Materialism	Idealism
– the primacy in social life of the material production of objects (economy)	– the primacy in social life of ideas and values, derived from culture, in people's minds, motivating their actions

Figure 1.5 Materialism and Idealism.

guarantee of truth any more. For Nietzsche, a radical critic of the Enlightenment, the natural sciences in fact fabricate knowledge rather than produce objective 'facts'. In so doing, scientists claim power for themselves over others by exercising their 'will to truth'. This hostility to positivism has been very marked in subsequent German thought (see Chapter 3). It was also taken up in the French context in the 1970s by Michel Foucault, who follows Nietzsche in arguing that sciences are in fact mechanisms of claiming power for those who formulate them (Chapter 8). If the natural sciences cannot produce objective knowledge, there is no ultimate Truth. There are only multiple forms of knowledge, each fabricating their own specific truths. This is Nietzsche's *epistemological relativism*. The aim is to show the fabricated nature of all so-called 'truths', pulling apart systems of knowledge to demonstrate how they are products of particular social relations. Here too is the start of 'deconstruction' (Chapter 8), which shows how particular systems of knowledge which claim to be true and coherent, are actually internally contradictory and incoherent. These are themes that would in the late twentieth century come to be central to post-modernist thinking (see Chapter 9).

Conclusion: After the Classics

Throughout the rest of this book, traces, remnants and echoes of the classical theorists will be apparent. It can be objected that given they are all 'dead white European males', so caught up in the undoubtedly sexist – and by today's standards, often racist – ideas of their times, that their concepts must be handled cautiously or even rejected altogether (Sydie, 1987). Contemporary writers have sought to deal with these issues by bringing in voices – of women, of people of colour, of the lower classes – from the past hitherto silenced, either at the time or in the subsequent defining of what counts as classical theory. Early feminists like Charlotte Perkins Gilman, and critics of racist thought such as W. E. B. DuBois, are now on the classical theoretical agenda, and will in future be increasingly utilized by contemporary theorists seeking inspiration (Edles and Appelrouth, 2007).

Some critics today see *all* classical theory as being totally out of date, completely irrelevant for present-day social circumstances that have changed radically over the last century (Beck, 2000). But ironically, much of what these critics present as their own wholly new ideas are in fact very much indebted to the classics. Even when the classics are rejected, much of what is presented as replacing them owes a hidden debt to them. A more serious issue is that we cannot treat what the classics said as timeless truths, expressed in eternally valid concepts. Classical theory's concepts reflect, mostly unintentionally, the times in which they were created (Somers, 1996). What the classics argued cannot be said to be true for all times and places. All the ideas inherited from the classical authors need to be constantly updated and re-worked. In many ways, this is what modern social theory is constantly doing. As social circumstances change, so too do theories about society have to be transformed. Modern social theory is the story of those transformations.

Further Reading

Heilbron, J. (1995) *The Rise of Social Theory*. Cambridge: Polity.

Levine, D. N. (1995) *Visions of the Sociological Tradition*, 2nd edn. Chicago: University of Chicago Press.

Löwith, K. (1993) *Max Weber and Karl Marx*. London Routledge.

Turner, B. S. (1999) *Classical Sociology*. London: Sage.

Wagner, P. (2008) *Modernity as Experience and Interpretation: A New Sociology of Modernity*. Cambridge: Polity.

2

Functionalist and Systems Theory Paradigms

Functionalism was one of the major viewpoints in classical social theory, being developed particularly by Émile Durkheim and Herbert Spencer. In the middle of the twentieth century, it was further extended, most notably by Talcott Parsons, whose work we will focus on in this chapter. In the 1950s and early 1960s, Parsonian functionalism was the dominant paradigm in social theory in America and in some other countries. It sought to provide a general, unified account of all types of 'systems', including social systems. To that end, Parsons re-worked certain ideas of the classical theorists, most notably Durkheim and Spencer, and located them within a systematic theory that claimed to demonstrate the essential functional processes and mechanisms that produce social order.

But from the late 1950s onwards, the Parsonian vision came under forceful attack by critics who claimed it vastly overemphasized the consensual nature of social order, underplaying or ignoring altogether issues of conflict and dissensus. By the early 1970s, it seemed that the Parsonian system was in tatters, and that its attempt to provide a general, all-encompassing paradigm for social theory and research had failed. Rival theoretical positions had sprung up to replace it, leading to a strong fragmentation of the social theoretical and sociological fields. Whether the critics of Parsons were fair to him remains an open question. Once the dust had settled, attempts were made, especially from the 1980s onwards, to rescue and re-work key functionalist themes identified by Parsons. It is to these developments in the ongoing fortunes and misfortunes of functionalist theorizing that we turn to in this chapter.

Classical Evolutionism

Functionalism in large part derives from classical theory's ideas to do with *evolution*, which in turn took inspiration from nineteenth-century biology. 'Evolution' here does not mean Darwinian notions of 'survival of the fittest', involving competition between different species for survival. Instead, so-called 'classical evolutionism' is about processes involving increasing *structural complexity*, whether of organisms or societies.

The central idea taken from biology is that all organisms develop from early stages where they are simple in form, to later stages where they are more complex in form. A particular species of organism is seen to evolve over time, from simplicity to complexity. This involves moving from a condition where it has only a few elementary parts that are all alike, related to each other in simple ways (like the parts of an amoeba), towards a situation where it has multiple parts, all very different from each other, connected to each other in complex ways (like the organs of mammals) (Sztompka, 1993).

The movement from simplicity to complexity involves the process of *differentiation*. Over time, each part of a simple organism divides up into smaller parts, and each of them in turn divides up into smaller parts, until the organism's structure becomes a multiple number of parts that are related to each other in complex ways. At the start of the evolutionary process, each of the few simple parts will have multiple jobs to do to keep the organism alive. But as the organism moves towards complexity, each of the newer specific parts created by the differentiation process takes on its own particular role in ensuring the organism survives. So whereas a part of a simple organism takes on multiple tasks (i.e. functions), a differentiated and specific part only undertakes one specific task (i.e. one function) (Lopreato, 1990).

Sometimes classical evolutionary thought emphasized that the differentiation process happened spontaneously, without any external pressures compelling an organism to become more complex. But sometimes it was stressed that the organism had to be regarded in light of the *environment* around it. For an organism to stay alive, it must *adapt* to its environment effectively enough to be sustainable. In particular, it must have means of extracting sufficient energy from the environment to stay alive: for example, an animal has to eat, so as to convert energy from its environment into energy for sustenance. Evolutionary thought assumed that organisms that were more complex would be better at achieving these purposes than those that were simple, as the parts of the former would be more efficient at fulfilling their functions than the parts of the latter which had multiple tasks to carry out.

These biological ideas were applied to the history of human societies, in order to discern what was unique about modern society, which was regarded as the most complex society that had yet existed. One could say, as did in their own specific ways Durkheim (1964 [1893]) and Spencer (Stark, 1961), that social evolution was strongly akin to biological evolution. On this view, social organization (society) was *like* an organism, moving over history from simplicity to complexity, from a few simple parts related in simple ways, to multiple, task-specific parts connected in complex ways. Social evolution is seen to involve the increasing *structural differentiation* of human social organization, leading away from small-scale societies with simple and undifferentiated parts, to large-scale societies that are ever more complex because they have multiple parts charged with specific functions. Such societies are highly adapted to their environments, because they have specific parts which do specific things, especially to do with the processing of energy from the environment and transferring that energy to other parts. Over human history, societies appear which have more parts than in previous societies, and where the parts are ever more clearly demarcated and separate from each other. Classical evolutionism was of the view that over time, societies have become ever more centred around distinct, specialist systems each with their own specific tasks – the economic system concerns itself only with the production and circulation of goods, the education system only with the education of young people, and so on. This involves a separating out (differentiation) of what before were tasks or activities that were done together (Sztompka, 1993).

Structural differentiation was seen to apply, for example, to the world of work. In a simpler society, work is part of, and organized by and within, kinship and family relations. The medieval European peasant household was both a family unit and a work unit. People did not, as they do in modernity, leave the family home to work – they worked within the home, for the family. But modernity involves the structural differentiation of work and family: most people leave their home to go to work, to be paid wages by an employer they have no familial, or even personal, connections to. A new, typically impersonal, separate sphere called the 'economy' arises in modernity, separated from the family system, which now itself becomes a separate sphere, distinct from others (Smelser, 1959). So modernity can be seen as a type of society based around distinct spheres, each organized in its own distinctive ways, and each having its own distinctive sort of tasks to perform.

Here we find the beginnings of later theories that are 'structural-functionalist'. Complex societies, especially modernity, which is the most complex, evolve distinct and separate spheres (structures), which are regarded as performing certain tasks (functions), which contribute to the overall survival of the social order, which is a social *system* (and which is seen to be like an organism). The structures and functions are particularly concerned with adaptation to the system's external environment (i.e. everything outside of it, including the natural world). The social system has to adapt to its environment effectively, or it will fall apart – just like an organism that fails to adapt to the environment around it will die. Just as a biological organism requires energy from its environment (e.g. an animal eating food it has found), so too does any social system. The social system has a structure – in modernity called the 'economy' – which has the function of gaining energy from the environment, processing that energy, and sending it to other parts of the system which require it, in order that the whole system keep operating.

A 'modern' kind of social system is characterized by multiple, separated structures, each with its own concerns and its own distinctive tasks. This raises the issue of *integration*. How do parts that are separate from each other still work with each other in ways that are 'functional' for the whole system? If each of the parts becomes wholly disconnected from each other, the system will fall apart. So what holds complex modern social systems together? According to Durkheim's influential answer, it was 'common culture', shared by all individuals in the social system, which ensured the system's ongoing functioning. In his later work Durkheim (2001 [1912]) described how a common culture works to keep both simple and complex (modern) social systems functioning. Durkheim follows Kant in arguing that the culture of a group makes sense of an otherwise chaotic external world (see Chapter 1). Culture divides the world up into binary oppositions: sacred/profane, moral/immoral, allowed/forbidden, etc. These ways of thinking get ingrained into the mentality of the society's members as they grow up. These are reinforced periodically at particular ceremonies involving directly or indirectly all members of society. Particular 'totemic' symbols, invested with a strong sense of sacredness and reverence by the group, are crystallized representations of the very group of people worshipping the symbols – that is, they are sacred representations of *society itself*. Thus a culture centres around particular sacred symbols – e.g. in modernity, things like national flags and national anthems – which are condensed symbolizations of society for the people in that society. Regular ceremonies using these symbols revivify the sense of people in the society have that they are indeed members of that society, creating feelings of being bonded with each other. Through collective ceremonies and symbols, a common cultural framework is reproduced over time, as well as evolving to fit changing social circumstances. So the social system itself creates and reproduces

---

From simplicity to complexity

Structural differentiation

Modernity
Highly complex social order, with multiple parts, differentiated from each other, each with their own specific functions

Durkheim – common culture binding differentiated parts of society together

---

Figure 2.1 Summary of Classical Evolutionism.

over time its own methods for allowing for its own ongoing functioning. This social 'lubricant' – or 'glue' – involves commonly held cultural values. These values create particular norms of interaction i.e. socially expected styles of behaviour. These norms guide individuals in their interactions, allowing these to be predictable and patterned in the ways the system requires for its ongoing operation. It is common culture which binds the otherwise separate parts of complex modern social systems together. This Durkheimian idea of a common culture ensuring smooth functioning of the social system as a whole is central to the ideas of Parsons, as we will now see.

Talcott Parsons: Systematizing Functionalism

The American sociologist Talcott Parsons [1902–1979] was probably the most influential social theorist of the post-Second-World-War period up until the early 1970s (Holmwood, 1996). Parsons sought to make functionalism into a general, systematic social theory that would inform not just sociology but all the human sciences. As such, he operated at the level of very general abstractions – for which he has been amply criticized (Mills, 1959; Andreski, 1972) – but also at the level of empirical applications of his general concepts.

Although his theorizing has a reputation for being very difficult to read, the central points are easy enough to understand, as they are extrapolations from the original ideas of Spencer (evolution towards social complexity; social-structural differentiation) and Durkheim (analysis of what keeps different parts of the system working together; common culture). Parsons coupled these together with a diverse array of other ideas, including Freud's ideas about childhood socialization (see Chapters 1 and 3), and his colleague Bales' analysis of the interactions among small groups (Parsons and Bales, 1956). Parsons was also mindful of the Durkheim-inspired functionalism of early twentieth-century British social anthropology, which in the vision of Radcliffe-Brown (1965) saw social institutions as patterned sets of relationships, centred around individuals carrying out allotted roles, the function of which was to maintain the social system. From the 1930s through to the 1970s, Parsons produced an evolving body of work which in various different ways aimed to be the definitive statement on what 'society' is, how it works, and how modernity operates.

His first book, *The Structure of Social Action* (1937), identified what it saw as a convergence between various schools of thought in classical theory as to solving a problem set for subsequent thinkers by the seventeenth-century political philosopher Thomas Hobbes. If, as Hobbes claimed, individuals were essentially selfish, calculating to promote their own self-interests at the expense of everyone else, then there would be a 'war of all against all', random chaos with no social order possible at all. But clearly social order *was* possible as there were instances of it all around to see. So the 'Hobbesian problem of order' was: how is this order achieved and reproduced over time? Parsons believed that certain classical theorists had made contributions to the answer to this, but their individual responses needed to be synthesized. While Weber had correctly noted that we must attend to the motivations of why individuals act, Durkheim had also pointed out how social values and norms guide action. So a rounded account of all the factors involved in action – what Parsons calls the 'unit act', the basic unit of sociological analysis – would have to account for all of the following factors:

(a) the *actor* (the person doing the action)
(b) the *goal* (the aim s/he wishes to achieve through the particular action in question)
(c) the *means* (the methods s/he chooses in order to achieve that goal)
(d) *situational conditions* (the *material* environment in which s/he acts – this includes constraints on possible actions by factors such as: the actor's biological make-up, the physical-natural world around the actor, the presence of other actors)
(e) *norms, values,* and *ideas* (the *ideal* environment in which s/he acts, i.e. the *cultural context*)

So action consists of a person, with particular goals, choosing certain means of achieving them, and these choices are made within conditions, both material and cultural, that constrain the choices and means. Action is 'voluntaristic' – the person chooses what to do (this is more like Weber). But it is the surrounding culture that defines for her what her goals are, what means there are to achieve them with, and what choices should be made (this is more like Durkheim). A social system is made up of sets of unit acts. The system can exist over time because individuals are constantly motivated to choose the sorts of actions which result in patterns which reproduce the system. It is cultural values guiding, but not wholly determining, actions which make possible social order.

Parsons After the Second World War

Parsons had originally intended to 'work up' from the smallest element of society, the unit act, to large-scale, complex social institutions. But after the Second World War, he moved in the opposite direction, seeking to explain how large-scale social structures shape individual behaviours (Parsons, 1951, Parsons and Shils, 1951). All interactions between humans are seen to involve (a) biological organisms (human bodies); (b) human minds (psychologies); (c) social relationships between at least two people; (d) culture (the language that is used by people, the values and norms that guide their interactions).

The first factor, the human body, points to the *behavioural system*, which we will return to later. Elements (b), (c) and (d) point to the existence of the *personality system*, the *social system* and the *cultural system* respectively (see Figure 2.2). These are systems because they each have 'environments' (made up of the other systems), and have internal elements that are internally connected to each other. The aim is to analyse two things: (1) the operation of each of the systems, the sub-systems within them, and the sub-systems within the sub-systems; (2) the ways the four systems interact

---

Biological organism – Behavioural system
Human mind – Personality system
Social relationships – Social system
Culture – Cultural system

Figure 2.2 Parsons' Four Systems.

with each other in relations of interdependence and interpenetration (Parsons, 1961).

It is assumed by Parsons that the cultural system (the common culture that all people in the system share) will ensure at least a minimum level of integration within both the personality system (i.e. an individual will have a relatively coherent personality shaped by culture) and the social system (enough to make actions and interactions coherent over time). It is also assumed that the cultural system will ensure at least minimal levels of connection between the personality and social systems. Otherwise, these could not be called 'systems' at all.

This all exists at the level of theoretical models. Really existing systems have to be studied empirically to see how internally coherent they are, and how well connected they are to other systems. This is a crucial point. Critics have often accused Parsons of ever-emphasizing system coherence and inter-system integration. In his studies of empirical systems, especially those of the USA of his own period (e.g. Parsons, Platt and Smelser, 1973) he may have been guilty of this to some extent, but only for contingent reasons, not for those that flow *necessarily* from his general theory. Parsons is *not* claiming that particular empirically existing systems will always be coherent and integrate with each other – they may well not. But he *is* saying that to use the notion of 'system' at all, we have to assume at least some minimal level of internal coherence over time within what we are taking to be a system, otherwise analysing human life in terms of systems would be impossible.

Social systems are made up of 'roles'. These are specific positions in the division of labour – bus driver, teacher, doctor, etc. – and the social expectations associated with them, i.e. what people in this role normally do, and how they are expected to act. When people enter the roles, they engage in social activities, acting with others in culturally prescribed ways. The values and norms shaping the roles come from the cultural system – it is in this way that the cultural system penetrates and structures the social system. Quite simply, culture guides action and interaction. The roles allow for the social system *to be a system* (i.e. relatively coherent over time), as they allow for people to act and interact in predictable and thus patterned ways. The roles indicate what in a concrete interaction – e.g. doctor and patient – should happen, in line with the participants' culturally shaped shared expectations.

Because they are based around norms, roles dictate what counts as proper and improper conduct in an interaction. When what is defined as improper interaction occurs, the rule-breakers are breaking norms and so risk sanctions, ranging from mild disapproval to severe formal punishment, depending on how serious the 'offence' is regarded. Norms and sanctions work to prevent interaction from becoming so disorderly that the social system cannot operate at least minimally. Such ideas derive in part from Durkheim, but Parsons added to these the Freudian notion (see Chapters 1 and 3) of how childhood socialization makes the individual internalize cultural dispositions, in this case the norms associated with role-expectations, so that they seem 'natural', often go without question, and are given commitment. More broadly, the cultural system shapes the personality system (the individual psyche) in terms of what individuals think is important, what their aims are, and what they think is the 'right' thing to do in any specific circumstance. Here we see the interpenetration of the cultural system (norms), the personality system (internalized norms in the psyche) and the social system (individuals acting in ways prescribed by roles). This leads to the generally 'automatic acceptance as the way of thinking and communicating' by individuals of the norms that guide roles (Parsons, 1961: 976).

The Pattern Variables

The norms embodied in roles derive from more general values in the cultural system. If we examine a particular society's cultural system, then the values within it will be locatable on one side of a fundamental divide. Here Parsons (1951: 67) follows the typical classical theoretical construction (see Chapter 1) of a binary division between 'modern' and 'non-modern' (or pre-modern) societies. The 'pattern variables' describe the differences between typically 'modern' and 'non-modern' cultural values (see Figure 2.3).

Non-Modern	Modern
Affectivity	Affective neutrality
Collectivity orientation	Self-orientation
Particularism	Universalism
Ascription	Achievement
Diffuseness	Specificity

Figure 2.3 The Pattern Variables.

Affectivity/affective neutrality involves whether a particular cultural system promotes highly emotional or very impersonal ways of thinking and acting.

Collectivity orientation/self-orientation concerns whether a culture system promotes identification by a person with the group to which they belong, or individuality and individualism.

Particularism/universalism is about whether the cultural system promotes thinking that is context-dependent, or based on abstractions and universally applicable rules (e.g are employers legitimately allowed to hire people because they are in their family, or is this denounced as nepotism? Job selection is based upon abstract criteria like choosing the applicant with the best qualifications).

Ascription/achievement involves whether, for a particular cultural system, the place a person occupies in society is based on custom and tradition – they were born into that role – or whether places in society are regarded by the cultural system as being won on the basis of merit, effort, achievement of qualifications and suchlike.

Diffuseness/specificity concerns whether the cultural system demands that an actor view an object or person in terms of their whole personality or being, or in terms of very narrow criteria. For example, do I have to know all about the woman at the supermarket till in order to interact with her, or is the nature of my interaction with her so narrow that I don't need to know anything about her except how to interact with her as a social type i.e. as someone merely acting out a specified role? (see Chapter 1).

The pattern variables are ideal-types, stressing extreme contrasts. But the point of them is to understand how particular sets of cultural, personality and social systems work. A cultural system creates specific sorts of personalities that expect to interact according to certain norms in particular types of roles. So a non-modern cultural system creates personalities who view the world, expect to interact, and expect to inhabit roles, all of which involve in various permutations the non-modern pattern variables. But a typically 'modern' cultural system produces people, roles and interactions all involving the modern side of the pattern variables. Modernity produces distinctively 'modern' behaviours, all the actors expect that, and so interaction can happen in orderly and predictable ways, which reproduce the social system.

This applies in the social system generally (the realm of human interactions), and also in its various specific differentiated parts, or sub-systems as Parsons calls them, such as the economy, the education system, the religious system, and the medical system. Each sub-system has a specific role to play in the overall social system. The specific roles that people have to carry out within a sub-system reflect this (e.g. teachers are expected only to carry out education-related roles in the education system and not any other roles; doctors are supposed only to carry out medicine-related roles in the medical system, and so on).

Role-expectations have to be similar enough between the different sub-systems so that as people move between them, they do not get totally confused, so undermining the integration of the subsystems with each other. If I usually operate in one sub-system (e.g. education) and I move into another (e.g. medicine) for whatever reason (e.g. because I am sick and need to see a doctor), then I can move smoothly between one sub-system and the other because the new sub-system uses the same pattern variables as the system I am used to. So if I am a teacher in a modern education system, I know that my professional role is to grade papers fairly, on the basis of their merits and not on whether I like the student or not. I am using typical modern pattern variables. If I think that the doctor I go to as a patient treats me as fairly as any other patient, I feel – generally only at a semi-conscious level – reassured, because the doctor is using in her sub-system the same pattern variables as I recognize from my own sub-system.

But if the doctor acts in light of norms I can't understand – for example, seems to be overly interested in my private life in ways that seem irrelevant to the consultation – then I will feel uncomfortable, perhaps even to the point where our interaction breaks down altogether. I was expecting interaction to be guided by modern pattern variables, but the doctor broke the rules by acting in light of non-modern pattern variables (wanting to know *all* about me, not me simply as a patient). There will be integration between sub-systems only if there are cultural values, centred around the pattern variables, that are general enough to guide the norms that apply in a wide range of social sub-systems. There has to be a common culture that is broad and flexible enough to guide interaction in potentially very diverse circumstances, ranging from, as here, university classrooms to doctors' surgeries. Without this, the overall social system could not work, because its various sub-systems would be totally out of synch with each other, and people could not act predictably and smoothly in all the various situations they might find themselves in in a modern, complex society.

Parsons' Structural-Functionalism

Parsons' structural-functionalist ideas can now be presented. They derived in part from his colleague Bales' study of small group interactions (Parsons and Bales, 1956). When a small group of people has to solve a task, it has to do a number of things. It must:

(1) solve the task by adapting to its environment (e.g. use readily available tools);
(2) work out methods to solve the problem;
(3) get people to cooperate with each other and smooth out problems and tensions;
(4) (especially if the group is going to solve a number of tasks over time) build up norms of solidarity so that it moves from a mere collection of individuals to being a coherent 'team'.

From these four requirements Parsons builds an account of how *systems of action* operate. The needs or functional requirements of *any* system of action (social or otherwise) involve a) how the system relates to its external environment; and b) how the system regulates all its constituent parts i.e. how the system regulates itself internally.

A further two principles that Parsons includes concern whether processes are to do either with the means by which goals are attained (the instrumental principle) or with integrating and coordinating the elements involved in those processes (the consummatory principle). Taking the four dimensions together creates a four-fold box, the famous 'AGIL' model (Parsons and Smelser, 1956) – see Table 2.1.

Each term shown in the table (Adaptation, etc.) describes a functional process. Each process is a sub-system of the overall system of action. Each sub-system is given a label (A, G, I or L), which is shorthand for its role in the system.

Table 2.1 The Action System – AGIL Model.

	Instrumental	Consummatory
External	A Adaptation	G Goal Attainment
Internal	L Latency	I Integration

The 'A' sub-system involves 'adaptation'. This is the functional process that concerns the system's instrumental relations to its external environment. This is the process whereby the constraints and opportunities afforded the system by its environment are responded to. This is also the process whereby the system attempts to control the environment in ways that resources are gained that satisfy the system's needs.

The 'G' sub-system, which is both 'external' and 'consummatory', involves 'goal attainment'. This is the process whereby the system's goals are formulated, and resources – gained in the Adaptation system – are deployed to meet those goals. The 'G' sub-system is the system's decision-making apparatus, its 'brain'. It decides what should be done to meet system needs.

The 'I' sub-system, which is 'consummatory' and 'internal', involves 'integration'. This co-ordinates the various component parts of the system in the direction of their operating together in order to meet the goals set by the 'G' sub-system. It is this function which attempts to resolve any internal disturbances the system may face concerning friction or conflict among its parts.

The 'L' sub-system, which is 'internal' and 'instrumental', is the 'latency' function. The role of this function is *pattern maintenance*. That involves the creation and maintenance of the motivations that inspire action in service of the system.

Reading the boxes in reverse direction, an action system is a process involving motivations pursued over time (L) to pursue certain goals (G) using certain means (A), with each part of the system acting in a co-ordinated way with the others (I). A successful action system is one in which the goals are indeed met. There will have to be balanced interactions between all four processes to allow this to happen.

This all relates back to Bales' small groups. For a small group of people, A is them adapting to circumstances and finding resources to allow for the problem-solving; G is them working out ways to solve the task set; I is making sure that all people in the group work together effectively; and L involves group norms so that all of this keeps happening over time.

It is Parsons' contention that the AGIL model can be used to analyse *any* sort of system, or sub-system of a system. Particular systems can be viewed as sub-systems of other systems, rather like a set of Russian dolls, one placed inside the other. This procedure allowed Parsons to locate the systems described above – the cultural, social and personality systems

Table 2.2 The Four Sub-Systems of the Action System.

Adaptation	Goal Attainment
Behavioural organism (body)	Personality
Latency	**Integration**
Cultural System	Social System

Table 2.3 The Social System as an AGIL System.

Adaptation	Goal Attainment
Function: Economic processes	Function: Political processes
Structure: Economy	Structure: Polity
Latency	**Integration**
Function: Socialization processes	Function: Social solidarity processes
(Culture)	Structure: Societal community

– inside the AGIL framework, along with the one we mentioned but have not yet dealt with, the behavioural system.

As Table 2.2 shows in any action system, adaptation to the environment is done by the behavioural organism, i.e. the human body. Choosing goals and how to achieve them is carried out by the individual personality (the psyche). The social system has an integrative function, as it coordinates all the actions of individuals into patterned interactions. The cultural system has the latency (or 'pattern maintenance') function as it ensures that over time its values inspire and guide the actions being undertaken. Again, there has to be balanced interchanges between all four elements for the action system to operate effectively. Note that this is an elaboration of the original 'unit act' idea described above.

Parsons says that we can open up the Integration/Social System box in Table 2.2, and see that it *itself* has four dimensions. That is, the social system has A, G, I and L components too, all of them functional processes (see Table 2.3).

Each of the four functional processes is carried out by a particular social structure (hence this is a theory of structural–functionalism, where particular social structures carry out particular social functions).

The most important sub-system is the Integration sub-system. Its purpose is to secure co-operation among members of the group in the social system and to give them a sense of collective solidarity and community. The social structure that carries out this function is the *societal community*, comprised of networks of social groups, organized in specific ways in particular empirically existing societies, and it both expresses and maintains the common culture.

The A sub-system involves the Adaptation of the social system to its environment. This involves gaining resources through production and distribution of goods. The social structure that carries out this task is the *economy*.

The G sub-system involves the Goal Attainment function of the social system. This involves the ways in which the goals of the system are formulated, and how people in the system are mobilized to carry out these goals. This is the 'brain' of the system, so the social structure that carries out this function is the *polity*, the political decision-making body i.e. the government.

Finally, the L sub-system ensures Pattern Maintenance within the system. This means that the fundamental cultural values and norms of the system are maintained. This is done through processes of *socialization*. Unlike the other sub-systems, this one does not have a specific social structure to carry out its functions. Instead, the maintenance of cultural values is carried out in a more diffuse and hidden (hence 'latent') fashion. The main mechanisms whereby socialization occurs are the family and education systems, but these are part of the societal community rather than forming a separate social structure of their own. In essence, the L sub-system involves the common culture, and it both reproduces and is reproduced by the institutions of the societal community which it is embedded within.

This model is a general one applicable to *all* social systems. In less structurally differentiated (simpler) systems, specific institutions may have more than one function e.g. in peasant societies, the family has both economic and political functions. In the most structurally differentiated societies – especially modern America for Parsons – there can be separate institutions carrying out just one specific function, but even here functions may be carried out by more than one structure, and a structure may be involved in more than one function (e.g. modern governments do not only have political functions but economic ones too).

Regardless of the level of actual social complexity, the general model also has to account for interchanges between the different functional realms, for they have to communicate with each other and achieve some sort of minimal level of balance between each other. It is important to note that Parsons is not arguing for *perfect equilibrium* between the functions and their respective structures. But he is saying that there has over time to be a certain level of *moving equilibrium* whereby the parts relate to each other, if the social system is to continue as a system and not break down altogether. There can be friction between parts, but if there is too much, the system will no longer be a system. If the system is to remain *as* a system, then as its structures change, so too will the relations between them have to evolve to maintain a moving equilibrium. Parsons is not saying this will happen in any particular empirical situation, only that this is what would logically have to happen if the system is going to be maintained.

The relations between each part of the system involve *transactions* and these are mediated by *symbols*. Each part possesses particular *media of exchange*, which are the symbolic forms through which the transactions between the sub-systems take place. In a highly differentiated society, the Adaptive sub-system's structure, the economy, relates to the other three sectors via *money*. The Goal Attainment's structure, the polity, has *power* or *authority* – the capacity to create conformity and loyalty on behalf of those on the receiving end of it – as its medium of exchange with the other parts. The Integrative function's structure, the societal community, uses *influence* (the capacity to persuade people to act in given ways), rewarding and recognizing individuals for carrying out roles in norm-governed ways.

Beyond Parsons

From the late 1950s onwards, and especially in the late 1960s and early 1970s, Parsons' ideas came under very heavy attack from all sides. In a period of political turmoil involving such issues as the Vietnam war and student protests against it, Parsons' vision of modern societies seemed to be more redolent of the apparent stability of the 1950s than of a politically highly troubled era (Gouldner, 1970). Parsons' apparent optimism about the nature and future of modern societies – especially the USA – seemed to put him at odds with radical critics of those societies (Holton and Turner, 1986). He was accused of being a conservative servant of the social status quo, rather than the neutral social scientist he claimed to be. Functionalism in general was accused of being by its very nature politically conservative, seeking to find social stability and cultural consensus where none existed.

Some critics argued that Parsons placed far too much emphasis on common culture and 'ideal' factors. Conflict theorists (e.g. Dahrendorf, 1959), inspired by Weber and Marx, argued against the emphasis on common culture to be found in Durkheim and utilized by Parsons. There might be cultural consensus in very simple social orders, they argued. But in the more complex situation of really existing modern societies, the cultural realm might be endemically conflictual rather than consensual, expressive of the different interests of rival social groups. In modernity, even in cases where there is something like a 'common culture', it is because dominant groups have succeeded in imposing their values on other groups (see the ideas of Gramsci – Chapter 3). So the system may 'function', but not in everyone's interest, but for the interests of a minority who have 'captured' the common culture. Marxists and Weberians regarded culture as a site of struggle whereby some groups dominate others, and make the social system run for their benefit. But Durkheim and Parsons could retort that even if this is true, it still implies their shared view is correct – that for any kind of social system, a common culture of at least some sort is an absolutely necessary part of its operation.

The issue of 'consensus' versus 'conflict' as rival ways of theorizing society was taken up by Lockwood (1964), who claims that Parsons confuses two different things: 'social integration', which involves 'the orderly or conflictual relationships' between individuals, and 'system integration', which concerns 'the orderly or conflictual relationships between the parts of a social system' (Mouzelis, 1974: 396). Conflict theorists concentrate on the former, functionalists like Parsons on the latter. For Lockwood, Parsons cannot see these are separable matters, because institutions (the level of system integration) are seen by him to operate around norms guiding action and interaction (the level of social integration). But what if system integration does not automatically lead to, or is not congruent with, social integration? What if the 'system', far from involving harmonious social relations among individuals, actually dominates them? This is the idea that Jürgen Habermas used to re-work elements of Parsonian systems theory for the purposes of developing a critical theory of how 'system' (today, capitalist economy and government) dominates 'lifeworld' (everyday social relations), putting a critical twist on Parsons' apparent conservatism (see Chapter 3).

Other critics alleged Parsons placed far too great a stress on social-structural and functional factors, as opposed to individual actions (Holmwood, 1996). The individual's mind seems to be wholly structured by the common culture, compelled to think only in socially required ways. This means that actors are being theorized not as active human beings with the capacities to choose different courses of action , but as 'cultural dopes' who carry out the instructions for social action given to them by the common culture's norms and values (Wrong, 1961). He had thus betrayed the point of his early work on the 'unit act', which was intended to account for individuals making choices in guiding their actions, by taking on board a too simplistic version of Freud's understanding of socialization as internalization of cultural values.

But Parsons could respond that his theoretical model of cultural, social and personality systems took account of the fact that in really existing systems, there could be a lack of integration between these. If there is very strong friction between them, then the system they are part of will collapse. Again, to talk of a 'system' at all assumes at least minimal integration between the three domains of cultural, social and personality systems. So a defence of Parsons would involve saying that the general model makes relatively modest assumptions, not the vast assumptions about continuing cultural consensus and system reproduction that the critics alleged. Thus maybe his ideas *can* handle issues to do with cultural dissensus and social dissent by individuals, and matters of conflict and social change, which the critics claimed they could not. Social change is examined through the idea of *moving equilibrium* between the various parts of a society. It is never said that any really existing system must have, or even could have, *perfect* equilibrium between its parts. Whether this is a good way or not of analysing social change is up for debate, but it *is* an analysis of phenomena of social conflict and change which critics alleged Parsons' ideas could not handle at all.

For a time, Parsons' theoretical reputation was dragged through the mud by radical critics. Once the dust had settled, by the later 1970s and 1980s it seemed safe for some thinkers to return to Parsons and functionalist theory more generally, in order to put forward systems theories that could avoid some of the pitfalls into which Parsons' version had apparently fallen. It was already clear from the work from the 1940s of Parsons' contemporary Robert K. Merton (1949) that a more modest functionalism that apparently made fewer controversial assumptions was possible. Merton's version of functionalism is well known for its distinction between 'manifest' and 'latent' functions: institutions and activities which have either a use for the social system that actors are aware of (manifest functions,) or which they are completely unaware of (latent functions) but which the unintended consequences of their actions produce (e.g. no one participating at an international football match thinks they are engaging in the kind of collective ritual Durkheim described, but they are, without knowing it, for it helps reproduce loyalty to the 'nation' among participants).

Just as important are Merton's dilutions of strong functionalist claims made by the British social anthropologists like Radcliffe-Brown mentioned above. One cannot assume that what is functional for 'society as a whole' (if such an entity actually exists) will be functional for all groups and individuals within it. It may in fact be *dysfunctional* for some of them: there are losers as well as winners. Relatedly, a social institution might be retained in a society if it is functional not for the 'whole society', but for powerful groups within it. Thus Merton places issues of power and conflict between groups right at the heart of functionalist analysis. Finally, one cannot assume that just because an institution exists that it must be essential for the system. What are essential are the system's requirements – in Parsons' terms, the four functional processes of AGIL – and not the particular institution that is apparently fulfilling them. Different institutions may fulfil the same requirement. If that is true, then it exonerates functionalism from the charge of being innately conservative. Functionalism cannot legitimately argue that a particular institution is the *only* one that can meet a system requirement, as another institution theoretically could do the same job. So the nuclear family form is not a necessary part of modern society, because single parent families could carry out the same function of socialization of children into the common culture. In this way, Merton had shown how flexibility could be built into functionalist thinking.

By the mid 1980s the Marxist ideas used to attack Parsons were much less widespread and accepted in American sociology than they had been a decade or so earlier. Thus scholars like Alexander and Colomy (1985), who called themselves 'neo-functionalists', were in a position to mount a revivification of what they saw as the better side of Parsons' ideas, and reject their weaker side 'by denying its conservative ideological implications and demonstrating its capacity to breed an appreciation of power, conflict, and change' (Camic, 1985: 694). Individuals' actions were regarded as being more creative and wilful than Parsons' focus on roles had implied. Social integration was understood as a possibility that *might* be achieved by systems, not as something they necessarily or automatically attained. Relations between a system's parts were regarded as open-ended and pluralistic, rather than mechanical and pre-ordained as earlier functionalism had implied. How successful or not neo-functionalism was in recasting Parsonian ideas was hotly debated at the time (Joas, 1985).

Luhmann's Systems Theory

An alternative use of some Parsonian ideas was formulated by the German sociologist Niklas Luhmann [1927–1998], his version of systems theory being nowadays more widely cited than neofunctionalism, cer-tainly in continental Europe. One notable feature of Luhmann's theory is that unlike most other forms of social theory, it is not concerned with issues of 'structure' and 'agency'. This is because it operates at the levels of social systems and their internal forms of communication, and not at the level of how individuals are shaped by, or can shape, social structures.

Luhmann (1982) assumes that structural differentiation is the major process by which modernity has been created, generating separate spheres of social life (education system, media system, economic system, and so on). In his earlier work, Luhmann's focus was on how each system deals with the environment around it by 'reducing complexity'. That is, each system only focuses on a very limited set of phenomena in the world around it, ignoring everything else. Thus the economic system only focuses on what it regards as 'economic' phenomena (money, markets, profits, etc.), and ignores every other aspect of the world.

Luhmann's (1986) main conceptual innovation rests in his later work's focus on the 'autopoietic' nature of differentiated social systems, and on communication within and between systems, as the central features of social existence. Here he combines evolutionary and Parsonian ideas with those of the philosopher Ludwig Wittgenstein on 'language games'. Auto-poiesis is a process where a thing reproduces itself out of itself – that is, it makes itself anew out of its own existing elements. So the 'autopoietic' nature of social systems means that each particular system (the economy, the education system, etc.) creates its own elements, and so in that sense is constantly 'self-creating'. Each system is self-organizing. It draws its own boundaries, these boundaries determining what is (or rather, what the system regards as being) 'inside' the system, and what is 'outside' it (i.e. what constitutes its 'environment'). Each autopoietic system is 'closed', in the sense that it operates completely according to its own logic of operation and its own criteria of relevance. Each system has its own particular form of communication, which underpins how things work within the system itself and how the system deals with other systems in its environment. For example, in the modern economic system, the world is divided up into what is 'profitable' and 'not profitable' and it is on this basis that the wider world is made sense of, and communications about it are formulated, by the economic system. The modern legal system divides things up into legal/illegal; the scientific system divides things up into true/untrue; the art system divides things up into what counts as 'art' and what does not, and so on.

Each communication made in a particular system refers to other communications made in that system, and it is the ongoing flow of communications within the system that keeps the system going. Following from this, each system deals with its environment (i.e. all other systems) in its own particular way, classifying in its own specific terms what is relevant or irrelevant about the environment, and how environmental factors are to be defined and dealt with. In that sense, each system only 'sees' what its definition of reality allows it to see, and it cannot see any other aspect of reality, remaining 'indifferent' to other factors that other systems might discern. Thus the economic system is 'indifferent' to 'moral' issues, except as these might impact upon the profitability of certain economic transactions. As each system is self-enclosed and self-reproducing, it is not guaranteed that any system will 'fit' well with any other.

For Luhmann, the complexity of advanced modernity is characterized by multiple relations between different systems that each have their own, potentially highly mutually incompatible concerns, their own specific modes of communication, and their own logics and ways of operating. As each system is autopoietic (self-generating), they each run according to their own specific logics of operation. Different systems thus tend not to be well integrated with each other, because they understand the world, and each other, in very different ways. This is very far from a simple functionalist vision where all elements of a social system are tightly bound with each other. For Luhmann, 'society' is the social system which encompasses all the other social systems – it is the system of systems. Contemporary society is therefore without a centre, as it is made up of multiple different systems that are self-enclosed and operate according to their own distinctive logics.

The systems do not at all overlap, because each runs according to its own communications and ways of making sense of the world. But they do connect with each other, in the sense that for one system, all the other systems are its 'environment'. A system deals with other systems by translating into its communications the specific concerns embodied in the communications of the other systems. For example, a company exists in the economic system. If the business-people want to exploit for a new product a novel scientific finding which has been discovered by scientists operating within the scientific system, they have to translate certain scientific system communications about the finding into terms that the economic system can understand. Will the finding allow us to make a product that is profitable, or not? Will the finding allow us to make a product that is better than that sold by our competitors?

So when communications from one system enter into another system, they have to be transformed so that they make sense within the system they have entered. Luhmann refers to such processes as different systems 'irritating' each other. In addition, some institutions exist which 'structurally couple' different systems together. Thus a university couples together the scientific system with the education system, and the people who run the university have to find ways of coordinating the two systems, allowing them to communicate meaningfully with each other (Van Assche and Verschraegen, 2008).

Although Luhmannian theory is notoriously difficult to read for the uninitiated, it has stimulated interesting novel ways of understanding the systemic aspects of human societies (Schinkel, 2010). It is open to criticism for implicitly bringing into social theory a certain kind of conservative politics, which accepts rather than criticizes existing social conditions. From the point of view of a rival theory of major social institutions,

---

Knowledge
Theory of autopoietic (self-generating) systems

Structure/Agency
Replaced by a focus on communications within systems

Modernity
Multiple, self-regulating autopoietic systems; translations of communications between systems as 'irritations'.

Figure 2.4 Luhmann's Systems Theory.

namely Pierre Bourdieu's field theory (see Chapter 10), the key flaw in Luhmann's vision is that it does not allow for a critical sociological analysis of how some fields (especially the capitalist economy and government) can come to dominate and control the operations of other fields, such as the media and education. This is also the thrust of Habermas' idea of system 'colonization' (see Chapter 3). For Luhmann's critics, he over-emphasizes the closure of each system, omitting to analyse how systems can be hijacked by other systems and the powerful groups who control them.

Conclusion

For some critics, such as Giddens (see Chapter 10), functionalist theorizing of all varieties is today more a historical artefact than a living theoretical force. It seems to be rooted in some of the worst aspects of classical theory, especially its reliance on nineteenth-century biological ideas that are now wholly out of date (Turner and Maryanski, 2008). Contemporary theories of social evolution reject the kind of simplistic models of evolu-tion of a single organism accepted by the likes of Spencer and Durkheim, in favour of looking at social evolution in terms drawn from Darwinian natural section: like animal species, some societies, or elements within them, survive and others disappear because of selection processes among rival entities competing in an environment (Collins, 1988b). So all analyses of modernity as the product of increasing structural differentiation have to reflect back on the assumptions, based in outmoded biological meta-phors, upon which they are founded. And this affects any present-day attempts to think in functionalist ways, because functionalism has always been concerned to work out how structurally differentiated social struc-tures fit together. Nonetheless, as functionalism was so central to social theory in the classical and early post-classical periods, understanding it remains crucial for comprehending later theoretical innovations which reacted against it. New forms of neo-functionalism may yet develop in future, picking up some of the more productive elements of the function-alist edifice.

Further Reading

Holmwood, J. (1996) *Founding Sociology? Talcott Parsons and the Idea of General Theory.* Harlow: Longman.

Sanderson, Stephen K. (2007) *Evolutionism and its Critics: Deconstructing and Reconstructing an Evolutionary Interpretation of Human Society*. Boulder: Paradigm.

Sztompka, P. (1993) *The Sociology of Social Change*. Oxford: Blackwell.

Thompson, K. (2002) *Émile Durkheim*, 2nd edn. London: Routledge.

3

Marxist and Critical Theory Paradigms

Marxist forms of analysis have made very important contributions to the development of social theory. In addition, Marxist theories have often been crucial foils for non-Marxists, from Max Weber to Anthony Giddens, to sharpen their ideas against. Certain thinkers, like Pierre Bourdieu (Chapter 10), have taken particular Marxist ideas and adapted them for their own purposes.

Since the death of Marx in 1883, there has been no one entity called 'Marxism', but rather a plurality of different – and often mutually antagonistic – Marxisms, created by different sorts of people for different purposes (McLellan, 2007). This diversity was in part because Marx intended his ideas not to be purely academic speculations, but rather practical guides to the ongoing political struggles of the working class, and the Communist Party which claimed to be guiding them. Marx was wholly against the idea that 'theory' was something only professors did in universities. Theory was a guide to practical political action, intended to diagnose the current state of capitalist society, to discern how it was changing, to discover how it would or could be overthrown through socialist revolution, and to examine how revolutionary change was being blocked by the activities of the ruling classes.

The older Marx felt uncomfortable with the term 'Marxism', as it suggested a dogmatic, unchanging viewpoint, rather than a theory that would change as social conditions altered. Since Marx's death, there has been a whole series of different attempts to define what Marxism 'is'. Divergent groups claiming to be Marxists have attempted to identify both what Marx 'really said' or what they think he should have said. There have been wide-ranging disputes over Marx's original writings, with different groups of scholars having their own specific interpretations of particular Marxist texts. For those impressed with the more directly economic and allegedly 'scientific' aspects of Marx's ideas, it is texts from Marx's later period of writing, such as the multiple volumes of *Das Kapital*, that have been presented as the essence of his thinking. But for those wishing, as they see it, to rescue Marx and Marxism from an overly 'economistic' and 'scientistic' understanding of his theory, the most suggestive works are those of the younger Marx, when he was writing under the heavy influence of Hegel (see Chapter 1).

Reacting against the view of Marx as primarily an economic determinist – the notion that the economy in direct and straightforward ways shapes and controls the rest of society – those who have favoured his earlier writings have tried to recover what they see as the 'Hegelian Marx', a writer alive to social complexity and contradiction, and the capacity of ordinary human beings to shape society at least as much as it shapes them. The conflicts and controversies between those advocating a more 'scientific' and economistic Marx, and those advocating a more philosophical, humanistic and 'Hegelian' Marx, very much shaped the contours of Marxism in the century and more after his death, as we will see.

In the twentieth century, many different types of Marxism sprang up in different regions of the world, reflecting the broader political cultures of those contexts. What this meant was a fracturing of Marxism. The most notable for our purposes was the division into 'Eastern Marxism' – involving the official political doctrines of the Soviet Union, the Communist state set up in Russia in 1917 that claimed to operate according to Marxist principles – and 'Western Marxism', the various reactions against Soviet Marxism formulated by left-wing thinkers in Western Europe and North America. The divergence between these two major types of Marxism very much shaped the nature of the Marxist theories that have made a mark within subsequent social theory. Two of the most important versions of Western Marxism are the 'critical theory' associated with the Frankfurt School, and hegemony theory, first formulated by Antonio Gramsci. Although these have certain similarities, they also propose quite distinctive versions of Marx, and lead in rather different directions, both conceptually and in terms of the kinds of politics they imply. In this Chapter we will examine both of these versions of Marxism, to show the influences they have had, and implications they still hold, for the practice of social theorizing.

Keeping Up With the Times

The history of Marxist thinking since the death of Marx has very much involved endeavours by Marxists to keep up with changing social and political circumstances, by adapting Marx's original ideas to fit these new circumstances and to explain them.

A very major problem in this regard was that Marx had predicted that socialist revolution was imminent, and that the collapse and destruction of capitalism was inevitable (Marx and Engels, 1968 [1848]). Marx also believed that the socialist revolution would begin in the most advanced capitalist countries – especially Great Britain and the USA – because it was only where the capitalist economy was at its most developed that the conditions would be right for revolution. Revolution could not happen in less advanced capitalist countries, or countries where capitalism was still in its infancy. What actually happened historically seemed to contradict completely Marx's predictions. Socialist revolution did not in fact occur in the advanced capitalist countries, but in the much more economically 'backward' context of Russia, where capitalism barely had a foothold in the early twentieth century. The Russian Revolution of 1917, led by Lenin and the Bolshevik party, seemed thoroughly to contradict Marx's assertions as to where socialist revolution would happen, because the Russia of that time was primarily a feudal economy, and not the advanced capitalist economy that Marx thought was the necessary condition for successful revolution (Hobsbawm, 2011).

So at the end of the First World War, Marxists were left facing a number of troubling questions. Why was it that revolution could occur in contexts that Marx's theorizing had ruled out? How should Marxists outside of the new Soviet Union relate to the kinds of Marxism propounded first by Lenin, then after his death in 1924, by his successor, the new Soviet leader Joseph Stalin? Most importantly, why had revolution not occurred in those Western countries where capitalism was highly advanced?

Two possible answers suggested themselves. The first was that Marx's predictions had been entirely wrong. But to reject Marx's views about revolution brought into doubt many of his other ideas, perhaps his whole system of thought, and this possibility many Marxists were not prepared to entertain. The second possibility allowed the question of the absence of revolution in the West to be answered, while preserving Marx's focus on looking at contemporary societies for signs of revolutionary possibilities in them. On this view, revolution had not occurred in the West because it had been blocked by various factors in capitalist society. Capitalist society had been somewhat more resilient in preserving itself than Marx had envisaged. But by identifying the reasons for the blockage of revolutionary change, Marxists could seek to fight against and remove these obstacles, preserving Marx's belief that revolution would happen in the future.

Most Marxists in the Western countries agreed that there were two major forms of resistance to revolution (McLellan, 2007). These were *physical repression* and *ideological repression*. The first refers to how the ruling classes in a society have at their disposal armed forces – the army, the police, etc. – which can be deployed to subdue and intimidate the population at large, and to arrest or execute revolutionary leaders. But the use of direct, brutal physical force is only ever a temporary solution on the behalf of the ruling classes. Large numbers of people can be intimated for short periods of time, but will eventually rise up against those that oppress them. For any ruling class to remain in power over longer periods of time, it has to use more subtle means of self-preservation. To ensure long-term social stability, it will have to convince the broad mass of the population that current social arrangements are *legitimate*: that the people in charge are legitimately in control, and that everything is naturally as it should be. The ruling class or classes can never rely just on physical means of control through armed force. Ideological control is at its most effective when it never occurs to ordinary people that there is anything wrong with the social order in which they live. This is when ruling class ways of think-ing are so endemic among the populace that the latter sees no need for revolutionary activities, but instead embraces the social status quo (Althusser, 1971).

Throughout the twentieth century, it seemed to many Marxists in Western countries that their task was to update Marx's original ideas to a context whereby capitalist society had, by and large, been successful in blocking revolutionary change through the means of ideological repres-sion. The aim became to identify the mechanisms whereby ideological repression occurred, to discern how successful or unsuccessful such mech-anisms were in particular contexts, to understand how socialists and com-munists could undermine these mechanisms by revealing their hidden workings to the working classes – the people who were being subjected to them – and to find and encourage revolutionary forces and energies that could undermine the mechanisms of ruling class ideological control. So a two-fold search seemed necessary: to find the – primarily ideological – forces that hindered revolution, and to discover trends and tendencies that resisted ideological manipulation by the ruling classes, and which pressed towards revolutionary outcomes.

Marx had understood the power of ruling class ideologies to capture and control the ways in which working-class people thought. But he had believed that the working classes would in one way or another see through such ideologies and reject them. The failure of revolution to materialize in the advanced capitalist countries, led to later Marxists acknowledging that mechanisms of ideological repression were much stronger and resilient than Marx had thought. These Marxists began to put more emphasis on *culture* – that is, ideas, symbols and ways of thinking – than had Marx, because it was culture, dominated by ruling class ideologies, which seemed to be the main brake on revolution. Marx had generally put emphasis on the economy (the 'economic base') as the realm that drove the rest of society, downgrading the importance of cultural factors (placing these in the less important 'social superstructure', see Chapter 1). The new breed of Marxists in the West from the 1920s onwards emphasized much more the power and social importance of culture. They began to think that Marx had only examined how the economy created and controlled culture, when what was required now was to analyse how culture – dominated by ruling class ideologies – could also profoundly shape and control both the economy and other parts of society, such as politics (Jay, 1974).

The re-working – or sometimes outright rejection – of Marx's base/ superstructure metaphor by some Marxists stemmed in part from its perceived inability to identify the reasons for the absence of revolution in Western countries. This re-working of Marx also seemed necessary because of the increasing dissatisfaction among Marxists in Western countries with 'Eastern Marxism', the official Marxism of the Soviet Union. After the death of Lenin in 1924, power in the Communist Party accrued more and more to the increasingly dictatorial Stalin. By the end of the 1930s, Stalin had crushed almost all internal opposition to his rule, sending tens of thousands of potential opponents to prison-camps, and killing off anyone thought to pose a major threat (Medvedev, 1989). In this way, the democratic elements of the early period of the Soviet Union were destroyed. Marx had thought that revolution would create a society where individual freedom would at last be possible. But as the Soviet state became ever more repressive, Marxism was set up as the official 'religion' of the state, in order to encourage compliance among the population to the rule of the Communist Party elite. Perversely, a theory opposed to religious belief and aimed at human emancipation became the religion of an oppressive state apparatus.

The kind of Marxism that Stalin and the Communist Party propounded was called Dialectical Materialism, and it emphasized the most simplistic aspects of Marx's ideas. Marxism was said to be a wholly 'scientific' and 'objective' analysis of society, rendering it into a simple kind of positivism. There were said to be fixed 'laws' of social life, just as there were fixed laws of physics and biology. The view was propounded that the base/ superstructure model was simply correct and without flaws. Overall, it was asserted that Dialectical Materialism was wholly true and completely beyond criticism (Kolakowski, 2005).

As Marxists in the West came more and more to realize the totalitarian nature of the Soviet Union – although this was a slow process, taking place from the early 1930s through to the death of Stalin in 1953 and beyond – it seemed clear that Marxism would have to be rescued from the clutches of the Stalinists, and fundamentally renovated, both to avoid the traps into which Stalin's Marxism had fallen, and also to keep up with the changing nature of social conditions in the Western countries.

One of the major resources the Western Marxists had to draw upon were the works of the younger, Hegel-influenced Marx, because Stalinist Marxism drew upon some of the more crude elements that could be found in Marx's later works. Many of the early Hegel-inspired texts had not been published in Marx's lifetime, but only appeared sporadically over several decades. The first major 'Western Marxist' was the Hungarian scholar Gyorgy Lukacs (1971 [1923]), whose work played up the Hegelian elements to be found in Marx. One of his central Hegelian–Marxist ideas was the *social totality*. Here every single part of a society is regarded as being complexly interrelated with all other parts. Changes in one part of the totality would have ramifications for all the other parts, but these effects would be indirect rather than direct. This is because it is the totality, made up of all the parts, which shapes the nature of each individual part. There are therefore no direct relationships of one part shaping or controlling another (e.g. the 'economic base' shaping the 'social superstructure'). Culture is not shaped directly by the economic base, but by the totality of the society in question, which is made up of all the various parts. Conversely, the 'economy' is shaped by the totality too, and does not have the direct power to shape every other element of society that the base/super-structure model implies.

Lukacs also argued that Marxism is fundamentally about the *critique of reification*. Drawing upon the Hegelian ideas about alienation and fetishism to be found in Marx, Lukacs described reification as involving a situation whereby people perceive as an objectively existing, independent and real 'thing', what are in fact fluid and constantly changing social relationships between individuals and between groups. Reification occurs in a capitalist society when the capitalist economy is regarded as a 'thing' that has a life, and even a mind, of its own. This is typically expressed today in media reporting of 'the markets', where financial markets are presented as if they existed wholly independently of human intentions and activities. This makes them seem like 'natural' phenomena, like weather conditions, that cannot be controlled by human intervention, but must just be accepted, whatever the consequences. Treating the financial markets as independent things with wills of their own is to reify – that is, to represent as *thing-like* – what is not a thing at all, but only the fluid social relationships that pertain between particular human beings. The financial markets are simply the results of people like bankers and financial traders interacting with each other in certain sorts of social relationships. Reification occurs when these concrete social relationships are forgotten about and suppressed, in favour of thinking that the markets exist wholly independently of the people who constantly make them. But if traders, bankers and others ceased to engage in financial transactions tomorrow, then there would be no such 'thing' as the market. For Lukacs, the aim of Marxism is to identify and break through reified thinking, and to point out that what seems to be thing-like and thus unchangeable (the market, capitalist society in general) in fact are merely social relationships that can be changed.

The Frankfurt School

Following Lukacs' lead, the Frankfurt School produced a re-worked version of Marxism – which they dubbed 'critical theory' – that tried to avoid the dangers of Stalinist Marxism, and to identify both the ideological repression mechanisms of capitalist society, and possible means of overcoming them. The Frankfurt School was made up of the group of scholars associated, directly or indirectly, with the Institute for Social Research, a partly autonomous research centre established within the University of Frankfurt in 1923 (Wiggershaus, 1994). The 'early' version of the School refers to the personnel associated with it from the 1920s to the 1960s. The 'later' Frankfurt School refers to the group centred around Jürgen Habermas [b. 1929], who became director of the Institute in the late 1960s.

The Institute in its earlier days was very interdisciplinary in character, involving at different times specialists in the fields of sociology (Theodor Adorno [1903–1969], Leo Lowenthal [1900–1993]), philosophy (Adorno,

Max Horkheimer [1895–1973], Herbert Marcuse [1898–1979], Walter Benjamin [1892–1940]), Freudian psychology (Erich Fromm [1900–1980], Marcuse), literary, musical and cultural studies (Lowenthal, Benjamin, Adorno), and political economy (Friedrich Pollock [1894–1970]). Most of these scholars had family backgrounds in the educated German-Jewish upper middle class, and this class-basis has often been the source of criticisms of their ideas, as we will see. Although dealing with different fields of study, and despite certain divergences in opinion, the work of the individual members of the Frankfurt School generally cohered around certain common principles, namely to develop new, non-dogmatic Marx-inspired thinking which could identify and combat mechanisms of ideological repression (Held, 1980).

The period in which the early Frankfurt theorists lived was turbulent, involving the rise to power of Hitler and the Nazi Party in Germany, something Marx had certainly not foreseen. One of the central themes of early critical theory was that there were strong similarities not only between the totalitarian regimes of Fascism and Soviet Communism, but also between these and the so-called 'democratic' Western countries. This was not just a matter of intellectual conviction, but produced also by the life experiences of the members of the School. Forced to leave Germany after the Nazis had taken power, most of them made their way to the safer environment of the United States. The shock of arriving in the USA created a profound impression on the critical theorists. The USA was supposedly 'the land of the free', but it seemed to be worryingly like Nazi Germany and Soviet Russia in important ways. The mass media – which had grown hugely in size and social importance since Marx's time – in both totalitarian and supposedly 'democratic' countries were seen to be powerful agencies of social control and ideological repression, with cinema and radio being used as powerful propaganda tools controlled by elites to control the wider populace. The Frankfurt analysis of the mass media was the first major social theoretical analysis of media forms and their apparent effects on audiences.

The great intellectual enemy of critical theory was the positivist attitude towards science, an attitude that informed both Soviet Marxism and the highly statistical sociology dominant in the US. For positivism, social science is modelled on the natural sciences, searching for general 'laws' of social life, through perfectly neutral means of investigation, leading to the collection of objective 'facts' (Halfpenny, 1992). But for critical theory, positivism is not neutral; it works in the interests of the most powerful groups in society (Horkheimer, 1972c). By collecting superficial data that only depict the *surface* aspects of society, positivism cannot penetrate underneath the surface, in order to reveal the true *essence* of that society. Positivism reifies social reality. The aim of critical theory is to uncover the *hidden workings* of society, which otherwise remain out of sight. Critical theory rejects the mere appearance of a society, especially how that society thinks about and represents itself, in favour of uncovering what it is *really like*. Critical theory must reject the ways of thinking that are common in that society. It must be utterly sceptical of *everything* (Maier, 1984). Critical theory therefore rejects people's own understandings of the world, as these are thoroughly shaped by ruling class ways of thinking.

Positivism pretends to be unbiased and neutral, when it in fact operates in the service of ruling groups. Critical theory does not claim to be 'unbiased', because it sees such a situation as impossible. It instead explicitly allies itself with certain values, most fundamentally the human desire for *happiness*, which is understood to be the desire for a society free of domination, that is, the control of ruling classes over subordinate classes (Horkheimer, 1972b). On this basis, critical theory wants to show how things could be very different from how they are at present. Critical theory has a *utopian* element to it, looking towards a better future. However, it is today impossible to imagine directly what a better future society might look like concretely. So critical theory looks to a better future *indirectly*, through comparing the high ideals a particular society has about itself with the degraded reality of that society. Thus capitalist society imagines itself to be characterized by individual freedom. But looking at this society in a critical-theoretical way, it is seen to be actually organized in ways that utterly restrict individual freedom, while giving the illusion that freedom is possible. Critical theory shows a society's *hypocrisy*: how it makes positive claims about itself, but fails to live up to those claims. Critical theory points out this contradiction and tries to develop a situation where the positive values the society proclaims are held up as indictments of it, showing people that the way they live could and should be changed. Society's values can be turned against it, and this method of trying to encourage people to see the world around them differently, and make them change society for the better, was called by the critical theorists *negative dialectics* (Adorno, 1990).

As noted, some of the early Frankfurt scholars believed that the mass media had become the central pillars of ruling class ideological manipulation and control of the broader population. In particular, Adorno and

Knowledge
Critical theory; anti-positivism; negative dialectics

Structure/agency
Social totality
Social structure strongly shapes thought and agency

Subjectivity
Very malleable by dominant ideologies

Modernity
Total administration; dominance of culture industry

Figure 3.1 Summary of Adorno and Horkheimer's Critical Theory.

Horkheimer (1992 [1944]) drew on the ideas of, among others, Sigmund Freud and Max Weber, conjoining these with notions taken from Marx, in order to analyse this situation. They argued that in Marx's time, capitalism was characterized by *competition* between different capitalist companies. But by the mid twentieth century, capitalism had entered into a *monopoly* phase, with competition being replaced by economic control exercised by vast conglomerates, like the Ford motor company. In this situation, cultural factors, in particular cinema and radio (and after the Second World War, television), were becoming ever more crucial to capitalism's ongoing functioning. Culture was ever more at the service of the capitalist economy, as what previously had been a separate economic base and a cultural superstructure merged into one massive system (totality) that dominated all the individuals within it (the same sort of problem that Weber had earlier identified – see Chapter 1). Social life becomes increasingly characterized by bureaucratic administration and intrusive authorities, a condition of 'total administration' where the major bureaucracies – capitalist conglomerates working under conditions of economic monopoly, and government apparatuses – control (almost) all aspects of an individual's life. Culture becomes ever more tightly integrated into the system of total administration, helping to destroy critical thinking among the population at large.

Adorno and Horkheimer called the new realm of media, leisure and entertainment, embodied most tellingly in the Hollywood system, the 'culture industry'. Here, huge media corporations produce the films, TV, newspapers and magazines for consumption by the majority of the population. The Culture Industry exercises an almost total monopoly over cultural life, working in the service of the social status quo. Culture becomes thoroughly commodified, i.e. made up of standardized products made only to be sold and mindlessly consumed by audiences, rather than thoughtfully read or viewed or listened to (Adorno, 1996). Culture was now blatantly a large-scale financial operation, and not the harbour for the socially critical thoughts of artists and intellectuals that it had been previously, in the nineteenth century. All the artistic styles of the past were now ransacked in order to create advertisements for the products of monopoly capitalism, like mass-produced fridges and cars, the consumer goods that the capitalist-administrative system was buying off the working class with, making them ever more passive consumers incapable of thinking for themselves (Horkheimer, 1972a). All genuine creativity had disappeared, with culture, entertainment and leisure now soul-less activities controlled by bureaucracies. To disguise the totally standardized and repetitive nature of its products that rolled off the cultural production lines, the Cultural Industry coated them in *pseudo-individuality*, making each product seem to be distinctive and unique, when actually it was exactly the same as all the others (Adorno, 1996).

The nature of the Culture Industry's audience remains one of critical theory's most controversial claims. Here Freudian ideas were melded together with Marxist ones (see Chapter 1). Freud had argued that society moulds the unconscious level of the individual's mind as much as it does the conscious part. One early critical theorist, Erich Fromm (1994), conjoined this to Marxist concerns by arguing that the demands of capitalist society, such as the requirement that individuals buy consumer goods to keep the economy working, were instilled into the unconscious of every person. The individual's mind, especially the unconscious dimension, is like a blank slate upon which ruling class ideologies get inscribed. For Adorno and Horkheimer, the Culture Industry's products promote conformist ways of thinking in audiences. Constant exposure to them reduce the mass audience's capacity for critical thinking. Thus listening to pop music, with its simplistic content and musical structure, promotes a lack of thought on the behalf of listeners, whereas listening to the complex musical structures of a Beethoven symphony promotes a much more thoughtful response, not just to the music but to social life in general. Adorno and Horkheimer made a strong distinction between 'art' on the one hand and 'mass culture' on the other, the former defined as promoting critical thinking and the latter said to encourage only passivity and

conformity. By being difficult to understand, the best works of art encouraged critical thinking. But such artworks were so difficult to comprehend
that they were beyond the grasp of most people. It is the erosion of critical thinking by the Culture Industry that keeps the populace pliant and
submissive. Desires to consume Culture Industry products and consumer
goods were not genuine expressions of an individual's will, but were the
product of false needs implanted into people's unconscious by the Culture
Industry (Horkheimer, 1972a). Thus the Culture Industry reproduced
itself, by making sure that the false needs it has created are only met fleet-
ingly, necessitating its consumers perpetually to come back for more of
the same.

By the 1960s, these ideas were under severe attack, including from other
sorts of Marxists. It seemed to many that Adorno and Horkheimer in
particular had betrayed Marx by being far too pessimistic and ignoring
potentials for social change. The result of their extreme anti-positivism
– with its great suspicion of empirical data about society – was seen to be
that their version of critical theory ended up being more like a dogma
than the supple new type of Marxism, attuned to changing social conditions, it had initially been designed to be. The pessimism and negativity
of their theory was connected by critics to their pre-war upper-middle-
class backgrounds, making them seriously ill-equipped to deal with contemporary culture, especially youth culture (McGuigan, 1992). The strong
division of 'art' versus 'mass culture' was strongly criticized, with critics
alleging it vastly over-simplified the nature of popular culture, and failed
to see the socially critical elements at work within it (Fiske, 1989). Their
Freud-inspired 'blank slate' view of the human psyche was also criticized,
critics not accepting the assumption that the human mind was always
completely open to external manipulation.

A New Beginning: Jürgen Habermas

By the late 1960s, it seemed to many that Adorno and Horkheimer's
Frankfurt colleague Herbert Marcuse (1991), who tried to ally his strongly
Freudian version of critical theory to emerging social movements such as
the anti-Vietnam peace demonstrations in North America and Europe,
had more to offer politically and theoretically. His more optimistic and
dynamic position suggested that critical theory could continue to embrace
changing social conditions rather than just reject them. The younger

generation of critical theorists, led by Jürgen Habermas, realized that just as the earlier Frankfurt thinkers had sought to re-work Marx in order to understand new social conditions, so too would critical theory have to be revamped once more.

For Habermas, the conceptual bases of earlier critical theory were too narrow to be workable. Habermas (1972) rejected what he saw as the overly restrictive sense of rationalization that Adorno and Horkheimer had inherited from Max Weber. They had overemphasized how the development of modern society was primarily about huge increases in instrumental-rational forms of control over people and things, through such means as bureaucratic domination of individuals. What this missed out was the *promise* of modernity; how rationality, far from enslaving everyone, in fact promised emancipation and freedom. In this way, Habermas sought to save a more positive sense of reason and rationality, inherited from the Enlightenment, from the negative understanding of these fashioned by Weber (see Chapter 1).

Weber, Adorno and Horkheimer had all concentrated on the negative side of modernity. But modernity was more than just a bureaucratically organized prison. It also had the *potential* to liberate people from forms of power held over them, and from the grip of tradition. The earlier critical theorists had been correct to show how, as it had actually developed, modernity had 'gone wrong', developing in ways characterized by the domination of the capitalist market and the state over people's thoughts and actions. But modernity's as-yet unfulfilled promise was to create ways of living that were free of domination, or at least could resist it. The task of critical theory was not just to note negative developments, as earlier Frankfurt thinking had tended to do; it was also to identify and to encourage more positive developments.

Habermas (1972) at this period regarded critical theory as being like a psychoanalyst, treating a patient – here the patient was modernity itself. Critical theory was like a talking cure, encouraging the patient to see how their consciousness was blocked and repressed by forces they could only dimly perceive. By making clear what those forces were, the 'therapy' enabled the 'patient' to overcome these blockages and repressions so as to come to a better self-understanding and to be more autonomous – that is, to be in charge of one's own destiny, rather than be the prisoner of forces one could not control. The aim was to make modernity see its own more positive side, and strive towards making it develop that side further, thus coming to control and overcome its negative side, the elements of over-rationalization and total administration highlighted by earlier, Weber-inspired critical theory.

Habermas' goal, then, was to identify and promote the better sides of modernity and to counter its worst sides. What counted as the more positive side of modernity was already apparent in his earliest work from the early 1960s (Habermas, 1989 [1962]). Here he had shown how, in eighteenth-century Europe, a special sort of social arena had arisen: the 'public sphere'. This was a space, both mental and physical, where educated middle-class citizens could converse freely with each other on important political and philosophical matters. They would meet, for example, in the newly opened coffee-houses to be found in the centre of cities. The conversational freedom of this sphere rested in the fact that no particular group or institution – the government, dominated by the aristocracy – or the capitalist market, dominated by rich merchants, and later by capitalists – controlled it.

It was a world where the best – i.e. most reasoned, most valid and most evidence-based – argument would win over others, or at least had the potential to do so. A consensus could be reached among everyone engaged in an argument, because eventually everyone would see what the best, most reasoned argument was. This is what is meant by the phrase 'discursive democracy' – a space where the manner in which people engage in discourse with each other is organized democratically. Arguments did not win just because a powerful person was making them. At its best, the public sphere was a special space where arguments were made that were free of the influence of power. Tradition and custom had very little place here, as decisions were made on the basis of the most reasoned argument, and not because tradition dictated a particular course of action. The middle-class public sphere of the eighteenth century thus embodied the promise of modernity. Modern social organization held out the possibility of creating spaces, both physical and mental, where the positive side of reason – arguing in a rational way to prove your point to others – could win out over the negative side of rationality, the side characterized by bureaucratic administration and restrictive control.

Unfortunately, by the nineteenth century the negative side of rationality had triumphed – capitalist market and government had become so powerful, they had smothered the public sphere, vastly reducing its scope and its potential power. For example, the public sphere had not just operated on a face-to-face basis – the new institution of newspapers meant that rational discussion could happen among people who had never met each other, whether they lived in the same city or same country, or even lived in different countries. But in the nineteenth century, the promise of newspapers in this direction was undermined as they became ever more about government imperatives (pumping out state-sanctioned propaganda) and capitalist market demands (selling commodities through advertising rather than engaging in thoughtful discussions). The external forces associated with government and capitalism came more and more to control the public sphere, eventually dissolving it altogether. But even with the dissolution of the public sphere, the aim of critical theory today was to identify and help create new spaces where discussion could happen in genuinely democratic ways. These spaces could then come to resist, and in future tame or even overcome, the forces of power associated with capitalism and government. These spaces would have to be less restrictive than the eighteenth-century public sphere, as it only admitted people of a certain type: highly educated, middle and upper-class males. But a realm of rational argument implied that anyone could be allowed to join in – e.g. women, the working classes – as long as all participants agreed to the rules of the game, that is, to be open to the force of the best argument, and not be dogmatic and closed-minded.

Habermas developed these ideas in various ways throughout the 1970s and 1980s. Most important here is what he argued about the nature of *language* as the basis for revived critical theory, and how he deduced a theory of modern society from this. The ideas about language are the roots of Habermas' revived critical theory, and these constitute a very different grounding of critical theory from that proposed by the earlier Frankfurt thinkers. Habermas (1984) argues that there are certain essential elements of human language. Each time one person says something to someone else, that person implicitly makes these claims:

(1) that their assertion is intelligible (i.e. that it is a meaningful statement that can be understood by the other person)
(2) that their assertion is true (i.e. that what they are claiming is indeed truthful)
(3) that they are justified in what they are saying (i.e. they are saying what they are saying with good reason)
(4) that they are being sincere (i.e. that they do not intend to lie to the other person)

'Undistorted communication' happens when the speaker can successfully defend all four of these criteria, that is, when both speaker and recipient are convinced that what has been said was intelligible, true, justified and sincerely put. Most of the time, all of this is implicit in conversations. But if the listener questions the speaker's claims, then the speaker will have to defend herself, producing reasoned evidence to demonstrate that what she is saying meets the various criteria. Habermas' claim is that there is rooted inextricably in the nature of human language itself orientations towards reasoned interchange between people. This is 'communicative rationality'. Anyone who uses language always implicitly presumes they can justify themselves as regards the four criteria above. This holds out the possibility of language being not a form of power and domination (as structuralists and post-structuralists like Foucault had argued – see Chapter 8), but rather as the means through which people can engage in reasoned ways with each other, reaching rational consensus on issues.

Communicative rationality is the positive rationality that Habermas wants to champion against the negative rationalization processes identified by the early Frankfurt thinkers. Habermas (1984) posits what he calls the 'ideal speech situation', a condition where communicative rationality is fulfilling its full potential. This is a situation where communicative rationality is completely free to work as it should. In such a situation:

(1) Every person (who is competent to speak and act) is allowed to take part in communication.
(2) Everyone is allowed to question any assertion made in the communication.
(3) Everyone is allowed to introduce any assertion into the communication.
(4) Everyone is allowed to express her own attitudes, desires and needs.
(5) No speaker is prevented, by internal or external coercion, from exercising her communicative rights (i.e. the rights to 'free speech' above)

So the ideal speech situation is where people communicate wholly rationally, free from coercion and power, be that from inside the group conversing (e.g. if a man tried to intimidate women, or an older person attempted to silence younger people), or outside it (when the principles of the capitalist market or government 'infect' the conversation, and stop it being freely willed by the participants). Everyone is treated the same, and all treat each other as equals, regardless of who they are outside the ideal speech situation. Thus a working-class female factory worker would have the same discursive rights as a rich male business executive. Wealth, class, race, gender and other social characteristics are not relevant and are excluded.

The ideal speech situation is thus an imagined situation where language is allowed to be at its most rational, at its most 'undistorted'. The people in it use their powers of communicative rationality to discuss, debate, provide reasons and evidence, and eventually reach a rationally agreed consensus on what they are debating. Although it is an imaginary situation, it is rooted in the real nature of language (the four criteria mentioned above). Habermas' point is that the ideal speech situation shows us the rational and freedom-producing potential of language – a potential implicit in all uses of language, in all conversations. Critical theory's aim is to identify and encourage the building of spaces where people's conversations can be as much like the ideal speech situation as possible. The eighteenth-century public sphere had been one such space. Although Habermas formulated these ideas well before the advent of the internet, it is easy to see how it could be claimed that the World Wide Web opens up a whole range of possibilities for free, unconstrained communication and agreement-building between all sorts of people, including from different regions of the world (Bohman, 2004).

The ideal speech situation operates as Habermas' normative ideal. This is how things could be if we had a society that was more equitably organized. This is the positive promise of modernity: the capacity to build institutions and spaces that operate according to the requirements of the ideal speech situation where communication is 'undistorted'. But it also allows us to see and to measure the negative side of modernity. We can look at particular contexts and discern how close to or far from the ideal speech situation they are. Contexts that are very far from it can be characterized as operating around 'distorted communication'. This is when the rules of the ideal speech situation are broken, and powerful individuals, groups and institutions get to impose their ideas on everyone else. Instead of being used to reach rational consensus, language is used to dupe and to bully people into submission. So the realm of newspaper journalism today can be viewed as a realm with very high levels of distorted communication – it involves propaganda aimed at fostering the interests of powerful groups, rather than rational discussion among equally treated citizens. Marx had measured capitalism against a normative ideal, the liberatory society that was communism. Earlier critical theory, through 'negative dialectics', had measured capitalist society against its own noble-sounding claims. What Habermas does is to encourage us to measure actual situations against the ideal speech situation, and see how wanting or not they are.

Habermas' understanding of the nature of modern society flows from this approach. Taking inspiration from the systems theory of Parsons and Lockwood's critique of it (see Chapter 2), he argues that modernity is split between two main realms – 'system' and 'lifeworld'. The system is made up of the institutions of government and capitalist market. They promote the sorts of rationalization Max Weber had criticized, including commodification (things are looked at in terms of their monetary value only) and bureaucratization (the state's bureaucracies, especially the legal system, control multiple social spheres). 'Lifeworld' (see Chapter 4) is made up of the social relations between individuals, and especially the communicative rationality involved in social relations. The problem with modernity as it is currently organized is that power (emanating from the state) and money (emanating from the capitalist economy) come increasingly to 'colonize' the lifeworld, such that negative rationalization comes more and more to dominate the lifeworld's communicative rationality, taking modernity ever further away from embodying contexts akin to the ideal speech situation.

The aim for Habermas is to reverse this process, so that instead of the lifeworld being colonized by the system, the reverse would happen – that communicative rationality, and its democratic impulses and potentials, moves out of the lifeworld and infiltrates and restructures the system. That way, the institutions of the state could be re-established around 'discursive democracy', which in turn could create laws which bolstered rather than undermined the communicatively rational dimensions of various lifeworlds. Critical theory identifies possibilities and opportunities for extending such processes. While Marx had proposed the revolutionary working classes as the group that would bring about social change for the better, Habermas (1987) proposes new social movements – the Green movement, women's and gay rights groups, and so on – as the agents of change, resisting lifeworld colonization and promoting positive transformations in the 'system'.

In proposing these solutions to the dilemmas of modernity, Habermas had moved quite far from the original Marxist bases of Frankfurt critical theory. The Marxist focus on economy and production of goods was dropped in favour of a focus on language and communicative rationality. Everything hinges on how convincing the account of language is, and it

---

Knowledge
New type of critical theory; critical theory as social therapy; centrality of language; communicative rationality; ideal speech situation

Structure/Agency
Structure = 'system'
Agency based in communicative rationality

Subjectivity
Shaped by both rationalization/system, and communicative rationality/lifeworld

Modernity
System and lifeworld; colonization of lifeworld by system; possible reshaping of system by lifeworld

---

Figure 3.2 Habermas' Critical Theory.

has been criticized by many as being too idealistic and abstract to be satisfactory (Crespi, 1987). Post-structuralists and post-modernists (see Chapters 8 and 9) have also felt that Habermas is guilty of purveying grand metanarratives which are the epitome of outdated modernist thinking (Lyotard, 1984). Habermas has also been accused by Marxist critics of throwing the baby out with the bath-water, in that he has ditched many of the less tenable assumptions of earlier Frankfurt theorizing, but in so doing has relinquished the still highly relevant Marxist ideas of social class and exploitation. For these critics, Habermas is a Weber-inspired liberal who has betrayed what is still vital in Marxism (for discussion of Habermas, see Outhwaite (2009)).

An Alternative: Antonio Gramsci's Marxism

Another very influential form of Marxism beyond Frankfurt critical theory was suggested by Antonio Gramsci [1891–1937]. A leading thinker within the Italian Communist Party in the 1920s, Gramsci was imprisoned for several years by Mussolini's Fascist regime, dying shortly after he was released. Gramsci's major theoretical text is *The Prison Notebooks* (1971). Given the conditions under which they were written, the notebooks contain jottings that are fragmented and which it requires an effort of interpretation to be able to join together. The key Gramscian notion is that of 'hegemony', which takes on various meanings in the *Notebooks*. Here for ease of understanding, we will concentrate on two major meanings.

Gramsci's ideas are very much part of 'Hegelian Marxism' favoured by Western Marxists. Gramsci (1971: 626) was of the view that 'everyone is a philosopher, though in his own way and unconsciously, since even in the slightest manifestation of any intellectual activity whatever, in "language", there is contained a specific conception of the world'. Everyone has the capacity for thought, and thus for the capacity to engage in meaningful activities, actions that need not just reproduce society the way it currently is, but can change it, including in ways that are (for the Marxist) for the better. Gramsci saw human life in general, and the struggle between different social classes more particularly, as involving the clash of contesting views of the world, of different images and understandings of what human beings are like and what society is and could be. This version of Marxism is about *mental warfare* – how the ruling classes attempt to impose their world-views on the subordinate classes, and how the latter can resist this and foster their own social visions, which can help to change society.

Gramsci was one of the first Western Marxists to claim that physical repression by the ruling classes is never enough to secure a stable social order that works in their interests. Ideological and cultural repression is also required. The first aspect of hegemony involves ideas familiar from other versions of Marxism: ruling class ideologies are the dominant ideas in a given social order. The ideas of the dominant classes are the dominant ideas. These ideas are propounded by the intellectual group or groups within, or working in the service of, the ruling classes. For example, right-wing journalists can be seen as the group who systematize and propound the ideas of ruling elites in business and government. Due to constant exposure to these ideas, people in the lower classes come to believe them, and in so doing cannot conceive of society being any other way than it currently is. In a strong condition of hegemony, the ideas and world-views of the lower classes are squeezed out by ruling class ideas, made marginal and given little public exposure. In this way, the world-view and ideas of the ruling classes can come to shape *everyone's* ideas. This is how the rule of the ruling classes comes to seem to everyone – especially those classes which are dominated and exploited – as natural and inevitable. Thus when ruling ideas and world-views are hegemonic, they infiltrate every part of life, shaping the common-sense thinking of the lower classes. The pervasiveness of ruling class ideas means they become naturalized, taken-for-granted by everyone and rarely questioned.

This sense of hegemony thus refers to a condition where ruling class ideas are so powerful and persuasive, they ensure social stability by effectively outlawing and subordinating dissenting and critical thoughts and actions. This conception of hegemony is close to the situation outlined by Adorno and Horkheimer under conditions of total administration. But the second meaning of hegemony complicates the picture. Gramsci would have rejected the early Frankfurt theorists' Freudian understanding of the human psyche as simply a blank slate upon which ruling class ideas are written. Everyone always has the potential for creative, and thus critical, thinking that is not totally enslaved by ruling class ideas. The situation described above – one of strong ruling class hegemony – is only a possibility, and is never guaranteed, as Adormo and Horkheimer seem to have thought. Instead, Gramsci argues that actual social situations rarely exhibit very strong ruling class hegemony: such situations are the exception, not the rule.

On the second meaning of hegemony – which describes situations that for Gramsci are more common than conditions where ruling class power is very strong – the ideological domination of the lower classes by the upper classes is rarely guaranteed. Because individuals always have the potential to think beyond the ways ruling classes would want them to, the rule of the ruling classes is always potentially threatened. Thus ruling class hegemony is always potentially *fragile*. How fragile depends on particular social circumstances. Adorno and Horkheimer had assumed that domination by the 'system' was now almost inevitable. Gramsci advocates a more empirical approach, that looks to see where cracks in the system and challenges to it may be appearing. For example, prolonged economic crises leading to high levels of unemployment may make people in the lower classes that much more sceptical of the claims of government officials and business elites. As social, political and economic circumstances are constantly changing, they may throw up new, 'counter-hegemonic' forces, groups which have ideas that differ from and challenge ruling class ideas. These groups too can have their own intellectuals, who formulate and promote their world-views, challenging the established ideas that promote the status quo. In our own day, we might think here of people who lead protest movements, such as anti-war campaigns, as the kinds of intellectuals Gramsci has in mind. Societies are thus always relatively unpredictable and never uniform. Counter-hegemonic forces can appear in ways that may seem unexpected, changing and upsetting the existing social fabric (Adamson, 1981).

Ruling classes constantly face opposition and challenge 'from below', from social forces constantly exploding into existence. Ruling classes, especially their intellectual groups, must work constantly to manage this situation, but it is likely that their attempts in this regard will only ever be limited and temporary, complete control even for short periods being very unlikely. Taking inspiration from Gramsci's ideas, Laclau and Mouffe (1985) describe this situation as 'suture'. In medicine, this is the stitching used temporarily to hold the flesh over a wound together, to encourage the wound to heal. But the suture is only temporary, and may not work. In the same way, the ruling classes are engaged in the constant endeavour to patch up problems and conflicts that are constantly opening up in society – but their efforts in this regard will never be totally successful, as either the same problems arise again or new ones come along to take their place. The ruling classes must constantly work to secure their hegemony; it is never guaranteed, and especially in complex modern societies, is often more fragile than it may seem.

This is compounded by the fact that, Gramsci insists, there is no such thing as a ruling class in the singular. In modern social orders, the ruling class grouping (or bloc) is made up of different groups, each with their own specific interests and viewpoints. Groups such as government officials, business leaders and religious leaders have to work with each other

---

Knowledge
Hegelian Marxism

Structure/Agency
Humans as active, creative, potentially critical agents; individual actions can be structured by hegemonic ideas

Subjectivity/Identity
Shaped by both hegemony and counter-hegemony

Modernity
Complex, constantly shifting mixture of ruling class ideas and world-views, and counter-hegemonic challenges to these

---

Figure 3.3 Gramsci's Marxism.

so that the grouping they are in can retain hegemony. But they may not work well with each other, may not be able to reach compromises, and so their hegemony may be jeopardized. Even when the ruling grouping is relatively coherent, it can very rarely just impose its will on the other classes. It often has to compromise with them and do deals. For example, the welfare state can be seen as the result of compromises between ruling and lower classes – the lower classes get some protection from the capitalist economy (e.g. unemployment benefit), and in return the ruling classes achieve a more stable social order than if there was no welfare state.

Conclusion

In this chapter, we have outlined some of the main contours of Marxism as it has developed since the death of Marx. Although different versions of Marxism have certain overlapping themes, they vary considerably too. For early critical theory, especially in the work of Adorno and Horkheimer, the modern age is one of stifling 'total administration'. But for Gramsci, such a vision is too apocalyptic. Change happens constantly, and even under apparently totalitarian situations, there are forces working underneath the surface that may come in time to undermine or even overthrow the status quo. No ruling regime lasts for ever seems to be Gramsci's overall message and main contribution to Marxist theory. In this sense, his brand of Marxism provides a more optimistic corrective to early critical theory's tendency towards extreme political pessimism, and it connects with, although remains significantly different from, Habermas' attempt to rescue critical theory and to render it more malleable, relevant and up-to-date. It is likely that the twenty-first century will pay witness to as many diverse, and often unexpected, developments of the Marxist legacy in social theory as did the century just past.

Further Reading

Bottomore, T. (2002) *The Frankfurt School and its Critics*. London: Routledge.
Finlayson, J. G. (2005) *Habermas: A Very Short Introduction*. Oxford: Oxford University Press.
Hobsbawm, E. (2011) *How to Change the World: Tales of Marx and Marxism*. London: Little, Brown.

Joseph, J. (2006) *Marxism and Social Theory*. Basingstoke: Palgrave.
Kolakowski, L. (2005) *Main Currents of Marxism: The Founders, the Golden Age, the Breakdown*. New York: W. W. Norton.
McLellan, D. (2007) *Marxism After Marx*, 4th edn. Basingstoke: Palgrave.
Outhwaite, W. (2009) *Habermas: A Critical Introduction*, 2nd edn. Cambridge: Polity.
Therborn, G. (2010) *From Marxism to Post-Marxism*. London: Verso.

4

Phenomenological Paradigms

Phenomenological approaches to social life exist at the heart of contemporary social theory. They are endeavours to understand how the world is perceived and understood from the points of view of particular individuals and groups. The term 'phenomenology' derives from the Greek terms 'phenomenon', which in English means 'an observable occurrence', and 'logos', which means 'study' or 'analysis' of something. Thus the literal meaning of 'phenomenology' is 'the study of observable occurrences'. In a less literal way, phenomenology is the study of how a person or a group of people perceives particular things around them. Phenomenology is about trying to see how things in the world look from the point of view of the people one is studying.

Phenomenology seeks to understand how people conceive of the world around them. It involves the study of the *consciousness* of the person or people under investigation – how they see the world about them, how they understand it, and the feelings and emotions they experience when engaged in such perceptions. Phenomenology is concerned with how particular persons or groups of people see, perceive, understand, experience, make sense of, respond to, emotionally feel about and engage with, particular objects or circumstances. Phenomenology is also centrally concerned with individuals' actions and activities. It is interested in understanding how their conceptions and perceptions of the world around them allow people to act and interact with each other. In that sense, phenomenological approaches are 'actor-centred', concerned with the consciousness of individuals, and how consciousness drives and makes possible action and interaction, which are taken as the elementary components of social life.

Phenomenology is also concerned with *everyday life* – the ordinary, mundane contexts in which people operate. How these are created through actions and interactions, and how in turn contexts of everyday life make possible actions and interactions, are the foci of phenomenology. It was phenomenology which first stressed the idea of *practical consciousness*. This is the idea that most people most of the time think and act in semi-conscious, rather than fully conscious and self-aware, ways. We do most things in our lives not by fully thinking them through. Because we have learned how to do these things and have become habituated to do them over a long period of time, then we just do them without having to think very much about them. They are just 'second nature' to us.

I do not have to think very much about how to catch the bus every morning – I can just do it. When I go to the bus stop to catch the bus, I am in a state of practical consciousness – a semi-conscious state where I know what I am doing but without having to think explicitly about it. When I was a child, I had to learn how to get from point A to point B, I had to learn what buses were, I had to learn to cross the road without getting knocked down by traffic, I had to learn to use money to pay people –including bus drivers – for things I wanted. But over the years, all of these kinds of 'everyday knowledges' have become so habituated in my consciousness – have become so part of 'me' – that I know how to do the sorts of things connected with them without having to think it all through. I can do what I need to do 'practically', and not fully self-consciously. I do not have to work it all out in a completely thought-through manner. And when I do have to make some sort of calculation – e.g. which bus to catch to get me to work quicker – my calculation will also be worked out not in a fully rational and self-aware manner, but in a practical, semi-conscious way too. Only when I am put in a position where I have to account for myself in some way – for example, when I am asked by my credit-card company why I am late with my payments – do I move out of the semi-conscious state of practical consciousness and move into the state of self-conscious 'discursive consciousness', where I have to think through logically what I have done or am doing, and to justify why I have done those things. But most of the time, individuals operate in practical, rather than fully conscious ways.

For phenomenologists, it is this state of practical consciousness that lies at the root of all human social life. People's actions mostly happen in a state of practical consciousness, so it is this which makes possible action and interaction, and thus, ultimately, wider society and social order.

Phenomenology exists in social theory in a number of ways. First, there have been certain thinkers who have developed what they explicitly present as phenomenological approaches to understanding social life, especially to do with how individuals (or groups) perceive the world around them and make sense of it, and how practical consciousness is the basis for action and interaction. Phenomenological sociology and ethnomethodology are exemplars of this strain of thinking. Second, there have also been attempts to conjoin phenomenological themes like these to other forms of social theory, to use phenomenology to help explain such issues as power relations and the 'social construction of reality'. The ideas of Berger and Luckmann are central examples here. Third, phenomenological insights have come to seem crucial in recent social theory, such as that of Bourdieu and Giddens (see Chapter 10), because phenomenology is seen to supply a necessary stock of ideas to do with how people perceive and act, which can operate as correctives to more 'objectivist' and 'structuralist' approaches which may overemphasize the power of wider social forces to constrain, shape and compel individuals' activities. In this chapter we will examine the various types of phenomenological thinking that have arisen in social theory, and the diverse uses to which they have been put. Throughout we will see how the central idea of practical consciousness has been understood in somewhat different ways by different thinkers.

Founding Phenomenology

We saw in Chapter 1 how much subsequent social theory owes to the foundational ideas of Kant. For Kant, we do not just simply and directly perceive the external world. That world is made sense of by some innate capacities of the human mind to order and structure the external world for us. We never have direct access to the world of 'noumena', things in and of themselves; all we ever perceive are things in the external world as perceived and structured by our minds – this is the world of phenomena. So the 'phenomenal world' – the world we can perceive – is as much a product of our minds as it is an external, objective 'reality'.

Phenomenology is a series of elaborations on the implications of what Kant was arguing. Following Kant, it seems clearly very important to work out how the human mind works, for in a certain sense it creates our sense of what reality is for us. As we can only ever perceive phenomena, rather than noumena, that means that we have to carry out a *phenomenology*, a study of how the world looks to the individual, and how human consciousness works. It is not just that human consciousness perceives the world – it also 'creates' it too.

In more recent philosophy, phenomenology was first developed as a form of investigation in its own right by the German philosopher Edmund Husserl [1859–1938]. Husserl was interested in how the human mind in general works, and how it makes sense of the world around it. For Husserl (1962 [1931]: 40), the object of philosophy was the study of the individual's 'stream of consciousness'. This is the sense of the world that exists in a person's head at every moment. Consciousness is like a 'stream' because it is constantly on the move, picking up on things in the world around the individual as they happen. Husserl was concerned with understanding the impositions of the mind in shaping consciousness as this pertains to the individual in general, and not with reference to specific individuals or groups (Roche, 1973). However, as it has developed over the last century or so, phenomenology in the social sciences has become less concerned with the nature of human consciousness in general, and more concerned with *particularities*: how *this* person (or persons) experiences and feels about *this* particular event, object or circumstance (Luijpen, 1969). This is because it is concerned with understanding what the world looks like from the viewpoint of the existence of an individual, as they exist in a shared everyday world (what phenomenologist call a 'lifeworld') along with other people that they interact with.

As phenomenology was taken up in the twentieth century for the purposes of social science, its focus shifted towards an emphasis on 'culture' – that is, the shared senses of reality and ways of perceiving and making sense of the world, to be found among particular groups of people or whole societies. The cultural context a person or group exists within clearly can profoundly shape how they experience the world around them. Phenomenology became concerned to unpick the ways in which culture affects individuals' experiences, which are now assumed to be shared by groups of individuals. Hence phenomenology started to look at conditions of inter-subjectivity (shared meanings and perceptions), not just those of individuals taken in isolation.

Alfred Schutz [1899–1959] was a central figure in importing phenomenological thinking and methods into sociology. Schutz (1967) was particularly concerned to extend the ideas about social action first developed by Max Weber, developing these by conjoining them to certain aspects of Husserl's understanding of human consciousness. Schutz (1967) endeavoured to develop some general phenomenological categories that could capture the nature both of individual and group experience, and of human social life more generally. His phenomenological sociology tries to give us words to describe the *details* and *particularities* of how specific people live their lives. The mundane, everyday world in which people operate is called the 'lifeworld' by Schutz (Harrington, 2000).

This is made up of the ways in which individuals view the world they are in, and ways in which they act within it. The lifeworld is formed by the culture of a particular group of people. The culture creates the 'commonsense' ways in which people experience the world. These are the ways through which people in a given cultural context make sense of and experience the world around them. These commonsense ways of perceiving and experiencing are generally not subjected to rational reflection or criticism by the people who work with them; they are generally just accepted without being thought about. This is called by Schutz the 'natural attitude', the habitual sense of the world a person has. The natural attitude is the mental disposition most people have most of the time – it is their sense of what is 'normal', 'everyday' and unexceptional. The natural attitude is only disrupted and called into question when something perceived to be extraordinary happens (e.g. a ghost appears to people in a lifeworld where ghosts do not normally appear). When it does, the habituated sense of what 'reality' is falls away, and uncertainty and anxiety reign. But most of the time the natural attitude underpins everything we think and do.

This focus on commonsense ways of thinking and reasoning – practical consciousness and practical reasoning – became the centre of subsequent sociological phenomenology. What has to be investigated is how people act in particular, mostly taken-for-granted, ways, as a result of living within particular lifeworlds. Lifeworlds make action and interaction, the bases of social life, possible. But these in turn come to shape and re-shape the lifeworld itself over time (Pressler and Dasilva, 1996).

Schutz also introduced a key issue into phenomenology, namely the division between the consciousness of the world held by the people we study, and the consciousness of us, the social analysts. This is the distinction between 'first-order' and 'second-order' categories. People in particular lifeworlds use 'first-order' categories – their typical ways of thinking and understanding, rooted in their practical consciousness, and used habitually by them in practical ways. So a 'first-order' category in my lifeworld would be that I know what a bus is and understand how to use it. The idea of 'bus' is one of my mental categories, which I use all the time in my actions and interactions, but without consciously reflecting on the fact that this is a category for me. If a social scientist were studying me, they would have to understand how the world was perceived by me and how I made sense of it. So the analyst would have to reconstruct the contours of my lifeworld – my everyday, taken-for-granted sense of the world, which is likely to be shared by the people around me.

That would involve trying to depict my mental categories, one of which is the idea of the bus as a mode of transport. When the analyst depicted my sense of bus – a first-order category – then she would have to describe it in her own language, in order to communicate to other analysts (or anyone else) what I was thinking when I took the bus. She would therefore have to describe in her words – second-order categories – what my first-order category was. Social analysis then is the second-order description of the first-order categories of a lifeworld. The analyst cannot hope to reconstruct fully the whole lifeworld of a particular person, for each lifeworld involves complex streams of consciousness, involving multiple taken-for-granted categories. But what can be done is for the analyst to reconstruct some 'typical' first-order categories that partially get at the complexity of a particular person's consciousness and lifeworld. These are 'typifications' – working models that get at what the thinking going on in a particular lifeworld looks like.

As it happens, at the level of the first-order categories of the lifeworld, individuals use particular sorts of typifications themselves all the time. My notion of 'bus' assumes that all vehicles of that shape, size and look are indeed the things I think are buses. My first-order category of 'police officer' assumes that all the people I meet who are dressed in the ways I habitually associate with police officers will indeed be police officers, and will act in the ways that my category of 'police officer' expects them to do. So individuals use typifications all the time, within their practical consciousness. They have to, because social interaction could not happen without those typifications. I have to assume that all instances I will encounter in the future of what I take to be 'buses' and 'police officers' will indeed turn out to be the things I expected them to be. Because if not, I could not live my life: I would not be able to travel, as I would not know what a bus is, I could not get help when in trouble, because I would have no conception that there was such a thing as a police officer. Ongoing everyday life is made possible by the individual having typifications to work with – these are the bases of all thought and action. But they are the bases of *inter*-action too. The lifeworld of an individual is made up of a series of typifications that the vast majority of people in that lifeworld share. This must be so because they could not interact with each other unless they had some shared typifications – all the passengers on the bus must know what a bus is, must know it requires payment, must know what the expectations of behaviour are when on it, and so on. So the life-world is made up of typifications, and is made possible by them. Human life is nothing other than the use of typifications in the practical conscious-ness of individuals. These first-order typifications are then described – necessarily never completely – by the second-order typifications of social scientists. From a phenomenological perspective, then, social theory and social science are (second-order) typifications of (first-order) typifications.

Schutz desired to produce some general categories that describe the basic 'architecture' of all lifeworlds. This could then be used to investigate how particular lifeworlds made sense of these general issues. In a given lifeworld, an individual is faced with interacting with, or at least dealing in some sense with, different kinds of people in a very general sense. These are: 'consociates' – those the individual interacts with closely and regularly, such as family and friends; 'contemporaries' – those that share the same lifeworld as the individual, but whom she does not know person-ally, including people she must interact with in fleeting ways, like those who work as bus drivers or shop assistants; 'predecessors', those people now dead who lived in the past; and 'successors', those who will live in the future.

An individual uses typifications in her dealings with all of these people. She may imagine what people in the future will be like. She will from time to time think of people in the past, and the only way really to do that is through typifications, like in our day 'the Victorians' and 'the Romans', which are highly stereotypical depictions – shared in modern lifeworlds – about what people in the past were like. The typifications used in dealings with contemporaries will also be highly stereotypical – these are the kinds of general categories like 'bus driver' and 'police officer' mentioned above, stereotypes necessary for the individual to interact with people of those types and to make sense of the world around her more generally. The least stereotypical typifications are used for consociates, the people an individual knows very well. But even here, typifications come into play: even if you know a person very closely, you are still tacitly (in your practical consciousness) using typifications. You know your father well but your lifeworld still supplies you with certain norms of what a father as a social category is, how such persons act and how they are to

Knowledge
Reworking of Husserl's phenomenology and Weber's action theory

Structure/Agency
Individuals' everyday understandings are rooted in and derive from the 'lifeworld'

Existence within a lifeworld involves the 'natural attitude'

In particular contexts, the natural attitude is structured by culturally specific and taken-for-granted stocks of meanings

Typifications

First order (actors') and second order (analysts') categories

Figure 4.1 Summary of Schutz.

be treated in interactions. So here the lifeworld, made up of typifications embedded generally invisibly in practical consciousness, shapes the individual's consciousness without them realizing it. All the other people in that person's shared lifeworld will have (roughly) the same typi-fication of 'father' in their heads, and that will shape in subtle ways their thoughts and actions. It is sometimes alleged that phenomenology is an individualistic approach to social reality, seeing the world purely through the eyes of an individual actor. But it is not just that, because by focusing on typifications – first-order categories shared by groups, or even whole societies – it is demonstrating how individual consciousness is structured and made possible by inter-subjective assumptions held by many individuals.

Constructing Reality

In the mid 1960s, Peter Berger and Thomas Luckmann (1991 [1966]) took Schutz's ideas and extended them. In a typical phenomenological manner, they argued that human consciousness must be seen as the ultimate root of all social phenomena. They claimed that 'social order is not biologically given or derived from any biological data in its empirical manifestations' (1991 [1966]: 59). Instead, the fact that there are any patterns and regulari-ties in human life is due to how human consciousness is structured. Social order is 'an ongoing human production', that makes possible action and interaction, but which also is produced and reproduced by these over time.

This view was akin to the ideas of symbolic interactionists (see Chapter 5). But they added to Schutz's basic categories one of the central aspects of classical social theory, namely the idea of 'alienation'. As we saw in Chapter 1, this is an idea derived originally from Hegel, and taken up, particularly in Germany, by a wide range of thinkers, including Marx, Weber and Simmel. All of them examined what they saw as the particularly alienating aspects of modern society – individuals seem dominated by large-scale social forces they think they cannot control. The original Hegelian idea had applied to all societies at all times. Hegel had argued that as humans interact with each other over time, they create social forces – such as values and norms – which in turn become institutionalized. What are actually human products come over time to seem as if they are natural and inevitable to the people who made them and their ancestors.

One can see Berger and Luckmann's combination of alienation theory and Schutz's phenomenology in what they regard as the essential aspects of all human life. 'Habitualization' is a key social process.

> All human activity is subject to habitualization. Any action that is repeated frequently [by individuals interacting] becomes cast into a pattern, which can then be reproduced with an economy of effort and which . . . is apprehended by its performer as that pattern . . . Habitualized actions, of course, retain their meaningful character for the individual although the meanings involved become embedded as routines in his [sic] general stock of knowledge, taken for granted by him and at hand for his projects into the future. Habitualization carries with it the important psychological gain that choices are narrowed. While in theory there may be a hundred ways to go about the project of building a canoe out of matchsticks, habitualization narrows these down to one. This frees the individual from the burden of "all those decisions", providing a psychological relief that has its basis in man's undirected instinctual structure . . . habitualization makes it unnecessary for each situation to be defined anew, step by step. A large variety of situations may be subsumed under its predefinitions. The activity to be undertaken in these situations can then be anticipated. Even alternatives of conduct can be assigned standard weights. (1991 [1966]: 59)

So social interaction produces habits that start to seem as if they had always existed. Typifications are produced which tell the people in a given lifeworld how to do certain things. To do any given thing (e.g. catching a bus), the person does not need to invent anew each time the way to do it. Working out the best way to do certain things also becomes habituated. These habituated ways of thinking and acting are called by Berger and Luckmann 'recipes' – they are formulas for doing certain things in certain ways.

The typifications and recipes are lodged in each individual's practical consciousness. As people are rarely put in situations where they have consciously to reflect on their practical consciousness, the typifications are experienced not as the social constructs that they are, but just as completely 'natural' ways of doing things. Human products – the typifications – have come through habituation to shape consciousness. But this is not perceived by the people with that consciousness. If they are asked why they do things in certain ways, people can claim it has something to do with 'nature', or with their 'biology' – 'it's just natural for men to drink more than women', and so on. But for Berger and Luckmann, there is nothing biologically determined about human behaviour. It is driven by typifications and recipes that are 'alienated' (they use the term 'objectified') products of earlier interactions. So what was once made by humans later on starts just to seem 'real'.

One of the major forms of 'objectified' reality is language. In the early history of any human group, language starts off as a set of sounds aimed at trying to communicate certain things. But over time it becomes more elaborate. Children born into the group who use the language start to think of the language as somehow 'real', rather than as a human product. They think the words they use directly refer to reality. But this is only how the lifeworld of the people who use that language perceive reality. It is not 'reality' in itself, because different languages and the lifeworlds they are embedded in and help create generate their own distinctive realities. The idea of the world having as many multiple realities as there are lifeworlds is a central view of this sort of phenomenology (see also similar ideas in Chapter 8).

So human interactions create typifications and recipes that become habituated and experienced as 'just the way the world is'. Once typifications and recipes are habituated they involve the process of 'institutionalization'. On this view, what we call social institutions – family relations, gender relations, relations of authority and subordination, and so on – are nothing other than alienated, objectified human products. The people in them generally experience them as real, natural and unavoidable. They think that this is the only way of doing things, the only way to perceive the world and act within it. Once institutionalization has occurred, this humanly shaped world seems as if it is not humanly shaped at all but just 'natural'. For each person, the 'world so regarded attains a firmness in consciousness; it becomes real in an ever more massive way and it can no longer be changed easily'. This is what Berger and Luckmann mean by 'paramount reality' – the lifeworld seems like a completely unavoidable sphere in which one lives. The forms of practical consciousness people customarily work with are so shaped by the lifeworld, that it is not experienced as a lifeworld at all, among possible other lifeworlds, but just 'reality' pure and simple. These ideas are Berger and Luckmann's phenomenological re-workings of Marxist ideas about 'reification' (see Chapters 1 and 3).

So interaction generates habituation and institutionalization. Once children are born into such a situation, they undergo 'internalization': socialization is essentially the inculcation of the typifications and recipes characteristic of the lifeworld of their parents. A new generation begins to see the world in light of the paramount reality of the parents' lifeworld. This means the children will think and act in ways that help reproduce the lifeworld, because the recipes and typifications are so embedded in their practical consciousness. So children begin to act like adults: everyone is engaged in interactions which assume the recipes and typifications, so reproducing these over time and confirming their apparently 'objective' qualities.

Berger and Luckmann very much emphasize the alienating effect of all social orders:

> ... institutions confront the individual as undeniable facts. The institutions are there, external to him [sic], persistent in their reality, whether he likes it or not. He cannot wish them away. They resist his attempts to change or evade them. They have coercive power over him, both in themselves, by the sheer force of their facticity, and through the control mechanisms that are usually attached to the most important of them. (1991 [1966]: 61)

As they sum the point up, 'society is a human product . . . [s]ociety is an objective reality' (ibid.). Society starts off as a human product, then through objectification, institutionalization and internalization processes, which happen over and over again, it comes to seem natural, and as a result, inescapable as far as the people in it are concerned.

The issue then could be raised: which groups control paramount reality, and how do they operate such that they reproduce this situation? Such a question takes phenomenological analysis in the direction of Marxism and other forms of 'critical' sociology (see Chapters 1 and 3). The implication of phenomenology that a lot of social power is not exercised intentionally by powerful groups, for they too may generally think that the social set-up that benefits them is 'natural' and inevitable too. This suggests that often power and domination are not consciously exercised by the powerful, because in the practical consciousness and lifeworld shared – at least to some degree – by powerful and less powerful groups alike, the current social situation is regarded as somehow simply 'the way things are'. These ideas as to the unintended reproduction of power and social inequalities through the means of practical consciousness were taken up by Pierre Bourdieu in productive ways (see Chapter 10). Such considerations also inform Dorothy Smith's innovative feminist blending of Marxism and phenomenology (see Chapter 11)

Berger and Luckmann also endeavoured to use this general view to understand the nature of modern society. Following the classical theorists, they saw modernity as a complex social order divided up into separate spheres, all quite distinct from each other: personal and family life, work, education, and so on. All of these have their own lifeworlds. Within work in particular, there are further sub-spheres, each with their own lifeworlds too: for example, the lifeworld of a science laboratory is very different, in

---

Knowledge
Reworking of Schutz's phenomenology

Structure/Agency
Ongoing interactions at first produce, then reproduce, typifications and recipes

Embedding of typifications in practical consciousness and lifeworld

Objectification/institutionalization/internalization

Paramount reality

Modernity
Multiple lifeworlds/overarching paramount reality

Figure 4.2 Summary of Berger and Luckmann.

terms of the typifications and recipes used there, from the lifeworld of a coal-mine. However, all these spheres are united by being part of the bigger lifeworld of a wider social whole, paramount reality, the ordinary, taken-for-granted sense of 'normality' embodied in everyone's practical consciousness, in whatever sphere they are operating and whoever they are, scientist, coalminer, or whatever.

Ethnomethodology: Accomplishing Reality

For Berger and Luckmann, 'society' starts to seem like a condition of complete alienation, a reality standing over and above the individual. They had taken phenomenology – perhaps without fully realizing it – forcefully in the direction of macro-sociology, as Durkheim did ('society' is different from, stands 'above' and profoundly shapes the actions and thoughts of people within it). Indeed, although Durkheim had assumed that 'society is real', Berger and Luckmann had sought to explain how such a situation had come about, and with what effects on people's consciousness.

Schutz's phenomenology did not have to be taken in this direction only, as another perspective taking inspiration from it, ethnomethodology, demonstrated. This is a type of micro-sociology first pioneered in the 1960s and particularly associated with figures such as Harold Garfinkel (1967) and Harvey Sacks (1972).

Schutz saw the aim of phenomenological sociology as getting at the details of how particular people experience things from inside their 'life-world'. This is also the aim of ethnomethodology. The word ethnomethodology refers to the *study of the methods people use to make sense of the social world they are part of.* Ethnomethodologists are intent on reconstructing what goes on in particular lifeworlds.

Like Schutz, ethnomethodologists are interested in describing in detail the actual ways in which people perceive and act upon the social world they live in. However, ethnomethodology adds to this focus a stress on how social actors (who are referred to as 'members' of particular social realities) are constantly in the process of actively achieving the sense of reality that they have. It is also the case that ethnomethodology seeks to abolish the Schutzian distinction between first-order and second-order categories, because it wants to find out what categories and forms of reason members themselves use, rather than impose on these the second-order constructions that social scientists usually draw upon to depict those first-order categories. Second-order categories hide the real nature of first-order categories. Hence ethnomethodology's attempted revolution inside social science – to reject the standard understandings used by analysts to understand people, in favour of analysing people through the means of those persons' own categories.

For ethnomethodology, the social realm is not something that exists 'outside' people's everyday thoughts and activities, and imposes itself on them, as Berger and Luckmann implied. Instead, society is seen as constantly *being accomplished* by people in their everyday actions (Garfinkel, 1967). As we have seen, Berger and Luckmann had said social order was 'an ongoing human production'. But they had emphasized that once certain products of human interaction (recipes and typifications) become 'objectified', they start to seem solid and inescapable.

By contrast, a key point raised by ethnomethodology is that any particular interaction, and any particular lifeword, is actually very *fragile*. Members have to work very hard – but generally without realizing they are doing so – to keep their shared sense of reality going. That sense of reality can break down if constant effort and vigilance are not applied. Members' realities, then, are not understood by ethnomethodologists as obdurate realities, bearing down on members from 'above' or 'outside', as Berger and Luckmann had implied. Instead, shared reality is something that must be constantly *accomplished* by members.

Ethnomethodologists are particularly interested in how members create the sense of reality they operate with through the means of certain *social competencies*. These are the resources that members deploy, generally in practical rather than fully reflective ways, in order to make their relations with other people comprehensible and meaningful. A particular form of social competence ethnomethodologists focus on is how people operate in particular contexts with a sense of the rules that they see as guiding activities in that context. But rules are not used mechanically by members. Nor do rules involve simple, repeatable recipes and typifications. These too have to be accomplished, that is, used skilfully in certain ways. The reproduction of a lifeworld is not guaranteed or likely, as Berger and Luckmann argue, but depends on what happens in the micro-interactions of members.

For example, Weider (1974) examines the unofficial rules of a hostel for prisoners on parole. He shows not only that everyday life in the hostel operates according to 'unwritten rules' as well as the official rules of the institution, but also that the residents *were well aware* of this fact. They know that an unofficial code exists, and use it as a resource in their everyday lives, commenting on it, criticizing it and making use of it as a reason for their actions. Thus when an official would ask a prisoner to do a particular task, the prisoner might refuse to do so, justifying his response by showing that such an activity (e.g. informing on another prisoner) was not acceptable according to the norms of the unofficial code. Both inmates and officials skilfully utilized their knowledge of, and competence in, the unofficial rules. Weider attempted to demonstrate what it feels like to be a 'member' in the particular social-cultural situation that was the hostel. This is a lifeworld, but one which exists in a more fragile and contingent way than Berger and Luckmann had understood it.

A related issue a particular kind of ethnomethodologist has looked at in some detail involves how conversations are managed between two or more people. This version of ethnomethodology is called Conversation Analysis (Sacks, 1972). According to this perspective, in order for a conversation to 'work', the participants must have a practical sense of how to conduct conversation. This involves knowing how to judge when it is appropriate for them to start speaking, knowing when the other person has finished speaking, and knowing what the appropriate response is to the other person's words. The 'work' certain words carry out in particular sentences is a special focus of the conversation analyst. Conversation analysis seeks to unpack the often subtle inflections of meaning inherent within particular words as they are used in particular conversational contexts. People engaged in conversation must work hard to keep the shared sense of reality embodied in the conversation going. When conversation fails to do this, 'repair work' is done to try to mend the failure.

Social order actively made and 'accomplished' by social actors ('members')

Social order and lifeworlds fragile

Members acquire socially marked and shared 'methods' which they use to 'construct' situations as meaningful

---

Figure 4.3 Summary of Ethnomethodology.

Existential Phenomenology

In sociology, the original, very abstract ideas of Husserl were progressively transformed in the direction of trying to understand specific situations involving particular individuals. Meanwhile, in twentieth-century philosophy, phenomenology developed in related ways towards the understanding of what the world looks like from the viewpoint of a particular human being or group. This orientation was called *existential phenomenology*, and is particularly associated with the German philosopher Martin Heidegger [1889–1976]. Heidegger (1988 [1927]) argued that ever since the ancient Greeks, Western philosophy had propagated distinctly abstract and theoretical ways of thinking about the world, and had ignored or downgraded actually the most important part of human existence, namely lifeworlds, and the lived experience of everyday existence (*doxa*) to be found in them. What should be the focus of philosophy is the human being's 'being-in the world' – their practical consciousness – and their existence in that world with other human beings – their lifeworld.

Heidegger echoed other developments in twentieth-century philosophy (see Chapter 8) by arguing that human beings can never know 'reality' directly but only as it is mediated and interpreted through language. So human life has an inescapably *interpretative* character. Human knowledge can never be 'objective' because any person's interpretation of reality is always undertaken from a particular point of view. Each person is located in a particular time and place (a lifeworld). They can only ever interpret things in light of that perspective, because they cannot escape their location in time and space even if they think they can. Each human being is 'always already' in a situation of having been 'thrown' into a particular lifeworld. Their view of reality will inescapably be shaped by the time in which they live, because each human being is a historical creation, moulded by the centuries-old lifeworld into which they were 'thrown' at the point of birth (Aho, 2005: 3).

So for existential phenomenology, the perception and consciousness of individuals are seen as being 'located' – in particular times, places and lifeworlds. Some of these Heideggerian themes were developed further by the French philosopher Maurice Merleau-Ponty [1908–1961]. Merleau-Ponty (1996) was concerned to transcend what he regarded as the age-old divide in Western philosophy between a conscious human mind and its passive, inert body (Schmidt 1985). For Merleau-Ponty, we can overcome this unhelpful way of thinking about human beings by seeing that the mind and the body are not two separate entities, but are always thoroughly bound up with each other. Mind and body are in fact just two aspects of the same substance, the individual human being. Each person is not just a subject, but a *body-subject*. This idea goes beyond merely saying that a subject *has* a body. Instead, the idea of body-subject is an attempt to express the idea that subjectivity and the body are not just interrelated, but completely indissociable. The body *is* the subject, and the subject *is* the body.

Merleau-Ponty analysed how the perceived space around them was experienced by particular body-subjects. Like other phenomenologists, Merleau-Ponty is concerned with practical consciousness, which is regarded as the opposite of natural scientific ways of thinking and perceiving, which are (supposed) to be purely logical in nature. Merleau-Ponty distinguishes between an *abstract* space perceived by sciences such as geometry, and a practical, 'lived' space perceived by body-subjects. Both spaces are products of particular ways of thinking and perceiving. 'Lived' space involves the spatial things, and relations between them, which body-subjects encounter in their everyday lives i.e. in lifeworlds (Priest, 1998). By contrast, abstract space is space as presented to a subject engaged in self-conscious reflection, not in practical activities (involving practical consciousness). This is space that is *thought* rather than practically *lived*.

Merleau-Ponty wanted to get away from a view that placed a fundamental divide between a conscious human mind on the one side, and an inert world of external objects confronting it on the other. He was, in a certain sense, going against Berger and Luckmann's ideas about 'objective' reality here. He wanted to see the ways in which the person and her environment are wrapped up in one another. Just as 'mind' and 'body' are seen to be interpenetrating entities, not separate substances, so too are the human being and the lifeworld s/he inhabits thoroughly bound up with each other. Merleau-Ponty points to a situation whereby the body-subject is constituted by his or her lifeworld, and the lifeworld is simultaneously constituted by the body-subject. Person and world are connected through practical consciousness; indeed, they both *are* practical consciousness.

For Merleau-Ponty, as in broader trends in the development of phenomenology, consciousness is always *situated*. This is because it is *embodied*. Perceptions of the world are never from a privileged, transcendental position, a 'bird's eye view'. Because each person is a body-subject, perception is fundamentally rooted in the *body* of each person. What each body-subject can see and experience is its own visual field – this is Merleau-Ponty's reformulation of the idea of lifeworld. The visual field is perceived from – and thus created by – the perspective of a subject who has a body (Merleau-Ponty, 1996). In fact, the visual field constitutes the body-subject while the body-subject constitutes the visual field (Schmidt, 1985). This is a 'dialectic of milieu and action' (Merleau-Ponty, 1965: 168–9). The world is a diversity of embodied subjects perceiving, constituting, and in turn being constituted by, visual fields relative to them.

What this means is that the human mind ('subjectivity') is not a pure consciousness that passively reflects on external objects, but is rather an *active* consciousness that exists in a *practical* relation to its visual field. Indeed, the body-subject *is* a form of practical consciousness. Each body-subject has practical knowledge of how to operate in its own visual field, and acts on the basis of that knowledge. The primordial condition of the body-subject is a state prior to reflective consciousness. Abstract modes of thought (those ways of thinking that are 'rational', 'logical', and 'calculating') are secondary products, generated on the basis of the pre-reflective forms of knowing and doing characteristic of the body-subject practically engaged in manoeuvring through its own visual field. Quite simply, 'doing' is prior to 'thinking'.

A good way of thinking about this redefinition of phenomenology is given by Merleau-Ponty (1965: 168–9; emphasis added) himself. He describes the movements of a soccer player on a pitch like this:

> For the player in action the soccer field is not a [geometrical] 'object' [existing outside of her practical consciousness] . . . [Instead the soccer field] is pervaded with lines of force (the 'yard lines'; those which demarcate the 'penalty area') and is articulated into sectors (for example, the 'openings' between the adversaries) which call for a certain mode of action and which initiate and guide the action *as if the player were unaware of it*. The field itself is not given to him [sic], but present as the immanent term of his practical intentions; the player becomes one with it and feels the direction of the 'goal' for example, just as immediately as the vertical and the horizontal planes of his [or her] own body. It would not be sufficient to say that consciousness inhabits this milieu. At this moment consciousness is nothing other than the dialectic of milieu and action. Each maneuver undertaken by the player modifies the character of the field and establishes

new lines of force in which the action in turn unfolds and is accomplished, again altering the phenomenal field.

So the perceived space changes as the player moves around the pitch. The pitch and the player are not two separate things. The player and the pitch are one single moving process, united through the player's practical consciousness. Another way of saying this is that we should be trying to understand action (movement on the pitch) and interaction (how the player connects with other body-subjects playing the game in constantly changing relations) from the point of view of examining the player as a body-subject. When we do that kind of phenomenology, we see that standard divisions between mind/body, internal/external, self/other, thought/action, all dissolve, because all of these things are in fact parts of one process, the dialectic of 'milieu and action', involving the body-subject and his or her constantly changing visual field.

Merleau-Ponty's account of such matters is a philosophical one. But it has been taken up, applied and transformed by social theorists. The notion of the body-subject and its practical consciousness has been taken up by Pierre Bourdieu and placed at the centre of his theory of 'practice' (see Chapter 10). Recent sociological work (Crossley, 1995) has argued that without a basis in the idea of body-subjects, phenomenology specifically and social theory more generally remain far too abstract. Previous phenomenological approaches have believed they have effectively got down to the nitty-gritty level of practical consciousness. But this consciousness has been regarded abstractly in a literally dis-embodied way, a person's perception and actions being analysed without reference to how their mind is rooted in their bodies, thus ignoring the fact that minds and bodies are part of the same concrete practical processes. Practical consciousness has been examined in ways that forget that 'practices' – the activities of a person – are not just mentally located (in 'consciousness') but in the

---

Re-working of Heideggerian existential-phenomenology
Intertwining of mind and body: body-subjects
Visual field: dialectic of milieu and action

Figure 4.4 Merleau-Ponty's Existential Phenomenology.

body too. Indeed, mind and body are the same thing. This view involves reorienting phenomenology away from its previous bias towards the minds of persons, towards how their minds *and* bodies simultaneously enact those practices. It also focuses phenomenology more systematically than before on the specifically *bodily* practices of people in everyday life-worlds, reminding us that social interaction is not only a disembodied, mental process but a fundamentally *bodily* thing too (Howson and Inglis, 2001).

Conclusion

It is appropriate to end this chapter with Merleau-Ponty's analysis of a soccer player. Although he took up Merleau-Ponty's ideas with enthusiasm, Pierre Bourdieu noted that there is a complete omission of questions posed by Merleau-Ponty in this regard about such standard sociological issues like who enforces the rules on the pitch, who polices the stadium, in whose interests the game is being staged, and so on: all questions about the nature of power (Bourdieu and Wacquant, 1992). This is a common kind of complaint from more structurally oriented social theorists – the key absence in phenomenological perspectives are their alleged downgrading or complete ignoring of questions to do with social hierarchy and inequalities of power. This may be true to some degree. But the point of the work of Schutz was to work out a basic vocabulary that would describe the elementary elements of human consciousness and their relations to action and interaction. The point of ethnomethodology is to try to gain a novel sense of how people do things, avoiding the usual categories of social theory. These positions cannot fairly be criticized for not doing what they never intended to do. As we saw in the discussion of Berger and Luckmann, those authors explicitly factor issues of power into their analysis – perhaps too much so, ending up with a vision of 'society' that other phenomenologists would reject as far too static. In contemporary social theory, it is acknowledged that, taken on their own, phenomenological approaches cannot fully discern important dimensions of the social world. But equally well is it recognized that phenomenological categories are absolutely indispensable resources for social theorizing, especially the key idea of practical consciousness, that we would ignore at our peril.

Further Reading

Berger, P. L. and Luckmann, T. (1991 [1966]) *The Social Construction of Reality*. Harmondsworth: Penguin.

Crossley, N. (1995) 'Merleau-Ponty, the Elusive Body and Carnal Sociology', *Body and Society*, 1(1): 43–63.

Garfinkel, H. (1984) *Studies in Ethnomethodology*. Cambridge: Polity.

Moran, D. (2007) *Introduction to Phenomenology*. London: Routledge.

5

The Symbolic Interactionist Paradigm

Symbolic interactionism developed at the University of Chicago in the early part of the twentieth century, and was intimately connected with what became known later as the 'Chicago School' of sociology. It then spread to wider American sociology as the century progressed (Blumer, 1969: 1). A theoretical paradigm focusing strongly on the micro-level interactions between individuals, symbolic interactionism (henceforth SI) was influenced by the process sociology of Georg Simmel (see Chapter 7), early American pragmatist philosophy and the wider social and political culture of the time. From Simmel, SI assumes the view that society is neither a 'static' or 'sui-generis' entity preceding individuals, but instead forms a dynamic and constantly evolving process of actions, reactions and interactions on the part of concrete individuals. From Pragmatist philosophy it takes the view of human agents as inextricably bound up in the creation of the social and cultural contexts they inhabit, as they actively seek to resolve the practical exigencies of everyday life. The notion that social reality is always already ordered is therefore rejected by SI thinkers and instead recast as something that is actively 'achieved' through patterned and recurrent interactions. This means that unlike more structural paradigms, like functionalism (see Chapter 2), SI is always either implicitly or explicitly motivated by the problem of how it is that society is possible. Or, put another way, how it is that our experience of everyday life comes to assume the feeling of something 'natural', 'inevitable' and 'ordered' when in actuality things may always be very different and potentially chaotic?

The concern with the manner and processes by which social reality is 'made' or 'constructed' is a central motif for SI and leads to a bottom-up approach to theorizing not only social reality and its component structures, but individuals too. Individuals create social order through their patterned interactions while simultaneously social order organizes and lends structure to individual experience and subjectivity. The construction of individual selfhood features in large part in SI theoretical ideas. In particular, the important role of language in the creation of selfhood is emphasized. So too are other forms of human signification such as body posture, gestures, ways of talking, expressing emotions, and so on. Social structures and institutions are also regarded as constructions which are neither 'internal' or 'external' to human actors, but reside instead in the habitual patterns of interaction built up between actors. SI thinkers stress that all social structures, from the most mundane interactions through to large-scale institutions and macro-level phenomena, are the outcomes and aggregates of the actions of concrete individuals.

Over the last century, in the USA in particular, SI has continued to develop and remains to date a respected body of theoretical ideas, underwritten by a strong tradition of empirical research feeding into developments and innovations in qualitative research methods within sociology. SI thinking is not without critics, however. Proponents of more macro-theoretical positions question SI's capacity to account for social processes over long-term time-frames. This has led to SI ideas being taken in two directions: first, integration with some other concepts and ideas, as in the example of Giddens' (see Chapter 10) use of SI ideas in his structuration theory; and second, through the continued efforts of contemporary SI thinkers such as Gary Alan Fine to respond to these charges by applying interactionist concepts in innovative ways.

The chapter begins by outlining the roots of SI thinking, beginning with a discussion of the importance of Simmelian thought and early American pragmatist philosophy in moulding the foundations of the SI conception of social reality. Next we depict the key influences on SI from the philosophical work of Henry James and George Herbert Mead, and consider the sociological application thereof in the contributions of Herbert Blumer and Charles Cooley, emphasizing in particular their respective accounts of more 'macro' and 'structured' institutional phenomena. We will show the influence of SI ideas on the Chicago School's distinctive working methods and research techniques. This entails addressing the work of a number of thinkers including Everett Hughes, Howard S. Becker, and Norman Denzin, all of whom simultaneously utilized, as well as contributed towards the development of a range of ethnographic and interpretive research methods. The final part of the chapter considers the attempts by Erving Goffman to develop a general theoretical account of the social rules underpinning all social interaction. We conclude with a survey of the main criticisms of SI and the subsequent developments and innovations this has led to.

The Roots of Symbolic Interactionism in Pragmatist Philosophy

The kind of philosophy known as 'pragmatism' strongly influenced the SI view of social reality as 'emergent' and actively created through individual agency. Originating in American universities, where it dominated the philosophical scene until the 1930s, pragmatism was developed by philosophers such as C.S. Pierce, William James, John Dewey and George Herbert Mead (Mills, 1966). In spite of their divergent views of what pragmatism exactly constituted, all of these thinkers were united by their 'common stance against rationalist philosophy' (Shalin, 1986: 10; 1991).

Three main points unify all pragmatist thinking. First, pragmatist epistemology comprises an 'anti-spectator' theory of knowledge. As James (1955: 167 [1907]: 67) noted, 'for rationalism reality is ready made and complete from all eternity, while for pragmatism it is still in the making'. Following Darwinian evolutionism, pragmatism emphasizes the active relationship between knowledge and action, such that knowledge is not seen to exist 'out there' in the world waiting to be discovered, but rather is created through the purposive action of agents drawing upon past knowledge and experiences in order to negotiate the practical problems and challenges of the present (Almeder, 2007: 171).

Second, knowledge is seen as a tool that once acquired provides the means with which to achieve some previously inhibited course(s) of action. The ontological notion of human beings characteristic of pragmatism is of 'man-the-maker' or 'man-the-sculptor', actively engaged in a process of 'moulding' reality into a form best suited to the attainment of specific goals (Shalin, 1986: 225; 1991). Third, an idea or theory is considered 'successful' or 'true' if it accomplishes what it is required to; in other words, knowledge that is 'true' is knowledge that allows a 'community of knowers' to understand or overcome the problem/s confronting them (Pierce, [1955] 1868).

In addition to pragmatism, Simmel's distinct conception of society informed and shaped the earliest moments of SI (see Chapters 1 and 7).

During a period spent in Berlin, one of the important figures in the Chicago School, Robert Park [1864–1944], was taught by Simmel and through this connection many of the latter's ideas featured in the first Chicago School textbook written in 1921. Simmel was fascinated by the novel social arrangements hosted by the rapidly bourgeoning urban centres of the day, such as Berlin and Chicago. According to Simmel, the notion of 'society' refers to the sum total of all interactions, or 'forms of sociation', taking place at any given moment and his conception of society can be summarized like this (Rock, 1979: 39):

(1) Society is never pre-given or static but is instead an ongoing process or event.
(2) Human actors create reality, ensuring it is meaningful through a process of shared identification and conferral of meaning on situations, events and objects.
(3) The shared subordination of agents to these mutually created definitions of situations gives rise to taken-for-granted structures or 'forms' that comprise the true object of sociological enquiry.

On this view, society represents an ongoing and interactive process or 'event' realized and achieved through collective interactions of which a number are relatively fleeting and some are recurrent and enduring.

Regarded as the founding figure of classical pragmatism, William James [1842–1910] originally trained as a medical doctor before turning to study psychology and philosophy (Barbalet, 2007). James' influence upon the other SI thinkers Mead and Cooley was as profound as it was enduring (Parsons, 1968; Joas, 1985) and his contribution to the development of SI can be seen at two levels: first, in his view of individuals as 'interested' and 'creative' in their use of experience to impose structure upon the stream of consciousness which confronts them as they perceive the world around them; and second, in his 'dialogical' conception of selfhood as the product of intra-personal communication (Wiley, 2006: 6). James (1890: 402) argued that consciousness is structured by 'selective interest'. Selective interest enables individuals to direct their attention towards those aspects of experience relevant to them for achieving a particular course of action. James argued that reality is always in the process of being made, and that as individuals we are constantly bombarded with an overwhelming variety of potential courses of action and possible futures. Because the future confronts us as indeterminate and formless, biological evolution has disposed human beings to create determinacy and certainty

Individual Identity

Understanding subjectivity through the concept of 'dialogical self'

The self ('I') emerges through interaction whereby it becomes an object to itself ('Me')

The stream of consciousness is a potentially overwhelming mass of sensory information

Agency

Individuals impose structure and order upon consciousness through 'selective interest'

The main driver of selective interest is to attend to those aspects of reality that contribute towards the fulfilment of practical goals and objectives

Figure 5.1 James' Selective Interest and Dialogical Self.

where otherwise none exists. Prefiguring the later concept of 'ontological security' (for Giddens' use of this idea, see Chapter 10), James (1897) argued that the ambiguity of the future is a cause of potential distress for humans, and the desire to create predictability, a drive typically led not by reason but the emotions, is a very strong one.

James' account of perception tends towards a phenomenological account (see Chapter 4) of individual subjectivity. His most significant distinction in this direction lay between the 'I' and the 'Me'. The 'I' is the individual subject, or self, to whom reality is revealed through conscious-ness. During experience, the 'I' is engaged in a constant process of interac-tion with the 'Me', the name James gave to the self when contemplated as an object (Wiley, 2006: 8). James' identification of the stream of con-sciousness and the importance he attributed to it in self-communication remains a seminal contribution to the psychology of the self (Barbalet, 2007: Wiley, 2006: 7).

George Herbert Mead [1863–1931] was a philosopher and social psy-chologist at the University of Chicago. Mead's most important work, *Mind, Self and Society* (1967), was published posthumously, having been assembled from his 'student notes'. The text bears traces of various intel-lectual sources, including the philosophies of James and of Hegel (see Chapter 1). A social psychological account of human interaction first and foremost, nonetheless it is significant for sociological theorizing for two reasons. First, it emphasizes the centrality of language as a shared system of symbols and signs allowing for the emergence of selfhood and interpersonal communication generally. Second, it rebuts both traditional philosophical and behaviourist conceptions of selfhood by demonstrating the *emergent* properties of the self as realized in and through social action and interaction. The crux of Mead's social psychological model of selfhood can be summarized thus:

(1) Individuals acquire language through their attachment to and interaction within social groups.
(2) Language is the primary medium through which the concept of selfhood *emerges*.
(3) Individual selfhood is realized through linguistically mediated forms of social interaction and develops throughout the life course.

Mead's central contention is that the individual self is a profoundly social entity. Contrary to philosophic and behaviourist views of the self as an innate and fixed attribute of human beings, Mead stressed that the self is only realized through 'the act' – that is, during interaction with others (Denzin, 1992: 5). According to Mead, the self cannot be introspected as James and the phenomenologists had suggested, because it ceases to exist outside of social interaction. It is only through language that agents develop a sense of self and the capacity to be self-aware through an ongoing process of self-monitoring and reflection. As Mead (1967: 177) observed, self-consciousness only occurs when 'the individual becomes an object to himself in the presentation of possible lines of conduct'.

Throughout Mead's work the importance of 'language' is continually emphasized. This is because language comprises a system of symbols and signs that enable human beings to generate and signify meanings. It is because of language, for instance, that culture is possible because non-human animals are defined and limited by the stimulus–response model, which means that the gestures or signals they make or send are always tied to the specific context in which they arise. Language allows human beings to talk about or refer to things, people, situations and so on, in a way that is temporally and spatially divorced from the contexts in which they first occurred. Through language the temporal and spatial dimensions of human existence are opened up and extended in a way that prevents individuals, unlike animals, from being trapped in the immediacy of the present. We have already identified the centrality of language to the uniqueness of human communication. But language, Mead argued, also enables dialogue – different from mere communication as a one-off exchange between individuals – not only with others, but more importantly still, with one's own self (Cook, 1993). For Mead, language is the medium through which the individual self develops and is formed. Language does not simply describe the world; rather, 'it makes possible the existence or the appearance of . . . [a] situation or object' (Mead, 1967: 78). By referring to the process of objectification by which selfhood is brought into being, Mead takes over James' distinction between the 'I' and the 'Me'.

Reality as we experience it 'from the inside', and the source from which all consciously directed action springs, is referred to by Mead as the 'I', whereas the object of self-awareness that is one's own physical body as perceived by others, is referred to as the 'Me'. The 'I' stands for the idiosyncratic and creative aspect of the individual, whereas the 'Me' represents the social component born out of the internalization of social roles, behavioural patterns, values and codes of conduct. The 'Me' does not merely act as a constraint on the 'I' but is instead both enabling and regulating because it allows the individual to adapt, revise and review their actions in light of the perceived reactions of others. The self, then, is a *process* and not a fixed or static structure. The notion of others and their relation to the self, as well as the idea of self-consciousness, leads us onto Mead's concept of the 'generalized other'.

The notion of the 'generalized other' is vital to Mead's account of self-development, comprising the link between the individual and the social group to which s/he belongs. 'Generalized other' refers to the complex of social attitudes, normative regulations and ways of seeing the world internalized by the individual. It is a concept intended to explain how individuals learn to regulate and monitor their own conduct by assuming the perspective of a generalized and impersonal other. How does this happen?

Mead cites the example of game playing as a situation where children learn to assume the general perspective of all the other players collectively, as well as the divergent viewpoints of individual players. The ability to empathize with and see oneself through the eyes of the 'generalized other' is essential to successful inter-personal communication, because the reactions of others are intimately bound to and shape the constantly shifting parameters of a situation. Moreover, it is because of the

Individuals are self-aware actors

Key ideas of 'I', 'me', and 'generalized other'

The self is an emergent and socially acquired 'process', and not a pre-given or static entity

The self is linguistically mediated and only realised in and through social actions and interactions

Social order, like the self, is not a static, pre-given entity – it is an ongoing accomplishment

Figure 5.2 Summary of Mead's Ideas.

individual's capacity to contemplate themselves as an object, 'Me', from the point of view of the 'generalized other', that the self is able to lay claim to any autonomy at all (da Silva, 2007). This in turn allows for a unique perspective of the world to open up for the individual, which serves as the basis from which purposeful courses of action and self-considered interactions can be undertaken. Social interaction is possible because of language, which not only provides actors with a shared set of standardized symbols through which to communicate, but also enables them to reflexively (i.e. in a self-aware way) monitor themselves and others during the interaction process. Social order and stability are *actively accomplished* by actors through successful interactions and for this reason they can never be considered pre-given.

Although a highly influential figure in the development of SI, Charles Horton Cooley's [1864–1929] theoretical contribution is often neglected in favour of Mead's. As well as devising an account of the development of individual selfhood, Cooley constructed 'a general sociological theory of social action, of social order and social change' (Schubert, 2006: 51). Central to Cooley's treatment of the individual self's sense of identity is the concept of 'self-idea'. As with Mead, Cooley (1998 [1908]) allocates primacy to the role of language in the emergence of the 'self-idea', which develops in three stages. First, the 'self-idea' arises as a reaction to individuals anticipating how they appear through the eyes of others. Second, and closely related to this, individuals imagine how it is that others perceive and evaluate their appearance. Third, in doing so they experience 'self-feeling' as they imagine these evaluations. In his account of the 'self-idea', Cooley invoked the metaphor of the *looking glass*. Cooley claims that in the same way individuals use a mirror to observe their own bodies externally, so a sense of self is built up and acquired through the mediating and imagined perspective of 'significant others', i.e. those people around the individual with whom they constantly interact.

Cooley regarded society as an emergent entity structured through lines of individually pursued 'communicative action' (Schubert, 2006: 54). As an organic totality whose parts 'must be seen as parts of a living whole', Cooley (1998 [1908]: 9) conceived of society as the sum total of the sociation of all the reflected selves involved in social interactions. In other words, all parts of social reality are inter-related and thus derive their meaning and form in relation to the whole. For this reason, any change to the organization of society necessarily leads to the formation of new forms of individual selfhood because of the new perspectives onto reality opened up to individuals. For Cooley, social reality centres on the ongoing dialogue between personal identity, primary groups and social organization. 'Primary groups', such as the family, are 'characterized by intimate face-to-face association and co-operation' and are the elemental social units wider underlying processes of social reproduction and the creation of individual selves (Cooley, 1998 [1908]: 173). Within the primary group, individuals develop a sense of their own autonomy and also the capacity to define and manipulate situations whenever contradictions arise between themselves and significant others. Individuals go on to develop an awareness of the perspective of 'institutional values', eventually realizing, through continuous socialization, that the general rules and socio-cultural norms particular to different spheres of actions are often contradictory, which in turn disposes them to think and act as autonomous beings.

Cooley regarded social institutions as both abstractions that in actuality are made up of individual actors, in which only specific aspects of their total self are presented (Jandy, 1969). So for example, 'The American Constitution' has no meaningful existence other than as the 'traditional ideas of the people and the activities of judges, legislators and administrators' (Cooley, 1998 [1908]: 313–14). In making this point, Cooley was underscoring the notion that institutional stability is the product not of 'external social' or 'internal mental' factors but instead the generalized and habitual patterns of interaction enacted by individuals. More than this, the meanings and value of situations and objects become institutionalized when

Key concepts of self-idea, primary groups and socialization

The 'social whole' is comprised of inter-related parts that form to make an 'organic totality'

'Primary group' as the fundamental social group

Identity begins with the 'self-idea' and develops into the 'looking-glass self'

Identity develops through self-consciousness as we imagine ourselves through the eyes of others

Figure 5.3 Summary of Cooley.

their practical use or value for lending structure to reality is habitually testified to and reasserted over time. It was on this basis that, Cooley always maintained that while social structures and wider institutional forms remain largely stable, they are always potentially liable to change.

Also based at the University of Chicago, Herbert Blumer's [1900–1987] contribution to the development of SI was to 'map out a theoretical scheme of human society' based upon Mead's psychologistic model of social interaction (Mead, 1967: 41). Blumer developed and extended Mead's interactionism in a sociological direction (Housley and Atkinson, 2003: 3). Blumer was strongly influenced by various interactionist ideas. From Robert Park, he inherited the view of sociological research as an empirically led enterprise, remaining true to the world of observable phenomena. From W. I. Thomas he assumed the view of meaning as an emergent and collectively negotiated entity and not an 'inevitable' or 'naturally' occurring phenomenon (Fine, 1993: 63). Central to Blumer's work is the processual notion of 'self-indication', meaning that consciousness is a constant flow involving notation of events, objects and people as they enter into the individual's consciousness. Individuals only become conscious of things by indicating them to themselves. Self-indication is a pivotal concept for two reasons. First, because it draws attention to the way individuals proactively confer meaning on social situations and other people. Second, because such a process enables potential courses of action to be constructed, altered or revised altogether by the individual. Self-indication is the organizing concept upon which Blumer's entire model of society pivots. There are various aspects to it:

(1) Human action is built upon and guided by the meanings individuals and groups attribute to objects, people, situations, etc.
(2) These meanings are an emergent property of the social interactions that occur between individuals and groups as they seek to fulfil tasks and goals.
(3) The socially negotiated meanings of things are typically developed, modified and refined over time through ongoing social interactions.

Blumer's view of social reality regards it as an emergent process. The meaning of things is neither natural or inevitable, but instead socio-culturally specific. Meaning is a social product precisely because by acting in certain ways, individuals demonstrate their commitment to classifying a situation along particular lines. Crucial here is the notion that meaning is typically taken-for-granted whenever social interaction runs smoothly and coherently, but is always liable to break down whenever the definition of a situation changes or is altered. The application of meaning to an event or situation is a *process* and typically occurs as part of the final stage in the wider process of identifying, weighing up, checking and refining that meaning before a course of action is devised. Such a process is essentially an interpretative one, precisely because as a social phenomenon meaning is fluid and liable to change.

According to Blumer (1969), society comprises the sum total of all the 'joint actions' or 'social acts' taking place at a given moment. By 'social act' is meant the collective form of action that occurs when specific 'acting units' co-ordinate or 'fit together' their respective lines of 'action'. For this reason, the 'social act', also referred to as 'joint action', is the 'distinguishing characteristic of society' (Blumer, 1969: 70). Blumer understands the notion of the 'acting unit' as referring to anything ranging from individuals to social groups through to large-scale social institutions. By emphasizing that social institutions are always comprised of interesting individuals, Blumer (1969: 85) was asserting the view that sociological analysis 'has to respect and be congruent with the empirical recognition that a human society consists of acting units'.

Blumer identified a number of characteristics pertaining to social acts, the main one being that they cannot be reduced to the common behaviour of individuals, because each constituent actor occupies a unique position or viewpoint in relation to all others. Individuals who form part of a social act must have identified the situation in a way that is sufficiently aligned with the definition shared by all others. Such a view underscores the SI vision of society as a complex and ongoing process that is always in the making, and not some static, pre-formed system of structures that simply dictate how individuals act.

In spite of the precarious nature of social interaction that requires individuals constantly to check, modify and realign their behaviour and definition of a situation in line with one another, Blumer acknowledged that for the most part social reality is experienced as 'taken-for-granted', 'unchanging' and 'predictable' (this is a theme emphasized by phenomenology – see Chapter 4). Over time, individuals learn the accepted and legitimate ways of acting associated with a particular context. So society and social reality often *seem* stable to individuals, even though both of them are always potentially alterable through individuals interacting with each other over time.

The way in which society is organized has far-reaching ramifications for the taken-for-granted nature of individuals' actions, not only because it shapes the contexts in which actions occur, but also because it produces situations with pre-defined symbolic frames individuals use to interpret reality. In the case of 'traditional', pre-modern societies, for example, the comparatively uncomplicated organization of social relations leads to relatively stable and fixed categories of meaning being reproduced through interactions. After all, 'tradition' means exactly that – knowing precisely how to act because a situation and the expectations attached to it remain the same over time. In modern society, however, the patterned regularities of situations and interactions diminish as individuals increasingly unknown to one another are brought together through shared interactions (see Chapter 1). Increasingly, individuals are dislocated from situations where action is couched within a frame of taken-for-granted meanings and points of reference. Similarly, the 'symbols or tools of interpretation' drawn upon by actors may be inappropriate or incongruent for holding together the situations they encounter. It is hard to imagine in an increasingly global society, for example, that different sorts of individuals may have very different ways of understanding reality and acting within it. Thus 'modern' social life is much more open, ambiguous and sometimes precarious than is life in pre-modern social orders.

Structure/Agency
Society is the aggregate of individuals' purposive and intentional actions and interactions
Social structures constituted through 'social acts', and 'joint action'
Identity
Individuals and institutions are 'acting units'
Individuals reflexively monitor their identity and actions as they are realized through social interaction in an ongoing process of 'self-indication'
Modernity
Social interactions within traditional society are relatively stable, patterned and taken-for-granted
Interaction under modernity increasingly precarious and ambiguous

Figure 5.4 Summary of Blumer.

So far we have examined the account of selfhood, social interaction and social structure propounded by the founding fathers of SI. In the next part of the chapter we provide a conspectus of the subsequent developments in SI to develop at Chicago and elsewhere as these theories were re-worked and applied to a range of novel socio-cultural phenomena.

The Development of Symbolic Interactionism

Symbolic interactionism as a distinctive paradigm within sociological thinking emerged and developed at the University of Chicago at the turn of the twentieth century. Home to the earliest attempts at sociological theorizing in America, the development of SI spanned roughly three generations of scholars at Chicago (Denzin, 1992). In addition to the theoretical groundwork laid down by Mead, Cooley and Blumer, both W. I. Thomas and Robert Park also played prominent roles at Chicago in ensuring its ensuing dominance in American sociological circles up until the 1930s (Atkinson and Housley, 2003; Tomasi, 1998). Thomas and Park were active in the empirical application of the ideas of their more theoretically inclined colleagues. Thomas, for example, wrote the classic five-volume study *The Polish Peasant in Europe and America* published between 1918 and 1920

(Thomas and Znaniecki, 1984 [1918–1920]). The importance of this study lies in its use of qualitative data and research methods, which, along with a number of the earliest Chicago School monographs and studies, comprise some of the earliest sociological uses of archival research, life histories, documentary sources and ecological analysis (Bulmer, 1984: 6). Previously a journalist before switching to academic life, Robert Park spent a year in Germany and was taught by Simmel before returning to establish himself at the University of Chicago. Park was responsible for importing many of his former teacher's most influential ideas and concepts, as well as instilling within his students a strong awareness of the need for, and value of, empirically grounded research, particularly with regard to the qualitative research methods of urban ethnology and participant observation.

In the hands of the second and third generations of Chicago School scholars, such as Everett Hughes, Howard S. Becker, Anselm Strauss, Blanche Greer, Erving Goffman, John Lofland and Norman Denzin, a concern with qualitative research methods and their application became an established feature of intellectual life at the university from the end of WWII onward (Bulmer, 1984). Much of the empirical work undertaken by these thinkers dealt with the inter-relations between individuals, identity and institutional life.

Everett Hughes [1897–1983] devoted considerable time to studying the 'careers' of individuals within institutional contexts. Utilizing data from fieldwork gathered at a local hospital, participant observation and interviews, Hughes and his research team overturned a passive view of institutional socialization in favour of a more individual-centred account of the ways individuals both align their actions with, as well as subvert, the wider organizations they are drawn from.

Taught by Hughes, Howard S. Becker's [b. 1928] contribution to the development of SI particularly assumed the form of the study of 'outsiders' (Becker, 1963). Now regarded as a sociological classic, 'Outsiders' played a crucial role in laying down the foundations for 'Labelling Theory'. In it Becker examines the concrete acts and decisions individuals make on the road to becoming, for example, marijuana users, and how in turn they self-consciously manage this process. Becker draws attention to the fact that one does not simply or automatically 'become' a marijuana user, but rather learns to do so over time by adapting and learning to behave in ways that are consistent with a community of marijuana users.

Carrying forward the development of sociological research methods, Norman Denzin, who left Chicago for the University of Illinois, wrote the

'Research Act' (1970), an ambitious attempt at providing a detailed overview of the numerous research methods developed by the Chicago school. Of the methodological issues considered by Denzin, the concept of 'triangulation' remains the most influential. The development and suffusion of SI theoretical ideas with applied research methods is one of the most noteworthy aspects of the symbolic interactionist tradition, distinguishing it from 'pure theory' of some other theoretical paradigms, especially those developed in Continental Europe.

Tales of Goffman

Although he was only at the University of Chicago during a two-year period spanning 1952 to 1954, Erving Goffman [1922–1982] is widely regarded as one of the most influential proponents of SI thinking and methods (Drew and Wootton, 1988). While Goffman's work is often criticized for its lack of 'cumulative quality' (Giddens, 1988: 251), Manning (1992) argues that all of Goffman's work is more or less motivated by one simple question: how is social interaction possible in a society characterized by increasingly impersonal and often anonymous relations between individuals? Through his numerous and highly perceptive studies of micro-social interactions, Goffman sought to develop a general account of the essential elements of face-to-face interactions under the increasingly impersonal conditions of modernity (Burns, 1992). While Goffman was always vehemently against the view of social order as the product of the workings of some deep underlying 'social structure', he attached huge importance to the value and function of rules as the invisible codes governing human interaction.

Following Durkheim (see Chapter 1), Goffman viewed rules as the underlying codes structuring all human interaction (Collins, 1988a). For the most part, social rules constrain individual behaviour; they are also the necessary and often 'hidden' basis of social life. Goffman argued that more often than not social rules are indeterminate and non-prescriptive, yet somehow agents know when and how to apply and adhere to them. On this view, rules form the 'syntax' of everyday interactions without which the language of behaviour simply could not be comprehended (Manning, 1992: 78). Goffman claimed that the fundamental rules common to all forms of interaction must be logically structured and thus could be analysed as a result.

In addition to rules, Goffman also emphasized the importance of 'trust' for social interaction. During interactions, agents seek to put forward a positive self-image referred to by Goffman as 'face'. If an individual loses face, then it can undermine a social situation and social order in that situation is likely to break down. So as not to undermine the face projected by others, individuals regulate their behaviour in order that a 'rigid equilibrium' is maintained (Goffman, 1967: 45). Tact, for example, is something we use in order to prevent a loss of face, whereas the emotion of embarrassment occurs whenever the face we project cannot be maintained in light of other people's negative responses to us.

Goffman's work can be divided into various stages, each of which represents a different approach to thinking about social interaction and the mechanisms by which individuals attempt to manage themselves, other people and the social contexts they enter into. Goffman's style is a distinctive one due to his repeated use of metaphors as heuristic devices for thinking about social interactions.

The 'dramaturgical' metaphor is one such metaphor gainfully employed by Goffman (1959: 32), which he used to promote the view of everyday social life as akin to a theatrical performance, with individuals performing roles designed to influence one another. The notion of 'impression management' is an important one here, because it highlights Goffman's view of individuals as acting self-consciously in ways designed to present themselves in as favourable a light as possible. On this view, individuals play different 'roles' as part of their respective 'performances'. Furthermore, the 'audience' comes to know and expect a certain type of performance from a given actor in a way that ensures predictability over time. Performances can be located anywhere on a sliding scale from 'successful' to 'unsuccessful'. Good actors know how to demonstrate and convince others that their definition of the situation – the particular version of reality they are trying to advance – is the right one. This involves putting on and sustaining a convincing 'front'. 'Front' refers to 'a set of abstract stereotyped expectations' that allow the audience to understand what they can expect to happen. Fronts are important for adding 'dramatic realization' to a performance. In order to animate a front, 'props' are used and appropriate gestures, facial expressions and appropriate 'role attitudes' are adopted. The areas where performances are realized can also be thought of in theatrical terms, comprising 'front stage' and 'back stage' areas. 'Front stage' areas are where 'public' performances designed by individuals to put on successful and socially appropriate 'fronts' are staged. 'Back stage' areas by contrast are locations where individual actors feel that they are able to display to other people – generally those they are on intimate terms with – their 'real' feelings and thoughts, beyond most considerations of putting on a staged performance for the benefit of other people.

An important aspect of the performances individuals put on is the concept of 'role distance'. Sometimes individuals are required to stage performances in the enactment of a particular social role, such as a traffic warden, say, that can lead to them having to assume a particular front that goes against how they feel and think about their own personal identity. The concept of 'role distance' describes the psychological disparity between the role individuals are required to play and their personal sense of identity. As his career progressed Goffman dropped the dramaturgical metaphor of interaction, partly because it seemed to suggest an overly cynical view of individuals as highly manipulative and constantly dissembling.

In the later studies *Stigma* (1964) and *Asylums* (1961), Goffman shifted his attention to the subject of social deviance in order to cast further light on the social construction of selfhood and the ways in which threats to social order are dealt with and marginalized through processes of exclusion. Goffman highlights the importance of socially expressive props, resources and contexts in the maintenance and reproduction of individual selfhood, as well as demonstrating how individuals who flout the norms of social participation and interaction are marginalized or excluded altogether by other people. In *Stigma* (1964), Goffman analyses the behaviour of individuals whose identity is publicly held as 'soiled' or 'defective' in some way. Stigma threatens self-identity because it alludes to some aspect of the self that breaches the rules of social interaction. Mirroring Mead's distinction between the internal 'I' and the socially mediated 'Me', Goffman (1964: 2) distinguishes between 'virtual' and 'actual' social identity, the former referring to the socially legitimate version of self individuals present in public, and the latter referring to the self-identity they imagined themselves to possess in private. According to Goffman, stigma arises whenever the disparity between 'virtual' and 'actual' social identity becomes untenable and embarrassment ensues, or the interaction breaks down. In their attempts to avoid being stigmatized, individuals appropriate different strategies including 'concealment' through use of 'covers' (such as wigs), in the case of people who feel ashamed of being bald or somehow disfigured, or 'disclosure' which involves openly acknowledging the discrediting feature/s of one's identity.

Further focusing on deviance and the maintenance of social order was Goffman's most controversial work, *Asylums* (1961), an ethnographic study of everyday life in a mental hospital in Washington DC. Goffman begins by defining the mental hospital as a 'total institution', a concept taken over from the work of Everett Hughes and intended to describe types of institution where the time and space of inmates is totally controlled by an external source (Burns, 1992: 11). Examples of 'total institutions' include prisons, monasteries and military camps. On entering a total institution, individuals undergo a process of 'civil' death, the first stage in the broader process that is the 'mortification of the self'. The mortification of the self can take a variety of forms including the denial of both personal space and ownership of time, the presentation and circulation of socially discrediting information, and the stripping away of individuals' 'identity kits' (i.e. the resources individuals normally have to present their ideas of themselves both to other people and to themselves). All of these represent crucial stages in the 'career' of the individuals as they enter into the total institution (Goffman, 1961: 28–9).

In *Frame Analysis* (1974), written near the end of his career, Goffman sought to describe the processes by which social actors differentiate their experience of social reality by creating and drawing up boundaries around events and situations. Here Goffman drew upon Gregory Bateson's notion of 'frames' (Fine, 1993: 76), which he employs to describe the processes by which individuals seek to convince themselves and others that their reading of a situation or events is the 'right' or 'correct' one (Denzin and Keller, 1981). Frames are discursive (i.e. linguistic and symbolic) structures used by actors to 'organize' and 'define' social situations. Embedded in the notion of frames is the idea that certain things are included in the definition of a situation while others are left out, depending on which 'side' of the frame they fall into. Frames impose order on 'strips', strips comprising arbitrary slices cut from the ongoing stream of social activity as it presents itself to consciousness. Strips have the potential to be 'keyed', a process intended to transform their original meaning. Comedians, for example, are very good at keying 'primary frames' such that the meaning of events the comedian describes to an audience is altered in ways that provoke laughter and a sense of absurdity.

In *Forms of Talk* (1981), Goffman analysed radio programmes and the DJs who host them, paying particular attention to the special forms of talk that DJs use during their shows. Goffman argues that DJs develop a remarkable capacity for generating a flow of words

Individuals are like 'actors' presenting different version of 'self' in the enactment of different 'roles'

In order to 'perform' a given social role, actors must know the relevant 'script'

Modern actors must 'manage' the disparity between 'who they are' and the roles they are required to perform – 'role distance'

Modernity involves increasingly impersonal social interactions and exchanges

Social reality strongly demarcated into 'front stage' areas – 'public' life – and 'back stage' areas – 'private' life

The importance of frames and framing in social interaction

Figure 5.5 Summary of Goffman.

that contains only a very small number of mistakes or slippages. Goffman (1981: 146) refers to these carefully produced rhetorical strips as 'fresh talk'. The study also develops the notion of 'frame space', the processes by which DJs try to project a version of themselves designed to appeal to as many listeners as possible through the creation of a sense of familiarity and intimacy with their audience (Goffman, 1981: 128).

In summary, while Goffman never realized his goal of providing a totally conclusive account of the essential principles structuring all face-to-face interactions – the best attempt at this can be found in his final paper 'The Interaction Order' written in 1983 (Goffman, 1983) – nonetheless, his work remains to date the most sociologically insightful and extensive attempt to bring to light the micro-dimensions of interpersonal communication (Manning, 1992).

Assessing Symbolic Interactionism

Like all theoretical paradigms, SI is susceptible to a number of criticisms. Of these, the most recurrent is the view that its strong emphasis on analysing individual actors leads SI to neglect the notion of macro-level social structure. Because of the general disdain on the part of SI to attribute ontological status to the notion of social structure other than as the aggregate of individuals behaving in reproducible ways, SI has allegedly struggled to provide a persuasive account of the effects of macro-level forces such as political power and long-term historical processes (Giddens, 1990; Meltzer et al., 1975) although an attempt to think through exactly these kinds of issues and to defend SI from such criticisms is offered by Stryker (1980). More specifically, one criticism aimed at the SI concept of mind is its alleged down-playing unconscious of motives, goals and desires, the very issues attended to by Freudian and post-Freudian theory (see Chapters 1, 3, 8 and 11). In addition to this, the SI account of mind barely alludes to the role of emotions in guiding and shaping individual behaviour, a particularly ironic criticism in light of the emphasis placed by William James on the emotions in directing human consciousness. Mead's social-psychological concepts such as 'Me', 'I' 'Self' and 'Other' have faced much critical scrutiny, particularly as regards the imprecision of such terms, which makes it difficult to subject them to what some critics regard as proper scientific scrutiny (Charon, 2006). Because of their virtual immunity to scientific testing, some critics argue that Mead's concepts cannot be either operationalized or falsified.

In a self-conscious effort to respond to such critical commentary, SI has undergone a number of conceptual turns which in turn have led to it expanding its analytical remit as well as being adopted into broader conceptual structures (Fine, 1993). In recent times, SI has been brought to bear on a range of novel research topics far exceeding the traditional remit of SI thinking. A good example is the work of Arlie Russell Hochschild (1983), whose study of the 'emotional labour' undertaken by airline cabin-crew, *The Managed Heart* (1983), directly explores the hitherto under-theorized area of the relations between 'emotion work, feeling rules and social structure'. According to Denzin (1992: 74) the SI view of social actors as 'meaning makers' is very well suited to grasping the matter of how 'interacting individuals connect lived experiences to the cultural representations of those experiences'. Concentrating on the centrality of 'communication' for SI theory, Denzin (1992) argues that SI should switch its attention to the ever greater role played by novel forms of communication and technology in the production and representation of social reality and in particular the ways in which the individual 'self' is realized through novel forms of visual-media such as video-images, the internet and so on.

Another important contemporary figure in SI is Gary Alan Fine (1993: 2), whose work represents a direct attempt to go 'behind the generalizations and abstractions of more conventional institutional theory to examine how institutions operate in practice'. Fine (1996) draws upon ethnographic fieldwork and in-depth qualitative interviews undertaken across four American restaurants, in order to build up a picture of the lived experiences and collaborative activities of chefs, waiters, cooks, porters, barmen and other such workers. In addition to expanding, SI has been adopted by thinkers attempting to combine a number of theoretical concepts and ideas. Giddens (1988: 271), for example, attempts to provide a general sociological theory of 'structuration' by drawing upon the work of Goffman to draw attention to the fact that the 'routine aspects of everyday life have a great deal to teach us about the fundamental issues of human experience, action and consciousness'. (For Giddens' attempts in this direction, see Chapter 10.)

Conclusion

In this chapter we have examined the emergence and development of symbolic interactionism. Starting at the level of individual actors, the centrality of language to the development and articulation of subjectivity and self-awareness was explicated, before we turned to consider the role of inter-personal relations and interactions as the site for the realization and expression of individual identity. We also examined the SI conception of 'society', dealt with in most detail by Blumer and Cooley. Society is never pre-formed or static, but instead comprises an ongoing and dynamic process of purposively aligned lines of action, or 'joint acts', which, in spite of their collective character, nonetheless can always be reduced to the actions, interactions and reactions of individuals operating in concrete social contexts. We have also seen how SI developed and diversified over the twentieth century, acting as the conceptual backdrop against which thinkers such as Park, Hughes and Becker sought to develop a range of qualitative research methods. The ideas of Goffman continue to be highly influential today, in sociology and related disciplines. Although SI thinking is seen by critics as struggling to provide convincing accounts of various macro-level social phenomena, nevertheless the innovative application of SI ideas in recent years by the likes of Hochschild, Denzin and Fine has ensured that SI remains a highly insightful and versatile body of social theory whose emphasis on individuals and their interactions is a necessary corrective to any more structural understandings of human social life.

Further Reading

Charon, J. (2006) *Symbolic Interactionism: An Introduction, An Interpretation* Englewood Cliffs: Prentice-Hall.

Denzin, N. K. (1992) *Symbolic Interactionism and Cultural Studies: The Politics of Interpretation*. Oxford: Blackwell.

Fine, G. A. (2007) *Authors of the Storm: Meteorologists and the Culture of Prediction*. Chicago: University of Chicago Press.

Manning, P. (1992) *Erving Goffman and Modern Sociology*. Cambridge: Polity.

Tomasi, L. (1998) *The Tradition of the Chicago School of Sociology*. Aldershot: Ashgate.

6

Rational Choice and Exchange Theory Paradigms

Rational Choice Theory (RCT) and Exchange Theories conceive of human beings as acting purposively and rationally in the pursuit of goals and objectives. The view of human agents as rational actors derives from a number of diverse strands including the political philosophies of Thomas Hobbes and J. S. Mill, economic theories of human behaviour and game theory. Rational Choice theories first entered into sociology in the US during the 1950s and were aimed at counteracting the prevailing conception of individuals as 'passive', 'reactive', 'cultural dupes' allegedly portrayed within the work of Talcott Parsons (see Chapter 2). Instead, rational choice and exchange theories promote a view of individuals as 'purposive', 'proactive' and acting with 'intentionality'.

Both approaches emphasize that in their pursuit of goals and aims, individuals select the course of action most likely to incur the greatest 'gain' or 'profit', while simultaneously minimizing any personal 'loss' or 'cost' (Coleman, 1994: 166), with goals and objectives internally represented in the mind of the actor as a series of 'hierarchies of preferences' (Zey, 1998: 2). The word 'personal' is significant here because it points to a view of individuals as the sole determinants of social reality, a fundamental contention of RCT. RCT thinkers deny, therefore, the possibility that interactions can ever take place at a 'macro' level, if by 'macro' is meant anything existing over and above the actions of individuals. To this end, RCT and Exchange Theories recognize interactions as occurring either between individuals – intersubjective exchanges – or individuals and institutions. Moreover, the notion that institutions comprise anything other than aggregates of individuals, or that there exists a realm of inter-institutional exchange that occurs behind the backs of individual actors, is rejected entirely.

Since the emergence of RCT and Exchange Theories in the 1950s, subsequent generations of thinkers have sought to carry on and develop the notion of individuals as rational actors. One reason for this is the allegedly great practical success economic and political thinkers have met with when using Rational Choice models to predict and model human behaviour across a range of social contexts and scenarios. Additionally, and in the last thirty years particularly, the spread of neo-liberal economic policy across the globe has led to RCT being applied to an ever wider range of social and cultural practices, a move alleged to mirror the increasingly rational and instrumental approach to everyday life adopted by individuals across the world. During the 1990s, the combination of these factors led James Coleman to try to remodel American sociology along Rational Choice lines, by establishing RCT as the dominant conceptual paradigm for theorizing the nature of all human behaviour. Yet in spite of what appear to be very good reasons for taking seriously a number of the central tenets of RCT and Exchange theories, nonetheless such an approach to understanding human behaviour has met with and continues to receive criticism from virtually every social theoretical quarter.

This chapter begins by delineating the intellectual roots of RCT and Exchange Theories, in classical economic theory, game theory and behaviourist psychology. We then move on to address the definitive features of the exchange theories of Homans, Blau and Emerson, and, in so doing, consider the extent to which the RCT vision of individuals as self-interested and calculating developed as a response to the individual/ society relationship promoted by Talcott Parsons' functionalism. Following on from this, we turn to address more recent Rational Choice models, most notably Coleman's approach to understanding collectivities and organizations, and the ways in which these can inform our understanding of corporations and other organizations today. This leads into a discussion of the attempts made to apply Rational Choice perspectives to Marxism (see Chapter 3), a conceptual manoeuvre undertaken by Elster, Roemer and Przeworski. The chapter concludes by considering the wide range of criticisms of rational choice models of human behaviour, and considerations to what extent these require to be addressed in order for RCT ways of theorizing human behaviour to retain their usefulness in the future.

The Roots of Rational Choice Theory

Rational Choice Theory draws upon strands of thought deriving from neoclassical economics, utilitarian theory and game theory (Friedman and Hechter, 1988). Central to all RCT is the image of human beings as self-interested and calculating, a position developed most notably by the seventeenth-century English political philosopher Thomas Hobbes (Zey, 1998: 41). Hobbes depicts a stark vision of social life 'as a war of each against all'. Hobbes' apparently highly cynical view of human nature is rooted in his assumption that in human life the resources that people need and desire are finite and scarce, a situation inevitably resulting in conflict between individuals and groups as they seek to accumulate those resources.

RCT also draws upon aspects of neoclassical economic theory, most notably the concept of *homo economicus*. This is a concept rooted in the work of the English thinkers Jeremy Bentham and J. S. Mill. The former declared that human beings are governed by two masters, 'pleasure and pain', and that by their very nature individuals are disposed to pursue any course of action resulting in the former while minimizing the latter (Ryan, 1987). Directly influenced by Bentham, Mill adopted a similar view of human beings as possessed of a fundamental 'desire of wealth' or 'profit motive', which they rationally pursue within the economic sphere (Mill, 1968 [1829]: 139).

Moving forward in time to the 1950s, a further theoretical strand was added to RCT in the form of game theory. Game theory became integral to the development of RCT, in part because of the relative ease with which it has been applied to traditionally sociological areas of enquiry, ranging from the analysis of social class to the selection of marriage partners (Becker, 1976; Coleman, 1993b, 1994). Strictly speaking a branch of applied mathematics developed by economists, game theory provides a model for theorizing behaviour in 'strategic situations', where each actor acts rationally and on the basis of the information available to them. Games consist of two or more players (Elster, 1982). During games, players develop strategies intended to maximize their chances of obtaining the rewards or resources on offer. Rewards comprise either material benefits or anything that is recognized as valuable to the players involved in the game. Whether or not players are successful in their pursuit of rewards depends simultaneously on the strategy they adopt, and the choices and strategies adopted by all the other players. Game theory provides conceptual models for a variety of types of games. The type of game model characteristically drawn upon by RCT is that of the 'constant-sum' or 'zero-sum' game where one winner's gain is another's directly proportionate loss (Elster, 1982: 465). This is a model that depicts a scenario with limited, finite 'resources' or 'stakes' to play for. The 'variable sum game' (or non-zero-sum game), by contrast, refers to games where the sum total of all players' rewards is contingent on the strategy employed by each player.

RCT is committed to 'methodological individualism' (Hedstrom and Swedberg, 1996). In its purest form, methodological individualism is the view that individuals and their actions form the sole constituents and determinants of social reality, a position diametrically opposed to the types of methodological holism associated with the work of Durkheim (Chapter 1), functionalism (Chapter 2) and French structuralism (Chapter 8). Within sociology, methodological individualism is most closely associated with the work of Max Weber (see Chapter 1), although the concept was anticipated in the works of Bentham and Mill as well as the twentieth-century Austrian economist von Mises (Hodgson, 1986). Significantly, present-day thinkers who adhere to methodological individualism acknowledge the emergent properties of social structures – that is, social structures *do* exist, but only as aggregates of individuals' actions. They reject the view that these 'properties' are able to influence or interact with one another at a level beyond the individuals giving rise to them (Hedstrom and Swedberg, 1996).

Methodological individualism – the primary focus of social science is individuals and their actions

Social reality comprises the actions and unintended consequences of individuals pursuing goals through rational action

Social structures are regarded as the aggregates of the actions of individual actors and never as supra-individual entities

Individuals are self-interested, purposive, calculating, 'rational utility-optimizers'

Figure 6.1 Summary of Rational Choice Theory.

Exchange Theory

Exchange Theory is a close cousin of RCT. Whereas RCT concentrates primarily on the actions of individuals and their subjective intentions, Exchange Theory focuses upon the types of exchange relations that hold between social actors. Exchange Theory possesses three main attributes. First, it conceives of society as fundamentally born of the exchange relations among actors. Second, it regards social change as the product of the transactions occurring both between concrete individuals, and also between individuals and collectivities. Third, it seeks to understand how developments taking place at the micro and macro levels 'connect', which it does by using the term 'actors' as a way of denoting both individuals and collectivities. The term 'social structure' is used in a very specific sense by exchange theorists, in that it refers to the associations of exchange relations among actors – not only individuals but collectivities too – along whose lines valued resources are passed.

The founding figure of Exchange Theory was George Homans [1910–1989]. During the 1950s, Homans claimed that social science should focus upon and ground itself in the forms of behaviour common to all human beings. This markedly universalizing vision led Homans to explore human exchange relations as elementary forms of behaviour, which he sought to identify in the form of a number of law-like propositions. At the heart of his social psychological and 'behavioural' account of human exchange relations is the figure of the rational actor guided by the pursuit of valued rewards and the avoidance of punishment (Cook and Whitmeyer, 1992). The word 'behavioural' here is highly significant as Homans was very strongly influenced by the work of the radical behaviouralist B. F. Skinner [1904–1990].

The central concepts around which behaviourist thinking revolve are those of 'reward' and 'punishment'. According to Skinner (1957), all behaviour – human or animal – is directly shaped by rewards and punishments. Here behaviour is understood strictly by its external and visibly identifiable characteristics, and not as the physical enactment or outcome of *subjective* experience or *cognitive* processes. Moreover, behaviourism investigates the *observable* behaviour of an organism as a response to its environment (that is, to external stimuli). Drawing on this definition, Homans (1967) conceived of rationality not as a label for describing the most efficient ways of acting, but instead as forming an intrinsic element of behaviour directly oriented towards securing reward over punishment.

This led him to define human behaviour 'as a function of its pay-off: in amount and kind it depends on the amount and kind of reward and punishment it fetches' (Homans, 1961: 13).

Homans defines social interaction as expressive of voluntary behaviour, where one individual rewards or punishes the behaviour of another in a process of mutual reinforcement. For example, Homans argues that if an action leads to a positive outcome for an individual, the individual is highly likely to re-enact that action. There are various dependent variables that apply to this proposition, such as the length of the period exchanges last for, the length of time between actions and rewards, and the regularity with which a given action is rewarded. Where individuals are positively rewarded for acting in certain ways in a particular setting, it is likely that placed again within that same setting the individual will re-enact the same behaviour. Actions leading to valued outcomes are thus more likely to be undertaken.

While this may seem like an obvious point to make, the importance of this proposition lies in its inverse: punishment – a negative outcome – is far less effective for directing individual action than reward because it is very hard to know exactly how actors will respond to punishment. A good example is of children who often behave badly in order to gain attention, even if the kind of attention they receive is negative and involves being scolded by a parent. According to Homans' logic, it is far more effective to ignore the child completely and reward them only on those occasions when they behave well. Homans' 'deprivation-satiation' proposition states that the more often an individual is rewarded for a particular course of action, the less valuable subsequent rewards become. Thus, two individuals may reward one another so often for their mutually enforcing behaviour that the value of the reward is understood to diminish over time.

Similar to the law of diminishing returns in economic theory, the more individuals are exposed to certain behaviours so the likelihood they become conditioned to them rises, and in turn, their impact diminishes. The 'rationality proposition' refers to the likelihood that, presented with a series of possible courses of action, individuals will always undertake the one they are most likely to achieve and that leads to the greatest gain.

Through adopting the conception of individuals as rational and purposive, Homans (1967) devised a series of propositions intended to be true of all human behaviour in all social contexts. A strong adherent of methodological individualism, Homans understood social structure as

Knowledge
Behaviourism, methodological individualism, economic rational choice theory

Structure/Agency
Psychological reductionism

Individuals are the sole unit of analysis – social structure is aggregated individual behaviour

Social interactions have emergent properties but these are the outcome of psychological processes and not extra-individual entities

Figure 6.2 Homans' Elementary Forms of Behaviour.

changing over time as the behaviour of aggregates of individuals changes. This was not to deny that social interaction led to emergent properties, only that these should be explained with reference to the psychological processes of individuals and not any supra-individual entity. While Homans' influence on subsequent exchange theorists such as Blau and Emerson was significant, nevertheless his work has subsequently lapsed into relative obscurity, probably due to its failure to attend to the subjective apprehension of experience and complete refusal to acknowledge social structure at a supra-individual level.

Strongly influenced by Homans' conception of social interaction as grounded in relations of exchange, Peter Blau [1918–2002] recast the concept of social structure as an extended network of 'relations between individuals and groups' (Blau, 1964: 2). Acknowledging the importance of individual agency for understanding social life, nevertheless Blau emphasized the emergent properties of social relations and the need for sociological analysis to extend to a systemic level by focusing upon the emergence of social relations as they develop outwards from a sub-institutional (i.e. individual) level. Blau thus moves beyond the analysis of merely direct face-to-face interactions between individuals, in order to include exchanges between individuals and collectivities, as well as dialogues between collectivities, and in so doing represents an attempt to address the 'micro-macro' problem and the need to link the two levels of analysis.

In his most influential work, *Exchange and Power in Social Life* (1964), Blau set out his theory of social and institutional structure and exchange. Central to this is the role attributed to social norms and values, or more specifically value-consensus, in governing individual and organizationally mediated exchange relations. The function of social norms is to convert or replace *indirect* forms of social exchange for *direct* ones (Blau, 1964: 255). So, for example, lecturers are normatively bound by universities to provide students with assistance with their studies, in exchange for which they may receive gratitude from the student (indirect exchange) as well as financial remuneration from the institution (direct exchange). The point here is that the collectivity, in this case the university, has entered into an exchange relationship with the individual (the lecturer).

Another example Blau (1964) used of the macro-to-micro species of exchange relation is the example of organized philanthropy. Individuals with very high levels of personal wealth, such as members of the business community, make philanthropic contributions in order 'to conform with the normative expectations that prevail in their social class' (Blau, 1964: 260). On this view, contributions are not offered for the sake of the personal gratitude expressed by the beneficiaries, because any donations are mediated in an indirect way via charitable organizations. Rather, the reward philanthropists receive from their *indirect* acts of 'kindness' is the *direct* exchange of social approval from the wider social group to which they belong.

For Blau, 'social norms' are essential in mediating collectivity-individual exchanges, whereas the mediating variable underlying exchange transactions between collectivities are 'social values'. Common values, or more specifically a common consensus over particular values, function as the medium structuring social exchanges over time and across society. This is because individuals' adherence to shared values allows for 'social transactions beyond the limits of direct social contacts and for perpetuating social structures beyond the life-span of human beings' (Blau, 1964: 263). It is precisely because members of collectivities share the same values that they are able to enter into association.

While Blau continues to be regarded as a seminal figure in the development of Exchange Theory, his work has attracted a variety of criticisms. Blau tends, for example, to treat norms and values as pre-given social facts, as well as over emphasizing the integrative character of exchange networks, as opposed to the socially divisive and stratifying effects often arising from them (Heath, 1976).

Social structures are supra-individual entities or social facts that have emergent properties

Approaches social structure through the lens of exchanges between individuals but also between individuals and 'collectivities'

Emphasizes the role of social norms and shared values as mediating and necessary factors underpinning social exchange

Differentiates between 'direct' and 'indirect' forms of exchange

Figure 6.3 Blau on Individuals and Collectivities.

Richard Emerson [1925–1982] was a highly influential figure in the development of Exchange Theory. Emerson was the originator of Exchange Network Theory, a sophisticated attempt to surpass the micro-macro conceptual impasse identified by Blau, which invokes the concept of networks, and more specifically 'exchange network structures' (Cook and Whitmeyer, 1992). Sceptical of Homans' psychological reductionism and overly rational conception of individuals, Emerson regarded exchange networks as webs of social relationships between individuals and organizations which combine to form a network structure. For Emerson, it is these *relations* of exchange, and not individual actors *per se*, that comprise the focus for analysis. By 'actor' is meant 'a point where many exchange relations connect' (Emerson, 1972: 57). The value of this expansive definition of actors is that it can be meaningfully applied both to individual persons, and also to groups (i.e. collective actors) such as business corporations and even nation-states. Exchange networks range from a minimum of two actors, known as a dyadic exchange, all the way up to a societal level. Networks are extended patterns of exchange relations between individuals and/or collective actors. For a set of relations to qualify as a network, the relations between actors X and Y must connect to transactions between, say, actors Y and Z. Actors X, Y and Z merely interacting as part of a group does not constitute an exchange network. Valued resources are differentially distributed among actors, leading to potential and actual relations of exchange. These exchange relations combine to comprise a network structure.

To emphasize the view of social structure as networks of exchange relations between actors, Emerson distinguished between positive and negative network connections. Positive relations occur when, say, actor A's exchange with actor B positively affects the subsequent exchanges between actor B and C. But if the exchange relations between actors A and B are negative in a way that carries ramifications for the interactions occurring between actors B and C, this points to a negative connection. An example of a negative exchange includes the passing of information between a recalcitrant pupil's (A) former teacher (B) and his prospective teacher (C) such that the information exchange negatively impacts upon future exchanges between the new teacher (C) and the pupil (A).

A central feature of Emerson's conception of exchange networks is the notion of dependency. Emerson argued that social structure exerts an influence over individuals by making them dependent upon one another in order to achieve particular goals or ends. Emerson is refer-ring here to the increased interdependency of actors within modern society, a direct outcome of the ever more complex modern social order (see Chapter 1). The unintended consequence of this differentia-tion is that increasingly actors become inter-dependent with one another because no single individual, or sphere of activity, can claim total self-sufficiency.

In highlighting this increased interdependency, Emerson stressed the uneven distribution of power across social networks. Where an exchange relation holds between two actors, such that one is more dependent upon the other, this creates a disparity in social power. Emerson regarded power as an essential attribute of the relations conjoining individuals. His work has played an important role in the realization of a more relational

---

Individual 'actors' combine to make up social structures

The term 'actor' comprises any entity – 'human' or 'institutional' – where exchange relations meet

Individuals are linked through exchange relations that combine to form exchange networks

The sum total of a society's exchange networks comprise the total social structure

---

Figure 6.4 Emerson's Exchange Network Theory.

conception of social power, as opposed to the notion of power as a resource individuals possess to greater or lesser degrees depending on the uneven distribution of material resources.

Responding to Parsons

So far we have examined the main characteristics and proponents of RCT and Exchange Theory, as well as identifying their main points of convergence. In addition to this, however, a further very important point unites RCT with Exchange Theory – the shared rejection of the account of individuals' actions set out by Talcott Parsons (see Chapter 2). Highly sceptical of utilitarianism and the conception of individuals derived from economics as first and foremost rational and calculating (the idea of *homo economicus*), Parsons' work was an attempt to show that individual human action is always shaped and underpinned by socially derived norms and cultural values. Thus Parsons sought to replace *homo economicus* with *homo sociologicus*. Normative codes comprise the largely hidden basis of social order and are produced and reproduced through and by action, and not independently of it. Parsons was not denying the capacity of individuals to act rationally or make choices informed by rational reflection. His intention, instead, was to emphasize that any type of action, including rational action, is always undertaken in concrete social and cultural contexts which are structured by social norms and values.

Parsons' critics and detractors claimed he had gone too far, offering in place of *homo economicus* a model of social actors as 'cultural dopes', as reactive rather than proactive, and as the passive carriers of socio-cultural values and norms imposed upon them from above by 'society' (see Chapter 2). One of Parsons' most scathing critics – a Harvard colleague at the time – was Homans. In an article entitled 'Bringing Men Back In' (1964) Homans attacked Parsons for failing to acknowledge social actors as 'voluntaristic', that is, as capable of exercising agency. It was consistently and widely claimed that Parsons had vastly prioritized 'structure' over 'action' in his model of social reproduction, resulting in what many saw as a highly impoverished account of human agency. Rational Choice and Exchange theories of human behaviour emerged as a corrective to the view of social agents as overly socialized and almost completely denuded of any capacity to act in innovative and voluntaristic ways. That Rational Choice models had met with significant practical success in matters of economic forecasting and public policy was cited as proof of the analytical worth of such a position. It was for these reasons, and against this backdrop, that Homans first imported Rational Choice models of human behaviour into sociology.

From the 1970s onwards, RCT has developed along two markedly divergent paths. First, in the work of James Coleman, who did much to import RCT back into mainstream American sociology in the period after the dominance of Parsonian social theory had waned (Tilly, 1997). And second, at the hands of neo-Marxist thinkers who have attempted to supplement Marx's allegedly structural account of social relations with Rational Choice models. We now turn to the work of Coleman.

Coleman's Rational Choice Perspective

Described by Smelser (1990: 778) as providing 'the most ambitious effort ever to build a general sociology on the basis of the individualistic, utilitarian, rational actor', James Coleman [1926–1995] was the leading light of RCT in America during the 1980s and early 1990s. Coleman's (1990: 42) work can be read as a critical response to accounts of human agency that he held to be overly reliant upon explaining human behaviour on the grounds of 'external' forces, such as Parsons' normative determinism. Utilizing a combination of mathematical modelling and quantitative methods, Coleman's (1990: 13) Rational Choice model can be stated in relatively simple terms: 'persons act purposively toward a goal, with the goal (and thus the actions) shaped by values or preferences'.

The concepts of most significance informing this definition are 'actors' and 'resources'. Resources refer to anything individuals are able to 'manipulate' and have a vested interest in 'accumulating', whereas the term 'actors' denotes 'purposive agents'. The vision of social structure, or social systems, set out in Coleman's (1990: 29) work builds upon these definitions. The concept of social system can be broken down in the following way:

- a social system comprises at least two actors
- each actor controls resources that are of interest and value to the other
- the mutual valorization of resources disposes individuals to interact
- the desire of actors to maximize and realize their respective interests is what gives the character of their relations a 'systemic' quality

Coleman (1990: 5) views the task of RCT as explicating macro-level phenomena from a micro-level perspective, by taking as the 'natural unit of observation' the 'individual agent' or 'concrete person', a position he describes as a 'special variant' of methodological individualism (Heckathorn, 1997: 4). The task of sociology is to examine various levels of social interaction as they occur, but always connecting these back to the micro level of concrete individuals.

The levels of analysis comprise: *micro-to-micro* interactions; *macro-to-micro* interactions; and *micro-to-macro* interactions. An example of micro-to-macro relations includes members of a local community voting for their preferred councillor. Individual votes are tallied up and counted out, and the councillor with the most votes wins. An example of macro-to-micro comprises the range of potential candidates the council allows to stand for the position of councillor and that community members are able to select from. For Coleman there can be no such thing as macro-to-macro interactions, which he regards as ontologically 'untenable' or 'redundant'. That is to say, the notion of a social system can only ever be legitimately invoked if it is with recourse to individual actors and their concrete actions.

Coleman sought to apply Rational Choice models to a number of areas that traditionally had proven problematic for them. In addition to his novel accounts of unruly forms of collective behaviour, Coleman applied RCT models to the study of social norms, a phenomenon typically understood as existing at a macro-level. Keen to overturn this view, Coleman (1990: 242) contends that systems of normative values are not 'social facts' but instead are purposively generated and enforced out of individuals' self-interest. It is not *in spite* of the fact actors are self-interested that they adhere to social norms, but precisely *because* of it.

In other words, it makes sense for individuals to relinquish part of their autonomy by adhering to certain norms, such as not stealing for example, because in doing so they benefit from the regulative power such a norm exerts, in this case, the fear of punishment for those caught stealing. Recast within the vocabulary of reward and punishment, norms become effective when enough of a consensus is reached that some actors or groups have the right or power to decide which norms should prevail. Key here is the power of certain actors or social groups to reinforce the consensus by ensuring adherence to the norm through punishing those who fail to conform to it. Social consensus is thus reinforced by the threat of punishment, as opposed to reward, and is crucial to the reproduction of norms and, ultimately, social stability. A similar argument is used by Coleman in his analysis of socialization. Individuals internalize norms which realize their effectiveness by presenting the actor with the option of either conforming (reward) or being stigmatized (punishment).

Coleman dedicated considerable time to exploring the links between individuals and social structure, but particularly the micro-to-macro processes that result in one actor relinquishing their individual power and rights to another actor. Coleman regarded this unilateral transfer of power as giving rise to the most basic macro phenomenon, or structure, because it leads to the formation of a single 'acting-unit' composed of two interdependent, as opposed to independent, actors. The subordination of individuals' interests to large corporate actors was a pressing matter for Coleman, who regarded modern social relations as characterized by impersonality and the transfer of power away from individual actors towards their large-scale corporate counterparts.

Coleman's view of the development from 'traditional' society to modernity closely mirrors the classical theorists' views of this shift (see Chapter 1). His understanding of modernity is founded on the view that 'the primordial institutions around which societies have developed are being replaced by purposively constituted social organization' (Coleman, 1990: xv). By 'primordial institutions' is meant social formations including 'family', 'class', 'ethnic groups' and 'communities', whereas purposive structures means 'economic organizations (such as firms, trade unions, and professorial associations) . . . and government' (Coleman, 1990: 584). In modern society, the growing power of corporate actors erodes more traditional forms of social life, as increasingly individual actors are disposed to relinquish personal control to corporate actors.

On this view, corporate actors and concrete persons are ontologically similar inasmuch as both are motivated by the accumulation and redeployment of valuable resources in order to realize specific goals. The key issue for Coleman is one of securing the social responsibility of these corporate actors. It is notoriously difficult, for example, to call to account global multi-national corporations, precisely because of the highly diffuse nature of the power-relations constituting such large-scale actors.

The rising power of corporate actors has led to vast social changes, of which two are particularly significant for Coleman. First, modern social-structural differentiation (see Chapter 2) has led to a great number of the traditional functions of primordial institutions, such as the family unit,

Variant of methodological individualism

Individuals as self-interested 'utility-maximizers'

Micro-to-micro, micro-to-macro and macro-to-micro levels of analysis

Macro-to-macro level interaction cannot take place because this would imply social structures have a reality independent of 'concrete persons'

Decline and replacement of 'primordial institutions' such as the family with 'purposive structures' such as corporations

Figure 6.5 Coleman's Rational Choice Theory.

being reallocated to purposive structures (Coleman, 1993a). One example is that of secondary schools which are now vested with the responsibility of teaching 'life skills', such as cooking and money management, to young people, whereas previously these skills were taught by, and within, the family. The prime concern here is that an overly differentiated division of labour can lead to 'slippages' occurring between primordial structures like the family, and purposive institutions like schools, whereby both fail to provide actors with certain key skills essential for reproducing the social order. One response to this problem is more thoroughly to re-model the education system in a way that more fully provides young people with the skills and behaviours traditionally imparted to them by the familial unit. The second problematic aspect of modern social relations is the increasingly anonymous character of human interaction, such that communications are enacted between 'positions' in purposive structures like news media organizations, rather than between 'concrete persons' (Coleman, 1993a). Communication becomes ever more impersonal in nature potentially creating various social problems, including the undermining of democracy – a theme also dealt with in other ways by Habermas (see Chapter 3).

Rational Choice Marxism

In addition to the direction RCT was taken by Coleman, RCT significantly influenced the development of so-called 'Analytical Marxism' from the 1980s onwards. The term Analytical Marxism refers to a strand of neo-Marxist thinking powered by the conviction that in order to progress and remain analytically insightful, Marxism must abandon its traditional, Hegel-inspired emphasis on dialectical reasoning (see Chapters 1 and 3) in favour of the types of analytical tools and methods utilized by contemporary social scientists, especially economists (Roemer, 1986: 191; Elster, 1985). Analytical Marxism retains the substantive political and ethical concerns of classical Marxism (to do with class-based exploitation), while substituting Marx's dialectical method with more positivistic forms of reasoning indebted to economics (Mayer, 1994).

Rational Choice Marxism (RCM) developed through the 1980s and 1990s, with varying degrees of success. As the name suggests, RCM represents an attempt to integrate Rational Choice models and game theories with classical Marxism. Led by Jon Elster and John Roemer, the appropriation of these theoretical ideas was intended to deal with the conceptual deficiencies of classical Marxism, specifically with reference to the key Marxist notions of 'exploitation', 'class relations' and 'historical materialism' (see Chapters 1 and 3). Elster (1982: 469) argues, for example, that game theory is particularly well suited to Marxist thinking because it allows for a conception of the subject that 'can be a "we" as well as an "I"'. That is, actors can be collectives of individuals, and not just individuals alone.

It is claimed that classical Marxist notions of social class can be augmented by Rational Choice Theory in three main ways (Roemer, 1986). First, the notion of class struggle can be conceived as assuming a variety of forms. Second, Rational Choice models can explain the micro-foundations of class-struggle with reference to concrete individuals. Third, RCM's emphasis on concrete actors makes it possible to understand 'why' and 'when' social class is the relevant unit of analysis for understanding social change.

The defining feature of RCM is the attempted refutation of the view of Marx as a 'structuralist' or 'methodological collectivist'. Elster (1985) and Roemer (1986) reject the emphasis placed by other Marxist thinkers (see Chapter 3) on the role of social structure in determining the organization of human development and relations. Instead, they argue that the standard understandings of Marx lack any kind of micro-foundation or possibility for conceptualizing individuals as self-interested, rationally oriented accumulators of valuable resources. Elster (1982: 454) claims that in spite of the structuralist label often attributed to him, Marx was in fact a 'methodological individualist' because he regarded all social structures – their form and transformation – as 'explicable in ways that only involve individuals'. On this view, it is legitimate to invoke RCT as an alternative to the strong structuralist neo-Marxian theories devised by thinkers such as Cohen (1982; 1986) and Althusser and Balibar (1998 [1965]), allowing instead for Marxist thinking to be aligned with the view of individuals as rational agents and their inter-relations being founded on exchange relations (Elster, 1982; 1985).

In RCM, the concept of class relations, and 'class exploitation' specifically, have received much attention. Taking concrete individuals as the starting point for enquiry, Roemer (1982a) holds that 'social class' refers to the uneven distribution of resources among actors, and *not* some intrinsic property of modern social relations between individuals that necessarily result in exploitation for one or more parties. Rejecting Marx's notion of exploitation as directly linked to the notion of 'surplus extraction', and the by now virtually entirely discredited 'labour theory of value', Roemer (1982b) proposes a view of exploitation grounded in 'property relations', more specifically the uneven distribution of assets among actors. Class analysis thus 'requires micro-foundations at the level of the individual' (Roemer, 1982b: 513), because it no longer refers to a property of the relations actors are constrained to enter into under capitalism, but instead arises from the 'exchanges between differently endowed individuals in a competitive setting' (Elster, 1985: 7).

Roemer (1982b) extends his novel conception of class relations by developing a view of individuals as actively involved in determining which social class they belong to. As counter-intuitive as it may seem, Roemer (1982b) argues that by deciding whether or not to work for themselves (as self-employed), to work for others (as an employee), or to employ others (as an employer), individuals play the definitive role in determining their own social class location. Crucially, whichever option the individual selects is done on the grounds of 'optimizing strategies'.

Similarly, Przeworski (1985b: 97) argues that social class location is the outcome of a series of rational choices, and is not simply determined by the individual's relationship to the means of production (see Chapter 1). Przeworski (1985b) employs the example of Mrs Jones – a female landowner married to a machinist and the mother of an accountant son – to illustrate this argument. Mrs Jones confronts a number of possible choices regarding her social class location: she could sell her land; she could request her partner work overtime; or she could set up a shop with her son as the accountant. That Mrs Jones rationally selects to be a worker is because it represents the 'optimum strategy' leading to the greatest gain (Przeworski, 1985a; 1985b).

Recasting of Marxism in terms of methodological individualism
Social relations characterized by uneven distribution of various types of resources among individuals and class groups
Capitalism comprised not of necessarily antagonistic relations between social class groups, but actors who make rational choices about which social class group to be part of

Figure 6.6 Summary of Rational Choice Marxism.

In their efforts to 'make sense' of classical Marxism through the application of Rational Choice and Game theories, RCM has demonstrated a considerable degree of conceptual innovation (Roemer, 1986: 192). Yet RCM has consistently met with heavy criticism, not only from mainstream sociologists for the most part disdainful of Rational Choice Theory in general, but also from neo-Marxists, who view the application of RCT to Marx's work as a form of conceptual sacrilege (Nickel, 1992; Roberts, 1996). Undoubtedly, the value of conceiving of class exploitation as the outcome of the unequal distribution of resources among agents is that it opens up a conceptual window through which to let the individual back into Marxist thinking. Furthermore, exploitation can be conceptualized in relation to different types of society including socialism, and not just capitalism. Where RCM meets with serious critical resistance, however, is in relation to Marx's claim that inequality is a structural property endemic to certain types of social relationship (Roberts, 1996). This suggests that Marx's thinking is markedly more 'structuralist' than RCM thinkers will admit. A further problem with collapsing structural properties or social relations into the actions and choices of individuals is that it leads to a view of 'human nature as capitalist nature' (Wood, 1989: 55). In other words, RCM posits the notion of human beings as 'calculating' and 'selfish' without any reference to the systemic properties that compel them to act in self-interested ways. This leads to a conceptual tautology where agents are held to accumulate capital because, by definition, they are 'capital accumulators'.

Assessing RCT

More than any other sociological theoretical paradigm RCT has attracted a wide range of critical commentary (e.g. Bourdieu, 1990, De Haan and

Vos, 2003, Giddens, 1984). The most recurrent and potentially damaging of these is the contention that RCT cannot adequately conceive of individuals acting in ways that are not fully rational.

Influenced by Freud's (see Chapter 1) work on the human psyche, Norbert Elias (1994 [1939]) (see Chapter 7) argues that any 'investigation that considers only people's consciousness, their "reason" or "ideas", while disregarding the structure of drives, the direction and form of human affects and passions, can be of only limited value'. If so, then all varieties of RCT seem to be of limited use in understanding individuals' actions, as both the non-rational and subconscious aspects of action are not at all taken into account. Coleman's (1990: 18) response to the charge that individuals do not always act rationally – or at least appear not to – is to argue that where this is the case, the person observing the action has failed to discover the point of the view of the actor from which the act is in fact rational. On this view, even the seemingly most irrational acts can be construed as containing some rationality. Such a malleable view of what constitutes 'rational action' means that it can be extended to incorporate virtually any act of human behaviour. This may invalidate RCT because it can never be proven to be wrong in its explanations – it just keeps finding ways of saying that individuals are always highly rational, even when the evidence points in a contrary direction.

Feminist thinkers have similarly been critical of RCT, particularly the notion of human actors as always self-interested and calculating, which they claim is a fundamentally androcentric (male-centred) assumption (England and Kilbourne, 1990). Another key criticism is that RCT never really asks the question as to *why* individuals are self-interested – this is just assumed as a matter of course. Despite Rational Choice Marxists' attempts to turn Marx into a Rational Choice Theorist, Marx himself might have said that human beings are in fact not 'naturally' self-interested, but are compelled to act in such ways because of the logic of social relations under capitalism. In other words, how 'rational' or not individuals are very much depends on the social and cultural contexts in which they operate.

Another key form of criticism is that RCT has failed to understand how people actually think in real-life settings, their models of behaviour attributing far too high levels of self-conscious calculation to what are actually mostly activities that are not so self-conscious and thought-through. Speaking as a leading figure in symbolic interactionist theory (see Chapter 5), Denzin (1990) is forceful in his criticism of RCT, claiming that such a theoretical paradigm offers no solution to the problem of how society is possible in the first place. Denzin (1990) argues that it fails to distinguish between rationality as a 'transcendental ideal' (i.e. an ideal model) and rationality as it is actually constituted within the context of actors' every-day lifeworlds (see Chapter 4).

Likewise, according to Anthony Giddens (1984: 535–6) (see Chapter 10), RCM is fundamentally flawed, not because human beings are not capable of being rational, but because the overwhelming majority of routine day-to-day activity is enacted out of a sense of 'practical consciousness' and 'not a matter of deliberated processes of decision-making'. Rational choice theory thus fails to deal with the insights of phenomenology (see Chapter 4), which stresses the practical, semi-conscious side of human reasoning and activities. This point also informs Bourdieu and Wacquant's (1992) criticism of RCT. (For Bourdieu's re-working of the analysis of individuals' actions and choices in light of phenomenological concerns to do with 'practical consciousness' see Chapter 10.) Most of the time, people do not act in self-conscious, rational ways. As Bourdieu (Bourdieu and Wacquant, 1992: 45) notes, we can always acknowledge that individuals make 'ratio-nal' sorts of choices, 'as long as we do not forget that they do not choose the principle of those choices'. Individuals are free to choose which course of action to pursue, but only very rarely are they fully conscious of the socially instilled values against which a given course of action strikes them as more or less the appropriate one to pursue. In his study of the marriage patterns of the Kabyle people of Algeria, for example, Bourdieu (1977) observed that without ever consciously devising deliberative, rational strategies for securing the 'optimum' marriage partner, nevertheless indi-viduals in that context tended to do so without being able to explain exactly how such a situation had come to pass. They had operated according to the *practical rationalities* inherent in their social world and not in the fully self-conscious calculating ways RCT theorists imagine. On this view, people strategize, but in practical and semi-conscious ways. RCT attributes far too much self-consciousness to individuals – such a state of affairs may arise from time to time, because of special circumstances, but the normal course of human affairs is not covered by the kinds of models RCT theo-rists construct. They mistake their models for reality itself, but reality is more complicated than they can conceive.

Conclusion

In one way or another, classical theorists like Marx, Durkheim and Weber all sought to develop distinctively sociological theoretical frames and concepts as a corrective to what they regarded as the over-simplistic assumptions of individualistic and economic accounts of human actors and social relations that dominated in their day. Over one hundred years later, the various attempts to reintroduce Rational Choice models and concepts into social theory have met with similar, if not greater, levels of condemnation from social theorists of virtually every theoretical disposition. In order for RCT to remain a living theoretical tradition, it will have to take into consideration the various criticisms outlined here, which constitute mainstream social theory's current consensus as to the flaws and limitations of RCT and Exchange Theory.

Further Reading

Archer, M., and Tritter, J. O. (2000) *Rational Choice Theory: Resisting Colonization*. London: Routledge.
Coleman, J. (1990) *Foundations of Social Theory*. Cambridge, MA: Belknap.
Elster, J. (1985) *Making Sense of Marx*. Cambridge: Cambridge University Press.
– (1989) *The Cement of Society*. Cambridge: Cambridge University Press.

The Process Sociological Paradigm

In this chapter we discuss process sociology, formulated in large part by the German sociologist Norbert Elias. Process sociology is intended to avoid the conceptual pitfalls it sees both with 'subjectivist' and 'objectivist' forms of social theory (see Chapter 1). Process sociology rejects the idea that an individual is a puppet in large part controlled by social structures and institutions (as certain forms of Marxism and functionalism may imply – see Chapters 2 and 3). It also is critical of how micro-level, individual-focused approaches – like Rational Choice Theory and symbolic interactionism – cannot properly understand how individuals are constrained in their activities by social phenomena. Rather like structuration theories (Chapter 10), process sociology tries to transcend what it sees as an artificial divide between social 'structure' and individual 'actions'.

Instead, it conceives of social reality as an 'ongoing', 'dynamic' process, the defining feature of which is its constant mutation into new 'forms' and 'figurations'. The notion of 'process' is intended to bypass altogether the notion of society as a 'reified', 'static' entity which individuals 'step into', an already pre-formed 'thing' with a life of its own. In addition, process sociology regards individual personality ('psychological structure') as intimately bound up with the shape and organization of social groups. What is conventionally called 'society' is understood as a constantly evolving set of over-lapping and interconnected 'chains', or 'networks', of individuals. Society cannot be conceived of without reference to the individuals who comprise it. But individuals could not exist without reference to the social networks they form part of. This emphasis on the two-way direction of human relations – individuals 'make' society, society 'makes' individuals – is what gives process sociology its 'dialectical' character (see Chapter 1). Elias also contends that as modernity develops, the more tightly interdependent upon one another individuals become, this having important effects on the identities and 'psychological structures' of the individuals involved in modernity's characteristic types of interactional chains. Elias also focused on how the development of new chains and networks of interaction impact on people's bodies and their emotions. This approach was developed through his analysis of the 'civilizing process'. We will also consider his contributions to a range of issues, including the theory of habitus, the sociology of death, and the sociology of sport.

From Simmel to Elias

Norbert Elias [1897–1990] was a German Jewish intellectual forced to flee Germany by the rise of the Nazi regime. Arriving in England, Elias took up a post at the University of Leicester. Although many of his pioneering ideas were first formulated in the 1930s, his work was not very well known until the late 1960s, following the publication in English of his most celebrated work, *The Civilizing Process* (Elias, 1994 [1939]). It was only then that his reputation as an innovative sociological thinker began to be taken really seriously (Burke, 2005). Elias originally referred to his distinctive approach to the study of social reality as 'figurational' sociology, although he later changed this to 'process sociology' (Mennell, 1998, 2009).

Given his background, Elias was very familiar with the works of the German classical social theorists, and many other figures in Germanic intellectual life, such as Freud, whose influence on Elias' analysis of the 'civilizing process' is clear (Van Krieken, 1998: 13–16; Bauman, 1989a). Although also drawing on the ideas of figures such as Marx and Weber (though much less so on French thinkers like Durkheim, whose sociology seems far too objectivist from his perspective), the major classical source of Elias' approach is the work of Simmel (see Chapter 1).

For Simmel, the object of social theory is comprised of the 'dialectical' social relations binding individuals, and not the individuals themselves, or the groups to which they belong, or the social institutions to which they are attached. Entities like groups and institutions do not have independent existences of their own but are simply 'elements which are articulated and constituted in social relations' (Kaspersen and Gabriel 2008: 371). In other words, what objectivist social theory misunderstands as objectively existing social structures are in fact merely patterned interactions

among individuals. But Simmel also was of the view that these social interactions shape and change over time the nature of the individuals involved
in them.

Elias' debt to Simmel is quite obvious (just as Simmel's debt to Hegel
on dialectical processes is quite clear too – see Chapter 1). Simmelian
sociology provided a resource for overcoming what Elias regarded as
unhelpful dichotomies that he saw as plaguing previous social theory,
which divided the world up into abstract entities – individual/society,
structure/agency, social continuity/social change, etc. – which in fact did
not exist. Elias refused to reduce social reality into a series of independent
entities or reified parts, each characterized by its own alleged properties
and traits. Instead, following the lead of Simmel, he wanted to treat social
life as a constant 'flow' of interrelated 'figurations' or 'processes' made
up of individuals interacting with each other over time, thus reconfiguring
themselves in the process.

It is not concrete individuals that are the subject matter of sociology,
argued Elias (1970: 113), any more than it is some reified and static
notion of 'society' that exists outside of and above individuals and their
interactions (as both Durkheimian and functionalist theory seem to
imply). Rather, 'societies are composed of individuals, and . . . individuals
can only possess specifically human characteristics such as the ability to
speak, think, and live, in and through their relationships with other people
– in society'.

On this view, the *relationships* which connect individuals to each other
are no less real than the individuals themselves. This view underpinned
his vision of sociology as the study of the 'unintentional human inter-
dependencies that lie at the root of every intentional interaction'. Here
he was referring to the fact that individuals when they interact are dependent upon particular sorts of social connections with each other that
may well be invisible, partly or wholly, to them. Particular sorts of social
relationships are the unacknowledged conditions that make interactions
possible.

The Civilizing Process

Like the classical theorists before him, Elias sought to provide an account
of the rise of the distinctive cultural values, ideals and activities characteristic of modernity. Of particular concern for him was the prevailing
view of Western culture as inherently 'civilized' and 'rational' and so by

extension, morally and spiritually superior to non-Western forms of social organization. This was a very common idea in nineteenth-century Europe, and it lasted well into the twentieth century.

As a Jewish man whose mother is thought to have perished in the Nazi death camps, Elias was very sceptical of the allegedly 'civilized', 'enlightened' and 'morally superior' character of Western culture. Indeed, the main thrust of Elias' work is devoted to re-evaluating critically such self-aggrandizing notions held by Westerners, along with the related view of Western dominance over the rest of the world as the result of some sort of consciously determined and rationally directed social process.

In explaining the development of modernity, Elias puts forward the idea of a long-term, multi-linear, but ultimately one-directional movement which he refers to as the 'civilizing process'. This involved historical changes in the nature of social relationships. These relationships had become over time ever more rationally organized, a theme taken from Max Weber (see Chapters 1 and 3). They had also involved ever higher levels of control by individuals of their behaviours, their emotions and their bodies.

This long-term historical movement towards ever greater psychological and bodily restraint by individuals is self-imposed, and not the result of greater control forced upon individuals by some external social structure or social group. Thus he rejects a Marxist view that increasing control over the mass of the population is due to the conscious and deliberate control of a ruling class over them. The drive towards ever more powerful forms of self-imposed self-restraint is due to unintended reasons that no one could have predicted. It came about as the unintended consequence of changes in the nature of social relationships.

In *The Civilizing Process* (1994 [1939]), Elias endeavours to show how social relations in Western Europe changed slowly, but surely, from the later medieval and early modern periods onwards (early modernity having begun in about the sixteenth century). These changes would come, in ways no one at the time was conscious of, increasingly to shape the bodily and emotional aspects of all people in Western societies.

He tried to illustrate these changes using empirical data drawn from a range of sources. One major source were etiquette guides, which were read by aristocratic people in medieval and early modern Europe in order to learn what were acceptable and unacceptable forms of conduct. Such guides showed Elias that over time, individuals were advised by the authors of such books to regulate their behaviours and their interactions with each other ever more strictly. In the late medieval world (c. the fifteenth century), Elias claimed – following the ideas of the Dutch historian Johan Huizinga – that people were, by today's standards, quite uninhibited in how they acted. The typical medieval temperament was volatile, with individuals prone to mood swings that often led to acts of physical violence. Medieval eating practices were also far less constrained than ours are today. Individuals characteristically used their hands to eat from a communal pot while openly spitting and farting when they felt the urge. This was because norms were not in place that would have regulated these behaviours by defining them as shameful. Senses of shame, especially to do with sexual and bodily activities like urinating and defecating, were weak, if not non-existent. Typical medieval behaviours were characterized by far lower levels of emotional, bodily and psychological restraint than people in the West are accustomed to today.

But from the later medieval period onwards, and then especially from the seventeenth century on, the etiquette books and other historical sources show that more and more human behaviours, especially those to do with sex and bodily functions, came to be regarded as 'repugnant', 'distasteful' and the source of ever stronger feelings of 'embarrassment' and 'shame' on behalf of individuals. Concomitant with this process was the increasing segregation or removal of these distasteful forms of behaviour 'behind the scenes of social life' (Elias, 1994 [1939]: 99). Sexual acts could increasingly only take place hidden away from the gaze of other people, although they had been tolerated in public to some extent in earlier times. Likewise, defecation and urination, which previously had been allowable in the street and in public places, were hidden away in what were now designated as 'private' places: toilet facilities, for example, were installed in houses, hidden away in corners and behind doors, so that people could not see each other 'in the act'. To be caught with one's trousers down was now a great source of shame and embarrassment. People began increasingly to self-restrain their behaviours, avoiding what was thought to be shameful in the eyes of others. This was self-control, not control imposed by an external authority. As Elias (1994 [1939]: 443) describes it, 'the regulation of the whole instinctual and affective life by steady self-control becomes more and more stable, more even and more all-embracing'. People became increasingly disgusted with the sexual and defecatory aspects of their bodies, and they felt ever greater need to cover up these embarrassing features of their bodily life.

What were the reasons for this? Sigmund Freud (2002) had already traced out some of these developments, but in a very speculative way.

Elias wanted to offer a more empirically grounded analysis of why these changes had occurred. One issue he insisted upon was that, contrary to popular perceptions, new forms of bodily self-control (e.g. going to the toilet in hidden-away places so that others could not see you) did not develop for reasons of health and hygiene. The changes in behaviours pre-dated changes in hygiene by several centuries (Inglis, 2001). Behaviours did not change for reasons of social respect either, because as late as the nineteenth century people of superior rank, mainly the aristocracy, could behave in ways that would have been considered shameful if the lower social classes had carried out such activities. New, tougher and tighter practices of self-regulation only came to apply across all social classes in the nineteenth century.

So the civilizing process must have been created by other reasons – and these involved changes over time in the nature of social relations. Over time, social relations became more complex, and it was this complexification that drove the civilizing process, without anyone intending this to happen.

The increasing complexity of social relations overall was driven in large part by changes in social relations in a particular sort of social location, namely the royal and aristocratic courts of the late medieval and early modern periods. This had to do with changes in the nature of social groups. As modernity developed, the older dominant class – the medieval warrior elite, made up of barons and knights – went into decline. As a result, kings and princes became more powerful, and more and more people flocked to their courts. A new class of 'courtiers' emerged, and they had very different emotional and bodily dispositions from the intensely warlike, unrestrained warrior class. The courtiers had very different sorts of social relations with each other than had the warrior class with each other and the people beneath them. In the highly competitive life of the court, where the courtiers were constantly seeking the favour of the royal family, they had to watch each other very closely, monitoring everyone else's behaviours intensely, in order to make sure no one else was winning more prestige and influence than they were. Just as the courtiers had to monitor everyone else's behaviours, they also had to monitor their own behaviours too. So this new type of social relationship stimulated people to start self-regulating more than before, not just in terms of how they interacted with others but how they controlled their own bodies and their own faces (life at court requiring a 'poker face' that did not give away to potential enemies what you were thinking). So in a completely unintentional way, new standardized modes of conduct, involving ever higher levels of self-control, were created by the new social relationships. Over time, these new ways of acting spread out from the courts, into the towns and cities around them, being taken up by middle-class people. These more lowly individuals often took up the mannerisms and habits of the courtly aristocracy because they wanted to be seen to be as 'refined' as their social superiors. Elias notes, however, that the spread of the new attitudes and practices outside of the courts where they were first produced should not be understood as just a simple and inevitable process of the lower classes copying the upper classes. He illustrates the presence of counter-tendencies to this process, and attempts by socially inferior groups to resist the colonization of conduct imposed upon them 'from above'. Yet, on the whole, the new norms of self-regulation invented at court did spread out into the wider social order, changing it slowly but profoundly over time.

At the same time, another related change in social relations was happening. As we saw in Chapter 2, the rise of modern society can be seen as centrally involving 'structural differentiation', the development whereby separate social spheres – the economy, the education system, the government, etc. – become ever more independent of each other. As modernity developed, social life came increasingly to be carved up into discrete spheres: the family home, where most work was carried out in medieval society, now becomes purely private as more and more people go to work outside the home, in a place like a factory. Because social spheres became ever more separate from each other, a need arose for a shared and uniform stock of emotional and behavioural norms, so that individuals could know how to act in appropriate ways as they moved from one sphere from another (e.g. from home, to work in a factory, to the shops – all now separate areas of life). Shared norms of behaviour that applied across all spheres would allow people to interact in patterned and predictable ways (Elias, 1994 [1939]: 367).

In the rapidly growing towns and cities of early modernity, ever greater numbers of individuals, largely unknown to one another, came into contact and were forced to interact. These interactions, again unintentionally, began to generate standardized behavioural codes. These codes (again involving self-regulation) in turn shaped subsequent interactions. Accordingly, the socially shaped senses of shame and embarrassment came less to be associated with individuals of the upper classes only, and instead were viewed as characteristics of anonymous, generalized 'others'. More and more people now self-regulated their behaviours, because in their minds that was now the normal thing to do. They wanted to avoid being seen as dirty, coarse or shameful in the eyes of what they took to be 'society' in general, not particular other individuals. Over time, the codes of self-regulation thus generated became ever more strongly the underpinnings of all types of social interaction. The socially conditioned emotions of shame and embarrassment started to be thought about not fully consciously but in semi-conscious ways, becoming part of the implicit framework in which all social interactions were embedded. By the nineteenth century, the civilizing process had developed so much that the original reasons for it – changes in social relations – had been long forgotten. People now thought of self-regulation and the senses of shame and embarrassment which went with them as 'highly personal, something "inward", implanted in them by nature' (Elias, 1994 [1939]: 127–8). So what had started out as a social process was now seen by everyone as something both 'natural' and inevitable.

The Civilizing Process, Rationality and Habitus

So far we have concentrated on long-term historical developments involving large-scale shifts in the types of social relationships people engaged in. Elias emphasized that these apparently macro-level and highly 'impersonal' forces actually directly impinged upon individual psychological development in the most intimate ways. That is, they were simultaneously macro-level and micro-level in nature.

The Enlightenment view of human reason sees it as a 'universal' and 'disembodied' faculty of the mind, existing independently of human beings and the social formations they belong to (see Chapter 1). This is the sense of calculating individuals, coolly working out the best means to achieve particular goals, which Rational Choice Theory works with (see Chapter 6). Elias, by contrast, argues that 'reason' and 'rationality' are culturally specific and only arise out of certain forms of social figuration (i.e. certain types of social relationships).

Acting in calculating, instrumentally rational ways can only occur in social contexts where external social constraints – demanded by certain types of relationships – become internal 'compulsions'. This is because 'rational' behaviour requires a calculating quality that is only possible when emotional and impulsive drives are kept at a distance. Drawing in part upon Freud, Elias argues that the more individuals are able to resist the immediate demands of self-gratification and affective fantasies, the more likely they are able successfully to enact a course of pre-planned action aimed at the fulfilment of a long-term goal. Rationality and the emotions of shame and embarrassment increase in society at the same time because they derive from a common source, namely the new sorts of social relationships described above. Rational Choice theorists are therefore wrong to see rationality and calculation as universal properties of human beings. In the West, high levels of rational thought on the behalf of individuals is only made possible because of the changes in social relationships that we can call the development of the civilizing process. If modern society involves greater levels of rational thinking than other sorts of society, this is only because of the changing quality of social relationships involving ever greater levels of shame and embarrassment to be felt by individuals, thoughts and actions having ever more to deal with these issues in thought-through ways. So modern society is not as 'rational' as it likes to think it is. Moreover, what we take to be purely individual accomplishments – here, the capacity to think in rational ways – is actually an unintended product of changes in social relations.

As part of his work dealing with the intertwining development of social relations and individuals, Elias (1990, 1991) sought to develop a theory of 'habitus'. He viewed the modern separation of the academic disciplines of history, sociology and psychology as highly unfortunate. They should not be separated, as each is concerned with the same object, namely humankind and its development over time, albeit understood from somewhat different perspectives. Embedded in this view are Elias' concepts of 'socio-genesis' and 'psycho-genesis', which refer to the ways in which changes to the social organization of human groups interact with the psychological constitution of individuals, and vice versa.

Elias invoked the concept of 'habitus' to denote this inter-relationship of the social and the psychological (Cavaletto, 2007). Critical of Freud's account of the relations between the id, ego and super-ego as universally applicable in all societies at all times (see Chapters 1 and 3), Elias conceived of an individual's 'personality structure' as historically, socially and culturally constructed. Against Freud who claimed the relations between the id (the unconscious mind, including the human being's sexual desires) and the superego (the part of the mind which tries to control the id in light of social norms) are relatively static and unchanging, Elias argues that the extent of the intervention of the superego within the personality structure varies over time and is directly linked to developments driving the civilizing process.

The notion of 'national habitus' refers to the historically and socially constructed nature of the emotional, behavioural and psychological characteristics and dispositions of the members of a given nation. As a study intended to address a 'habitus problem par excellence' (Elias, 1990: xi), *The Germans* delineates the formation of what Elias sees as the typically 'German' personality structure, with the aim of explaining how it was that the Holocaust could have happened in Germany.

By examining the intersecting, long-term historical processes that included the ambiguous position of the German lands in relation to their neighbours, the constant threat of invasion this situation led to, and the dominance of the German military aristocracy in German society, Elias asserts his view of the indivisibility of psycho-genetic and socio-genetic developments. He illustrates how 'the fortunes of a nation over the centuries become sedimented into the habitus of its individual members' (1990: 19). In other words, he is interested in how German society – conceived of as involving particular sorts of social relationships – came over a long period to shape the typical personality structures of ordinary Germans. Definitive traits of the German habitus (i.e. typical personality structure) included a weak conscience unable to regulate itself without external pressure, hostility towards outsiders, constant fear of potential threats, and a high regard for war-like attitudes and behaviour. Through the specific nature of social relations typical of the German lands for centuries, a particularly 'authoritarian personality structure' developed, which Elias (1990: 423) saw as leading to the eventual emergence in the nineteenth century of an authoritarian state. This state went along with a culture in which democratic participation was unfavourably regarded and deference to authority as imposed from above – of which no greater example can be imagined than the figure of Adolf Hitler – was positively valued. Here, over many centuries of unintended changes in social relations, are to be found the roots of why many German people tolerated, if not embraced outright, the rise to power of the Nazis and their eventual engineering of the Holocaust. It is only by examining, through the concept of habitus, the long-term historical interplay between psychological and sociological factors, that more recent events can be explained. The Holocaust had very historical deep roots, social relations over time forming a habitus that could make possible the worst genocide in history. Elias' version of the reasons underpinning the Holocaust contrasts interestingly with another major social theoretical account of those events, namely Zygmunt Bauman's (1989b) analysis, which regarded the Holocaust as a highly rationalized event, very much characteristic of modernity because it was run on very bureaucratic lines. While Bauman emphasizes specifically modern forms of rationality as underlying the genocide, Elias roots the events in a much longer historical narrative encompassing socio-genetic and psycho-genetic factors. He also emphasizes that it involved the undoing of the centuries-long development of the forms of self-regulation developed in the civilizing process. The forms of barbarity enacted in the death camps were a 'de-civilizing spurt', reversing the wider civilizing logic of modernity that had developed over several centuries. For Bauman, modernity's rationality makes the Holocaust possible; but for Elias, it is the failure of the forms of rationality produced over centuries by changes in social relations that allowed it to occur.

Applying Process Sociology: Death and Sport

In the later part of his career, Elias sought to apply the insights of process sociology to a range of particular spheres of social life. While the research on the civilizing process focused on the development of self-regulation, his analysis of death and dying (Elias, 1985) highlights how discourses, images and representations of these matters have become throughout modernity ever more socially marginalized and cordoned off from everyday experience. As an unavoidable aspect of human experience, he argued that human solutions to the 'problem' of death have differed greatly through time and cross-culturally. As far as death today is concerned, 'without being specifically intended, the early isolation of the dying occurs with particular frequency' in modern social conditions (Elias, 1985: 2).

As a simultaneously personal and socially constructed event, death becomes increasingly removed behind the curtains of modern social life, as acknowledgement of the inevitability of dying is increasingly 'denied' or 'repressed' (Elias, 1985: 8). Due to advances in technology and scientific reasoning, 'nature', to which death is understood to belong, is increasingly viewed as something liable to manipulation and control by human beings. This has direct ramifications for how death is widely perceived in modern society. Death tends to be viewed as something that can be 'postponed' or 'put-off'. Increasingly today death is also represented as something that happens to 'other' people, not oneself. As the fact of death becomes more repressed, so the dying person – the living embodiment of the death process – increasingly figures as an unwelcome reminder of our own mortality. Hence they are marginalized to the peripheries of social life, hidden out of sight, just as centuries before, the 'dirty' aspects of human bodies were denied by being made ever more invisible. Elias (1985) uses the idea that modern society is 'death denying' to explain the increasing isolation of the elderly. They are shunned as they remind younger people of death, a possibility that the modern habitus cannot cope with easily. Because of long-term changes in social relations and habitus, dying has become a very lonely process, as people withdraw contact from the elderly and dying, because death seems so unbearable a possibility to our current ways of thinking.

Elias also applied process sociology to another dimension of social life, namely the practices of sport. Sporting activities extend back in time to the earliest civilizations, and the often highly emotional and aggressive attitudes and behaviours that can be present within sport were of interest to Elias. Of particular interest to him were the processes by which modern sportive practice has become increasingly less violent, and much more controlled and regulated than it was several centuries ago. Modern sport tends to imitate physical violence, rather than actually be violent itself. Together with his colleague Eric Dunning, Elias was keen to overturn the view that the social function of sport is to serve as a 'release' or 'safety-valve' for tension accrued in more 'serious', work-related spheres of modernity. Sport actually allows for the generation of excitable energy and tension. But it does this within a context of social relations which demand individuals adhere to strictly regulated behavioural and bodily codes of practice. Leisure pursuits and sportive practices are sites within which a controlled but pleasurable 'decontrolling' of emotional restraint is regarded as socially legitimate (Elias and Dunning, 1986: 65).

There were long-term historical reasons for this. Elias pointed to the relationship between the development of England's reputation as the 'home of sport' and the seventeenth-century process of 'parlia-mentarization' of English political life taking place at the same time (Mennell, 1998). He was not arguing that events in the political sphere exerted a casual influence on those in the sporting arena, rather that changes in the factional contests between individuals and political parties in Parliament helped produce the subsequent pacification of sportive practices. This was because certain aristocratic individuals, who were involved in making political life more peaceful by making politics a primarily parliamentary affair, rather than involving physical violence between rival groups, were the very same people who imported a similar pacifying outlook into the sporting pastimes they engaged in (Elias and Dunning, 1986: 40). Sport and leisure activities thus typically are consistent with the broader types of self-regulation characteristic of the habitus of the group of people who engage in those activities. Elias and Dunning also argue that the human need and capacity for self-control is precariously counter-poised by an opposing social-psychological tendency, one that leads individuals to seek out areas of life in which they can loosen control of their emotions – controlled by the sorts of self-regulatory norms we saw above – but in a regulated and relatively controlled manner. But disparities in this regard can exist within particular societies between different social groups. Socially marginalized groups, for example, may occupy a social location that to some degree immunizes them from the civilizing drive towards self-restraint. So if 'football hooligans' typically come from lower working-class backgrounds, then the reason they are so 'violent' at and around football matches would be that they come from a group where the norms of self-regulation have only an insecure foothold.

Such claims by Elias and his colleagues have often led to quite heated disputes about the appropriateness of process sociology for understanding sporting phenomena (Giulianotti, 1999). More generally, in the later part of his life and then after his death, a body of critical commentary has developed around his work. Layder (1986: 372), for example, argues that Elias' concept of social relations does very little to advance the debate about social structure and individual action, because the emphasis Elias gives to the notion of social interdependency is already present in other theoretical paradigms. As regards the analysis of the civilizing process, some critics have argued that members of 'traditional' types of society, including medieval Europe, were in fact far more closely bound to each other than people in modernity have been, and thus subject to far higher degrees of social control. One could argue that precisely because modern life is characterized by rising numbers of impersonal interactions with people completely unknown to us, the pressure towards self-restraint is diminished because how any given individual perceives another carries far less importance than in pre-modern social contexts (Lasch, 1985). A significant number of commentators have criticized Elias' use of the work of Freud as highly problematic (Burkitt, 1991). Perhaps the most recurrent criticism of Elias is that he provides an overly socialized account of the human psyche, which fails to take seriously Freud's contention that certain psychological drives operate independently of, or indeed against, the social realm. If Elias has inadvertently introduced an 'over-socialized'

Knowledge
Process sociology; dialectics of social relations and individuals; long-term historical approach

Structure/Agency
Individuals constituted by, and constitutive of, interdependent 'networks' or 'figurations' of relations

Individuals are 'processes'

Social relations produce habitus

Intertwining of psycho-genesis and socio-genesis

Modernity
Result of the civilizing process
High levels of self-regulation
Occasional de-civilizing tendencies

Figure 7.1 Summary of Elias' Process Sociology.

conception of the individual, as was arguably done by Parsons (see Chapter 2), then that would seriously undermine his claim to have overcome the structure/action divide, putting him closer to structuralism and objectivism than he thought he was.

Conclusion

Regardless of the problems that critics have identified, Eliasian process sociology has had a lasting impact on social theory, sometimes in tacit ways. As a former colleague of Elias at the University of Leicester during the 1960s, Anthony Giddens was influenced by the processual image of social reality, and that arguably informs to some extent his own structuration theory (see Chapter 10). Elias' ideas also provide useful counterpoints to the work of two other major theorists: in the case of Bourdieu (see Chapter 10), it is interesting to compare how each of them uses the concept of 'habitus'; and in the case of Foucault (see Chapter 8), it is useful to contrast the latter's account of individuals' self-regulating activities with those offered by Elias. Perhaps the most appealing aspects of process sociology are its attention to empirical data to make its claims, and its focus on long-term historical developments, a necessary corrective to naïve, presentist forms of analysis which refuse to delve into the past in order to understand the historical construction of present-day social conditions (Inglis, 2010).

Further Reading

Mennell, S. (1998) *Norbert Elias: An Introduction*. Dublin: University College. Dublin Press.
– (2007) *The American Civilizing Process*. Cambridge: Polity.
Van Krieken, R. (1998) *Norbert Elias*. London: Routledge.

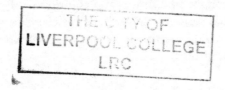

8

Structuralist and Post-Structuralist Paradigms

Structuralism was a radically new way of regarding social and cultural phenomena that was invented in the early twentieth century. It claimed to discern structured patterns in phenomena that seemed on the surface not to possess these. It claimed to be able to go beyond everyday perceptions of things, to penetrate beneath the surface of apparently random and chaotic cultural forms and social activities, in order to see the patterns and structures that lurked underneath. The early twentieth-century structuralists were followed in the 1950s and 1960s by a new breed of structuralist authors in France, such as Barthes, Lacan and Althusser, who were keen to update the ideas of the pioneers and apply them to the social conditions of the time. Once many of the limitations and problems of this wave of structuralism had become apparent by the late 1960s, structuralism mutated into post-structuralism, and other thinkers, most notably Derrida, stepped forward with radicalized versions of the original structuralist ideas. The career of the highly influential thinker Michel Foucault straddled both the structuralist and post-structuralist waves of French thought, developing in the process a strong challenge to previous accounts of social order and change.

In this chapter we examine the ideas of the figures just mentioned, illustrating continuing themes within structuralism and post-structuralism. These ongoing concerns include their challenges to conventional ideas as to the nature of the individual person's psyche as being rational and unified; their rejection of claims that science was completely objective; and their disavowal of the notion that society was moving in ways that made it ever more conducive to individual freedom and liberation. Structuralism and post-structuralism were concerned to shatter these and related myths, and to propose alternative and more sophisticated accounts of human life and the nature of modernity. How successful they were in this regard is still open to debate, as we will see.

Innovations: Durkheim and Saussure

One of the major early structuralists was Durkheim (see Chapter 1). In his later writings (2001 [1912]), he regarded cultural forms, especially religious ones, as being highly structured. All religions were seen to divide the world up into *sacred* and *profane* things. Drawing on Kant's ideas, Durkheim argued that religions use this binary structure to make sense of the world for the people who believe in that religion. They classify the world into things regarded as sacred, good, moral (etc.) on the one side and, profane, bad, immoral (etc.) on the other. A religion is a processing mechanism, dividing the world up into two parts, so that believers can make sense of the world and of themselves. It is not just religions which do this, but all cultural forms, including secular ones (Alexander, 1988).

Another early structuralist was the Swiss linguist Ferdinand Saussure [1857–1913], who developed his ideas independently of Durkheim but about the same time. There are certain affinities in their ideas, especially the notions that underneath surface mess and chaos there are regular patterns, and that meaning is only possible because of hidden structures that the people who use them are not aware of. While Durkheim was a *social* structuralist, Saussure's was a *linguistic* structuralism, and subsequent intellectual culture in France has witnessed both mixings of the two sets of ideas, and also fierce rivalry between them, with social scientists such as Pierre Bourdieu taking up and defending more Durkheim-inspired ideas, and humanities scholars such as Derrida and Baudrillard more influenced by Saussure's legacy.

Saussure's major claim is that language is structured in certain ways that are not immediately discernible. In a compilation of his lecture notes published after his death, Saussure (1959 [1906–11]) outlined several key distinctions. The first concerns the terms *langue* and *parole*. In French, *langue* refers to the idea of regarding language as a structured system. A *langue* is more than just the sum of all the linguistic capacities of all the people who speak it. A *langue* exists above and beyond each of these individual speakers. It is a structured system in and of itself. It is made up of a collection of words, and a set of rules for putting them together in particular ways so that they seem meaningful to speakers and listeners. For speakers to make their utterances understandable to others using the same *langue*, they have to obey these rules of how to put sentences together. Specific uses of speech (utterances) made by individual speakers are called *parole*. *Langue* (the overall system) is more important than *parole*, because particular instances of *parole* are just utterances that follow the rules set by *langue*. To really understand how language works, one must focus on *langue*, and not the specific uses of it made by individuals.

The task then is to discern the structural features of *langue*, understood as a system. This involves looking at how that system operates at a given point in time. The structures of that system can only be seen if we take a snap-shot view of it, freezing it in time. If we were to examine the historical evolution of a specific language, as linguists before Saussure had done, this would not allow us to see clearly the structural aspects of langue. Analysis has to be *synchronic* (looking at *langue* as if it has been 'frozen' at one point in time) and not *diachronic* (looking at *langue* as it has changed over time), to allow perception of *langue*'s hidden structures.

These structures in part involve what Saussure calls *signs*, *signifiers* and *signifieds*. Language of course is mostly made up of words and the rules for putting them together. But what words are and what they do has to be defined more precisely. Saussure replaces the term 'word' with that of *sign*. The sign is the basic constituent component of the system of *langue*. *Langue* is made up of a set of signs, which relate to each other in structured ways.

Signs themselves are made up of two components: *signifiers* and *signifieds*. The signifier is either the phonetic expression (sound) or written expression (a written symbol) of a certain mental concept (an idea). That concept is the *signified*. Saussure is not making the obvious point that a particular sound (a signifier) or a particular written symbol (again, a signifier) refers to a particular object in the world (the signified). On the view Saussure is rejecting, either the sound you make when you say 'cat', or the symbol you write when you want to describe a cat (the symbol 'cat'), actually refers to a real cat sitting beside you. Instead, his more radical claim is that a sign, combining a signifier and a signified, unites 'not a thing and a name [for it], but a concept and a sound-image' (Saussure, 1959 [1906–11]: 66). This is a very important reformulation of the nature of language. It is *not* the case that language is a set of words that refer to things existing in the world around us. Against common-sense (which is a typical structuralist orientation), it is not the case that when I say 'cat', or write the word 'cat', that I am simply referring to a 'real' cat.

Instead, language is seen to be made up of two related but separate structured systems. One the one hand, there is the *system of signifiers*: the particular sounds and written images a particular language involves. The second is the *system of signifieds* – the concepts (ideas) that these signifiers refer to. The relation between the two is that they are *mutually self-constituting*: they each make the other. In each particular sign, signifier and signified are 'intimately united, and each recalls the other' (ibid.). The signified (the meaning of the sign) is therefore indissociable from the signifier (the representation, in speech or writing, of that signified). The spoken or written signifier 'cat' (the word 'cat', either spoken or written down) does not refer to a 'real' cat. Instead, it refers to the *idea* of a cat. And that idea is itself constructed by the system of *langue*. A particular *langue*'s idea of a cat does not derive from anything to do with 'real' cats that live in the world. *The idea is purely a product of the langue itself.*

Real cats do not dictate what a *langue*'s idea of them is. Quite the opposite: it is the *langue* that dictates, for the people who speak that language, what the idea of a cat involves. One particular *langue* may have the idea that cats are household pets – thus speakers of that *langue* will view them in certain ways. But another *langue* may have an idea of them as wild animals or as vermin – speakers of that *langue* will then think of cats very differently from those whose *langue* defines cats as pets. Of course, there are 'real' cats in the world. But when we use either written or spoken language to describe them, we are not actually referring to those real cats, even if we think we are. Instead, when we use language, we are actually only ever referring to the *idea* of a cat that our *langue* uses and has constructed. Signifiers (written and spoken words) only ever refer to signifieds (the ideas of things in a particular *langue*), and *not those things themselves*. We may think our words refer to real things (e.g. cats) but they do not – they only refer to our ideas of those things. And those ideas are wholly constructed by our language. This is Saussure's linguistic twist on Kant's original idea that humans never have access to things in the world 'as they really are' (see Chapter 1). In sum, it is the language of a social group that fundamentally shapes their sense of reality. 'Without language, thought is a vague, uncharted nebula. There are no pre-existing ideas, and nothing is distinct before the appearance of language' (ibid.: 112).

Here we see the *arbitrary* nature of the sign. There is never any *natural* relationship either between signifier and signified, or between signified and the object it refers to. In terms of the latter, the signified is the idea of the object, as held in a particular *langue*, not the object itself. So particular *langues* are free to construct particular ideas of objects, as the objects have no power to constrain or shape these ideas. In terms of the former, there is no natural or necessary relationship between a given signified and a signifier. A signifier (a word, either spoken or written) is merely a sound or a written symbol, and so the fact that a *langue* uses that signifier to indicate a particular signified is purely a matter of convention within that *langue*. It so happens that in the English *langue*, the signifier 'cat' refers to a particular signified (the idea of a certain kind of animal). But *any other word at all* could have been used to describe that signified if the *langue* so defined it. We could use the word 'fnark', for example, to describe the same idea of the same animal, as long as everyone using English shared the convention that 'fnark' meant that sort of animal. So the word 'cat' has only an arbitrary – that is, non-necessary and non-natural – relationship to the signified it points to. Within a *langue*, any signifier potentially could be used to denote any signified. It is purely a matter of convention which signifier refers to which signified.

This seems to indicate potential for complete chaos – any word could potentially refer to any thing (or rather, the idea of a thing). But chaos does not occur, because *langue* works to impose order on the world and on the people who speak the *langue*. The *langue* imposes habits and customs upon the people who use it. Particular signifiers are habitually accepted by speakers as referring to particular signifieds. As the signifier 'cat' has for centuries in English referred to a certain signified (the idea of that animal), then English speakers just accept the word as referring to that signified. They think it is 'natural' that this signifier points to that signified, even when it is not natural but merely a convention. Thus *langue* involves arbitrary relations between signifiers and signifieds, which are made to look *as if* they are natural and fixed for ever. Speakers experience as natural what is actually arbitrary, conventional and linguistically constructed.

We have seen that *langue* consists of two systems, that of signifiers and that of signifieds. Each is a *system of differences*. Each of the elements in each system only have meaning because they are different from all the other elements in the system. So in the system of signifiers, each signifier possesses meaning only because it is unlike *all* the other signifiers. The signifier 'cat' has meaning only because it is different (it has a different sound when spoken, and has a different written form) from every other signifier in the English *langue*. A *langue* is a system precisely because each signifier in it has its separate meaning guaranteed by the fact that it does not sound or look like any other signifier in the system.

Saussure points out there are further structural relations in a *langue*. The first is the *syntagmatic* relation. This involves the ways in which particular words are joined together in sequences to form phrases or full sentences. The English sentence 'the cat sat on the mat' is a syntagmatic relation of words. It follows the rule of basic English grammar: noun (cat) is followed by verb (sat). Each of the signifiers in the sentence 'acquires its value only because it stands in opposition to everything that precedes or follows it' (ibid.: 123). So the signifier 'cat' here has a meaning (the signified, the idea of a feline) because it is not the same sound or written image as the other signifiers 'sat' and 'mat'. The other relation is the *paradigmatic* relation. Here signifiers take on their specific meanings through being contrasted with other signifiers that have somewhat similar yet also subtly different meanings (i.e. signifieds). So the English words 'tuition' and 'apprenticeship' refer to similar kinds of activities, but the English *langue* makes a subtle distinction between these two activities. This difference at the level of signifieds (meanings of the words) is mirrored at the level of signifiers: the words 'tuition' and 'apprenticeship' are different signifiers, made up of different sounds and different written symbols. Saussure regards the paradigmatic relations of language as something implicit within a person's knowledge of a given *langue*. Mostly we do not consciously contrast different words in this way, but implicitly we are doing so all the time. Only in this way do words make sense to the people who use them.

All this no doubt sounds like very dry linguistic theory, with little relevance to social theory. But much social theory, especially that coming out of France, is hugely indebted to Saussure's ideas and it is important

---

Langue (system)/parole (individual uses of the system)

Langue made up of systems of signs

Systems of signs are systems of difference

Sign made up of signifier (written word, sounds) and signified (the idea the signifier points to)

Language creates social reality

Figure 8.1 Summary of Saussure's Linguistics.

Discourses
- create their own 'objects'
- present these objects as 'real'
- present themselves as 'natural'

Figure 8.2 The Nature of Discourses.

to understand them. Later structuralism and then post-structuralism took up the Saussurean notion that social life is essentially made up of multiple different, but overlapping and mutually informing, systems of signs, all of which are structured and operate in the same ways as *langue*. Social life is seen to be made up of different 'languages' – different sorts of *langue* – each of which constructs reality in its own specific ways for the people who use it.

Each of these languages – or as later authors would call them, 'discourses' (see Figure 8.2) – is made up of systems of signifiers and signifieds, the meanings of which are dictated not by the 'outside world' to which they apparently refer, but to the internal relationships within each *langue* between all of its signifiers, and between all of its signifieds. Thus each discourse does not reflect or represent the things it talks about, as those things are not 'real' objects in the world. Instead, each discourse creates its own reality, and creates its own objects. A discourse *may seem as if* it is referring to real things; but it is actually referring merely to signifieds, its own construction of those things. People who use a discourse *think* that the words they use are neutral, simply and naturally referring to things in the world. Most people most of the time are unaware that their thinking has been shaped by particular discourses. They think that their ways of thinking and perceiving are just 'natural', giving them unmediated access to the 'real world'. But everyone, generally without knowing it, can only ever think and perceive in ways shaped by the discourses they use.

Following Saussure's insistence that *langue* is more important than *parole*, structuralism (and most post-structuralism) says that the particular uses individuals make of discourses are much less important than the discourses themselves. In a very profound way, each person is a prisoner of the discourses (*langues*) that they are forced to use to speak and think with. Discourses are at their most powerful when they are most invisible, when they thoroughly shape a person's perceptions at a wholly unconscious level. It is the nature of discourses to be wholly constructed and not in any way 'natural' (i.e. they are arbitrary), while at the same time seeming so natural to the people whose thinking they construct that they are not even noticed. Discourses disguise the fact they are constructed by 'naturalizing' themselves, coming to seem to those whom they influence that they are not even there. Structuralist analysis aims to reveal all of these things, and to reveal to people the discourses which tacitly shape how they think and act (Sturrock, 2002).

Analysing Myth

One of the first major thinkers to develop Saussurean ideas for the purposes of social science was the anthropologist Claude Lévi-Strauss [1908–2010], who analysed what he took to be the structural characteristics of a wide range of cultural systems, such as a particular society's myths, rituals, marriage rules, and kinship systems. Phenomena that were apparently random and patternless were regarded as being in fact strongly patterned. The underlying structural properties 'cannot be reached by purely empirical observation, or by intuitive consideration of phenomena, but result from measuring some basic relationships between the various elements' of each phenomenon (Lévi-Strauss, 1986 [1963]: 59). Thus analysis goes beyond the surface level of *parole* to get at the fundamental structures of *langue*. While Lévi-Strauss' ideas were very fashionable in France and elsewhere in the 1960s (Leach, 1966), they fell out of fashion in social theoretical circles thereafter. One reason for this was that he seemed to some critics to have drastically over-emphasized claims as to particular *langues* underpinning all social and cultural phenomena, allegedly finding underlying structures where none actually existed.

A form of structuralist analysis of the 1950s and 1960s that has lasted better than Lévi-Strauss', and is still widely taught and used today, is the critical reading of 'texts' (understood in the broadest sense of anything involving systems of signifiers and signifieds) developed by the literary critic Roland Barthes [1915–1980]. The younger Barthes (1988) developed a structuralist conception of how to 'decode' the significance of the systems of signs that are everywhere in modern, urban societies. Barthes combined Saussure's ideas with a Marxist understanding of power and ideology (see Chapter 3). Systems of signs (discourses) contain and present meanings which express the views of, and help to maintain the rule of, the ruling classes (1988: 155).

Structuralist analysis becomes an explicitly *political* exercise, carried out with the intention of exposing to view the forms of power contained within, and reproduced through, particular sign-systems and the texts they are found in. Apparently 'common-sense' views of the world are shown to be not 'natural' (as they are generally experienced by those using and influenced by them) but products of ruling class ideologies as these are expressed in discourses. Discourses hide forms of social power while simultaneously expressing and promoting them. The mass of the population think in ways thoroughly shaped by discourses expressing ruling class ideas, stealthily promoting these, making them seem natural and commonsensical, but at the same time hiding the fact that this is happening. The analyst has to stand outside of the discourses that everyone else is taken in by, so that people can be made to see the constructed and biased nature of the 'myths' that they live their lives by.

In *Mythologies* (1993 [1957]), Barthes endeavoured to reveal the nature of the discourses at work in a France increasingly influenced by discourses associated with consumerism and advertising. Apparently trivial and 'harmless' texts, like adverts for soap powder, embodied meanings created by ruling class discourses. 'Mythical' meanings and messages are those which work at two separate but related levels. The first level is *denotation*. This is the apparently basic meaning of the text. An advert for soap powder tells the audience that the product washes clothes whiter than rival products. The signifier (the advert) refers to a signified, the basic meaning of the object (the soap powder, which washes 'whiter than white').

But this is not the only meaning. Taken together, the signifier and signified of this denotative level constitute a further sign, which leads on to a second level of meaning. The denotative sign is transformed into a signifier of that other level of meaning. This is the *connotative* level, the mythical (ideological) level of the text. The connotative level of meaning is a language that *infiltrates* the primary language of the denotative level, and takes it over. In the soap powder advert, the connotative (mythical, ideological) meaning is that happiness resides in the purchasing of clothes and other consumer goods, and that happiness and pleasure can only be obtained through the means of capitalist consumerism. The advertising text works such that the mythical connotative language of consumer capitalism pervades the banal denotative language of the picture of soap powder. Advertising is a signifying system that in a subterranean way

---

Denotation: basic meaning
Connotation: hidden, ideological meaning, which infiltrates denotation

---

Figure 8.3 Barthes on 'Myth'.

encourages audiences to assume that it is *natural* and *right* to buy consumer goods. This is *naturalization*: making something contingent and not pre-determined – here, people accepting the system of consumer capitalism, and buying into it – seem totally *inevitable*. Thoughts about other possible ways of living are foreclosed by the ruling class discourse in favour of making current social conditions seem *eternal*. Capitalist society is thus made to seem as if it were both the only, and best, possible form of social organization, so helping to stabilize the rule of the ruling classes (Barthes 1993 [1957]: 139–40).

But this situation is generally not intentional on the behalf of those who construct and reproduce the discourse, such as advertising executives. They are likely to be as enslaved by such discourses, and unable to realize this fact, as the consumers they endeavour to reach. This is a condition of hyper-alienation: discourses create reality, and this is recognized neither by the less powerful nor (most of the time) by the powerful too. Everyone remains caught within the webs of meaning spun by discourses. Only the structuralist analyst can stand outside and see what is really happening.

This is a similar position to that of another important structuralist, the Marxist philosopher Louis Althusser [1918–1990], whose work was highly influential in the 1970s. In ways that very much echo Barthes, but using the language of Marxism in a more sophisticated manner, Althusser (1971) recast the Marxian account of how ruling class ideologies can come to control the thinking of the mass of the population into terms of sign-systems and discourses. Following Gramsci (see Chapter 3), Althusser argues that ruling class control of a society cannot be brought about by the use of physical force alone (by the police, army, etc. – institutions that Althusser calls the 'repressive state apparatuses'). This also has to be done by mental domination of the population. The institutions that achieve this are the 'ideological state apparatuses', such as the churches, the family, and the education system. All of these are based around and promote particular ideologies, embodied in particular discourses, each discourse defining reality in its own way.

The various discourses profoundly shape each person's ways of thinking and their sense of themselves (their 'subjectivity'). This is done through the process of 'interpellation'. When a person is confronted with a discourse that has thoroughly shaped their subjectivity, they 'recognize' themselves within it: the sense they have of themselves, created by the discourse, is reconfirmed constantly by ongoing exposure to the discourse. So the discourse of 'the family' shapes the subjectivities of women to make them think they are 'naturally' above all else mothers, who have primary responsibility for childcare. There is nothing 'natural' about this belief; it is the arbitrary product of the modern ideology of the family. Likewise, the discourse of the modern education system 'interpellates' pupils to believe that if they fail at school it is wholly their own fault, thus disguising the fact that children from lower-class backgrounds have to face systematic bias against them in the system, and it is that bias which makes them more likely to be educational failures than their upper-class counterparts (Bourdieu and Passeron, 1990 – see Chapter 10). So 'objective' features of social structure, such as class and gender inequalities, are disguised by discourses fundamentally shaping how people think and defining the world in ways that suit the interests of modern capitalist society's ruling groups. This is not deliberate manipulation by the ruling classes, as they are generally as much mental prisoners of discourses as are the lower classes.

A key problem that arises for both Barthes and Althusser is that their analysis suggests that only the structuralist analyst can discern all of these processes, for everyone else is so imprisoned within discourses that they cannot see the true state of affairs. Their analyses implied that structuralism was completely 'scientific', able fully to break out of the webs spun by discourses in order to see how things 'really work'. Critics (e.g. Jameson, 1972) soon began to think that such claims were not only naïve but

---

Repressive State Apparatuses
police, army, etc., using physical violence

Ideological State Apparatuses (ISAs)
ideologies/discourses using mental violence

Interpellation by ISAs of individual's subjectivity

Figure 8.4 Althusser's Marxism.

arrogant, falsely conceiving of almost everyone as a dupe of signifying systems. This is assumed at the level of theory, rather than convincingly proved by reference to empirical evidence.

Another serious problem concerned what happened if instances of *parole* involve more active and creative activities than Saussure had thought, and Barthes and Althusser had assumed? The possibility had to be examined that people who spoke and thought within particular discourses were not just prisoners of these discourses. Perhaps discourses could be used creatively by speakers, and that new ideas could be created which complicated discourses and changed them over time (Eco (1987 [1967])? That would raise the possibility that discourses might, under certain circumstances, be spotted by particular social groups *as* discourses, and be challenged or rejected. Discourses might have uneven and contradictory effects on people's subjectivities, not simply creating people who all thought in ways the discourses demanded (Hall, 1993 [1980]). This raised the possibility of analysts examining *counter-discourses* associated with the lower classes as well as discourses that operate in ruling class interests. Thus in the 1970s Michel de Certeau (1984) conceived of social life as an arena where the lower classes are constantly engaged in creative acts of *parole* that are subversive of ruling class and elite discourses. Acts of *parole* have the power to infiltrate, undermine and sometimes even destroy discourses, subverting them from within or ignoring them altogether. While such a position may well over-emphasize the power of *parole* as much as Althusser and Barthes overstated the capacities of *langue*, it was a useful corrective to the structuralist vision whereby human life seemed to be a terrible 'prison-house' of discourses from which there was no escape (Jameson, 1972).

Towards Post-Structuralism

By the late 1960s, the various problems of structuralism just mentioned were apparent enough to produce new ideas and methods, indebted to Saussure but not trapped by his original notions. These constituted the trend that would be called 'post-structuralism' (Harland, 2010). Post-structuralism shifted away markedly from structuralism's preoccupations with structure and patterns, and its claims to be objective and 'scientific' in its analysis of meanings in social life, towards concerns with the multiplicity and instability of meanings, and what it took to be the infinitely complex nature of subjectivities, now regarded as multiple and chaotic, rather than simply structured by specific discourses. Post-structuralism regarded itself as 'radical', but as part of the overall trend towards 'post-Marxism' in French intellectual life from the early 1970s onwards (see Chapter 12), it generally rejected Marxist politics and means of explanation, in favour of radicalism politically and methodologically closer to anti-Enlightenment philosophers such as Friedrich Nietzsche (see Chapter 1).

For Saussure, each signifier refers to a certain signified. The connection between them is arbitrary – a signifier only refers to a signified because of the convention within a given *langue* – but there is still a connection between them. Post-structuralism moves in the direction of a stress upon the *completely* arbitrary nature of the signifier, cutting off the signifier's connection to the signified. The *only* source of the signifier's meaning is seen to be its place in the system of signifiers, for now the signifier has no necessary attachment at all to signifieds, let alone the 'real things' they purport to refer to.

One of the main post-structuralist thinkers to deal with such issues was Jacques Derrida [1930–2004], whose philosophy combines a radicalized version of Saussure with aspects of phenomenological thought (see Chapter 4). The radical possibility Derrida (1978) points to is that there is no 'real world' at all, just images of it, and those images are completely arbitrary because they are not rooted in anything that would guarantee their truth. So language and other sign-systems (discourses) are not means of representing the world, for they can only ever signify themselves. Signs never point to the 'real' – there is no such thing – but only ever to other signs. Signs refer to signs that refer to other signs, in never-ending chains of signification.

Each sign-system and chain of signification is not stable but constantly subject to fluctuating shifts and changes, such that the meaning of each signifier is constantly open to alteration and disruption. The result is that each signifier does not relate to only one signified, but potentially to a multiplicity of them. In other words, signifiers are *polysemic* – they possess multiple meanings – rather than *monosemic* – having only one, stable meaning. There is only ever *difference*, i.e. meaning is generated purely through the differences between different signifiers, rather than on the basis of any capacity to represent what is outside of chains of signification (in the supposed 'real world'). Indeed, there is not and cannot be anything outside of signs. In order to press this point home, Derrida argues that the real nature of language rests not in *speech*, which seems to be connected to external reality in a direct way, but rather in *writing*, which is a wholly arbitrary series of signs and conventions. Writing does not represent the 'outside world'. Instead, writing creates its own multiple, plural, transient realities. The world is made up of different texts, each of which has constantly shifting and multiple meanings. Meaning is never stable, and the significance of anything is never fixed. Because all meaning is conventional and arbitrary, then everything is mutable and nothing is guaranteed (Harland, 2010).

The shift towards post-structuralist thinking had already been in some ways anticipated by the psychoanalyst Jacques Lacan in the 1950s. Lacan's (2007) re-working of the ideas of Freud (see Chapter 1) are closer to post-structuralism than structuralism because of his insistence on the instability of sign systems and the meanings they generate. Lacan's claim was that the human unconscious was 'like a language'. As a child learns about the world around it, and starts to speak language, it is being inducted into the 'symbolic order', that is, all the various discourses that make up the surrounding society. These discourses thoroughly structure not just the conscious mind but the hidden, unconscious dimensions of the mind too. The unconscious works in ways very similar to Derrida's sense of signification – endless, shifting, volatile signifiers endlessly referring to other signifiers. Thus the unconscious, shaped by the multiple discourses of the symbolic order, is constantly fluctuating, unsettled and transient. The individual constantly searches for a coherent ego and identity, but this is made impossible by the never-ending flux of the unconscious. Secure identity is therefore an 'obscure object of desire', constantly sought but never found or achieved. Lacan's writings are notoriously difficult and opaque, but this is a deliberate strategy to try to indicate the ever-shifting nature of the unconscious, which is always mutating and cannot be pinned down.

Lacanian theory has been highly influential on subsequent post-structuralist analyses of the complexities of identity, which stress the multiplicity of identities within one particular 'subject' (Žižek, 2006). While modern Western culture claims that subjects are coherent and unified, engaged in rational thought, they are in fact shaped by multiple discourses, leading to ever-shifting and ambiguous forms of personhood which never cohere around any single principle. A person's psyche is a site of contending, contradictory forces, characterized by multiplicity and instability of meanings and dispositions, rather than coherence and uniformity (Elliott, 2004). Taking their cue in part from Lacan, post-structuralists such as Julia Kristeva (see Chapter 11) and the later Barthes – whose position by the 1970s had shifted away from the structuralist outlook described above – emphasized that the ego is never unified but constantly bursting open and endlessly altered by the play of all the different discourses that have constituted it. As Barthes phrased it, 'the "I" is . . . a plurality of other texts' (Culler, 1983: 82). A person's mind is a text written upon by a multitude of discourses, creating endless incoherence and ambiguity.

This is the structuralist 'de-centring of the subject' – showing that the human mind is produced by discourses – taken to further extremes by post-structuralism, which views all phenomena as radically contingent. Instability, incoherence and being unsettled are the norm, both within people's heads and in the world at large. The politics of post-structuralism is to celebrate and extend this situation, and attempts to fix meaning or to render subjects coherent are both reviled and seen to be impossible anyway. Although post-structuralism is generally regarded as wholly antithetical to Marxism, nonetheless the two have been combined or have been made to enter into dialogue as the work of Laclau and Mouffe (see Chapter 3) and the later Derrida (1978) attest.

Michel Foucault: From Structuralism to Post-Structuralism

While these sorts of post-structuralist ideas have been very important in the development of subsequent cultural theory in humanities disciplines, a more influential body of ideas for the social sciences is that formulated by Michel Foucault [1926–1984]. Foucault embraced structuralism in the 1960s, followed by a movement towards post-structuralist concerns thereafter. While Foucault's work is often presented as if it were wholly unique and unprecedented (Halperin, 1995), it is better to see it as part of some broader trends of thought in France, both structuralism and the French tradition of 'historical epistemology', which connects in certain ways to Durkheim (Gutting, 2005).

Like other structuralists and post-structuralists, Foucault's targets were what he saw as the most important myths of modern society, especially 'science', 'humanism' and Marxism. These are seen as peddling various mythical notions: that scientific knowledge is wholly objective; that modern society is moving in a progressive direction, liberating subjects more and more from the hold of power; that power is primarily class-based; and that human subjects are fundamentally unified, rational egos, this latter being the central claim of 'humanism'.

Foucault's work, both earlier and later, was a sustained attack on these notions, which he saw as profoundly structuring modern social order. Foucault's non-Marxist politics involved a rejection of the 'metanarrative' of Marxism (see Chapter 3), with its claims as to modern society's liberation from power being undertaken by a unified revolutionary working class. Foucault aimed to replace this view of politics with a political sensibility more attuned to specific, micro-level struggles against authority by non-class-based oppressed groups, such as women, gays and prison inmates (Simons, 1995).

Foucault's earlier work is very much akin to other structuralist thinking of the early 1960s. In it he proposed an 'archaeology of knowledge', which involved two main dimensions (Foucault, 2001 [1966]). First, intellectual archaeology shows that the history of modern Western society essentially involves different successive 'layers' of knowledge-systems, which Foucault calls 'epistemes'. These are like Saussure's understanding of *langue*. A particular period of history involves the dominance of one particular episteme. All specific types of knowledge at that period are shaped by the episteme. The episteme defines what it is possible and impossible for anyone to think at that period. People can only conceive of things in ways that the episteme allows, and it is impossible for anyone to think outside of the boundaries set by it. The implication of this is that the idea that science has progressed constantly over the last several centuries, to become ever more 'objective', is mythical. Instead, there is no progress in knowledge, only the successive replacement of one episteme by another. By looking at the different epistemes, which exist in Western history in the same way as the layers in the ground uncovered by an archaeologist, we can see that history has no particular direction and that science and society are not progressing as time goes on. Thus archaeology of knowledge explodes some of the most cherished myths propagated by modern society about itself.

The second activity of archaeology involves examining the particular forms of knowledge that existed at the time of a particular episteme.

Archaeology of Knowledge
Search for *epistemes* and discourses made possible by them
Power/knowledge
Panopticon and surveillance

Figure 8.5 Foucault's Earlier Ideas.

Archaeology examines particular sciences – both natural (e.g. medicine), social (e.g. criminology) and a fusion of the natural and the social (e.g. psychiatry, psychology) – which claim to be 'objective', but are actually discourses which construct their own objects of analysis (signifieds). They bring into existence the very things they claim to be simply 'real'. In this sense, each discourse creates its own 'truths', which it then endlessly confirms. As a natural science like medicine has changed, it has moved from being one sort of discourse to another, with the new discourse imagining the human body in radically new ways from its predecessor. Likewise, as new social sciences were invented, particularly from the eighteenth century onwards, they claimed to investigate particular types of people – 'criminals' in the case of criminology, 'psychiatric patients' in the case of psychiatry – as if such types of people 'naturally existed'. But it is the discourses *themselves* that create the category of 'patient', 'criminal' and so on, such that these types of people are invented by the discourses themselves. It follows from this that power is not just negative, as Marxism claimed. (As we saw in Chapter 3, Marxism sees ruling class power acting as a negative break on working-class revolutionary activities.) Instead, if power is seen as the capacity of discourses to invent new categories of people, then power is productive and, in a certain sense, 'positive' because it has the capacity to create, not just repress.

A discourse creates the very things that it purports to study. When the discourse studies people defined as 'psychiatric patients', 'criminals' and so on, power is exercised upon those people. This is why Foucault understands *knowledge to be power, and power to be knowledge*, for the two are thoroughly interpenetrating.

The people labelled by a discourse often take on its labelling of them and start to believe its definition of who they are. Discourses tell those who are under their control what sort of person they are, why this category of person ('criminal', 'psychiatric patient', etc.) is deviant, and, by contrast, what a 'normal' person is. Discourses like psychiatry and criminology engage in 'normalizing judgements', which endeavour to remake the person so that they become like the ideal of the 'normal' person set up by the discourse. The knowledge specialists who create and operate the discourse – doctors, prison warders, etc. – collect vast amounts of information on the people who have been labelled, in order to know everything about them. This knowledge is used to try to turn these individuals into the 'normal' persons imagined by the discourse.

Unlike in the medieval world, where authorities exercised power over people's *bodies* (e.g. violently executing criminals, or whipping them), these new sorts of authorities are 'engineers of the soul': their aim is to reform the people under their scrutiny, by working on their *minds*, so as to create what the discourse defines as 'healthy' citizens (Foucault, 1977a). In the standard myth propagated by Western science since the time of the Enlightenment (see Chapter 1), sciences were invented, particularly in the eighteenth century, that were far more humane than previous ways of thinking were. But these sciences did not, as they claimed, help liberate people from the forces of power. Instead, argues Foucault, the discourses *themselves* were forms of power, which could control people in far more subtle, insidious and effective ways than had previously been possible. The medieval jailer merely had control over the bodies of his prisoners, but not over their minds. The new 'masters of discourse', like psychiatric doctors and other 'scientists', while claiming to free those they scrutinized, had far more effective power over those they controlled than did the jailer, because their power was over the minds and souls of the people they examined.

These 'scientific' discourses were exercised in newly created locations, like mental asylums and new types of prison. There the normalizing judgements of discourses were exercised upon those kept inside. These new sorts of institutions were designed to keep inmates under the constant surveillance of the authorities, those who wielded the discourses. Foucault takes as his exemplar of this situation a type of prison designed by English social reformer Jeremy Bentham in the early nineteenth century. The *Panopticon* ('all-seeing eye' in Greek) was a ring-shaped building with

> ... at the centre, a tower; this tower is pierced with wide windows that open onto the inner side of the ring; the peripheric building is divided into cells, each of which extends the whole width of the building; they have two windows, one on the inside, corresponding to the windows of the tower; the other, on the outside, allows the light to cross the cell from one end to the other. All that is needed, then, is to place a supervisor in a central tower and to shut up in each cell a madman, a patient, a condemned man, a worker or a schoolboy. By the effect of backlighting, one can observe from the tower, standing out precisely against the light, the small captive shadows in the cells of the periphery. They are like so many cages, so many small theatres, in which each actor is alone, perfectly individualized and constantly visible. The panoptic mechanism arranges spatial unities that make it possible to see constantly and to recognize

immediately. In short it reverses the principle of the dungeon; or rather of its three functions – to enclose, to deprive of light and to hide – it preserves only the first and eliminates the other two. Full lighting and the eye of a supervisor capture better than darkness, which ultimately protected. Visibility is a trap. (Foucault, 1977a: 200)

The prisoners are always under scrutiny from the guards in the tower. Their every move can be seen constantly, and the prisoners know this. But because of the way that the tower is designed, the prisoners cannot see if the guards are actually there. So power resides in the inequality of visibility between the two groups. The prisoners have to assume they are being watched, and this sense of being examined constantly becomes habituated over time. Even if no guards are actually in the tower, then the prisoners will still assume the guards are there. So it is the thought that one is being surveyed constantly that compels prisoners to *self-regulate*, to act in the ways demanded of them by the prison and its discourse.

A situation where self-regulation is endemic is one where the norms of discourse have thoroughly penetrated and shaped the dispositions of both mind and body. According to Foucault, these 'panoptic' principles spread out from prisons in the nineteenth century and infiltrated ever more types of institutions, such as hospitals, barracks, orphanages and schools, each with their own specialist discourses and techniques of power (constant visibility, normalizing judgements) that worked upon the minds and bodies of those within. Foucault's conclusion of the 1960s was that modernity narrates a discourse about itself as the liberation of people from the clutches of power, but in fact modernity is characterized by multiple discourses productive of ever more insidious forms of power. These are not controlled by a single ruling class, as Marxism claimed, but rather are invented and operated by multiple different sorts of knowledge specialist. If modern society is akin to the prison imagined by Weber and other classical theorists (Chapter 1), it is not because it is wholly rationalized and bureaucratized, but because of the multiplication of discourses, creating multiple forms of power, which create their own distinct subject populations.

These were Foucault's central structuralist ideas of the 1960s. In the 1970s, he, like many other French thinkers, shifted towards more post-structuralist ways of thinking (see Chapter 9). The guiding spirit of his post-structuralism is Friedrich Nietzsche (see Chapter 1), who had pioneered the idea of intellectual 'genealogy'. Genealogy was the post-structuralist approach that Foucault (1991 [1971]) replaced his previous structuralist method, the archaeology, with.

When the history of an idea that is dominant, and the truth and importance of which are widely taken for granted, is examined genealogically, then a radically new understanding of that idea comes into view. We see that that idea does not have a straightforward, cumulative history, developing slowly and becoming more sophisticated over the years. Instead, we see that the idea is not unified, but is actually made up of many different sources. It is revealed to be heterogeneous, not homogeneous. It is found to be made up of multiple discourses, even if its multiplicity is subsequently hidden, so that it looks more coherent than it really is. Ideas and discourses are revealed by genealogy to be 'unstable assemblage[s] of faults, fissures, and heterogeneous layers', as unstable as Lacan's unconscious and Derrida's signification chains (1991 [1978]: 82).

Genealogy also shows that the ways in which ideas become widely accepted are not necessary or inevitable, but rather are contingent, often purely accidental and random. This demonstrates the radically constructed nature of what counts as 'truth' – what we think of today as true and real is actually the product of contingent historical processes that could have been quite different from how they actually turned out. Ideas and discourses that seem to us today unavoidable and 'natural' actually are only accepted because of often quite random reasons. Foucault tries to 'denaturalize' our customary ways of thinking. We only think the ways we do because of historical accidents.

A key area Foucault applied the genealogical method to was the history of 'sexuality' (Foucault, 1981). One of the twentieth century's central ideas, in large part formulated by Freud and subsequently popularized by his followers (see Chapters 1 and 3), was that biological sex drives are strongly repressed by the norms of modern society: this is 'the repressive hypothesis'. But a paradox emerges: why is it that modern people talk so much about not being able to talk openly and without 'hang-ups' about sex? Genealogical analysis reveals that far from repressing (biological) 'sex', the norms associated with particular discourses have actually worked to create new forms of 'sexuality'. This has been going on for a long time. The widespread contemporary belief that 'sex' is vitally important in our lives, that it has to be 'repressed', and that to speak about sex is to 'confess' to others about apparently the most private things, can be traced back to the beginnings of Christianity:

... how is it that in a society like ours, sexuality is not simply a means of reproducing the species, the family and the individual? How has sexuality come to be considered the privileged place where our deepest 'truth' is read and expressed? ... Since Christianity, the Western world has never ceased saying: 'To know who you are, know what your sexuality is'. Sex has always been the forum where both the future of our species and our 'truth' as human subjects is decided. Confession, the examination of the conscience, all the insistence on the important secrets of the flesh, has not been simply a means of prohibiting sex or of repressing it as far as possible from consciousness, but was a means of placing sexuality at the heart of existence and of connecting salvation with the mastery of these obscure movements. In Christian societies, sex has been the central object of examination, surveillance, avowal and transformation into discourse. (Foucault, 1977b: 154)

We *think* there is such a thing as biologically based 'sex', that it is unchanging, that it is repressed by society (especially over the last few centuries), and that the only way to talk of it today is in a 'confessional' manner, not to one's priest as in the past but to one's psychotherapist. But these are ideas created by particular discourses, myths by which modern society operates. We have inherited these beliefs from Christianity and other historical sources for random historical reasons, not because they are true. What has actually happened is that every historical period has invented its own 'sexualities' in the plural. Sexualities are discourses as to what 'sex' is and what variants of it there are thought to be. Apparently 'deviant' forms of sex, such as homosexuality and paedophilia, are actually discourses, products of particular languages that have specific ways of talking about and defining what 'sex' is.

Foucault's point is that power does not *repress* something that already existed (here, biological 'sex'). Instead, power is *creative*, as discourses generate new forms of 'sexuality', which then can infiltrate the subjectivities of those people they are directed at. So the woman defined by the discourse of the 'science' of sexology as frigid or nymphomaniacal or sexually hysterical, is interpellated by the sexological discourse, her mind and her body coming to be shaped by it. New sexual 'perversions' were invented as new discourses about sex proliferated from the later nineteenth century onwards. People may believe that they have 'their own' distinct sexuality. But as sexualities are the products of discourses, then everyone's sexuality is a product of historical accident and the workings of power. That power does not 'repress' the 'pure' biological body. Instead, it creates new kinds of minds and bodies, and pleasures and experiences, which mirror and express the discourses of sexuality.

Foucault also points out (following Hegel – see Chapter 1) that power produces resistances to itself. Thus in the nineteenth century, the older idea of the 'sodomite' (understood as a random, aberrant freak of nature) was replaced by a new idea, invented by the discourse of the 'science' of sexology: this was the novel category of the 'homosexual', now defined as a categorizable 'type' of human being, not just a random freak of nature. Obviously this new category involved the workings of power over a certain population of men: sexology defined people labelled as 'homosexuals' in generally very negative ways. But the unintended consequence of the new category was that it 'also made possible the formation of a "reverse" discourse: homosexuality began to speak on its own behalf, to demand that its legitimacy or "naturality" be acknowledged, often in the same vocabulary, using the same categories' by which it was defined discursively (Foucault, 1981: 101).

In other words, those defined as 'homosexual' could over time come both to resist that category, and the discourse that created it, and also to use it for their own purposes. The label may be a form of power, but the people who are subjected to it can use the label in resistive ways, challenging the ways they are defined by the discourse. The label 'gay' becomes a form of pride, not shame.

It is these kinds of thoughts that led to the later Foucault's conception of power, involving a rejection of the Marxist notion that power is a property, held by particular institutions like a ruling class or the state. Power is instead complex, made up of shifting sets of relations, productive both of categories involving control and of counter-categories set against those forms of control:

> By power . . . I do not understand a general system of domination exercised by one element or one group over another, whose effects . . . traverse the entire [society] . . . It seems to me that first what needs to be understood is the multiplicity of relations of force that are immanent to the domain wherein they are exercised, and that are constitutive of its organization; the game that through incessant struggle and confrontation transforms them, reinforces them, inverts them; the supports these relations of force find in each other, so as to form a chain or system, or, on the other hand, the gaps, the contradictions that isolate them from each other . . . The condition of possibility of power . . . should not be sought in the primary existence of a central point, in a unique space

Genealogy of Knowledge
Influence of Nietzsche
Revealing complex history of established ideas
Power productive, not just repressive
Power creates resistance to itself

Figure 8.6 Foucault's Later Ideas.

of sovereignty whence would radiate derivative and descendent forms; it is the moving base of relations of force that incessantly induce, by their inequality, states of power, but always local and unstable. Omnipresence of power: not at all because it regroups everything under its invincible unity, but because it is produced at every instant, at every point, or moreover in every relation between one point and another. Power is everywhere: not that it engulfs everything, but that it comes from everywhere. (1981: 121–2)

This view of power is a serious rejection of standard Marxist ideas that power is the domination of one class over others, exercised through the power of the government to secure the domination of the ruling class(es). Instead, it reflects post-structuralist concerns to do with the complexity, multiplicity and above all instability of power relations. In this sense it has a lot in common with the 'post-Marxist', post-structuralist analysis of power offered by Laclau and Mouffe (see Chapter 3). Marxists have responded that Foucault ignores far too much the ongoing importance of class-based domination (Smart, 2002). At the same time Foucault was writing, the ongoing importance of class power was advocated in French social theory by Pierre Bourdieu (see Chapter 10). However, even more than a quarter-century after his death, Foucault remains a major figure in social theory, and it is difficult to imagine any understanding of what power is and how it operates in social life that did not seriously engage with his ideas.

Conclusion

In this chapter we have surveyed the development of earlier structuralist thinking into later post-structuralist theory. Although the contemporary consensus is that earlier structuralism is too limited an approach to use in a wholesale way today, nonetheless it is still rewarding to read authors like Saussure, Barthes and Althusser, because even if we cannot accept their ideas in full, they remain suggestive for understanding certain aspects of how sign-systems and discourses operate. As structuralism mutated into post-structuralism, more sophisticated and supple accounts of society and culture were formulated, the most important of which in social theory were Foucault's contributions. Post-structuralism remains a highly influential resource for theorizing today. Both structuralism and post-structuralism are at the roots of post-modern ways of thinking, and it is to these that we now turn.

Further Reading

Harland, R. (2010) *Superstructuralism*. London: Routledge.
Smart, B. (2002) *Michel Foucault*. London: Routledge.
Sturrock, J. (2002) *Structuralism*, 2nd edn. Oxford: Blackwell.
West, D. (2010) *Continental Philosophy: An Introduction*. Cambridge: Polity.

9

Post-Modernist Paradigms

From the mid 1980s onwards, words that became unavoidable throughout the social sciences and humanities were 'post-modernism' and 'post-modernity'. They had become *the* fashionable terms to use when talking about cultural and social issues. Claims were made, both inside universities and among cultural commentators like journalists, that Western societies had undergone such fundamental changes in the last few decades that one could no longer understand them as being 'modern', in the senses that the classical sociologists had understood that term (see Chapter 1). Instead, new 'post-modern' social and cultural situations had emerged, which were radically different from the 'modern' society they had allegedly replaced. It was argued that the understanding of these new conditions would mean abandoning established forms of theorizing, and embracing new, properly post-modern ways of thinking and seeing in order really to discern what was happening. In the 1980s and early 1990s, it seemed that post-modernist thinking was thoroughly shaking-up and undermining previously dominant theories and paradigms. But by the late 1990s, the high-tide of post-modernism in the social sciences and humanities was receding. By the early 2000s, post-modernism and post-modernity had themselves come to be seen by many as rather dated concepts. Now that the hype has died down, what remains of post-modern thinking that is still of interest and value?

In this chapter, we will first examine the various contexts from which post-modernist thinking derived and took inspiration from. Then we will turn to look at the main post-modernist thinkers, and their distinctive views on what post-modernism and post-modernity are, especially Jean-François Lyotard and Jean Baudrillard. We will then see how Marxist critics accused post-modernism of both ignoring and covering up the iniquities of the capitalist system. By reviewing the claims of the post-modernists, and the counter-claims of their critics, we can move towards an understanding of what today may be more and less useful in the post-modernist legacy.

What Are Post-Modernism and Post-Modernity?

Post-modernist thought emphasizes transgression and rejection of established parameters and boundaries, and radical scepticism about any attempts to identify the nature of something once and for all (Hassan, 1985). So it is paradoxical to try to give a single, fixed definition of post-modernism, post-modernity, post-modern culture and so on. This would defeat the purpose of post-modernist thought, which is to escape from what it sees as 'essentialist' ways of thinking, i.e. attempts to fix the meaning of something for ever.

A crucial feature of the intellectual terrain that constitutes post-modernism is its (deliberate) confusion of different ideas and attitudes. The values of confusion, mixing and mess were what post-modernist authors championed over what they saw as the overly restrictive notions that underpinned their great enemy, modernist thought (also known as 'modernism'). For post-modernists, modernist thought is characterized by a desire to create fixed categories which claim to be utterly true and objective. A central tenet of post-modernist thought, by contrast, is that claims to know something comprehensively and objectively are fictions. Things and their meanings are instead anarchic, refusing to be captured in the overly simplistic terms that modernist thought operates with, especially in its so-called 'scientific' versions.

Post-modern ideas centre around a rejection of what are taken to be the typically 'modernist' ideas of scientific knowledge, certainty and order. The opposite principles of subjective understandings, uncertainty and disorder were stressed and championed. Although post-modernist thought is suspicious of dualisms, which it takes to be overly simplistic and constraining, nonetheless the differences between modernism and post-modernism can be represented in a basic manner as involving the oppositions illustrated in Figure 9.1.

These emphases placed post-modernists in opposition not only to modernist thought but also the society they take to be its embodiment, namely modernity, which is usually seen (distantly following Max Weber – see Chapter 1) as a social order based around a bureaucratic and repressive form of rationality. The defence or pursuit of a more anarchic and irrational – and therefore more fluid and open – society informed the political desires of most post-modernist thinkers. Post-modernists also often viewed the transition from an *industrial* economy

Modernism	Post-Modernism
Stasis	Movement
Social and cultural innovations	No real innovations possible any more
Design	Chance
Certainty	Uncertainty
Rational control and order	Anarchy and disorder
Uniformity and regularity	Multiplicity and mess
Belief in objective knowledge	Scepticism about all forms of knowledge
– Science produces Truth	– Relativism; Science loses its monopoly on truth
Belief in social progress	No belief in anything
– the future will be better than the past	– the future is unpredictable – OR the future involves the endless recycling of past styles

Figure 9.1 The Values of Modernism and Post-Modernism – from a post-modernist's point of view.

Modernity	Post-Modernity
Rational order and control: bureaucracy	Anarchy and irrationality: beyond bureaucracy
Industrial economy	Post-industrial economy
Importance of social class	Decline, or death, of social class
Identity singular; conferred by society	Identities plural; freely chosen by individual
Coherent social order	Incoherent, fragmented social (dis)order
Coherent culture; shaped by class structure	Incoherent, kaleidoscopic culture

Figure 9.2 The Nature of Modernity and Post-Modernity – from a post-modernist's point of view.

(based around factories and heavy industry) to a *post-industrial* economy (based around information technology, and electronic flows of information and knowledge) as one of the major features distinguishing modernity from post-modernity. These points are summarized in Figure 9.2.

The movement towards a post-industrial economy was seen by post-modernists to have involved several very important changes in how people thought and acted – especially how they thought about themselves (Lash and Urry, 1987). While in modernity social class had fundamentally structured social order, post-modernity was seen to be a period when social class was much less salient, or was absent altogether in terms both of how society was organized, and how people thought of themselves. From this perspective, the typically 'modern' individual first and foremost saw themselves as the member of a particular social class. But the typical post-modern individual would see class as only one factor among many informing their sense of themselves – their identity – if they took account of social class at all (Pakulski and Waters, 1996).

In modernity, it was the wider social order that had conferred upon the individual their sense of who they were, and how they were to be seen by others. Once this identity was conferred, it was very difficult to change, and probably could not be changed at all. But under the conditions of post-modernity, the nature of society itself had changed, from a relatively strong coherent social order to one characterized by multiplicity, fragmentation and a lack of coherence. Under such conditions, there was no longer a strong and unified 'society' or social class structure which could confer identities on individuals. Instead, the fragmented nature of post-modern social reality encouraged – indeed forced – individuals to forge their own identities and sense of self.

This they could do by choosing from a wide range of identities available to them in the kaleidoscopic cultural supermarket that was post-modern culture, where practically every sort of self was available to be adopted for one's own personal use. Thus whereas in the first half of the twentieth century a person's identity as, for example, a heterosexual working-class woman was imposed upon them by the wider society in which they lived, a society that allowed no deviations from that conferred identity, in post-modern conditions it was possible to pick, mix and discard identities, senses of self, and the ways of acting that were associated with them, as one pleased. While not all post-modernist thinkers emphasized the liberation of individual subjective freedom, they generally agreed that while modernity had been a coherent social and cultural order centred around an industrial economy and stable social classes, the post-industrial world of post-modernity was far looser, more complicated and characterized by multiplicity and movement, not modernist stability and predictability (Featherstone, 1991).

The Origins of Post-Modernism

Although post-modernist thinking very much took off in the mid 1980s, its intellectual roots can be traced back to the late 1960s. At this period, certain sorts of intellectuals could look around at the society and culture of the time, and start to discern the beginnings of the sorts of changes described above. The first glimmerings of the shift to a post-industrial economy could be seen, with, for example, the widespread appearance of computers in workplaces for the first time (Bell, 1976), and the increasing ubiquity and importance of advertising culture, with its emphasis on superficial effects over deep meanings (Baudrillard, 1996b [1968]). If current society was describable as 'modernity', then it seemed logical to call the new post-industrial social order coming into view 'post-modernity'. Likewise, if one was thinking about culture, in the sense of arts and aesthetic matters, since the early twentieth century, the latest and most advanced new works had been labelled 'modernist' (Calinescu, 1987). But new kinds of art from at least the mid 1960s onwards seemed to be breaking with the conventions of 'modernist' art. These could plausibly be called 'post-modernist' because they seemed to have something radically novel about them. Such thoughts were formulated by a range of different intellectuals and artists, especially in the United States and France, in the fields of architecture, the arts and philosophy.

For some younger American architects of the time, modernist architecture was seen to be dying. Modernism in architecture was associated with styles that had been developed since the 1920s, which emphasized geometrical shapes, straight lines and plainness of design. Such architecture was primarily ascetic in temperament, avoiding bright colours and non-geometrical shapes. The iconic figure of this style was the Swiss architect Le Corbusier [1887–1965], who had pioneered the notion of architecture as being based around a 'spirit of order'. Modernist architects influenced by Le Corbusier believed that the urban environment could be fundamentally rebuilt using their designs, to eliminate all forms of disorder. But what had been novel and progressive in the 1920s had by the early 1970s come to seem rigid and authoritarian. Many modernist designs for housing estates in America and Europe had become alienating slums rather than the utopian communities their designers had hoped for (Jencks, 1992).

For younger American architects like Robert Venturi, post-modernist architecture was the way ahead, as it had the potential to turn the values of modernism upside down. It would reject 'a view of life as essentially simple and orderly' in place of an outlook that viewed the world as 'complex and ironic' (Venturi, 1966: 23). In post-modernist design, there was to be 'richness of meaning rather than clarity of meaning' (ibid.: 17). This was to be achieved by mixing-up different styles that had previously been kept apart, producing collage effects expressing disorder and chaos. The new architecture took different established styles (e.g. gothic, art nouveau) and 'quoted' from them in ironic and playful ways, rejecting the perceived humourlessness of modernism.

The early post-modernist architects found inspiration from the casinos of Las Vegas (Venturi et al., 1977 [1972]). The facades of the casinos involved juxtaposing a wide variety of otherwise incompatible styles, like ancient Rome and Egypt together with nineteenth-century Paris. Each of these was a *pastiche* of the original, a clearly fake rendering of the original style. The mixing together of all these faked styles broke all the rules of modernism. Purity and coherence were ditched in favour of chaos and mess. Modernism's desire to separate rigidly 'high' and 'low' cultures was rejected in favour of muddling these up. Post-modernism involved the blurring or destroying of all the boundaries that modernism had created and wanted to police. Post-modernism in the arts celebrated popular culture like TV shows, comic strips and trashy magazines, the very things that modernism despised because they were not proper 'art' (Huyssen, 1984).

Post-modernist architects noticed that the gaudy facades of the Las Vegas casinos also hid what was behind them, namely the bland modern buildings – in simple, block-like shapes – that housed the hotel and gaming spaces. Everything in Las Vegas appeared only on the surface. There were no hidden meanings to be discovered and decoded. The hidden, difficult-to-understand meanings of works of art were one of the main focal points of modernism in the arts (see the modernist ideas of Adorno in Chapter 3). Las Vegas expressed a cultural condition where there were no hidden meanings, only surface meanings that either were very easy to understand or were completely meaningless. Post-modernists liked the way that Las Vegas 'meant' nothing: when you scratched its surface, no hidden depths were to be found. This was what liberated it from the overly serious modernist search for supposed hidden meanings. Two possibilities emerged from this situation, each of which characterizes different strains of post-modernist thinking. On the one hand, the shallow, all-on-the-surface culture of Las Vegas points to a world where all meaning has evaporated. In this sense, post-modernism is about the death of meaning. But, on the other hand, the wild mixture of styles at play on the Las Vegas strip could be taken to indicate not the absence of meaning, but in fact a situation alive with multiple meanings, where individuals are free to interpret meaning in any ways they want.

Both these more optimistic and more pessimistic strains in post-modernism had associated political dispositions. If post-modernity was a world evacuated of meaning, then the political stance of the intellectual was merely to report passively on this state of affairs – the position of Jean Baudrillard comes close to this. But if a more optimistic view of post-modernity is adopted, where there are multiple meanings which can be actively interpreted and combined by individuals according to their fancy, then politics is about celebrating and augmenting this condition of multiplicity. Thus post-modernist architecture was intended to be much more 'democratic' than its modernist predecessor. In the latter, the meaning of the building had been under the control of the architect. But given the multiple combinations of style and effect in post-modernist architecture, the meaning was now seen to be much less fixed, and much more open to the interpretative imaginations of members of the public. It was not the architect – or any other kind of artist – who dictated what the building – or any other cultural product, like a painting or sculpture – was to 'mean'. Meaning was democratized, because individual audience members were free to use their own imaginations to say what the thing they were viewing meant. Optimistic post-modernism saw itself as liberatory of human capacities for imagination and freedom of thought, freeing these from the dead hand of modernist dogmas. But pessimistic post-modernism regarded the post-modern epoch as one where imagination was dead, smothered by an excess of meaning, such that there was no real meaning left any more.

The response to post-modernist innovations by modernist critics in architecture and the arts was that post-modernism was cynical, shallow and lacking a critical perspective on art's social and political functions (Huyssen, 1984). Modernists were appalled by what they saw as the super-ficiality and triviality of post-modernism, arguing that it was in fact a disguised means of supporting the social and cultural status quo, because it lacked critical perspectives on issues such as power and exploitation.

From Politics to Philosophy

At the same time as these post-modernist innovations were happening, especially in the USA, post-modern impulses were beginning to be felt in philosophy too, especially in France. This trend was rooted in French social and political conditions of the time. Throughout the 1960s, France was split between politically conservative forces headed by President Charles de Gaulle, and radical anti-establishment voices, located in the Communist-dominated trades unions and in the newly radicalized student movement. In May 1968, tensions that had been simmering for several years burst out into the open, with mass demonstrations, riots and violent clashes between student protestors and police. The hopes of the student movement expressed in the 'events' of May 1968 involved the desire to build a freer, more democratic France centred around a socialist economy. Marxist theories of various types were loudly advocated, and seemed to be able to guide the revolutionary events that were unfolding. But after initial successes where it seemed that the protestors might topple the government, the latter seized the initiative, this being made possible in large part because of splits in the anti-government movement. The government regained the upper hand, and the political status quo was re-established, fracturing the student movement and leading to a series of fractious recriminations (Bourdieu, 1988).

The apparent failure of the May 'events' had a profound effect on the younger generation of intellectuals, some of whom had been directly involved in the protests, while others had publicly supported them from the sidelines. The key post-modernist philosophers who emerged in the 1970s were of that generation of French intellectuals who grew very disillusioned with radical politics in general, and Marxist politics in particular, after the failure of 1968. It seemed to many that the promises of Marxism – that revolution was inevitable and would create a better society – were false. Many intellectuals thus moved towards 'post-Marxist' outlooks (Therborn, 2010). These often retained the anti-establishment nature of Marxist thought, remaining unconvinced of the claims that the existing system made for itself, especially the idea of 'progress'. This was the notion that society today is already very good (democratic, egalitarian, liberating for the individual, etc.), but in the future it will evolve into something even better. This notion was common to both defenders of capitalist society *and* their apparent enemies, Marxist thinkers.

Post-Marxist philosophies rejected the idea of 'progress' in both its capitalist and Marxist versions, claiming instead that there was no particular direction in human history, and that there was no way of telling what the future would be like. In addition, post-Marxist philosophies rejected most of the other central tenets of orthodox Marxism, especially the claim that Marxism was the only true science of society and as a result was the only way of having 'objective' knowledge about social conditions. In this way, Marxism's scepticism about the social status quo was retained, but its positive diagnoses about how to study society and how to change it, were ditched. Along with Marxist certainties, other grand claims about the nature of reality, including social reality, were subjected to sustained criticism, and rejected in favour of what were seen as less grand, over-arching accounts of the social world. Post-modernist philosophy was very much a product of the post-Marxist tenor of French thought in the after-math of 1968.

One of the leading proponents of post-Marxist ideas was Jean-Francois Lyotard [1924–98]. Lyotard's post-modernism is essentially an argument about the nature of knowledge. It concerns how knowledge has become fractured and fragmented in 'the post-modern condition'. This was the title of his most famous book (Lyotard, 1984 [1979]), which began life as a report for the government of Quebec, making it one of the oddest documents ever commissioned by government officials. Lyotard drew upon two earlier philosophers who have often been presented as anticipa-tors of post-modernism, namely Friedrich Nietzsche (see Chapter 1) and Ludwig Wittgenstein. Each in their own ways had argued that modernist philosophy falsely claimed that there could be unproblematic, objective knowledge of the natural and social worlds, and that science was the key to absolute truth. Both had presented radical ideas about how there is no one single truth but rather only a series of particular, localized 'truths' in the plural. (These ideas were also important for Michel Foucault, another post-Marxist thinker – see Chapter 8.) Nietzsche and Wittgenstein seemed to have anticipated the central post-Marxist and post-modernist theme: that no one perspective (e.g. Marxism) or method of generating knowl-edge (e.g. natural scientific experiments) had a monopoly on truth, even though they claimed to possess this. Instead, truths were plural, and were relative to particular times and places. What counted as 'true' in one context might count as untrue in another. There was no way of deciding which truth was truer than others. The fundamental uncertainty and contingency both of human life and of knowledge about it, had to be acknowledged.

This is why Lyotard famously defines post-modernist thought – and more broadly, the contemporary social and cultural condition of post-modernity – as 'incredulity towards metanarratives' (1984 [1979]: xxiv). 'Metanarratives' are overarching, apparently all-encompassing accounts or stories, that purport to explain most or all things in the world. Contemporary social and political metanarratives tend to focus on what they see as human freedom and emancipation. Among these are the liberal belief in increasing democracy and progress as modernity has developed, and the Marxist idea of communist revolution and the complete emancipation of the working class in a future communist society. These were the central ideas that have, according to Lyotard, underpinned the development of Western modernity. And, like all meta-narratives, they are not true. They are fictions, the ideas of particular interested groups who pass them off as being of universal interest and applicability.

Lyotard insists that knowledge is always particular and subjective, rather than universal and objective. Different groups each have their own 'narratives', their own particular ways of understanding the world and themselves. What must be recognized is that each of these 'mini-narra-tives' is in and of itself valid, and that one cannot be evaluated or criticized from the point of view of another, because no narrative is more true than any other. Lyotard's view of knowledge is that it is inevitably and always disparate and fragmented. Knowledge has always been like this. But in particular societies, specific metanarratives have operated to cover this up, from Christianity in medieval Europe, to liberalism and Marxism in modernity.

In this sense, what can be called typically post-modern conditions of uncertainty and subjectivity have always been part of human life. They were part of modernity too, even if such a society was based on covering up this condition (Readings, 1991). So for Lyotard, the 'post-modern con-dition' is less a period in history (as some other post-modernists have argued) and more a kind of mindset that has existed for a long period of time in different societies. But this mindset, based around the acknowl-edgement of uncertainty and epistemological insecurity, has for the most part been subjugated by metanarratives which confidently announce their own monopoly on the truth.

However, for Lyotard the contemporary situation is distinctive, in that for the first time, the post-modernist mindset has become the predomi-nant one, with the effect of widespread 'incredulity towards metanarra-tives' among all sectors of the population. This is because in the present day, most people do not believe in the allegedly absolute truths and certainties that the metanarratives of modernity (liberalism, science,

---

Knowledge
post-modern analysis of metanarratives; epistemological relativism

Subjectivity/Identity
post-modern scepticism

post-modernity as scepticism of metanarratives; proliferation of specific narratives

---

Figure 9.3 Summary of Lyotard.

Marxism, etc.) emphasized. Thus contemporary Western society is describable as 'post-modernity', for it is a social order based around typically post-modern ways of thinking, a mindset that embraces relativity and contingency, and rejects the claims of metanarratives. Such a society has relinquished what have to be seen as the delusions of modernist knowledge, and has embraced the principles of doubt and a lack of certainty about anything.

Media and the Death of Reality

Along with Lyotard, the other major post-Marxist thinker who very much shaped subsequent post-modernist philosophy was Jean Baudrillard [1929–2007]. Baudrillard took some of the major emphases of post-Marxism in philosophy, and used them to examine what he regarded as the central social and cultural trends of post-modernity.

Baudrillard's early works, published in the late 1960s and early 1970s (1996b [1968]), drew very much on the post-structuralist thinking then emerging as part of post-Marxist trends in philosophy (see Chapter 8). These works regarded contemporary social life as a realm where material reality was disappearing, not just being hidden but in fact actually being wholly replaced by systems of signs, leading to 'a world no longer given but instead produced' by endless series of signifiers (1996b [1968]: 29). In such a context, all objects become manufactured commodities, deprived of any meanings they may once have possessed.

Baudrillard here was using the concepts of *use-value* (the uses people can put particular objects to) and *exchange-value* (the monetary value of those objects) that Marx had worked with. But as his thought developed, Baudrillard, in line with other French thinkers of the time, became more and more dissatisfied with Marxian ideas. Baudrillard (1975) claimed Marxist analysis was wholly outmoded, because while Marx had analysed the production of *commodities* (products made for sale in the capitalist market), he did not account for what was under post-modern conditions the key factor of social life, namely the production of *signs*. In such a situation, the meaning of an object comes not from its use-value (e.g. the meaning of a pair of jeans is the warmth they afford to the wearer), but from its commodity-value (e.g. the meaning of the jeans is dictated by the designer label attached to them). It is not the object's material qualities that are important and recognized by people, but rather it is the symbolic value, projected onto the object by systems of signs (discourses), that is seen and believed to be the important thing. So the jeans in themselves, as a material product, count for little or nothing; what seems to people to be important is their symbolic value – in this case, whether they have a designer label or not, and if they do, what the designer label tells us about the person wearing the trousers. The meaning and 'reality' of the material object (the physical pair of trousers) is obliterated in favour of the symbol (the designer logo). Given this, Baudrillard rejected Marxism because he believed it was founded on a certain myth, the idea that ultimately the value of any product can be explained by the amount of labour that went into making it. The value actually rests in the symbolic meaning projected onto the object by systems of signs, not the object itself or the production process that made it.

Contemporary capitalism is seen by Baudrillard (1975) to be much more irrational, uncontrollable and beyond human intervention than Marx could have imagined. Baudrillard sees this system as operating according to its own complex, possibly unknowable logics rather than being manipulated by a ruling class. The idea of class-based domination is relinquished by Baudrillard in favour of seeing systems of signs as wholly autonomous of other factors, and running away from human control, towards ever more frenzied forms of directionless change. Systems of signs and symbols have taken on a life of their own, and this is the essence of the post-modern condition. This is the post-modernist version of the modernist idea of alienation (see Chapter 1), where things (in this case symbols) originally made by human beings come to take independent existences of their own, dominating and controlling the people who made them.

Baudrillard also argues that under post-modern conditions, there can be no distinction between truth and falsity, a myth that Marx and other modernists had uncritically believed in. Nowadays there is no 'reality' based in use-values to compare to the falsity of exchange-values. Instead the whole value of a thing rests in its sign, which is completely on display. Marxist theory is defunct, because it relied on making a distinction between the surface appearance of a situation (its ideological representation) and the actual truth of it (the power of a ruling class to control other classes). In post-modernity, everything is on the surface and entirely open to view. There are no hidden depths to be penetrated. As Marxism cannot understand this situation, a new, fully post-modern type of thinking is required. This involves 'surfing' along the surfaces of systems of signs and symbols, watching how they mutate and transform, without trying to find a more profound truth behind or below them. Post-modernist analysis accepts that all that exists are surfaces with no substance underneath or beyond them.

Baudrillard (1983b) applied these ideas to the mass media, the most important feature of post-modernity according to him. He emphasizes the utterly unpredictable and irrational nature of the signs and symbols that travel through the media today. These are like 'blizzards' of information, involving constantly undulating transfigurations of meaning. The key idea here is 'simulation'. This does not involve the creation of 'false' systems of images, as Marxism argued, because 'truth, reference [to 'real' objects] and objective causes [of events] have ceased to exist' (1983b: 6).

Drawing on a key idea of structuralism (see Chapter 8), Baudrillard argues that particular signs and symbols now do not stand for the objects they apparently refer to. Instead, real objects no longer exist, and signs and symbols *create* the objects they supposedly merely reflect. Such signs and symbols are *simulacra*. Instead of reality being reflected in images, images now create reality itself. This is the condition of *hyperreality*. Post-modern culture involves a reality created solely by shifting and unstable systems of symbols and signs. There is nothing 'real' being hidden by this hyperreality. The only reality we have any more is the fabricated reality produced by systems of signs and symbols, especially in the media. There is a 'death of the real', a situation not intended by anyone, or controlled by any powerful groups. It is just the result of the unstoppable and uncontrollable proliferation of reality-constituting symbols in a media-dominated world (Baudrillard, 1996a). The media claim to represent external reality. But they in fact fabricate it.

Baudrillard understood Disneyland theme parks as expressions of hyperreality. Their fake European palaces and make-believe world of cartoon characters obviously point to a world of simulacra, of signs and symbols that have no hidden meanings. Baudrillard also regarded Disneyland as having a particular social function: it exists in order 'to conceal the fact that it is the "real" country, all of "real" America, which *is* Disneyland . . . Disneyland is presented as imaginary in order to make us believe that the rest' of America is real. In fact it is 'real' America which is now hyperreal (Baudrillard, 1983b: 25). The ideas associated with Disneyland do not hide social reality, they do not seek to cover up the exploitative nature of American capitalism, as Marxists would claim. Instead, Disneyland is a good examplar of post-modernity because what it hides is the fact that there is nothing to hide. America – and by extension, all advanced capitalist countries – is now in a hyperreal condition where all meaning lies wholly on the surface, and there is nothing beneath the surface that needs either to be hidden by powerful groups or uncovered by radical critics like Marxists.

Under conditions of hyperreality, information and meaning are both utterly clear and totally incoherent at the same time. The clarity Baudrillard refers to as the 'obscenity' of communication. Because there are no hidden depths to images, and all their informational content is on the surface, their meaning is utterly apparent. They are obscene in the same sense as pornography is obscene: everything is totally clear, nothing is hidden, everything is on the surface (Baudrillard, 1990b: 181). But at the same time, hyperreality is a situation where things become ever more unclear. There is so much information being produced by the media that it all starts to make no sense. Think of the masses of different TV channels, pumping out vast amounts of information twenty-four hours a day. The multiplicity of different messages sent out, encompassing everything from news reports to soap operas, music shows and historical dramas, create at the level of meaning chaos that is utterly incoherent. Information overload leads to feelings of 'vertigo' and 'ecstasy' among those exposed to these media – which is everyone in a post-modern society. There is so much meaning constantly available, and wholly unavoidable, that nothing makes sense any more in the 'dizzying over-multiplication' of messages and symbols where 'all sense is lost' (Baudrillard, 1990a: 9).

Today the mass media can no longer operate as propaganda tools for powerful groups, as Marxists wrongly still think. The identification of certain messages as propaganda requires identifying a 'real' situation

Knowledge
post-modern 'surfing' of hyperreal signs

Subjectivity/identity
post-modern apathy and information overload
post-modernity as hyperreality and proliferation of simulacra

Figure 9.4 Summary of Baudrillard.

which they disguise. But this distinction is obliterated by hyperreality. Baudrillard's (1995) most infamous claim was that the Gulf War of 1991 'did not happen'. That war played out as a televized media spectacle like a film or video game, rather than as coverage of a 'real' event. The series of signs and symbols that purported to describe what was really happening were actually only simulacra, images which claim to represent external reality, but which in fact construct that reality. The first Gulf War was experienced by the vast majority of people in the world, with the exception of the tiny minority actually doing the fighting, as if that war were like a Hollywood film or a video game. The reality we perceive has become so thoroughly mediated, it has become pointless to try to unpick truth from fiction any more. Baudrillard also argued that we should not think that audiences are at all influenced by the messages they receive from the media, as Marxists like those in the early Frankfurt School had believed (see Chapter 3). In hyperreality, the 'masses' are wholly disinterested and impassive, believing nothing at all. Information from the media 'flows through them . . . but diffuses throughout them without leaving a trace' (Baudrillard, 1983a: 2). They are not alienated, because there is no 'reality' to be alienated from. They are not deceived, because deception is impossible in a hyperreal world where all meanings are on the surface.

Back to Marx?

Post-modernism was a central part of post-Marxist trends in philosophy. Post-modernism very much had Marxism in its sights, understanding it both as a modernist metanarrative which could not possibly explain all the things it purported to, and as rooted in modernist distinctions, especially truth/falsity and surface/depth, which could no longer apply in conditions of hyperreality. In response, Marxist critics had some very barbed things to say about post-modernism.

The endeavour to slay what was seen as the post-modernist monster was taken up by those advocating a classical Marxist position, such as Callinicos (1989a). For authors like this, post-modern theory was simply an uncritical form of thought that hides the realities of capitalist society by passing the latter off under the more acceptable label of 'post-modernity'. Post-modernism had nothing to teach Marxism, because the central institution of contemporary societies was the capitalist economy, and ideologies continued to circulate which operated to hide the exploitative and iniquitous reality of capitalist society. Marxism had to continue to pursue its analytic strategy of revealing what existed beneath the surface glitter of capitalist social order, distinctions between true and false continuing to be relevant as long as capitalism continued to disguise its own nature, as it necessarily had to.

For Marxist critics, post-modern culture was seen to be little more than the thinnest of dressings upon the aggressive capitalist socio-economic orders being fostered in the 1980s by Ronald Reagan and Margaret Thatcher. By denying there is no reality underneath the surface of simulacra, post-modernism denied the truly exploitative, cruel and harsh realities of contemporary capitalism that are, for Marxists, at the root of all forms of culture today (Kellner, 1989). Generally speaking, Marx's original base and superstructure model (see Chapters 1 and 3) continued to be true, in that where post-modern theorizing had gone seriously wrong was in underplaying the importance of the capitalist economic base, still the most important part of any social order, and the entity which created the various cultural forms which post-modernists like Baudrillard so adulated.

Some Marxists were prepared to cede more ground to the post-modernists, seeking to tame post-modernism and utilize some of its insights, rather than to kill it off completely. For the Marxist geographer David Harvey (1989), the term 'post-modern' did indeed accurately depict the kind of cultural superstructure produced today by a new phase of the capitalist economy in a period of 'flexible accumulation'. For Harvey, Baudrillard's emphasis on constantly and rapidly changing systems of signs and symbols being characteristic of post-modern culture is correct. But Baudrillard fails to account for how and why this situation is created. Post-modern culture is produced by a radically new form of flexible capitalism which has appeared since the 1970s. 'Flexible accumulation' is the key characteristic of a post-industrial economy. In this context, goods are still manufactured, but not in the manner of fixed production lines that remain in particular countries for decades, as had been the case in 'modernist' capitalism up until the 1970s. Under the regime of flexible accumulation, companies respond much faster than before in exploiting opportunities in new markets. Capitalist production becomes ever more geographically mobile, for example rapidly laying off workers in one country when production is to be moved to another country to exploit emerging opportunities such as lower taxes and wages. At a more purely post-industrial level, flexible accumulation has involved capitalism finding new ways of generating profits, engineered through instantaneous electronic flows of communication across the globe, such as through playing currency markets, corporate raiding and asset-stripping (Harvey, 1989).

This economic situation is characterized by dizzyingly rapid movements of both information and people operating 'in ways that seem almost oblivious of the constraints of time and space' (Harvey, 1989: 164). It is this state of affairs – involving new and complicated senses of time and space – which produces what the post-modernists called post-modern culture, a condition of permanent flux and uncertainty. In sum, Harvey claimed that present-day culture was certainly post-modern, but it had been produced by the development of something essentially 'modern', namely the capitalist economy, its restless pursuit of profits and its tendencies towards innovation and global expansion.

Another major intervention came from Fredric Jameson, an American follower of the early Frankfurt School (see Chapter 3). His argument was neatly encapsulated in the title of his major work *Post-modernism: Or the Cultural Logic of Late Capitalism* (1991). Adorno and Horkheimer (1992 [1944]: 126) had arguably anticipated post-modernist themes of hyperreality back in the 1940s, when they had warned of how the Culture Industry creates a situation whereby 'life is becoming indistinguishable from the movies'. Jameson's (1991) Frankurt-style analysis attempted to take these sorts of insights further. Post-modern culture does indeed exist, but has to be seen as the cultural expression of 'late capitalism'. This is understood, in similar fashion to Harvey, as the novel form of global capitalism that has developed since the 1970s in which transnational companies, tied to no particular home country, are involved in a 'vertiginous new dynamic' (ibid.: xix) of rapid and ever-changing transactions spanning every part of the globe (for more on globalization processes, see Chapter 12) .

For Jameson, post-modern culture embodies this state of affairs. On his view, post-modern culture is primarily about *style*. Not only is

---

Post-modern culture:
depthless; fragmented; hides real conditions

Capitalist economic base:
globalization, electronic communications, rapidity of movement

---

Figure 9.5 Summary of Marxist Responses to Post-Modernism.

style celebrated over substance and meaning, but the former comes dangerously close to obliterating the latter. Jameson wanted to instigate a critical reading of post-modernist culture that could see through its fetishization of style, so as to reveal its hidden effects on social life. Jameson indicates that post-modern culture does not create any new styles of its own, but rather plays about with parodies and pastiches of previous styles. Jameson singles out for particular attention films made in the mid 1980s, such as David Lynch's *Blue Velvet*, which involved deliberately 'fake', hyperreal representations of small-town America in the 1950s. In such movies, the 'real' 1950s – a society characterized by repressive norms to do with gender roles and sexual repression, rampant racism, and condemnation of any sort of non-conformity – are ignored, replaced by the flat surfaces of images taken from 1950s films and TV series. The past is reduced to being a mere succession of stereotypical images. The real history of oppression and exploitation is conjured away in favour of Disneyland-type hyperreal surfaces. Thus audiences are encouraged to forget how things really were, and not to think critically about how things really are today. Post-modern culture encourages uncritical thinking, because it compels people to remain at the surface of things – even though there is a reality underneath the surface, and a very ugly reality at that.

Conclusion

The claims of Fredric Jameson illustrate the fact that the fundamental dispute between Marxists and post-modernists came down to two issues: whether there was a reality beyond simulacra, and if there was, was Marxism the right means to understand it, or an arrogant and outdated metanarrative that falsely claimed to have a monopoly on the truth? The debates between post-modernists and their critics ran throughout the 1980s and on into the early 1990s. By the mid 1990s, the use of the words 'post-modernism' and 'post-modernity' began to wane in social theory, and 'globalization' more and more became the centre of attention. Having been a very fashionable position in the 1980s, at the present time very few social theorists would use the label post-modernist to describe themselves – fashion has moved on. But we can still pose the question as to what remains of interest and use in post-modernist thought.

There are some areas where post-modernism continues to have a positive impact on social theorizing. First, post-modernist criticisms of meta-narratives have led to a general sensitization in the world of social theory about the perils of uncritically making grand claims for particular theoretical systems. Lyotard's points as to how confidently proclaimed meta-narratives can crush other, more particular forms of knowledge, have been a lesson learned by many theorists. Today it is probably markedly more difficult to make grand, sweeping statements about how particular theories have vast explanatory capacities than it was in the 1960s, before post-modernism's claims about the contested and fragmented nature of knowledge were widely known. Second, although often very overstated, Baudrillardian ideas about a world constituted in and through mediated symbols have come to have special resonance in a situation that would have seemed unlikely when Baudrillard started writing in the 1960s, namely the endemic presence of the internet, its increasingly complex virtual universe, and its far-reaching, if uneven, ramifications for social order and social action. Perhaps Baudrillardian ideas are now, and will be in the future, more provocative than ever. Finally, contemporary Marxism had to contend with the various post-modernist challenges, and in so doing it emerged both with its older ideas sharpened up and with new understandings of present-day capitalism. Marxism today owes something to its post-modernist foes, not least due to the fact that it had to enter into new cultural terrains where it had not trodden fully before. Even if post-modernism in some ways is a museum-piece of the 1980s, its presence continues to be felt in various diffuse but constructive ways in social theory today.

Further Reading

Bauman, Z. (1997) *Post-Modernity and its Discontents*. Cambridge: Polity.

Featherstone, M. (1991) *Consumer Culture and Post-Modernism*. London: Sage.

Harvey, D. (1989) *The Condition of Post-Modernity: An Inquiry into the Origins of Cultural Change*. Oxford: Blackwell.

Jameson, F. (1991) *Post-Modernism: Or, the Cultural Logic of Late Capitalism*. London: Verso.

10

Structurationist Paradigms

Structuration theory is one of the central dimensions of contemporary social thought. It involves ambitious attempts to reconcile what authors in this area see as the unsatisfactory nature of all previous forms of social theory. From a structurationist perspective, previous social theories throughout the twentieth century could not give a satisfactory account of how societies are made and remade over time. They could not explain properly how societies are made by individuals and their interactions, at the same time as acknowledging how social forces, institutions and structures influence and shape those individuals and their interactions (Schatzki, 1997).

As we saw in Chapter 1, Marx (2000 [1852]) had already made this point when he said that people 'make history but not in conditions of their own choosing'. Human beings make the societies they live in, but not in ways they have complete control over. This is because they inherit from the past particular ways of thinking and acting, these very much influencing how people act and think in the present. But people are not completely prisoners of the past – when people act and interact with each other, they do not just reproduce what has come before, they also change it, either intentionally or unintentionally. From a structurationist viewpoint, what one must explain is both *social reproduction* (social order being reproduced over time by people continuing to act in ways inherited from the past) and *social transformation* (how social order is changed by people, intentionally or unintentionally, through their interactions).

Previous social theories are seen by structurationists as privileging one of these dimensions over the other. Thus the various kinds of Marxism (Chapter 3) seem to overemphasize the power of class-based societies to persist over time, reproducing class relationships of power and domination. Likewise functionalist theory, especially that of Parsons (Chapter 2), overly focuses on how social systems reproduce themselves, regarding individual actors as mere 'cultural dopes' who carry out actions and interactions which the social system requires them to do. These sorts of theories are seen as putting too much stress on social reproduction, at the expense of social transformation. They do so because they start with unsatisfactory concepts of 'society' and 'social structure', and then deduce how these allegedly dictate what individuals do. They are thus overly 'objectivist', examining things solely from the point of view of how social structures compel particular forms of action. On the other hand, various kinds of micro-sociologies, including Weberian action theory, symbolic interactionism, ethnomethodology, and Rational Choice Theory (see Chapters 4, 5 and 6) are seen as over-privileging individual actions and interactions, failing to explain satisfactorily how these are shaped by broader social factors and how they contribute to the reproduction and transformation over time of wider social order. These sorts of theories put too much stress on social transformation, at the expense of social reproduction. They do so because they start with unsatisfactory concepts of 'individuals', 'actions' and 'interactions', which are too 'subjectivist' – examining things solely from the point of view of actors – to give a satisfactory account of how social order is maintained and transformed over time (Hollis, 1977).

Structuration theory therefore seeks to overcome what it sees as the failings of earlier social theory, avoiding both its 'objectivist' and 'subjectivist' extremes, seeking to overcome these by forging a new terminology to describe how people both *create and are created* by social order, and how the interacting activities of individuals leads to both social reproduction and transformation. The very word 'structuration' attempts to indicate that the things conventionally referred to by the words (social) 'structure' and (individual) 'action' are not separate entities, but in fact elements of one single process, the 'constitution of society', as Giddens (1984) puts it. The two most important contemporary theorists of structuration are Anthony Giddens [b. 1938] and Pierre Bourdieu [1930–2002]. Both have attempted to escape what they see as the endless oscillation in previous theoretical endeavours between 'objectivist' and 'subjectivist' orientations. Both have attempted to abolish the conventional divide between 'structure' and 'action', by radically redefining the terms used to describe social order and the activities of people within it.

From the 1970s onwards, they both put forward distinctive visions of structuration, that have in common a focus on social 'practices' rather than 'actions'. Practices are everyday activities that are routinized. 'Social structure' is just simply routinized practices, and the memories in people's heads that allow them to keep doing those practices in those ways over time (Reckwitz, 2002). Thus 'social structure' and 'society' are not 'things' existing outside of individuals and their practices – they *are* those practices. Instead of seeing what individuals do as 'actions' produced by conscious choices (as does Weberian Action Theory and Rational Choice Theory), a focus on practices draws from phenomenology (Chapter 5) the idea of 'practical consciousness', the notion that what most people do most of the time is neither wholly conscious (as Rational Choice Theory in particular would have it) nor wholly unconscious (as certain sorts of Marxism and functionalism would see it), but semi-conscious. People are 'knowledgeable' in that they know how to do all sorts of everyday activities; but many of these activities are done without consciously thinking about how to do them. We just 'know' how to greet people we meet in the street; we just 'know' how to buy groceries at the supermarket. But we do not usually reflect on this knowledge, as it is part of the stock of taken-for-granted knowledge that makes up, and makes possible, our everyday 'lifeworlds'. This, then, is the realm of 'practices', which constitute social order, and which in turn are shaped by social order. It is practices which lead – generally unintentionally – to both social reproduction and social transformation. It is practices which are at the heart of structuration processes, and a focus on them is meant to avoid lapsing into the old, unsatisfactory terminology of 'structure' or 'action', allowing us to see more clearly how societies are both maintained and transformed.

Despite their shared focus on structuration and practices, there are very significant differences between the ideas of Bourdieu and Giddens. Although both draw on phenomenology, the other streams of thought they each draw upon differs markedly, Bourdieu looking more to certain ideas about power in Weber, Marx and Durkheim, and Giddens looking more to ethnomethodology and the philosophy of Wittgenstein for understandings of interaction. This divergence is because of their brands of structuration being developed for somewhat different purposes, including political purposes. Bourdieu regarded his sociology as one aimed at revealing the nature and operation of *forms of domination* (which Bourdieu calls forms of 'symbolic violence'), especially by the higher classes over the lower classes, but also by men over women, and ethnic majorities over ethnic minorities (Lane, 2000). This is clearly related to Marxism, although Bourdieu is far from being a mainstream Marxist, for equally well he could be called a radical, left-wing inheritor of Weber's analyses of power. In his later life Bourdieu took on the role of public intellectual, becoming an outspoken critic of neo-liberal policies in France and elsewhere (Bourdieu, 1998a). By contrast, although it was developed from the late 1970s onwards, in the 1990s Giddens (1994b, 2000) put his structuration theory at the service of the 'third way' politics associated with Bill Clinton and Tony Blair, which endeavoured to recast 'soft left' social democratic politics into an age of global capitalism. Structuration theory was also used by Giddens to diagnose contemporary social and cultural change, including globalization processes (Giddens (1990) – see Chapter 12) and transformations in self-identity and intimacy (Giddens, 1991, 1992).

For Bourdieu's account of structuration, present-day social circumstances are marked by very high levels of 'symbolic violence', whereby elites dominate the broader population. On Giddens' more optimistic account, the present-day social order is understandable as the 'late modern' condition, which contains within it forms of self-liberation and freedom that are historically unique. Thus while Giddens' structuration views of the 1990s and after led him to focus on such issues as new types of intimate relationship that he sees as developing among people in all social classes, Bourdieu's (1999) vision remained focused more on the forms of 'social suffering' endured by the poor and marginalized, a focus that he had maintained ever since his earliest research in the 1960s.

As their structuration theories were developed for different purposes in different contexts, and then applied to different sorts of empirical issues, it is not surprising that critics should have found particular sorts of flaws in their ideas. The majority of criticism aimed at both thinkers (Calhoun et al., 1993, Held and Thompson, 1989, Bryant and Jary, 1991) tends to imply that despite their endeavours to develop structurationist positions that were neither 'objectivist' (too much stress on how social structures dominate individuals) or 'subjectivist' (individual agency is overemphasized at the expense of an adequate understanding of social structure), each ends up falling towards one side of the old structure/action divide, Bourdieu towards the former pole, Giddens towards the latter. How valid these conventional criticisms are remains to be seen. In what follows, we will first examine Bourdieu's structuration position and the uses to which it has been put, before turning to do the same for Giddens' approach.

Bourdieu's Structuration

It is important to note that although Bourdieu has been represented outside of his native France, and particularly in the English-speaking world, as a 'social theorist', he strenuously resisted that label, because he saw it as indicating a certain kind of thinker who engages only in philosophical speculation, rather than engaging in empirical sociological research about particular dimensions of social life (Santoro, 2011). For Bourdieu there is a fundamentally important relationship between empirical data, research methods and 'theory'. Each is a crucial element of the research process (Bourdieu, Chamboredon and Passeron, 1991). Diverse methods of research, from large-scale surveys to detailed ethnographic studies, must be used in order to investigate a particular situation (Inglis et al., 2000). One cannot just theorize in isolation of actual research and data, although these in turn have to be guided by thinking of the utmost philosophical sophistication. Bourdieu was particularly well placed to carry out such a programme, having been trained in philosophy as a student but then having turned to ethnographic research in his earliest work on Algerian society in the early 1960s (Lane, 2000). Bourdieu insisted he was not interested in making grand theoretical claims, but rather was engaged in examining particular substantive areas ('fields') of social life that existed at particular times and places, such as the fields of education (Bourdieu and Passeron, 1990), cultural production (Bourdieu, 1993a) and cultural consumption (Bourdieu, 1992a) in contemporary France.

Drawing inspiration from a wide range of sources, including both Marx and Weber, Bourdieu argues that all aspects of social life must be examined in terms of the power relations they embody (Honneth, 1986). Bourdieu sees the main aim of sociology in Enlightenment terms (see Chapter 1) as the exposing of the power of elite groups in society, power mechanisms that would not be fully open to view without the sociological exposure of them. This 'exposure' element is somewhat alien to Giddens' structuration theory, which, drawing on micro-sociology, emphasizes more the 'knowledgeability' of individuals, while Bourdieu regards power relations as often occurring without actors being fully conscious of their operation. This is one reason why some critics regard Bourdieu's position as not a true structurationist one, giving equal weight to 'structure' and 'action', but rather as merely a disguised version of Marxism which looks at how social structures and ideologies force individuals, especially in the lower classes, to reproduce through their activities the social structures which dominate them (Jenkins, 1982).

Despite these criticisms, Bourdieu regarded his position as successfully mediating between 'objectivism' and 'subjectivism'. He claimed these are transcended by his key concept of *habitus*. This term is meant to describe both how social conditions act upon and shape individuals' actions, and also how people are – within certain limits – capable of creative responses to the situations they find themselves in (Reay, 2004). That is the essence of structuration for Bourdieu.

A habitus (plural: habitus) is essentially the characteristic ways of thinking, feeling, acting and experiencing shared by all members of a certain group of people. It is defined as a 'system of practice-generating schemes which expresses systematically *the necessity and freedom* inherent in' the collective conditions of life of a certain group of people (Bourdieu, 1992a: 172; emphasis added). Habitus involves *both* the socially shaped dispositions *and* creatively generated activities (practices) of individuals belonging to a particular group. It describes the conjunction between how social structures act on individuals in that group, *and* how individuals actively respond to the social situations created by those structures. Thus a person's habitus generates practices that are characteristic of that particular habitus. Those practices then can either reproduce or transform the social situations individuals operate within.

An important contrast with Giddens is that Bourdieu's structuration theory places emphasis on social groups, particularly the ways in which an individual's habitus is reflective of the habitus of a broader group to which they belong. Giddens focuses less on groups and more on individual 'agents'. For Bourdieu the primary social group in modern societies are social classes, and so the habitus of an individual will be reflective of the habitus of a wider social class. Although Giddens was an important theorist of social class in the 1970s (Atkinson, 2007), his structuration theory rejects the Marxist focus on class, in favour of a more general account of individual agents in the abstract, while class is a constitutive part of Bourdieu's structuration approach. This contrast also marks their divergent understandings of the role of power in social life. While Bourdieu understands power as domination by one or more classes over others, and involving processes whereby the dominant class(es) seek to make their power seem legitimate in the eyes of the dominated, Giddens understands power as the capacity of individual agents to act otherwise than they might have (see below). He also regards power as involving ways in which individual agents can use resources to make possible their practices. Each thinker here has taken up different strands within Max Weber's diverse writings (Callinicos, 1989b).

Returning to habitus, Bourdieu sees it as encompassing *both* objective *and* subjective, passive *and* active, and 'material' *and* 'ideal' elements. The more 'objective' and 'material' aspects of a habitus are the life-conditions of the group possessed of that habitus (e.g. whether they are economically wealthy or not, whether they possess power or not, etc.), and the socialization processes that make people part of that particular group. Socialization involves the inculcation of the habitus into the individual. From birth, individuals are instilled with the values, ideas and attitudes of the group. Such socialization does not just happen at the purely *mental* level, it also happens at a *bodily level* too. Socialization embeds in the physical constitution of an individual 'the most automatic gestures or the most apparently insignificant techniques of the body [such as] ways of walking or blowing one's nose, ways of eating or talking' (Bourdieu, 1992a: 466). Childhood socialization (another factor less emphasized by Giddens) means that both the mind and body of the individual are shaped in ways typical of the group's habitus, their characteristic ways of thinking and acting. Even the tiniest details of an individual's behaviour, such as the way they walk or talk, reflect the habitus of the group, in most cases this being a social class (albeit inflected by gender and ethnicity factors too). While Bourdieu sees the tiny details of a person's social interaction in light of their childhood socialization into a particular culture (following the earlier French anthropology of Mauss (1973)), Giddens focuses more on the sorts of interactional details phenomenologists, ethnomethodologists and symbolic interactionists look at, especially how individuals have to put a lot of effort into keeping interactions with others 'on track' (see Chapters 4 and 5).

For Bourdieu, generally speaking individuals are not fully aware that everything they do is expressive of the habitus they have been socialized into. Instead, the habitus disguises itself by making people see the world in common-sense ways, and these ways generally do not allow actors to turn their critical reflection upon the habitus. People just experience things 'as they are', mostly without realizing that what they experience as 'common sense' is actually the result of habitus. This commonsensical view of the world is *doxa*, the unexamined ways of acting that are at the root of each person's (often class-based) existence in the world (1977: 80, 164).

One important aspect of habitus in this regard is that it 'adjusts expectations to reality', that is, it tends to make a person's 'subjective' mental outlook on life mesh with the 'objective' social conditions they find themselves in. Habitus would, for example, work to adjust an economically very poor person's expectations such that they would not expect to have champagne and caviar for breakfast every day. Habitus works such that this thought would probably never enter into such a person's head, remaining outside their range of possible thoughts. As Bourdieu sees it, people generally do not reflect back on their habitus, as it just seems 'natural' to them to think and act in the ways they usually do.

It is only when they are in contexts where habitus does not 'work smoothly' that people can become conscious of the fact they have – indeed, they *are* – a habitus. For example, if I am born into the working class and spend most of my time with other people who share the same working-class habitus, then generally my habitus will be invisible to me. The typically 'working-class' ways of thinking and acting that I embody in my everyday life will go unchallenged if everyone around me generally thinks and acts like I do. I will understand the ways I think and act merely as normal and natural. But if I go into a context – for example, an upper-class wedding party – where how people think, act, interact and talk seems very unfamiliar to me, I may start to realize that I am 'very working class', because the ways I dress, talk, eat and so on are very unlike how these upper-class people do these things. It is only when my customary activities (practices) seem to fail or be inappropriate for the setting I am in, that I would realize I have a habitus at all, for otherwise the habitus generates my practices without me realizing this.

Here we encounter some main criticisms of Bourdieu's account of habitus. First, it might overstate the power of habitus to generate a person's practices. If so, it seems to fail to be a structuration theory, as it simply seems to be saying that 'social structures' through means of socialization inculcate a class-based habitus into a person, and then all that person's practices are simply functions of the habitus. This is simply another way of saying that structure determines action, and seems to push Bourdieu in the direction of Parsons (see Chapter 2) (Jenkins, 1982). But Bourdieu can defend himself by claiming that habitus does not *determine* a person's practices. Instead, habitus has a creative side, allowing a person to make decisions about what to do. These decisions will generally not be fully conscious, but will be enacted at the level of 'practical consciousness' i.e. at a semi-conscious level. Bourdieu insists that habitus does not just simply compel people to do what wider social structures demand of them. Habitus creates possibilities for action, but, he adds, it always provides a limited set of possibilities (Reay, 2004). We are all constrained by our habitus, at the same time as it enables us to do things. But it never gives us complete freedom to do anything at all: we can only choose from the set of options it gives us.

Critics further allege that Bourdieu radically underemphasizes the amount of 'reflexivity' habitus allows, especially in present-day social conditions (Mouzelis, 2007). That is, Bourdieu underestimates the degree to which people can be aware that they have a habitus, and that by being aware of this, they can change their practices so that they are not prisoners of the habitus. This is the thrust of Giddens' views on 'post-traditional' social orders, where individuals are forced to reflect on themselves, what they are and what activities they will engage in (see below). Bourdieu would respond that such criticisms miss the point that most of the time the workings of habitus are invisible to most people, even in so-called 'late modernity', and that authors like Giddens overestimate the degree of reflexivity in everyday life – most of the time people operate at the level of practical consciousness only (Skeggs, 2004).

Playing Games

Bourdieu worked out his account of habitus and practices by deploying metaphors of *games*. Each social context ('field') a person finds themselves in involves playing the particular game associated with that context. To be able to play the game at all requires the person to feel the game is worth playing. The feeling held by actors that the game is worth playing is the *illusio* of the game (Bourdieu, 1998b: 77). This is the sense both that the game is worthwhile participating in, and that the stakes involved in playing it are worth pursuing. This feeling is embedded in the unconscious of the actor, within the habitus, and the importance of the game is never fully reflected upon. People generally just accept that the things they do are what they do, as they live within the common-sense terms (*doxa*) of their habitus and of the games they are accustomed to play.

In that sense, the practices involved in game-playing are generated at an unconscious level. However, individuals *are* aware of what they are doing, to the extent that they are capable of engaging in particular forms of interaction with others, that is, of being able to 'play' the games they are engaged in. The practices – the forms of playing – that the game involves are to that degree consciously engaged in. Most game-playing happens at the level of practical consciousness (Bourdieu, 1993b, 1998b). Without fully reflecting on it, actors have a *feel for the game*. If a particular 'move' in the game *feels* right, it will be carried out, but if it *feels* wrong, it will not be. These feelings derive from the criteria of rightness and wrongness vis-à-vis particular games embedded in the habitus. In their playing of games, actors are constantly deploying *strategies*: these are actions oriented towards achieving something without the actor being fully aware (or indeed fully unaware) of what s/he is trying to achieve (Bourdieu, 1977). So practices (ways of playing games) are generated in ways beyond the full conscious awareness of actors, as they are produced by the habitus. But the person has a practical (semi-conscious) sense of how to play the games they play.

Modern societies involve a range of separate structures where particular sorts of games are played. These structures Bourdieu calls 'fields', and this is his redefinition of the conventional term 'social structure'. Classical sociologists like Spencer and Durkheim described modernity as involving a high level of *structural differentiation* (see Chapters 1 and 2). Modernity was split into different, relatively separate spheres: the areas of politics, religion, education, media, etc. For Bourdieu, sociology examines both the relations *between* these fields, and also the games and game-playing that happen *inside* each field. If, as in modernity, a field is strongly separated from other fields, the game will have its own particular *rules* (i.e. legitimate ways of playing the game), *resources* (i.e. the assets on which players can draw upon to try to win the game) and *stakes* (i.e. the benefits that come from being successful in the game). Bourdieu had an 'agonistic' view of social life: individuals and groups are in constant competition with each other. The competition is the game-playing, with all participants seeking, without generally being fully aware of it, to win the game and thus dominate all the other players. This was another idea taken from Weber (Bourdieu, 1991b).

Bourdieu was interested in creating models of how games within each field worked (Lizardo, 2010). The models were to reveal the total dynamics of the game that the participants themselves could not see fully. Bourdieu was less interested in studying actual interactions among players, because he thought this only scraped the surface of the dynamics of games, and was more interested in analysing the deeper structural underpinnings of the game (Becker and Pessin, 2006). He wanted to reconstruct the different possible 'positions' within each field that particular players could occupy, with each position being seen to generate its own distinctive 'position-takings', i.e. specific ways of playing the game.

Why a particular person gravitates towards occupying a particular position in the field and the game, is due to two interrelated factors. First, the person's habitus will propel them towards occupying certain sorts of positions and not others. For example, in the present day a person with an upper-class habitus brings with them to most games certain sorts of socio-cultural advantages, such as being seen by others to 'speak well' (this is explained more below). These advantages often will allow them to enter a field and occupy quite a high position within it. By contrast, for Bourdieu a person with a lower-class habitus will lack those advantages, and so when they enter the same field they will likely occupy a much lower position in it than their upper-class counterpart. (The paradigm case for these dynamics is the education field, as we will see below.) So one's habitus strongly influences the position a person occupies when they enter the field at first, and what positions they subsequently occupy within it. Particular types of people tend to occupy particular sorts of positions: people with more upper-class habitus generally occupy higher positions in most fields, whereas people with lower-class habitus generally occupy lower positions in most fields.

Second, each position in a field is created by a specific *amount and type of capital*. 'Capital' is the fourth of Bourdieu's central concepts of structuration, along with *habitus, practices and field*. Capital involves both *resources* – the ways in which actors can play a game – and *stakes* – what players are playing the game to get more of, i.e. the advantages that can be won or lost by playing the game.

There are three types of capital (Bourdieu, 1993b: 32–3). The first is *economic capital*: the level of monetary resources a person has at their disposal. The second is *social capital*: the amount of resources a person has in terms of networks of relations with other people. This involves how many people they have relationships with, and the *types* of people that they are involved with. You have high social capital if the people you habitually interact with, and the social contacts you can draw upon, are wealthy and powerful; but you have low social capital if the people you know are economically poor and powerless.

The third type is *cultural capital*: the cultural resources that a person possesses. This is the amount of socially recognized prestige attached to a person's various practices (e.g. how 'well' they are seen to talk, how 'distinguished' their activities are seen to be by others). It is also the amount of knowledge a person has about cultural matters, such as knowing about 'the arts'. It is partly embodied in the educational qualifications a person possesses. The higher the qualifications a person has, the richer that person is in cultural capital.

Economic capital – money

Social capital – social connections

Cultural capital – 'knowledge of legitimate culture'

Specific forms
– educational capital
– linguistic capital

Figure 10.1 Bourdieu's Three Types of Capital.

There are also *particular types* of cultural capital. One such is linguistic capital (Bourdieu, 1991a), which involves the varying levels of social validation given to different ways of speaking, these forms of speech being class-based. Lower-class speech is less socially valorized than upper-class speech, so an upper-class person possesses more linguistic capital than a lower-class person.

All of this is fundamentally connected to habitus. Being possessed of a particular habitus equips one with a certain amount of each of the types of capital, with higher class habitus providing much more capital for a person than lower-class habitus. Quite simply, the higher the class you are born into, the more advantages (in the form of capital) you will have at your disposal, and these advantages are crucial for the successful playing of all the games of social life.

In addition, the particular positions within fields are associated with particular amounts of specific types of capital. Each field involves a game centred around the winning of a particular kind of capital that is unique to that field. So the field of education is centred around the winning of 'educational capital' (i.e. gaining the highest-level qualifications). Recall that educational capital is a specific form of cultural capital.

A high position in a field is associated with the possession by the persons who occupy that position of large amounts of capital relevant for that field. A low position in a field, by contrast, is associated with the possession by the persons who occupy that position of small amounts of that capital. High positions in a field are occupied by players of the game who dominate other players. Low positions are occupied by more unsuccessful players, who are dominated by the more successful players who occupy higher positions. To get into and then retain over time a high position, a person must have accumulated high amounts of capital relevant for the field. To get stuck in a low position means one has failed to accumulate much capital relevant for the field and the game played in it.

So the *amount* of field-relevant capital a person possesses is the basis for how successful they might be in the game in each particular field they are involved in (Bourdieu, 1990: 117). But it is not just a question of *how much* capital of each type one has at one's disposal. Relative success or failure in a field depends also on whether the *type* of capital one has is appropriate to the particular game being played within it (Bourdieu, 1993b: 34).

Thus a large amount of economic capital might be very useful in a direct way within the field of *big business*, where the reputation of a businessperson rests on how much economic capital s/he possesses (or how much other players in the game *think* s/he possesses). But in another field where cultural capital is the most important factor, economic capital might only have an indirect benefit for its holder.

For example, in what Bourdieu (1992) calls the 'field of cultural consumption' (e.g. involving the buying of 'artworks'), cultural capital (for example, being seen to know a lot about different types of 'art') can be much more useful than a direct utilization of economic capital (i.e. just spending money). Other players in the field may well find it 'common' if someone is seen to be throwing lots of money about buying paintings without apparently knowing very much about art. This is the typical activity of the 'nouveau riche' person, who is seen by more established players of the game of buying 'art', as having a lot of money but no real 'taste'. Think, for example, of how snobbish the reactions would be from people like art gallery owners if a reality TV star, coming from a working-class background but having recently made a lot of money, were to start buying artworks – they would be seen as having enough money to do this (economic capital) but as having no real taste (i.e. insufficient cultural capital). The reality TV star would be regarded by the art gallery people, who are established players of the game and possessed of high levels of field-relevant capital (here, cultural capital), in negative ways: as a low-level player who, through gaining a lot of money has ideas above their station, and so who is very common, vulgar and stupid. This is one way in which those occupying higher positions in this field try to dominate those occupying lower positions, by 'putting them down'. Bourdieu emphasizes that individual players feel these things mostly in semi-conscious, *practical* ways, rather than as a result of explicit awareness and reflection.

Here we come to one of Bourdieu's central claims, one which gives his version of structuration its politically radical colouring. For Bourdieu, the structuration of society involves the interplay of habitus, capital, practices and fields. In contemporary societies, this structuration tends to play out in a particular way. Social transformation can and does happen. But for Bourdieu, for the most part structuration in contemporary capitalist societies operates in the service of a certain kind of social reproduction. The reproduction of class-based social inequalities in modern societies is due to the fact that, although there can sometimes be upsets for the powerful and unexpected triumphs for the weak, in all games played across all fields, *the winners keep tending to win and the losers keep tending to lose.*

This is so both at the level of individuals and the groups they make up, these groups being social classes. Fields are not level playing-fields. Instead, they are organized – generally unintentionally – to favour players from upper-class groups and to disfavour those from lower-class groups. This is because in order to win games and remain dominant within them, each player must have a lot of field-relevant capital *and* the skills and capacities to play the game effectively. The habitus of the upper classes, and the relatively large amounts of economic, social and cultural capital associated with it, allows upper-class players to be generally successful game-players. But for players with lower-class habitus, they will lack these forms of capital, and so will be seriously disadvantaged in the games they enter into. They will find it difficult to gain capital in each field, because they came into those fields poorly equipped with capital in the first place.

This all works out at the level of practical consciousness i.e. the players are not fully aware of all the dynamics the analyst can see, although they are aware, in 'practical' ways, of the nature of the games they are engaged in. The person with high levels of field-relevant capital will have an advantage over the less well-equipped player because s/he will both feel more 'comfortable' playing that type of game and will know how to enact more effective techniques of play than the less advantaged player. The player without much cultural capital will feel 'awkward' in a game s/he feels unfamiliar and uncomfortable with. (Think of how at ease the art gallery owners would be at a new art exhibition, and how ill-at-ease the reality TV star may be, because they feel 'ignorant' and are afraid of being mocked by those players who are familiar with the 'art' game.) These feelings of unease derive from the habitus being badly attuned to the

Knowledge
Combination of various theoretical positions (including Marxian, Weberian, Durkheimian and phenomenological theories)
Aims to identify, and demystify, forms of domination and 'symbolic violence', exercised by dominant over subordinate groups

Structure/Agency
Structurationist position, with empirical focus on class-based social reproduction and class-based competition
Central concepts of habitus, practical consciousness, practices, capital, games and field.

Identity
Class-based identities; subject to some alteration through engagements in different fields

Modernity
Structurally differentiated fields, centred around particular forms of capital, and organized to favour domination by upper classes through game-playing.

Figure 10.2 Summary of Bourdieu's Social Theory.

nature of the game. The lower-class player, lacking relevant capital, has not been trained appropriately for this type of game by the habitus, whereas someone raised within an upper-class habitus will feel much more at ease in this game.

Bourdieu and Education

One of the most important fields which Bourdieu claimed these dynamics were to be found in was the educational field (Bourdieu and Passeron, 1990). For Bourdieu, education is a competitive game where those with upper-class habitus will almost inevitably win the game, and those with lower-class habitus will be very likely to lose – as can be seen in statistics to do with upper-class success and working-class failure as regards educational qualifications (Reay, 2004). The *winners keep winning, losers keep losing* logic of social reproduction goes on despite modern Western schooling systems being apparently based around the notion of meritocracy. This is the idea that if you are 'naturally intelligent' and work hard, no matter what your social background is, you will get good examination grades and thus be able to get a 'good' job. For Bourdieu (1998c: 52–3), there is a 'hidden agenda' in educational systems but it operates, and has effects, generally beyond the full consciousness of the people involved. Teachers may genuinely think that they are being meritocratic in their assessments of their pupils. But teachers themselves have been socialized by the educational system that trained them into operating in un- and semi-conscious ways with 'high culture' – the culture associated with high levels of cultural capital and thus the culture of the upper middle class (the dominant class in contemporary societies for Bourdieu) – as the norm against which to assess their pupils (Bourdieu, 1998c: 22).

This has huge consequences for how children from different backgrounds fare in school. Pupils are both regarded informally and formally classified (e.g. in examinations and essays) as being 'bright' or 'gifted' because they have capacities, such as the ability to speak 'confidently' and to express themselves in 'sophisticated' ways, which are associated with having high levels of cultural capital, gained from being raised in upper-middle-class homes. Children raised in lower-class homes, who lack such cultural capital, are therefore assessed in much more negative ways.

This has little to do with 'intrinsic' levels of intelligence. For Bourdieu, what the school system tests is not how 'naturally' intelligent – or unintelligent – you are, but how much cultural (and other types of) capital you have got. If you speak in local, working-class dialect at home, this is not going to help you in your schoolwork, because school is based around speaking and writing in 'standard English', the very language that upper-middle-class people all across the country use at home. This gives them an advantage: they already feel very comfortable in the school's linguistic environment, whereas children who normally speak in other ways generally feel quite alienated from what they view as 'posh' speech (Bourdieu, 1991a). Pupils are regarded as being intelligent or stupid, 'promising' or 'failures' less on any intrinsic merits they have and more on the basis of whether they display more upper-middle-class traits or not, that is, how much cultural capital they have at their disposal (Bourdieu and Passeron, 1990: 52).

In turn, children internalize the judgements made about them by teachers, with upper-middle-class confidence in oneself being confirmed by school experiences, and the lack of confidence among working-class and lower-middle-class children also being confirmed by school. Most of this goes on at the level of practical consciousness – and that is why it keeps happening, because no one is fully aware of the consequences of their practices, which in effect reproduce upper-class privilege, through successful game-playing, and lower-class failure, through unsuccessful game-playing. The aim of social theory and research, then, is to expose these mostly hidden workings, in order that the dominated lower classes may come to realize what is going on and try to change it.

Assessing Bourdieu

Bourdieu's writings became hugely influential across the social sciences internationally from the early 1990s onwards. There arose a veritable industry devoted to applying, criticizing and re-working his ideas (Silva and Warde, 2010). For present purposes, the key issue is whether or not Bourdieu's structuration theory actually achieves what it claims – to transcend the objectivist/subjectivist divide – or whether it is in fact just a repackaged kind of objectivism, especially of the Marxist variety (Martin and Szelenyi, 1987). For some critics (e.g. Alexander, 1992), Bourdieu's notion of habitus is ultimately deterministic in that it implies that an individual's practices, created by early socialization into a class-based lifestyle, remain fixed and unchangeable in later life. People seem to be 'preprogrammed' to operate always in the way habitus demands of them. In this way, social reproduction is assumed always to take precedence over social transformation.

Bourdieu could respond that his structuration theory does not examine habitus in isolation but always in relation to specific fields. How a person's habitus responds to the field depends on the specific circumstances of competition within the field at any point in time. As the field changes, it requires creative responses on the behalf of individuals, to which habitus responds. So while the latter *constrains* behaviour, it does not *determine* it. That would mean that the *winners win, losers lose* logic was a *tendency*, not an *inevitability*. In his later work, Bourdieu (1990a) emphasized that not all lower-class people *necessarily* fail in the games they play, for upward social mobility is possible under certain field conditions. Likewise, it is not guaranteed that upper-class individuals will automatically be successful in the games they play: there is the possibility, depending on field conditions, of *downward* social mobility, where individuals can end up with less capital than their parents had.

However, Bourdieu remained of the view that *on the whole* contemporary societies exhibited forms of structuration that exhibited high levels of class-based domination and social reproduction. This, he said, could be verified with empirical data: it is a statistically provable *fact* that people with less capital do indeed tend to lose the games they play, passing this disadvantage on to their children. As Bourdieu (1993b: 25) summed up his position: 'the degree to which the world is *really* determined is not a question of opinion: as a sociologist, it's not for me to be "for determinism" or "for freedom", but to discover necessity, if it exists, in the places where it is' – and that can only be done by using a broad range of empirical research methods, not by 'theory' alone. His views in this regard are quite strongly differentiated from those of the later Giddens, who stresses more the contemporary undermining of older forms of social determinism, and the rise of more reflexive forms of agency whereby social transformation is more the norm than class-based social reproduction.

Giddens' Structuration

At least as ambitious as Bourdieu's attempt fundamentally to rethink the inherited categories of social theory are Giddens' endeavours in this direction. Giddens' intellectual career has over the last forty years encompassed the criticism of earlier social thought, the production of a new general theory of structuration, and its application to diverse empirical conditions of what he views as 'late modernity' (Cohen, 1989).

In his writings of the 1970s, Giddens (1971, 1976, 1979) set out – rather in the manner of Talcott Parsons before him (Kilminster, 1991) – to discern what was both useless and still usable in earlier forms of social theory. A very significant part of that exercise was his critique of all positivist positions within social science, which are seen to be based on a mistaken search for general laws of social life (Cohen, 1987). Such laws do not exist because – and here Giddens (1984) agrees with the hermeneutic tradition in social theory (see Chapters 1 and 4) – human beings are thoughtful, knowledgeable and creative, acting in ways that cannot be wholly predicted in advance. Positions such as functionalism, structuralism and orthodox Marxism have to be rejected because of their unacceptable downgrading of human agency. In his work of the 1970s and early 1980s, Giddens (1981, 1984) also took issue with other aspects of Marxism, seeing it as far too economically reductionist. He downgraded its central concept of 'capitalism' to being just one of four key institutional complexes of modern social order, along with surveillance, military power and industrialism.

Giddens was also critical of micro-sociological positions like symbolic interactionism, Rational Choice Theory and exchange theory, for their inadequate understandings of how human activities – now called by Giddens 'practices' rather than 'actions', carried out by 'agents' rather than 'actors' – are patterned and can persist over time and space (Turner, 1986). Giddens drew selectively on a wide range of sources, including Wittgensteinian philosophy, hermeneutics, ethnomethodology and the micro-sociology of Erving Goffmann, in order to produce what he regarded as a necessary corrective to previous slippages into objectivism and subjectivism. This was a theory of structuration that was deliberately posed in very general terms, a general 'ontology' of human agency in the world (Giddens, 1984).

Giddens' primary focus is on 'agents' and some forms of their practices. These agents are regarded – contrary to positivism, Marxism and functionalism – as knowledgeable, that is, capable of exercising agency in and through their practices (King, 2000). The 'ontology of potentials' indicates that every agent can potentially have acted in a way different from the way they happened to do in any given case. The agent is always presented with some kind of range of options, even in the most constrained empirical social circumstances. Even a slave has agency of some variety (Cohen, 1987). But this agency – 'the capacity to make a difference' – need not be intended or conscious. It is simply the capacity to transform a situation in some way, even without being aware of that or to know the consequences of what one does when one 'makes a difference'. After all, we are dealing here with semi-conscious practices, not self-conscious 'actions'.

Here Giddens is keeping open at the general level the possibility of social transformation as much as social reproduction: practices always have the possibility of changing, and are never simply guaranteed to be reproduced over time. Whether practices alter or stay the same in any given case depends on the kind of really existing society we are dealing with. For Giddens (1990), 'traditional societies' tend to involve the reproduction of practices over long periods of time, whereas modern and especially 'late modern' societies tend much more to social transformation, issues we will return to. Some critics (e.g. Archer, 1990) understood Giddens to be saying that agents *always* have a great deal of freedom to do as they want, free of the constraints of 'social structure'. But he responded

(1984: 169–80) by saying that there well may be many factors constraining the agency of empirically existing agents. But this does not alter the general *theoretical* point that agency in general has to be defined as the capacity to 'make a difference', because otherwise no social change would ever be possible if agents had absolutely no option but to do what they have always done in the past.

Agents have to be knowledgeable about what they are doing, otherwise human social life would be impossible. This is because

> . . . the production of society is a skilled performance, sustained and 'made to happen' by human beings. It is indeed only made possible because every (competent) member of society is a practical social theorist; in sustaining any sort of encounter he [sic] draws upon his knowledge and theories, normally in an unenforced and routine way, and the use of these practical resources is precisely the condition of the production of the encounter at all. (1976: 15–16)

So people 'make' society. What we conventionally call 'society' 'is created and recreated afresh . . . by the participants in every social encounter' (1976: 15). 'Society' is simply what we 'do', in our practices, all the time. If we ceased to carry out practices, there would be no 'society'. But, echoing the point made by Marx above, 'the realm of human agency is bounded', for 'the constitution of society is a skilled accomplishment of its members, but one that does not take place under conditions that are wholly intended or wholly comprehended by them' (1976: 160). So people make society, but through resources and materials inherited from the past. Those in turn are the products of previous generations' practices, who also inherited from their ancestors the conditions under and through which they make society. This inheritance from the past is simultaneously enabling and constraining: it makes possible certain courses of action while making others less likely or impossible.

A brief depiction of Giddens' structuration account of practices involves saying that 'society only has form, and that form only has effects on people, in so far as structure is produced and reproduced in what people do' (Giddens and Pierson, 1998: 77). In other words 'structure' does not exist 'outside' or 'beyond' people. Rather, structure is simply made up of people's practices as these occur over time. Structure is not some 'thing in itself' separate from practices, but rather it is simply patterns of practices. As practices change, so too does structure; but by the same token, as structure changes, so too do practices.

Agents are 'skilled' performers of practices. Practices are techniques and procedures of doing things that require certain amounts of skill. Practices are carried out mostly at the level of practical consciousness, involving taken-for-granted ways of thinking that are not generally commented on by agents. Practices happen without being self-consciously thought through by the agents. Sometimes, however, agents operate at the level of 'discursive consciousness', i.e. reflecting upon and putting into words procedures that they usually just 'do' without much reflection or comment. (Think of how difficult it is for footballers in post-match interviews to describe in words – discursive consciousness – what they have been doing on the pitch – practical consciousness. They 'know' how to play the game, and so are skilful agents in the sense Giddens, Bourdieu and others using phenomenological ideas describe, but they are not accustomed to put this into words and to reflect upon it consciously.)

Agents know at the level of practical consciousness how to do certain things. 'Mutual knowledge' is the tacit, taken-for-granted knowledge shared by all agents who do, or can, engage in a certain practice or set of practices. This knowledge is based around 'rules' of how to do things, which everyone who does those things knows, but again these rules operate at the level of practical, not discursive consciousness. These rules encompass both how to do certain things, and what is defined by the mutual knowledge as the 'right' and 'wrong' ways of doing them. Rules persist across large numbers of people and over time because they are lodged in agents' heads, in 'memory traces' (1979: 64), which can be passed on from parents to children. (Here we come close to Bourdieu's views about socialization and habitus.)

When agents are engaged in practices, they have to draw on 'resources', in order to try to do what they are doing. Resources that agents can draw on are of two types: 'authoritative' ones involve the agent being able to get *other people* to do what is required (e.g. a mother using her authority in a family to get children to tidy their room), while 'allocative' ones involve the agents' attempts to control *objects* (e.g. using an object like a car, rather than walking, to go to the shops). An agent's capacity to carry out their practices is very much influenced by what resources they have at their disposal, and how skilled they are at using them. (There is an echo here of Bourdieu on 'skilled' players of games.)

In his general theory, Giddens left open the possibility of *both* social reproduction and social transformation. The former is understood as the reproduction over time of agents' practices, these remaining relatively stable across time. Social institutions (e.g. a certain sort of family organization, a certain sort of economic arrangement) that persist over time are understood as sets of practices that have become routinized, and are carried out repeatedly by the majority of agents connected to them across time and space. For example, the institution of a 'university' only exists because many agents constantly carry out the practices that are part of the mutual knowledge involved in 'being a student' and 'being a teacher'. These practices persist over time and also over space: you don't stop 'being a student' just because you have left the lecture theatre and gone to another space like McDonald's. But if most agents stopped carrying out these practices, the institution of the university would disappear.

A social institution only exists because all of those involved in it keep 'making' it constantly. The same applies to what is conventionally called 'social structure'. Here we come to another central concept, the 'duality of structure'. Giddens (1979: 5) radically redefines what earlier theory means by 'structure' when he says 'structure is both medium and outcome of the reproduction of practices'. 'Structures' make practices possible – they are the 'medium' by and through which practices happen. But 'structures' are only ever the 'outcomes' of practices that have previously happened.

So 'although structure shapes the conduct of human agents, it is only through that conduct that it itself possesses any effectivity'. Moreover, structure 'may itself be modified by the activity of which it is [both] the unacknowledged condition and unanticipated consequence' (Callinicos, 1989b: 137). In other words, 'structure' is what makes practices possible, though agents are generally unaware of that. And structure is what is produced as the unintended consequence of agents' practices. Given that, structure can shape practices. But in turn practices can either reproduce structure or change it. When the former happens, there is social reproduction (practices stay constant over time), and when the latter happens, there is social transformation (practices change).

For Giddens social structures do not reproduce *themselves*, as some critics of Bourdieu think his theory implies. According to Giddens, it is always agents and their practices that reproduce or change structures, depending on circumstances. After all, 'structure' is simply made up of *rules* (in agents' heads, in their practical consciousness) and the *resources* agents can draw upon in their practices. Rules and resources ('structure') make practices

Knowledge
Focus on 'knowledgeable agents' and the 'ontology of potentials'

Structure/Agency
Structurationist position

Central concepts of agents, agency, practices, structure as rules and resources, structure does not exist independently of practices

Modernity
Modern society utterly distinct from 'traditional', pre-modern societies

Analysis of 'late modernity', its distinctive forms of structuration, new sorts of social relationships, and highly reflexive forms of identity construction

Figure 10.3 Summary of Giddens' Social Theory.

possible. (Bourdieu claims it is habitus that makes this possible.) Simultaneously, practices create and recreate rules and resources (i.e. rules and resources are the *outcomes* of practices). In sum, *structure (as rules and resources) creates practices, and vice versa.* Therefore structure only exists in practices, and in the 'memory traces' in agents' practical consciousness, and has no existence external to these.

Assessing Giddens

A lot of the critical response to Giddens' general theory has involved complaints from those such as Marxists (e.g. Callinicos, 1989b), 'critical realists' (e.g. Archer, 1990) and others (Sewell, 2005) that he has conjured away 'structure', giving it a strange quasi-existence where it only exists as 'memory traces' in agents' heads. For these critics, social structures should be seen as having independent existences of their own, in the manner that Marxism and functionalism have pointed to. For a critical realist like Archer (1990), human life is ultimately not characterized by a 'duality' – of structure and agency – but a dualism, between 'individual' and 'society'. This is because each individual is born into an obdurate set of social relations that pre-exist them and which they can generally do very little to alter. Other critics (Mouzelis, 1995) have claimed that Giddens' understanding of structure is not a general theory of human life, but just a description of certain particular situations; other situations are better described as involving a fundamental opposition between individual and society.

These criticisms are connected to another common complaint – that Giddens has overstated the extent of agency in human life (Layder, 1994). This involves a dispute about the 'capacity to make a difference' by the agent that Giddens puts at the heart of his theory. For critics, including Habermas (1982), Giddens overestimates the degree to which agents produce social relations, meaning his structuration theory fails to bridge the structure/agency divide, coming down on the agency side of it far too heavily. Giddens could respond that the critics remain stuck in the old objective/subjective dualism, attacking him using objectivist, structuralist thinking his theory has indeed transcended. This would also apply to critics like King (2000) who regarded Giddens as actually coming down on the objectivist side of the dualism, because of his allegedly faulty conception of rules as overly determining agency.

Those critics who saw Giddens as overemphasizing social transformation rather than social reproduction omitted to note the strong emphasis on 'ontological security' in his mid-period writings (e.g. Giddens, 1979). This was understood as the unconscious level of the human mind, which seeks a sense of stability in its relations with the outer world, especially with other people. This drive for mental security can create an orientation not towards social transformation but to the reproduction of established social relations and ways of doing things. This emphasis went against the apparent overemphasis on social transformation that the critics found in Giddens' concept of the agent, and arguably illustrates Giddens' attempt to deal with agents *both* reproducing structures and transforming them.

Giddens and 'Late Modernity'

Once he had codified structuration theory, Giddens (1990) turned towards applying it to the trends and dilemmas of the contemporary world. His orientation now was to see things through the lenses of 'late modernity' and 'post-traditional' social order. The typical forms of structuration in pre-modern societies tend towards the reproduction of practices, because practices in such situations tend to reproduce and reinforce the customary rules agents operate with. But in modernity, 'tradition' starts to break down, with practices more and more likely to have as their consequences the re-working of previously established rules. This process speeds up markedly in the 'late' modernity that has developed since the 1970s.

How other theorists have diagnosed late modernity and its relations to globalization processes are depicted in Chapter 12, as are Giddens' own contributions to such matters. Here we can say that for Giddens, if premodern social orders generated tendencies towards reproductive structuration and the cultivation of ontological security, the contemporary period is marked by strong, often apparently uncontrollable global social forces (Giddens, 2002). These lead to constant transformations in structuration and an undermining of older forms of ontological security. The 'late modern condition' is one of uncertainty and constantly shifting boundaries, these both creating and created by socially transformative structuration.

Giddens endeavoured to discern both the negative and positive dimensions of late modernity. If forms of ontological security are under threat through constantly reconfigured structuration processes, it is also the case that the late modern condition heralds unprecedented freedom for individual persons to construct their own lives and senses of self, even if for ever more people, this sense of self-creation is a necessity and not a choice. 'De-traditionalization' means the removal or destruction of older social rules, such as the expectation to stick to fixed gender and sexual roles, to get married, and to have children. Individuals are both allowed and compelled by late modern forms of structuration to create their own senses of self, and invent their own rules and practices, rather than have these dictated by older codes such as social class membership (Giddens, 1992).

The late modern agent is a 'reflexive' one, constantly engaged in having to create a coherent sense of self out of an ever expanding range of possible models. This is a major point of difference with Bourdieu (1999), who argued for the ongoing salience not just of class-based structuration but of class-based identities too. Whether one agrees more with either thinker probably has a lot to do with how sympathetic one is to their broader political views as much as their theoretical position. For those on the more radical left, Giddens' account of the late modern agent is a generalization of the lifestyle of privileged upper-class people to the entire population (Skeggs, 2004). But for those more attuned to Giddens' 'third way' politics (1994b, 2000), his later work will be more appealing, as it strikes chords with various dimensions of contemporary experience, not just among the higher classes, for example, the idea of the 'pure relationship' (Giddens, 1992) entered into for purely individualistic reasons and not forced upon individuals by social obligations.

Although Bourdieu carried out his own empirical researches, Giddens has left the task of empirically testing his theoretical account to others, the results sometimes indicating support for his claims (Gross and Simmons, 2002) and other times not (Jamieson, 1999). At the purely theoretical level, a curious irony may be that Giddens' ideas about individual self-reflexivity in late modernity suggests a divide between individual and society – the self-reflexive person confronts wider society as something alien to her – rather than the understanding of structures and practices constituting each other that is the heart of the structuration theory, perhaps returning Giddens to the very dualism of 'structure' and 'agency' his earlier work may in fact have already transcended (Bagguley, 2003).

Conclusion

The structuration theories of Giddens and Bourdieu are in some ways overlapping and in other ways very different. The differences have a great deal to do with the broader political orientations of both thinkers. However, they both stand as the most sophisticated general theories of human social life that are available at the present time. It is possible to cross-fertilize them in various ways, using parts of each to inform the other, rather than seeing them as simply wholly antagonistic. For example, it is possible to see the kinds of reflexive agency Giddens highlights, as being particularly within the capacities of those sorts of people Bourdieu would regard as being possessed of high levels of various sorts of capital. More simply, the rich and socially privileged are more likely to be able to exercise certain sorts of agency and reflexivity than those who are poor and lacking in various forms of privilege. It will be fascinating to see how the reputations of both thinkers and their ideas develop and change over the next several decades – including through the sorts of structuration processes each described so evocatively.

Further Reading

Bryant, C., and Jary, D. (2001) *The Contemporary Giddens: Social Theory in a Globalizing Age*. Basingstoke: Palgrave.
Calhoun, C., LiPuma, E. and Postone, M. (eds) (1993) *Bourdieu: Critical Perspectives*. Cambridge: Polity.

Craib, I. (2011) *Anthony Giddens*. London: Routledge.

Giddens, A., and Pierson, C. (1998) *Conversations with Anthony Giddens: Making Sense of Modernity*. Cambridge: Polity.

Grenfell, M. (2008) *Pierre Bourdieu: Key Concepts*. London: Acumen.

Swartz, D. (1998) *Culture and Power: The Sociology of Pierre Bourdieu*. Chicago: University of Chicago Press.

11

Feminist Paradigms

Mapping a Complex History

Feminism is rather like Marxism in that, unlike some other paradigms covered in this book, it is far more than a primarily academic exercise. Intellectually, it encompasses a diverse range of political ideas, theories and empirical studies. Academic and intellectual forms of feminism are always in one way or another related to the broader feminist political movement. But just as that movement is diverse, so too are its relations to what we can call feminist social theory. The key thing is that feminist thought, again like Marxism, has practical purposes: to change the world, not just to observe it.

In a broad-brush way, we may say that feminism as a political movement takes as its objective the challenging of what it sees as the oppression of women by men, and widespread sexual and gender inequalities. An oppressive social order, centred around or at least involving in significant ways, inequalities between the genders, is 'patriarchal' (Walby, 1990). Feminism may be defined politically as the challenging of that state of affairs, and the desire to change it, replacing it with a more equitable social order. But how to define patriarchy, how to contest it, and what more specific aims are desired, all vary between different sorts of feminists and feminist groups (Gottfried, 1996).

The development of feminism politically involves a very rich and diverse history that we cannot possibly cover comprehensively here. This history begins with the first stirrings of 'first wave feminism', involving early pioneers like the English author Mary Wollstonecraft [1759–1797], writing her defence of women's rights in the 1790s, and protesting against conditions of unequal and unfair treatment of women by men. The first wave of feminist political activists and thinkers stretched through to the early twentieth century, encompassing in Britain the famous Suffragette movement, which fought for women's right to vote at a time when women were denied the vote in almost all countries of the world.

'Second wave' feminism of the 1960s and 1970s involved a resurgence of feminist forms of consciousness and action. It is at this period that the international women's movement, a broad and loose collection of different types of feminist groupings stretching across many countries, really began to make its mark on broader social and political life. Although the movement was very diverse, certain themes were common across the spectrum of groups involved. These included the notion that 'the personal is the political'. Thinking this way involved arguing that issues and phenomena previously defined as non-political and 'private', were in fact highly political and therefore matters of public concern. Forms of oppression that happened in the home, from domestic violence through to women doing unpaid labour for men under the guise of 'housework', were now defined not as the 'personal' problems of individual women, but as both symptoms and products of wider, oppressive sex and gender relationships and forms of social organization (Rowbotham, 1993).

Second wave feminism also highlighted the importance of 'consciousness raising'. Just as Marxists argued that the point of Marxian thinking was to break through ideologically conditioned commonsensical ways of thinking, in order to reveal the real mechanisms of oppression by the ruling classes, so too did much feminism in the 1970s aim to show women how they were dominated by social processes and institutions which worked in the service of men, either all men, or especially those in higher social positions. Although the feminist movement was made of many different kinds of groups and associations, another element which united many of them at this period was the idea of 'sisterhood', the idea that all women, regardless of other differences, had certain things in common, notably shared forms of male oppression which, by joining together as a transformative political movement, they could overcome. As feminism sought to transform all sectors of society, it made sense to seek to change fundamentally one such sector, the university world, at that time arguably a highly patriarchal institution. It was at this period that feminist politics started to infiltrate the academy, with the beginning of dedicated women's studies programmes teaching feminist ideas, and the (slow) transformation of existing disciplines in the humanities and social sciences (Farganis, 1994).

Third wave feminism, which has been developing since the late 1980s, is a more diverse and fragmented phenomenon than the second wave, which has perhaps not found a clear identity yet. This is probably connected to the fact that younger feminists today are women who were brought up at a time when the society around them was already beginning to feel the influence of feminism socially and politically, sometimes in obvious ways, such as in the passing of sexual equality legislation, and many others more tacit and subterranean. The nature and ongoing social and political relevance of feminism remain contested at the current time, and it is certainly not clear what the feminism of the late twentieth and early twenty-first centuries will subsequently be deemed by people in the future to have achieved.

This diversity of feminism at the level of political practice is mirrored today by its diversity at the level of theory, which is simultaneously a set of political formulations and a body of intellectual ideas. Again in a broad-brush way, it is the case that probably all feminists would agree with the statement that 'women's position within society is not a natural phenom-enon, but a social, political and economic product, which is reflected and perpetuated' by male-centred – and mostly male-produced ways of think-ing and acting (Harding, 1991). A patriarchal social order is seen to be socially structured and culturally reproduced. But how different sorts of feminist theory understand these issues varies very much, depending on their political allegiances, and their understandings of the key concerns of social theory, such as particular conceptions of social order, social inequality, culture, identity and agency.

It remains the case, though, that there is a general correspondence between particular sorts of feminist politics, and the specific type of theory that these both draw upon and generate. For Liberal feminist poli-tics and theory, the key issue to be dealt with is *equality*, between what are taken to be 'men' and 'women'. For Marxist (or more broadly, Social-ist) feminism, the central focus is the analysis of *exploitation*, by all men over all women, but particularly by ruling class men. For Radical femi-nism, the orientation is the analysis and overcoming of *patriarchy*, defined as a social order where the group made up of all men oppress the group made up of all women, and where all social institutions both express and work to reproduce and reinforce this state of affairs. Finally, post-modernist feminism (also definable as post-structuralist feminism) wishes to point out issues to do with *differences* (between men and women, and between different *kinds* of women), and the *social and cultural construction* of reality by gendered discourses and ideas.

In this chapter, we will encompass some of the diversity of the history and contemporary state of feminist social theory. One important issue worth mentioning here is that while other paradigms covered in this book have a fairly unproblematic relationship with the classical social theorists, taking up and transforming their ideas often quite happily, for various reasons particular sorts of feminism have been more sceptical of the so-called 'classical legacy'. After all, the classical thinkers wrote in a historical period where highly patriarchal ideas, practices and institutions were the norm, and this is reflected in their ideas in all sorts of ways, both obvious and not so obvious (Sydie, 1987). That is why certain sorts of feminist thinkers may feel that the classical legacy is primarily the expression of the patriarchal dispositions of 'dead white European males', and may prefer to look for intellectual resources elsewhere. Such sources of inspiration could include neglected pioneering feminist thinkers of the classical period, such as Charlotte Perkins Gilman, who wrote brilliantly about the disastrous effects of patriarchal conditions on women's mental and physical well-being (2004 [1914]). Other sources of inspiration can include the works of male thinkers whose ideas either explicitly challenged contemporary sex and gender categories, such as Foucault (McNay, 1992) (see Chapter 8), or whose ideas can be taken in this direction by feminists today, such as Lacan (see Chapter 8).

The importance of post-structuralist thought in much contemporary feminist theorizing does suggest a breaking on the behalf of at least a substantial number of feminist thinkers with the classical social theorists, especially those of a more explicitly sociological disposition. It is difficult to try to think what a self-consciously Durkheim-inspired feminist position would look like today, even if one can easily plot out the historical connections between Durkheimianism and feminism historically (Lehmann, 1994). This is not to deny, though, the interest for some feminist thinkers that may still reside in certain works by particular classical thinkers, one of the more obvious being that of Marx's collaborator Friedrich Engels (1978 [1884]), which tries to connect systematically the history of class-based domination to the history of patriarchy.

In much feminism produced over the last twenty years or so, older, more sociological concerns about 'structure' and 'action' (or agency), and more Marxist concerns to do with relations of exploitative commodity production, have taken something of a backseat in comparison to more post-modernist concerns with subjectivities and identities, which have flourished. That may be a function in part of where the major feminist theorists are institutionally located, often tending to be humanities scholars rather than social scientists. Such thinkers might more accurately be called 'cultural theorists' rather than 'social theorists', in that their primary concerns involve issues to do with language and cultural forms, treated in ways more familiar in the humanities than in what has traditionally been called 'social theory', with its roots more in the social sciences, and in sociology in particular. However, the blurring of some intellectual boundaries over the last two decades, particularly through the influence of post-modernism, has created a new hybrid genre called 'social and cultural theory' (McLennan, 2006), which allows more literary and philosophically inspired feminist theories to enter into the awareness of social theory authors and readers.

From Liberalism to Marxism to Radical Feminism

Feminist social theories have complicated relations to the various wings of the feminist political movement. Nonetheless, there exists a fairly straightforward relationship between the liberal wing of the feminist movement and liberal feminist thought. Liberal feminism is the oldest of the various sorts of feminist political activity and theorizing, dating back at least to the time of Wollstonecraft.

Its aim is the defence and the augmentation of the 'rights of women'. It takes as its central political and analytical focus issues to do with 'equality' – the identification of existing inequalities between men and women, and their reformation. Issues that liberal feminism has focused, and continues to focus, on include women's political rights (e.g. the winning of the vote), economic rights (allowing women to have more financial independence), the pursuit of equality in the workplace (e.g. through equal pay legislation), and the promotion of some cultural changes (e.g. legislation to enhance a culture of mutual respect between the sexes, such as in workplaces) (Cornell, 1998).

These goals are to be achieved by the reform of the institutions of the liberal, democratic, capitalist social order. It is thought that reform of the existing social order will be sufficient to eradicate inequalities. More revolutionary changes are not required, as the basic structures of society can be reformed in order to allow them to promote equality. Reform is often pursued through parliamentary and legal means, especially the enactment of equalities legislation, rather than through other, more non-establishment means. Liberal feminism is very much the mainstream feminism of the present-day, being widely subscribed to by politicians and journalists. It is embedded in government bodies such as Equal Pay Commissions and in legislation. A particular concern of contemporary liberal feminism is the issue of the 'glass ceiling', whereby legislation is said to have so far failed to prevent inequalities in certain domains of life, especially the workplace, where women continue in many kinds of employment to suffer lower rates of both pay and promotion than their male counterparts (Okin, 1989).

Liberal feminism today speaks of 'gender inequalities', but considered in light of other sorts of feminism, it may as well be using the older term 'sex inequalities', and related phrases like 'sex discrimination', because it tends to conceive the categories of people involved in the inequalities it is seeking it eradicate as 'men' and 'women', persons who have genders, but whose genders are rooted in their biological sex. This is precisely the kind of conception of gender – as essentially rooted in fixed sexual dispositions – that post-modernist feminism in particular takes exception to.

There is a strong affinity between, on the one hand, liberal feminism as political practice and as way of defining issues, and the stream in social science of 'feminist empiricism' on the other (Abbott and Wallace, 1999). This part of mainstream social scientific positivism believes that the social world can be captured directly, either qualitatively through interviews and related research techniques, or, more often, quantitatively, through statistical means (e.g. depicting unequal pay rates for men and women in particular occupations). Feminist empiricism is part of, and accepts with some caveats, the research practices and conceptual orientations of wider mainstream empirical social science. Feminist empiricism by and large accepts the mainstream's ideas and concepts. Where these are found to be a problem (e.g. techniques that define a household's social class position by reference to the male breadwinner's occupation), it is thought that any 'faulty' conceptions can be corrected to become 'non-sexist'. Ideas of value neutrality and scientific 'objectivity' are not objected to, as feminist empiricism's widespread use of statistical approaches attests.

It is obvious why other forms of feminist politics and theory would find much to criticize in liberal feminism, condemning it for multiple reasons for being at best naïve, and at worst actually an unwitting accomplice of a social order far more unpleasant than it can admit. Clearly for other sorts of feminist, the liberal position is not nearly radical enough, being blind to how social order, both in the past and in the present, is *fundamentally*, rather than just contingently, structured in ways that favour males. For other kinds of feminism, the central epistemological problem with liberal feminism is that it uncritically accepts 'andocentric' (male-centred and -produced) definitions of what a 'human being' is. It takes on board all sorts of deeply held prejudices of a male-dominated cultural context, and falsely essentializes the male / female and sex / gender divides that post-modernist feminists in particular object to. Overall, it is understood to be more a 'tool of the system' than a means really to transform that system.

If liberal feminism is the type of feminism that has the longest history, then Marxist – or more broadly, socialist – feminism can trace its roots back to the later nineteenth century. Feminist ideas and activities have had a complex relationship to the communist and socialist political move-ments over the last 130 years or so. As noted above, a major reference point for Marxist feminists has been the pioneering work of Engels (1978 [1884]). This is a key source for subsequent attempts to formulate a 'mate-rialist' feminism that could deploy the ideas of Marxism to understand (much) more fully than Marx himself had managed the nature of sex- and gender-based exploitation. The view that derives from Engels is that throughout history, women have been both economically and politically subordinated by men. Successive 'modes of production' – the notion Marxism uses to understand social orders based around the exploitation by ruling classes of subordinate ones – have been structured to control women, both in terms of their work, and also in terms of their reproduc-tive capacities. Women have been exploited in ways that differ from those of men, in part because of their ability to give birth to new members of society. Marxist feminism connects the standard Marxist notion of rela-tions of production (how work is socially organized such that ruling classes control and exploit lower classes) to another factor, namely social relations of biological reproduction (how families are socially organized, and the ways in which childbirth and childcare have economic ramifica-tions) (Barrett, 1980).

With the characteristic Marxist focus on economic relations and factors as the dominant institutions in any social order, Marxist feminism's diag-nosis of modernity sees the exploitative social relations of capitalism as its main focus of attention. Capitalism is seen to subordinate and exploit both the working classes and all women, understood as a group encom-passing upper as well as lower-class females. Thus women who occupy a social position at the overlap of these intersecting modes of exploitation – working-class women – are seen as being the most exploited of all social groups, especially because they are seen to be subject to exploitative social relations that operate in the interests not just of the upper classes but also of working-class men. A working-class 'housewife' works in ways that means she is exploited both by her husband and by the broader forces of the capitalist economy. In the social conditions of the advanced capitalist societies of the mid twentieth century, women were relatively marginalized from the 'public' sphere (the world of work and politics) and relatively confined to the 'private' world of the domestic sphere. Under capitalism the type of labour associated with the domestic sphere, namely cooking, cleaning, tidying etc., is not recognized as work at all, leading to the widespread view of women as mere consumers, highly dependent on their spouses.

A particular focus for Marxist-inspired feminism in the 1970s was the nature of 'housework', which was seen as a particularly compelling example of the intersection between class-based and gender-based modes of exploitation (Oakley, 1974, 1976). Under the contemporary phase of capitalism, for reasons deeply embedded in the social structure and not just due to the contingent cultural dispositions of the category of males called 'husbands', the kind of domestic labour conventionally called 'housework' was not regarded as 'real work'. Women were compelled to engage in domestic tasks without wages, it presumably never occurring to most women in that position that wages were a reasonable request given the amount of labour they were giving 'for free'. This was a form of exploitation necessary for the capitalist economy. A male breadwinner may well personally benefit from his wife's domestic labour, but for Marxist feminists the real cause of this exploitation rested in the very structure of the capitalist economy itself. By providing for the needs of male workers, females ensured that the workforce was kept functioning in the service of the economy. Just as the male worker was exploited at work, his wife was exploited at home, both by him directly and the overall capitalist system indirectly. In essence, capitalism required all the women put into the social position of 'housewife' to be massively exploited, but this process was disguised by ideologies which presented domestic labour as just naturally 'women's work' that was neither exploitative nor important enough to merit being given a wage.

The increasing appearance of women in diverse parts of the workforce in more recent times is interpreted by Marxist feminists not as some kind of 'liberation' from domestic tyranny, but rather as a function of structural changes in the capitalist economy, as it seeks new sources of cheap labour to exploit. The fact that women are more likely to be found in low-paid, low-skilled, part-time, insecure forms of employment is interpreted not – as liberal feminism would – as a matter of inequality that could be fixed through legislation and social reform, but rather as a neces-sary structural feature of a particular phase of capitalism. The search for profits through cheap labour necessitates the recruitment of a historically disadvantaged group – women, especially of the working classes – who have little power to resist the imposition of such features of exploitation as poor working conditions, non-unionized workplaces, and so on (Eisen-stein, 1979).

Just as Marxist feminism could berate its liberal counterpart for exces-sive naivety, merely scratching the surface of deeper structural issues, so too could other types of feminism lambast Marxism for what was con-strued as its far too narrow focus on issues to do solely with the economy and work. As in broader criticisms of Marxism (see Chapters 1 and 3), Marxist feminism is seen to downplay far too much or ignore issues that are not directly economic in nature (Sargent, 1981). Likewise, when it does touch upon other issues, especially to do with cultural forms and ideas, it construes these solely in light of their expressing certain ruling class ideologies which hide vested interests. Post-modernist feminists in particular would claim that there are far more complex issues to do with gender and culture than merely saying that cultural forms express the ideologies of capitalism. This is an overly reductionist and essentialist view of gender matters, which ultimately always subordinates gender phenomena to issues of class and economic exploitation, other forms of exploitation and domination being seriously downplayed. In essence, Marxists might be able to think about capitalist exploitation, but their conception of patriarchy is far too narrow (Hartmann, 1979, Jaggar, 1983).

The critique of what was seen as the excessively narrow lens of Marxist feminism led in the 1980s to attempts to broaden analysis so as to locate the issues Marxists focused on alongside other forms of oppression. Thus the British sociologist Sylvia Walby (1990) proposed a model of patriarchy composed of six analytically distinct but empirically interrelated elements: household production, which refers to women's domestic labour; women's exclusion from, and subordination within, the labour market; State endorsement of patriarchal policies; inter-personal violence as perpe-trated by men against women; sexuality and the differences in 'rules' gov-erning the sexual conduct and practices of men and women; and finally, culture and the perpetuation of exploitative representations of women in the media and magazines such as *Cosmopolitan* (Walby, 1990: 98). The first three of these were plausibly explicable in Marxist terms, but the latter three only in simplistic fashions by Marxism, and even the Marxist interpretation of the third – the patriarchal nature of government – was open to question due to Marxism's historical difficulty in theorizing a more complex view of what the 'State' is than merely claiming it is a straightforward tool of ruling class power.

An important part of the critique of the Marxist approach was formulated by Radical feminism, a position that began to be influential in the early 1970s (e.g. Millet, 1977 [1970], Firestone, 1972). It eschewed the Marxist tendency to reduce gender relations to class relations. Instead, it argued that the focus of analysis should be 'patriarchy' per se. This is a type of social order *wholly and primarily* structured around the interests of males. The central social division is not between ruling and subordinate classes as the Marxists claimed, but between *all* men on the one side and *all* women on the other. A patriarchal social order is one that is centred around at the deepest levels the *systematic* subordination of women by men. This elementary fact is reflected in *all* social institutions, and in all ideas and cultural forms. It is through the latter that the former are reproduced over time. For Radical feminism, all social institutions are oppressive, not just work and the economy as the Marxists thought, but also the typical organization of the family, and the media. Patriarchy was seen to have at its root both physical and symbolic male violence towards women. Domestic violence was seen not as an accidental happening, dependent on the dispositions of particular men, but a structural feature of the current family set-up per se. Likewise, pornography is a widespread feature of culture and media in patriarchal society, and not for accidental reasons – it is the symbolic expression of a society centred around male control, of, and hatred of, women (Brownmiller, 1975).

For Radical thinkers, Marxism had committed the same mistake as liberalism, its apparent diametric opposite. They had failed to see that women and men are radically different. They have different interests. For all males (whether they realize it or not), the central interest is the ongoing maintenance of patriarchy. For females, the central interest is the rejection and overthrow of patriarchy, and the construction of anti- and non-patriarchal social relations. Because all females are fundamentally different from all males, Radical feminism could posit a 'universal sisterhood' that united all women, for they all had common interests. Consciousness-raising processes could make individual women see how patriarchy really worked, beneath the surface of things, making women realize that they were part of one overall group that had to overcome its own means of oppression. So many of the aspects of traditional Marxism – social structural explanations, ideology, highlighting of the hidden nature of oppression to the oppressed – were used and re-worked by Radical feminists, at the same time as they rejected what they saw as Marxism's misguided focus on class rather than patriarchy as the central analytic category.

The flaws that critics of Radical feminism discerned are fairly obvious. Critics alleged that the central idea of patriarchy as the root and cause of all things was overstated, and perhaps more simplistic than the Marxist overemphasis on class. The power of males over women was said to have been very overstated, partly as a result of a failure to focus on social divisions between different types of males in different social positions. What had been seen as male-centred conspiracies were explicable as more contingent phenomena (e.g. the role of pornography could be linked not only to male violence but to the need for media organizations to make money out of 'sex' as well). Post-modernist feminists, who would appear on the scene in the 1980s, were very sceptical about claims as to 'universal sisterhood', stressing instead that in complex contemporary societies, there

---

Liberal Feminist Theory
Aim: equality

Method: mainstream social science

Subjects of analysis: 'men' and 'women'

Social order: liberal democratic; reformable

Marxist Feminist Theory
Aim: revolutionary transformation of class and gender relations

Method: structural analysis

Subjects of analysis: dominant and dominated classes; women as part of class structure

Social order: class-based exploitative social relations produce exploitative gender relations; capitalism structures patriarchy

Radical Feminist Theory
Aim: analysis and transcendence of patriarchy

Method: analysis of fundamental sexual divide

Subjects of analysis: females and males as distinct groups with divergent interests

Social order: patriarchal relations reproduced in all social spheres

---

Figure 11.1 Liberal, Marxist and Radical Feminisms.

exist multiple different groups of women, divided by age, class, ethnicity and other factors, and their various identities and senses of themselves could not just be dismissed as the unfortunate products of false consciousness instilled into them by patriarchy.

Towards Post-Modernism

From the 1980s onwards, post-modernist themes became ever more central in feminist theory, if perhaps not as much in the feminist political movement. Post-modernist feminism can also be called post-structuralist feminism or 'cultural turn' feminism. This is because post-modernist philosophy, in which it is located, derives primarily from post-structuralist ideas (see Chapters 8 and 9). Post-modernist feminism was often produced by scholars located more in humanities departments than in the social sciences, where one might have been more likely to encounter thinkers of liberal and Marxist persuasions. It can be called 'cultural turn' feminism as it draws upon and contributes to a broader shift in social theory that took place from about the mid 1980s onwards, mapped out in Chapters 8 and 9, in which new forms of theory were produced that were focused less on the 'material' issues of work and economy that concerned Marxists, and more on what were taken to be the constantly mutating complexities of culture.

Given the sources it drew from, post-modernist feminism was more markedly philosophical than the other feminisms we have looked at, much of it being produced by French philosophers like Luce Irigaray, Julia Kristeva and Hélène Cixous, and later on by those in other countries following their lead (e.g. Grosz, 1994). The central focus for these thinkers is the ways in which female 'subjectivity' is constrained by textual and cultural forms as defined and dominated by men. Central resources for post-modernist feminism included the ideas of Foucault, Derrida and Lacan, and general post-structuralist ideas of how 'discourses' shape reality (see Chapter 8). In line with broader post-modernism, post-modernist feminism is associated with a radical social constructionist position. On this view, there is no 'reality' to be found behind and beyond social constructions. Discourses are seen thoroughly to shape the realities people experience (Stavro, 1999).

However, unlike the nihilistic philosophy of post-modernists like Baudrillard (Chapter 9), which completely rejected the possibility of any sort of theory motivated by a positive political project, post-modernist feminists also were of the view (potentially contradicting the post-modernist point about there being no realities beyond discursive constructions) that discourses are created by powerful groups (of males), and that one can identify and expose male-centred discourses. Post-modernist feminism very much pitched itself against what it saw as natural science's dominating role in contemporary culture, and its drive to fix gender and sex categories that were in fact infinitely mutable, because culturally constructed, and so open to challenge and being changed. Science was attacked as a modernist 'metanarrative' (see Chapter 9) which oppresses women, by seeking to justify a strict division of all people into two distinct 'sexes'. This is oppressive because it denies and imprisons people's capacity to choose their own identities. In the condition of post-modern liberation you can choose whoever you want to be: man, woman, straight, gay, transgender and other possibilities. A key aim of post-modernist feminism was to 'deconstruct' so-called scientific claims to truth, showing these to be the discursive fabrications that they are. The political aim was to change the broader culture such that its repressive apparent stability (operative around dyads like male/female), was changed to a liberating condition of the instability of all categories and all claims to truth. Post-modernist feminism sought the liberation of people's subjectivities through the destabilizing possibilities afforded by the deconstruction of all metanarratives and discourses. A corollary of this position was that the Radical feminist view of universal sisterhood was mythical. Instead, *differences* between different kinds of women were to be celebrated and cultivated. There was no single female identity, but multiple and fragmented identities, a condition to be furthered through the exhilarating deconstruction of all fixed systems of thought.

Within a post-modernist and post-structuralist world-view, female liberation comes about not by following the outdated modernist promises of Marx (see Chapter 9), but through developing theory based on more promising sources, such as the ideas of the psychoanalyst Jacques Lacan. We saw in Chapter 8 that Lacan's very distinctive re-working of themes from Freud argued that as a child learns about the world around it, and starts to speak language, it is being inducted into the 'Symbolic Order', that is, all the various discourses that make up the surrounding society. These discourses thoroughly structure not just the conscious mind, but its hidden, unconscious dimensions too. These discourses come to affect profoundly the tumultuous, churning morass that is a person's unconscious. One of the foremost Lacanian feminist thinkers, Julia Kristeva

(1997), develops this notion, regarding the Symbolic Order as structured by patriarchal discourses. She argued that prior to acquiring language, children pass through a 'semiotic' stage, which co-exists with the Symbolic Order. It is here that they learn to express emotions and feelings. Kristeva regards this stage as a 'maternal' one, which is antagonistic to the patriarchal Symbolic Order. Liberated individuals are able to 'flit' or 'play' between the maternal and patriarchal psychic realms, rather than being imprisoned unconsciously within the ways of thinking demanded by the latter.

Another leading feminist adaptor of Lacan, Luce Irigaray (1985a; 1985b [1977]) argues that all that is known in mainstream society and culture about women and sexual desire is known from a male perspective, resulting in a vision of women she calls the 'masculine feminine'. Irigaray's (1985b: 28) aim is to overturn this vision so that women are understood and conceptualized on 'their own' terms, as the 'feminine female'. Throughout the history of Western thought, women have been represented as the 'sex which is not one', The woman has been continually depicted negatively as an entity that is lacking, as something that is 'not-men' (Irigaray, 2004). The woman's identity and sexuality are represented in this way in light of 'phallogocentricism', the patriarchal view of the world expressed in and through language as defined by men. This vision tries to freeze the meaning of 'female' and define it in highly negative ways. The task of theory is to liberate women from this way of thinking. They must be encouraged to see that in contrast to male sexuality, women's sexuality has plural dimensions, unlike men's, which is monolithic. A woman's multiplicitous sexuality has the power to change her identity, to allow it to escape from the grip of the phallogocentric culture it has had to operate within.

Not all post-modernist feminism is wholly rooted in French philosophy. The ideas of the leading American post-modernist feminist Judith Butler also draw on ideas from Anglo-Saxon philosophy of language, particularly J. L. Austin's (1962) notion of 'speech acts'. This is the idea, which has certain things in common with French structuralist philosophy (see Chapter 8), that language does not describe the external world, but rather creates it. Austin's view is that when someone says something about a thing in the world, it may seem like they are describing a really existing thing, but in fact they are actually bringing that very thing into existence. The act of speech brings into existence the very thing that the speech act seems merely to describe as if that thing was already there.

Butler uses this idea to make a dramatic claim: there is no such thing as sex. More specifically, she means that the category 'sex', in the sense that there is a biological thing called a 'male' and a biological thing called a 'female', is just that – a category, a mental construction, not something that actually refers to 'real' things in the world. There are not really 'men' and 'women', only persons we label that way. But because this labelling goes on all the time, we *think* the labels refer to real entities.

This is a radical claim to make as it is, but it also goes beyond what previous forms of feminism had assumed. In the 1970s, one of the major underpinnings of much feminism was to say that sex (as biology) and gender (characteristic traits of 'masculinity' and 'femininity') are different (Oakley, 1972). Patriarchal thought had fixed the two together: a person is born a man or a woman, so those born as 'males' must 'naturally' have 'masculine' traits (e.g. confidence, aggression) and those born as 'females' must 'naturally' have 'feminine' traits (e.g. nervousness, passivity), and these are unalterable as they are rooted in the person's 'sex'. Feminism had challenged this by saying that gender is in fact socially shaped, created through socialization of the child, and because it is not rooted in biology, it is alterable. The connection between sex and gender was broken. That meant it was impossible to condemn some women for having 'masculine' traits and some men for having 'feminine' ones, because there was no 'natural' gender.

Butler's point is that this left untouched what she sees as another widespread assumption: that 'sex' is biologically rooted, determined and fixed, and that therefore there really is a simple division based on biology between 'males' and 'females'. Butler argues that this division too is a construction of patriarchy. Both gender and sex are not things people just 'have' – instead, these are what people 'do'. People 'perform' gender. They do so through what Butler (1990: 140) refers to as 'stylized repetition of acts' enacted through the most mundane 'bodily gestures', 'movements' and forms of comportment, that taken together produce the effect of a fixed and unalterable 'gendered self'. Gender is not the expression of 'sex'. Instead, the category of 'sex' – of 'male' and female' – refers not to 'real' things but in fact is constantly produced and institutionalized through forms of gendered discourse and practice. These are like Austin's 'speech acts' – they bring into existence what the people who are enacting them think they are just describing and which already exists. These gendered practices are undertaken not by a fixed-sex subject that exists prior to the act. Instead, the person doing those practices *becomes*, as opposed to already *is*, a 'woman' or a 'man' through repetition of those practices. For

Butler, the term the term 'sex' is a profoundly political one, precisely because it does not refer to anything 'in nature' and so can be contested, its destruction helping to undermine significantly patriarchal thought and practice.

Just as Butler challenges patriarchal relations through a critique of what is normally taken to be 'natural', so too does a fellow American, Donna Haraway, take issue with the patriarchal organization of science, and the gendered categories it produces which are disseminated through wider society. Haraway is highly critical of the widespread positivist view of scientific knowledge as 'objective', 'value-free' and 'disinterested', instead claiming that science is a product of 'capitalism, militarism, colonization, racism and crucially male domination' (Wajcman, 2004: 82). In spite of science's rhetoric as to its 'neutrality in political and social matters', Haraway (1989: 12; 1991) argues that scientific knowledge is no less 'ideological' than any other form of discourse. She regards the production of scientific knowledge as a social process (Haraway, 1988). Because of its social origins, Haraway embraces the possibility that scientific technology might be redirected so as to assist, rather than work against, womankind in overturning male oppression. She does not regard science as essentially patriarchal; but it does need to be radically reorganized.

In her criticism of scientific knowledge, Haraway (1988; 1989) invokes the notion of the 'god trick', which refers to the claims of scientists that the knowledge produced by them is 'omniscient' and 'all seeing'. The 'god trick' performed by science is only possible if the historically, socially and sexually contingent status of the knower – the subject who claims to know – is denied and concealed from view. Scientific knowledge is not disembodied truth, but situated knowledge born of historically and socially contingent practices that could have been quite different from the way they happened to be. So scientific ideas could have been quite different from the ways they happened to turn out. She examines how, for example, the emergence of primatology – the scientific study of primates – was a key development in the political ordering of the boundaries not just between 'nature' and 'culture', but 'male' and 'female', and 'science' and 'ideology' (Haraway, 1989). Haraway (1997) also analyses a series of experiments carried out by male scientists in seventeenth-century England, in order to emphasize that the social networks comprising the scientific community at that time were composed almost entirely of white European upper-class males. This male bias within the scientific community directly influenced the connections made as to femininity/passivity and

Aim: analysis of 'differences'; liberation through stimulation of cultural multiplicity

Method: analysis and deconstruction of discourses and texts

Subjects of analysis: gender categories as cultural constructions; subjectivities

Social order: cultural realm dominated by patriarchal discourses

Figure 11.2 Post-Modernist Feminist Theory.

masculinity/activity that came into being at this time, and which have continued to be an important part of patriarchal culture ever since. Just as Foucault sought to show how scientific discourses that claim to represent 'pure truth' are in fact marked by their historical conditions of production, so too does Haraway carry out such projects to destabilize what she and other post-structuralist feminist thinkers regard as the politically regressive and stultifying effects of so-called 'truths' that are in fact highly contingent and therefore alterable.

While the arguments of Haraway are grounded in careful collations of empirical evidence, the same cannot be said of all post-structuralist and post-modernist feminism. Like broader post-modernism, its feminist versions too generally prefer the free-wheeling speculation of a certain type of philosophizing, rather than grounding arguments in evidential bases. Its typically 'deconstructive' methods can seem more negative than positive – discourses are deconstructed and presented as constructions, but what the positive political outcomes of that may be remain unclear, which poses a problem for the women's movement as a political force. A postmodernist feminist approach can, however, be defended on the grounds that to criticize it for a lack of evidence assumes the terms set by male-dominated 'science', which is a meta-narrative now well and truly discredited. The only truth is the power to pull apart the discursive construction of forms of male power.

Phenomenological Feminism

The limitations of post-modernist feminism compel the search for other ways of theorizing gender oppression in the present day. One such approach is phenomenological feminism, which draws upon the ideas of phenomenological thought (see Chapter 4). With its emphasis on people's practical activities, it has a very different focus than post-modernist feminism's analysis of discourses and 'texts'. But phenomenological feminism links to post-modernist feminism through its concentration on practices, which it shares with Butler (1990, 1993), whose work is part of the 'practice turn' in social theory more generally (see Chapter 10).

A much-cited contribution to feminist phenomenology is Iris Marion Young's (1990) piece 'Throwing Like a Girl'. Young draws upon the phenomenology of bodily movement proposed by Merleau-Ponty (Chapter 4) in order to analyse typically 'feminine' modes of consciousness and the physical actions which are both motivated by and part of these. Young takes her cue from how at the present time typically 'male' and 'female' forms of bodily posture both seem different and are commonly presented as being different.

A nice example of this widespread phenomenon concerns Bill and Hillary Clinton. At the beginning of the 1994 baseball season, the then-President Clinton was photographed throwing the ceremonial first pitch of the season. At around the same time, but at another venue, Hillary Clinton was also photographed carrying out the same act. A number of newspapers the next day carried the two photos together. An interesting difference was made apparent in each of the Clintons' throwing styles. Bill 'had turned his shoulders sideways to the plate in preparation for delivery [and brought] . . . the ball forward from behind his head in a clean-looking throwing action' (Fallows, 1996: unpaginated). By contrast, Hillary was pictured throwing the ball with her 'body facing the target, rather than rotating [her] shoulders and hips ninety degrees away from the target and then swinging them around in order to accelerate the ball' (ibid.). While the President looked as if he was throwing effectively, the First Lady looked wholly ineffective in her stance. She was 'throwing like a girl'.

In a similar manner to post-modernist feminists who deny the importance of biological factors in gender relations, Butler argues that observable differences in male and female bodily movement are not rooted in 'sex', 'biology' or 'nature' – all patriarchal categories. Instead, the matter is explicable wholly in terms of culturally constructed gender categories. The differences in bodily use rest in how people in each gender category use their bodily capacities. Young sees such differences in bodily use as functions of different forms of socialization. In a patriarchal form of social order, women are brought up in ways that deny them the 'subjectivity, autonomy and creativity' that such a society accords to men (Young, 1990: 144). Women are encouraged in childhood to act in 'ladylike' ways, such as keeping the legs close together, and not using 'masculine' gestures such as walking with a bold stride. Such bodily dispositions are learned and acquired, not inevitable or innate, although patriarchal society presents the situation as if women are just 'naturally like that'. Males, by contrast, are taught implicitly and explicitly to walk, talk, throw, run and so on, 'like a man'. The common characteristic of all these male forms of bodily activity is one of confidence and openness, psychological and embodied qualities that a patriarchal society accords to men but not to women.

In a patriarchal context, therefore, the female 'body-subject' is one that tends to be less efficacious than its male counterpart. The space around the female is one that she has, through processes of socialization and enculturation, been discouraged from confidently reaching out towards. Women tend to be more corporeally *reactive* than active in comparison to men, who are more *active*, because the space that women 'feel' through their bodies seems more restricted to them than the space around the body felt by their male counterparts. For example, 'in softball or volleyball women tend to remain in one place more often than men do, neither jumping to reach nor running to approach the ball. Men more often move out toward a ball in flight and confront it with their own countermotion. Women tend to wait for and then *react* to its approach, rather than going forth to meet it' (ibid.: 146).

Patriarchal social conditioning means women tend to be less 'open' to the space they feel around them than men are. Moreover, 'women tend not to put their whole bodies into engagement in a physical task with the same ease and naturalness as men' (ibid.: 145). Women's bodily comportment, and the practical consciousness that goes with it (see Chapter 4), which tends to be much more tentative than that of men, has nothing to do with 'nature', and everything to do with the fact that patriarchal socialization creates a certain female sense of self. A patriarchal cultural context socializes women in light of its suspicion of feminine autonomy and confidence. While childhood socialization begins this process, this sense of self is constantly reinforced for women in adulthood by the – generally unconscious – practices of the social order around them. Everyone, both women and men, expect female bodies to act and be presented in certain stereotypical ways – 'being ladylike' – and if women break these norms

– e.g. 'sitting like a guy' – then they can face strong condemnation from other people, all of whom are constantly engaged in mental and bodily practices which unknowingly reproduce the dominant gender order all the time, through the most tiny details of how their bodies move and how they experience their bodies. The important point here is that Young, in ways similar to Butler's focus on practices, has suggested a way of connecting macro-level gender structures to micro-level experiences and activities. The shared use of Merleau-Ponty's phenomenology with Bourdieu (see Chapter 10) suggests that the model Young proposes can be seen as the gender-oriented version of what Bourdieu presents as an analysis of class-based forms of power, rooted in the body and practical consciousness.

Young's account, though, remains abstract, positing ideal-types of femininity and masculinity, rather than examining how these may work in specific micro-level contexts. This mirrors the high level of abstraction at which Merleau-Ponty operated. In the phenomenological tradition, ethnomethodology was intended as a way of avoiding abstraction by focusing on the most minute forms of human behaviour. It is on this strand of thinking that Dorothy Smith (1990) draws, combining ethnomethodological analyses of how individuals' sense of reality is created through micro-level activities, with both a feminist orientation and a Marxist critique of power relations in capitalist societies.

Smith contends that women's typical experience of reality is built upon 'a line of fault' between what they know and experience in their 'everyday/night' lives, and the linguistic and conceptual terms at their disposal for articulating those experiences. She claims that standard sociological concepts and ways of thinking about social life typically assume the character of 'objective', 'value-free' and 'taken-for-granted' knowledge and so are rarely called into question. Against this view, Smith argues that most social theorizing is undertaken by men because it is males who dominate the 'head world', occupying the professional positions within intellectual and public life given over to the supposedly 'rational' and 'objective' contemplation of social organization. Men are only able to occupy these socially prestigious and powerful positions because they depend upon women to attend to the most apparently mundane aspects of the lifeworld, such as cooking, cleaning, caring for children, etc.

Following a Marxist theme, Smith contends that under patriarchal conditions, women's work is systematically devalued, even though it is the necessary precondition for male-dominated 'headwork'. Male-defined concepts carry authority and are intellectually valorized, even though they are almost entirely divorced from the social and material conditions from which they arise. But only knowledge rooted in 'people's activities and material conditions thereof could be considered non-ideological'. This leads her to conclude that social science 'creates a construct of society that is especially discontinuous with the world known, lived, experienced and acted in' by women (Smith, 1990a: 36). Just as Marx had said that social theory must ally itself politically with the oppressed and root its understandings of the world in their experiences of it, so too does Smith (1987) argue that social theory must systematically reorient itself so as to incorporate and base itself in the views of reality experienced by women. This requires theorists to reposition themselves, rejecting mainstream social science, rooted in male visions and experiences, and locating themselves in the position of women, looking at the world from women's typical perspectives on it. This is part of broader feminist 'stand-point' theory, where social science's endeavours to be neutral and value-free are rejected as mythical and as tools of reproducing patriarchal social relations. Social theory and research are to analyse the world in ways rooted in the perspectives of women, for it is only in that way can they contribute to changing the world as it is currently ordered.

A key idea Smith uses to account for the subjugation of women is 'ruling relations'. These are the social relations which constitute the dominant social institutions: administrations, government bodies, corporations, and suchlike. These regulate modern society typically through impersonal and generalized media or 'texts', such as passport documents or tax declaration forms (Smith, 1990a, 1990b). Because modern society is increasingly knowledge-based (see Chapter 9), power is exerted through expert knowledge-systems which are defined as socially legitimate and authoritative (see Foucault's ideas – Chapter 8). Knowledge produced by psychologists, management consultants and other professional groups play a central role in supporting the 'ruling relations', because its 'expert' status makes it very hard for marginalized social groups to have their views of the world publicly represented. Women participate only marginally within these institutions, occupying lower positions within them than do men. For Smith (2000: 77):

> ... the ruling relations 'extract' the coordinative and concerting of people's everyday/everynight activities and subject them to technological and technical specialization ... and objectification. Coordination and

Iris Marion Young	Dorothy Smith
Merleau-Pontian phenomenology	Combination of feminism, ethnomethodology, Marxism
Patriarchal socialization of female and male body-subjects	
	Stand-point position
Everyday reproduction of gender practices	Ruling relations and their texts

Figure 11.3 Two Phenomenological Feminists.

> concerting are leached out of localized and particularized relations and transferred to modes in which they are subjected to specialized and technical development.

In other words, the activities of all oppressed groups – women, the working class, all kinds of minorities – are denied agency (see Chapter 10) because the ruling relations organize social order such that the dominant institutions control everyday life. So people living in a poor area have their everyday activities highly constrained by government officials, social workers, the police and so on. All of these use particular sorts of 'texts' as part of the apparatus of control: reports, files, documentation of all sorts, the use of which structures and reproduces the oppressive social order. This social order controls women particularly through texts which assume certain stereotypical understandings of sex and gender (e.g. that women offenders in court facing serious charges like murder are more morally culpable than men, because they have not only broken the law but they have also broken dominant gender codes which assume that women are 'naturally' more 'gentle' than men). In all sorts of unspoken ways, patriarchal ruling relations underpin the texts customarily used in everyday life, from psychology manuals to social work reports, and so spin a web of domination constantly reproduced through micro-level practices.

Conclusion

In this chapter, we have outlined the development of feminist social theory, which has always been simultaneously a form of intellectual activity as well as a political one, connected to broader political struggles.

Feminisms of various varieties throw down a challenge to the overall field of social theory. They illustrate the often gender-blind nature of previous forms of social theorizing, and of the need to transcend the blinkered forms of analysis that have resulted. In some sense, 'mainstream' social theory remains today 'male-stream' social theory, with many of the major authors male, and social theory being regarded by some feminist critics as primarily a 'man's game'. This is reflected in the frequent sequestration of 'feminist theory', it being defined as merely a sub-field of wider social theory, or as a separate entity altogether. 'Feminist theory' often gets treated as a mere 'add-on' to social theory courses and textbooks, rather than as something centrally constitutive of the field itself. This is very unfortunate, but it is a situation that can be changed. At its best, feminist theory has shown that genuinely new kinds of thinking, applicable to every dimension of society and every kind of person, can arise when one takes gender – and gender biases in knowledge production – as seriously as possible.

Further Reading

Grant, J. (1993) *Fundamental Feminism: Contesting the Core Concepts of Feminist Theory*. London: Routledge.

McLaughlin, J. (2003) *Feminist Social and Political Theory: Contemporary Debates and Dialogues*. Hampshire: Palgrave Macmillan.

Oakley, A. (1972) *Sex, Gender and Society*. London: Maurice Temple Smith Ltd.

Saul, J. M. (2003) *Feminism: Issues and Arguments*. Oxford: Oxford University Press.

Tong, R. P. (1998) *Feminist Thought: A More Comprehensive Introduction*. Oxford: Westview Press.

Walby, S. (1990) *Theorizing Patriarchy*. Cambridge: Blackwell.

12

Globalization Paradigms

Globalization has become in recent years an almost unavoidable word. It is used by a very wide range of people – journalists, politicians, business-people, political activists, religious leaders – who want to understand and represent the nature of the world in the present day. The term has become probably the most widely used buzzword of the early twenty-first century. It has come to have a wide range of meanings, both positive and negative.

Globalization's primary meaning in political and journalistic circles is to do with economic factors (Bourdieu, 1998). Both the right-wing supporters of 'global capitalism', in the form of trans-national corpora-tions (TNCs) and big business, and its radical left-wing critics, regard globalization as a fundamentally economic phenomenon, involving the creation of world-spanning free markets, and the global reach of capitalist systems of production and consumption. This is a new form of capitalism that is seen both by its advocates (e.g. Friedman, 1999) and its critics (Klein, 2001; Hardt and Negri, 2000) as thoroughly 'global' in scope. The expansion of capitalist markets across the world is seen to yield striking transformations in political, economic, social and cultural relations and regimes (Sklair, 2004). Whether one believes, as people on the political right do, that global capitalism brings with it jobs, opportunities, increas-ing wealth and higher standards of living, or whether one thinks, as do people on the left, that it leaves in its wake a range of social and environ-mental catastrophes, the shared belief among both right and left is that globalization is essentially a product and expression of multi- and trans-national capitalism.

There are other reasons why globalization has become such a ubiqui-tous buzzword. Environmental issues and problems that are widely under-stood as being 'global' in scope have been important influences in creating an overall political-intellectual climate in which the whole 'globe' is regarded as one single entity (Lovelock, 2000). Consciousness of the unin-tended consequences of human actions on the natural environment, and the set of partly uncontrollable world-wide risks that are attendant upon such actions, have helped to make diagnoses of globalization so omnipresent today (Beck, 1992).

At the same time as globalization became ever more present in public life, it has also come to figure as one of the most frequently used words across the social sciences and humanities. A very wide range of recent books and articles ask social scientists to make a 'global turn' in their thinking (e.g. Albrow, 1990; Robertson, 1992; Urry, 2000a, 2000b, 2003). This literature has been concerned with achieving at least two aims. First, to depict what globalization is, what it involves, how it works, and what effects it is having in different contexts and across the whole planet at the present time. These are the issues that we will unpack in this chapter, illustrating the different sorts of understanding of globalization that have been proposed by a range of different theorists coming from diverse schools of thought.

Second, the globalization literature has also aimed at transforming the nature of social theorizing itself. For many authors in this field, the phenomena associated with globalization seriously problematize traditional ways of theorizing 'society', as these were inherited from the classical sociologists and those of the post-First-World-War period (Mann, 1986; Albrow 1990). For one such critic, Ulrich Beck (2000: 24):

> The association between sociology and nation-state was so extensive that the image of 'modern', organized individual societies – which became definitive with the national model of political organization – itself became an absolutely necessary concept in and through the founding work of classical social scientists. Beyond all their differences, such theorists as Émile Durkheim, Max Weber and even Karl Marx shared a territorial definition of modern society, and thus a model of society centred on the national-state, which has today been shaken by globality and globalization.

In light of such critiques, the notion of a 'society' as a self-enclosed, bounded entity has come under heavy criticism. It seems highly unsuited for capturing the trans-national processes and phenomena associated with globalization (Outhwaite, 2009). The very notion of 'society' itself may have been rendered obsolete by the onset and deepening of globalization forces. Social theory should no longer primarily be concerned either with the idea of 'society' in general, or with national entities such as 'British society' or 'French society'. This is both because the realm of the 'social' is alleged to be no longer primarily contained within particular countries and states, and also because it is argued that there are today so many processes and phenomena that exist *beyond, across and above* the confines of nation-states that a focus on national societies would miss out what is most important and novel about a world being transformed by globalization processes. On this view, social theory that takes 'society' in general, or particular national societies, as its main concern is guilty of 'methodological nationalism' (Martins, 1974), falsely and unnecessarily restricting social life to what occurs *within* particular states, rather than looking at what happens at more 'global' and 'transnational' levels of human activity. According to John Urry (2000a, 2000b, 2003), for social theory to keep apace with an ever more globalized world, it needs to embrace a 'post-societal' paradigm, the terminology of which would be centred around notions of 'global networks and flows' (2000a: 186), which move across the whole planet, operating through and beyond the territories that national governments are now only partly in control of.

Whether or not one accepts that social theory has for too long been fixated on the notion of 'society', and whether this is a bad thing or not (Inglis and Robertson, 2008), it remains the case that conditions of globalization pose important challenges to social theory, compelling it to find vocabularies – either new or inherited from previous thinkers – to describe the phenomena associated with a globalizing world. In this chapter we examine the ways different sorts of social theorists have risen to that challenge. There are many different types of globalization theory, leading to

Culture – does globalization primarily entail cultural imperialism and global homogeneity?	**Politics** – does globalization thoroughly undermine the power of national governments?
Social Relations – how are social relations altered by globalization?	**Economy** – is globalization primarily a function of the global capitalist economy?

Figure 12.1 Four Dimensions of Globalization, and Key Questions About Them.

a somewhat bewildering array of perspectives on what globalization is, how it operates and what effects it has. A sensible way of categorizing these accounts is to divide them up into theories which emphasize either the *economic, political, social* or *cultural* facets of globalization. We will examine each set of theories in turn.

Globalization as Economic Processes

Despite their other differences, both right-wing defenders of capitalism and radical, often Marxist, critics of capitalism believe that globalization is primarily an economic set of phenomena, that have had profound effects on the world today. Despite the waxing and waning popularity of Marxist ideas in public discourses over time, it is quite ironic that contemporary popular discussion of globalization partly follows, although mostly unintentionally, the views of Marx and his collaborator Friedrich Engels. In the middle of the nineteenth century they wrote in the *Manifesto of the Communist Party* (1968 [1848]: 38) that 'the need of a constantly expanding market for its products chases the bourgeoisie over the whole surface of the globe'. What they were claiming was that capitalism contains within itself a dynamic that compels it, in its search constantly to make profits, to expand its markets all across the world. Capitalism seeks to bring every single person on the planet under its sway as both a producer of goods, from which it can extract profits, and as a consumer of those goods. Marx and Engels (1968 [1848]: 38) saw that this increasingly globe-spanning capitalism

> . . . batters down all Chinese walls [i.e. all national defences against it] . . . It compels all nations, on pain of extinction, to adopt the bourgeois mode of production . . . [and] to introduce what it calls civilization into their midst, i.e., to become bourgeois themselves.

All regions of the world would sooner or later be thoroughly transformed by capitalism, with traditions being swept away and replaced by a novel, world-encompassing social order centred on the search for profit. Both defenders and critics of capitalism in the present day share some of Marx's and Engels' views about globalization essentially involving the global spread of capitalism from the West to the rest of the world. Globalization is thus seen as 'the inexorable integration of markets, nation-states, and technologies to a degree never witnessed before . . . in a way that is enabling individuals, corporations and nation-states to reach around the world farther, faster, deeper and cheaper than ever before . . . [The end result is] the spread of free-market capitalism to virtually every country in the world' (Friedman, 1999: 7–8).

The sort of analysis pioneered by Marx and Engels was taken up in the early part of the twentieth century by V. I. Lenin, Bolshevik leader of the Russian revolution, who argued that by around the period of the First World War, capitalism had 'grown into a world system of colonial oppression and of the financial strangulation of the overwhelming majority of the population of the world by a handful of "advanced" countries' (Lenin, 1977 [1916]: 232). Taking up some of Lenin's analytical orientations in the present-day is *world-systems analysis*. Over the last three decades, this has come to be one of the most influential paradigms for analysing the dynamics of the world economy. The major pioneer of this approach, Immanuel Wallerstein (1974), has come to be seen as a major contributor towards 'globalization' debates, although he rejects the term 'globalization', instead focusing on different kinds of 'world-system'. His analysis is not based on a single academic discipline, because it does not accept the conceptual carving up of the social world into discrete spheres of 'society', 'economy', 'politics', and so on.

A 'world-system' for Wallerstein (2004: 16–17) refers not to a system that is necessarily world-spanning in scope, but to a system that creates its own distinct 'world'. It is 'a spatial-temporal zone which cuts across many political and cultural units', involving 'an integrated zone of activity and institutions which obey certain systemic rules'. A world-system is both multi-political and multi-cultural; it forms a system which pulls into the same orbit, and into patterned forms of interaction with each other, different political and cultural entities. World-systems rather than particular nation-states are to be the central focus of inquiry.

World-systems have 'core', 'peripheral' and 'semi-peripheral' regions within them, where particular sorts of economic activities take place. The core dominates and controls the whole system, using and exploiting the resources of the peripheral region. The role of the semi-periphery is to keep the whole system functioning effectively by connecting core and peripheral regions in ways that suit the core's interests. Wallerstein analyses the world-system that is the contemporary global capitalist economy. This system started to develop in Europe in the sixteenth century, involving the development of a single division of labour stretching from Ireland in the west to Poland in the east. Northwest Europe became the 'core' of this unit (first of all specializing in higher-skilled forms of agricultural production), the Mediterranean area the 'semi-periphery' (specializing both in high-cost industrial products like silks, and credit transactions) and Eastern Europe and the Americas 'the periphery' (specializing in the export of raw materials like grain and sugar).

By the twentieth century capitalism had become truly globe-spanning in nature, but from its very beginnings it was highly expansionist (2004: x). Over time, there has come to exist 'a single virtual world market . . . [acting] like a magnet for all producers and buyers, whose pull is a constant political factor in the decision-making of everyone – the states, the firms, the households, the classes . . . [It] is a reality in that it influences all decision making, but it never functions fully and freely' (2004: 25). Thus on this view, we are not, and never have been, dealing with national economies that exist in isolation from each other. Capitalist entrepreneurs always have sought to operate in the whole capitalist world-economy, even if that has sometimes meant pressuring governments to erect protective trade barriers for their benefit. Today's so-called 'globalizing' trends are only the most recent developments in capitalism's ever-growing global reach since its inception in the sixteenth century.

The capitalist world-economy is made up of 'many institutions – states and the interstate system, productive firms, households, classes, identity groups of all sorts – and . . . these institutions form a matrix which permits the system to operate but at the same time stimulates both the conflicts and the contradictions which permeate the system'. Thus capitalism *requires*, rather than abolishes, a multi-state system (see below). This is because 'capitalists need a large market . . . but they also need a multiplicity of states, so that they can gain the advantages of working with states but also can circumvent states hostile to their interests in favour of states friendly to their interests' (2004: 24).

'Core states' (primarily those in Western Europe and North America) are those which contain large amounts of highly profitable economic activities. 'Peripheral states' (e.g. those in Africa and parts of Latin America) are those that, by contrast, have high proportions of low-profit activities. Core states remain core if they manage to retain within their territories high-profit activities, while ensuring that industries that are becoming low-profit move from them to peripheral states. 'Semi-peripheral states', such as Brazil and India, and the actors within them, are both exploiters and exploited. They try to engage in what count at any one time as core-type activities, while trying to avoid becoming focused around periphery-type activities. For Wallerstein, states continue to be important players in the world-economy, controlling to varying degrees the movement of goods, capital and people. Core states operate to pressurize semi-peripheral and peripheral states to play the economic game according to the rules that act in the favour of the core states and the business enterprizes domiciled in their territories. The current 'hegemonic' (see Chapter 3) state in the capitalist world-economy is the USA, which dominates the inter-state political system, gets mostly to set the rules of the global economy, and can get what it wants through diplomatic means without having to resort constantly to violent methods.

As far as the future of the capitalist world-economy is concerned, Wallerstein, as a Marxist committed to the idea that capitalism sows the seeds of its own downfall, argues that it is doomed to self-destruct, opening up the path towards the building of a world socialist system. The system is currently reaching its limits in terms of profitability – costs are inexorably going up and profits are unavoidably coming down. This is in part because sources of cheap labour are drying up as more and more parts of the globe undergo some sort of industrialization, leaving fewer and fewer locales where labour is very cheap. In addition, the development of environmental consciousness among particular populations has compelled governments to lay more levies on polluting companies, driving their costs up. Also there has been growing since the late 1960s an anti-capitalist (and anti-American) cultural climate, in which people in all parts of the world are increasingly dissatisfied with the promises and practices of capitalism. Ironically, the system itself has brought to the fore an increasingly 'global' sense of its own shortcomings such that 'people are more fully aware of these issues today than a century ago . . . They are more aware, more willing to struggle for their rights, more skeptical about the rhetoric of the powerful' (2004: 89).

The global capitalist system is thus reaching its own finite limits, casting it into unavoidable crisis and decline. To his critics, this may sound more like a product of Marxist wishful thinking than hard-headed analysis of capitalism's relative robustness and staying-power over the long-term. Wallerstein has often been criticized for being too wedded to the terms of Marxist political economy (see Chapter 1), having far too narrow a view of the complexities of globalization, especially as regards cultural issues (Boyne, 1990). However, the focus on core, peripheral and

Analysis of 'world-systems'

Dominance globally of capitalist world-system since the sixteenth century

Splitting up of world into core, semi-periphery and periphery regions and countries

Core exploits semi-periphery and periphery

Figure 12.2 Summary of Wallerstein and World-Systems Analysis.

semi-peripheral regions within the world capitalist economy remains a highly influential one.

The effects of radically unequal economic arrangements worldwide are the focus of Zygmunt Bauman's (1998) analysis of the 'human consequences' of globalization. Bauman has been concerned to develop an ethically informed social theory which takes as its focus the nature and consequences of various forms of suffering induced by social and economic conditions. Globalization theory (e.g. Urry, 2000a, 2000b) often focuses on how people, money and goods are constantly moving across national borders. Bauman points out that the nature of trans-national mobility is of radically different sorts for different kinds of people. Those living in the 'global North' – the core countries of the advanced capitalist societies – generally engage in freely chosen mobility, moving from country to country for reasons such as business and tourism. But the vast majority of the world population, living in the 'global South' – the countries of the global semi-periphery and periphery – are generally *forced* to be mobile, for reasons such as seeking work when there is none to be had in their country of origin, or fleeing war and persecution. One of the hallmarks of the modern age as a whole, and the highly globalized version of it that has been created over the last several decades, are mass migrations, involving the movement and dispersal of millions of people from their places of origin (Papastergiadis, 2000). For Bauman, if mass migration is one of the central features of a globalized world-condition, then one of economic globalization's central features is its dividing of the world's population up into a minority of relatively – sometimes very – rich winners, and a vast majority of very poor losers, forced to leave their homelands to become the low-paid, exploited workers, domestic servants, prostitutes and asylum-seekers to be found on the social margins of the global North.

Globalization as Political Processes

Marx and Engels predicted that the creation of a truly world-encompass-ing capitalist market would severely diminish the power of national gov-ernments to control that goes on within their territories. This is a view held today by many observers on both left and right. From this point of view, capitalist markets are nowadays not just *inter*-national but in fact *trans*-national in nature. Information, goods, people and services move across and beyond national borders without respecting the territorial power of governments. This situation is seen to have certain severe reper-cussions for the degree to which national governments remain in control of their economic and other affairs. A state with unquestioned control over its own 'national' territory – the condition political scientists call 'sovereignty' – was an innovation of Western countries that was invented only as recently as the seventeenth century (Osiander, 2001). Over the last several hundred years, individual states have had (at least in theory) the power to run affairs within their own borders, without hindrance from other states. According to some analysts (e.g. Ohmae, 2000), what capital-ist economic globalization does above all is to undermine the power of the state within its own territory. If trans-national corporations (TNCs) such as Coca-Cola and Toyota can pick and choose which countries to situate their businesses within, if capital and resources are very geographi-cally mobile, and if all national economies are thoroughly bound up with each other, then it would seem to be the case that the capacity of the state to control its own economic affairs is undermined, perhaps seriously so (Held and McGrew, 2000). The degree to which states increasingly lack economic power – and thus other sorts of power too – within the present-day global system remains a contested issue, with some claiming the day of the nation-state is now well and truly over, and others arguing that claims as to the demise of the state are very overstated (Hirst and Thompson, 2000).

What most analysts would agree about, however, is that individual states today find themselves operating within a series of constraints that are probably much more developed than was the case before the Second World War. States have to work within an environment where they are hemmed in not just by the machinations of global corporations, but also by international law, international bodies like the United Nations and the World Trade Organization, inter-state bodies like the European Union, and global-level pressure groups like Amnesty International and

Greenpeace. The latter operate within what can be taken to be a nascent 'global civil society', a realm of political contestation and debate operating outside of the nation-state system and across national borders (Keane, 2003).

Moreover, in comparison to fifty years ago, national governments find it increasingly difficult to control information flows within their borders, with satellite television and the internet allowing people access to information and attitudes from potentially every other part of the world. The recent, rather desperate attempts by the Chinese government to control internet access by its citizens, shows just how potentially troublesome trans-national information flows can be to particular governments who desire control over the attitudes of their populations. The outcome of all these factors is that even the most dictatorial governments are arguably more constrained in their actions today than they have ever been, both in terms of what they do on the global political stage and how they deal with affairs within what is – theoretically – 'their own' national domain. What nowadays counts as 'inside' and 'outside' a particular state has been problematized by the economic and political dimensions of globalization (Albrow, 1996).

Globalization as Social Processes

A focus on the social dimensions of globalization involves reflection upon how globalization forces may be involved in the reconstitution of the nature and form of social relations today.

Echoing the views of many others, Waters (1995: 3) defines globalization as a 'social process in which the constraints of geography on social and cultural arrangements recede and in which people become increasingly aware that they are receding'. This definition usefully highlights the possibility that 'globalization' is not just about the 'world becoming smaller', but also that people's actions and beliefs are affected and changed precisely because they *believe* that is indeed the case.

Accepting this view of globalization has ramifications for how we can think about the forces that shape and influence people's actions and inter-actions. We should not see these forces as being either simply 'local' or 'national' in scale any more, as formed and operating within purely 'local' communities or within the boundaries of particular nation-states. This is because both the 'local' and the 'national' are nowadays bound up with wider, more global-level phenomena and forces (Robertson, 1992: 37). We have to examine how people who live within the borders of a particular state are affected by, respond to, and themselves help to create, forces that are trans-national in nature (Urry, 2000).

Anthony Giddens views globalization as involving 'the intensification of worldwide social relations which link distant localities in such a way that local happenings are shaped by events occurring many miles away and vice versa' (Giddens, 1990: 64). Thus 'what happens in a local neighbourhood is likely to be influenced by factors – such as world money and commodity markets – operating at an indefinite distance away from that neighbourhood itself' (ibid.).

In a similar vein, for Martin Albrow (1996: 88), globalization in part means a situation where 'global practices . . . exercise an increasing influence over people's lives', where 'global practices' could mean various things, from a big corporation closing down a factory in one country and moving it to another where costs are lower, to a non-governmental organization such as Friends of the Earth campaigning in national or local media.

The central point made by these thinkers is that under conditions of globalization what happens *here* is influenced not just by what happens *there* but in a whole series of *theres*. And what counts as 'here' can get fundamentally changed too. For the philosopher Martin Heidegger (1971 [1950]: 165), writing just after the Second World War, developing communications technologies were thoroughly undermining older relations between time and space: 'Distant sites of the most ancient cultures are shown on film as if they stood this very moment amidst today's street traffic. The peak of this abolition of every possibility of remoteness is reached by television, which will soon pervade and dominate the whole machinery of communication.' What this entailed was that now 'everything is equally far and equally near', a condition of 'uniform distancelessness' (ibid.: 166).

Held et al. (1999: 16) similarly regard globalization as involving transformations 'in the spatial organization of social relations and transactions – assessed in terms of their extensity, intensity, velocity and impact – generating transcontinental or inter-regional flows and networks of activity'. Given that social relationships are no longer primarily tied to 'local' areas and within the boundaries of states, then the people you work and do business with, the friends you have, the acquaintances you know, all could be located in geographically distant locales. A person's relationships and forms of interaction become increasingly unconstrained by geography and are no longer necessarily 'local' or 'national' in nature.

One of the most sustained attempts to theorize the changing nature of social relations – indeed the very nature of the 'social' realm itself – is offered by Giddens (1990), who sees globalization as the 'stretching' and 'disembedding' of social relations. His general ideas as to the nature of modernity were set out in Chapter 10. Giddens highlights the changing nature of time and space under globalizing conditions. When a jet aircraft can transport you a vast geographical distance from one side of the world to the other side in a fraction of the time it used to take by boat, then the connections that used to hold between time and space are shattered and new forms of time and space are created. In the nineteenth century, it took several weeks to travel by ship from Western Europe to the United States, whereas nowadays by plane it only takes a matter of hours. This alteration in time and space changes a person's perception of the nature of their social relations. If one's relatives live four weeks away by boat, then they will seem very far away, but if they live only six hours away by aircraft, they might not seem so far away at all. If they can be contacted almost immediately by telephone or through the internet, they will in some ways seem very 'present' even if they live on the other side of the world.

Giddens views globalization as a consequence and radicalization of modernity's recasting of the nature of social relations. Modernity has an inherent tendency to spread globally (1990: 63). This is because it creates the kinds of social relations that do not need to happen in particular physical locations between people interacting face-to-face. Modern communications mean a person can interact with others very geographically distant from them. Thus typically 'modern' social relations have the capacity to become 'disembedded' from particular, more 'local' and geographically specific locales. As modernity expands across the world, social relations are 'stretched' across indefinite levels of space, to the extent that, in theory, actions happening in any place on earth could have ramifications for any other place on earth, as long as adequate telecommunications systems are in place. The ensuing actions and interactions may well transcend the territorial boundaries of nation-states.

The particular mechanisms that create and allow the disembedding of social relations are two types of 'symbolic tokens', namely money and 'expert systems'. Money 'provides for the enactment of transactions between agents widely separated in time and space' (ibid.: 24). Expert systems are 'systems of technical accomplishment or professional expertise that organize large areas of the material and social environments in which we live today' (ibid. 27), such as medicine, engineering and law.

These have the capacity to 'remove social relations from the immediacies of context . . . by providing "guarantees" of expectations across distanciated time-space' (ibid.: 28). Both money and expert systems allow social relations to be stretched across long geographical distances and over indefinite periods of time, because they allow a certain form of predictability to social relations which is necessary for them to be practicable. No matter where in the world one happens to be, one can rely on certain sorts of social relations being possible, because of the presence of money and expert systems. This provides one with a certain degree of necessary 'ontological security', the knowledge that one is in a context where one knows how to act 'correctly' and that one may reasonably expect others to respond to you in relatively familiar and understandable ways (Giddens, 1991). Money can allow you to rent a hotel-room anywhere in the world. The expert system of medicine means that doctors trained within it will act generally in the same ways with you when you are a patient, regardless of what country you are in. Here we have a vision of the universal 'modernization' of social relations involving money and expert systems, with people in all parts of the world coming to engage in the same sorts of behaviours and expectations of trust in those systems.

This does not imply, however, that social relations become exactly the same in every part of the world. The effects of disembedding are 'not simply that localized influences drain away into the more impersonalized relations of abstract systems' (ibid.: 140), but that the latter can be *re-embedded* by human agents back into 'local' contexts, albeit local contexts increasingly characterized by mixtures of more 'local' and more 'distant' elements. Actual face-to-face encounters between expert-system 'professionals' (doctors, hotel clerks, etc.) and their 'users' (patients, tourists, etc.) are understood by Giddens (ibid.: 87–8) as involving re-embedding processes, which are 'encounters and rituals which sustain . . . trustworthiness', by bringing 'placeless' systems back into specific micro-level contexts. People have to have faith in the expert systems they use or rely upon. You want the expert system of aircraft engineering and safety measurements to be as trustworthy in any part of the world you are flying to as in your home nation.

But even despite re-embedding processes, the problem with disembedded social relations is that the more the abstract systems that make those relations possible require trust in them, the more possibility there is of that trust being diminished, or even brought into very severe doubt when

Stretching of social relations
Disembedding and re-embedding
Trust in expert systems
Risk management

Figure 12.3 Summary of Giddens on Globalization.

things go wrong. As Giddens (ibid.: 125) puts it, if 'disembedding mechanisms have provided large areas of security in the present-day world, the new array of risks which have thereby been brought into being are truly formidable'. We trust that aircraft engineers in airports will be as well-trained and diligent wherever we fly – but what if they are less so in some countries? Then the possibility of flying becomes a matter of risk assessment, working out how risky or not flying in and out of particular territories may be. Thus globalization involves the expansion of, and necessity of people regularly placing their trust in, expert systems. But this form of risk management itself breeds risks that have to be managed, which in turn can lead to a spiral of ever more risks and ever more risk-management.

Giddens' ideas about globalization and risk have affinities with the 'world risk society' thesis of Ulrich Beck. Beck's (1999) account of world-level risks is based in his analysis of the transition from 'first modernity' – the industrial capitalist society analysed by the classical theorists (see Chapter 1) – to 'second modernity', which Beck also calls 'risk society'. In first modernity, social order is relatively stable and coherent, based around industrial production, class-based identities and politics, nation-states in control of their own territories, beliefs in social progress, and faith in the natural sciences to produce socially beneficial knowledge.

However, according to Beck this society inadvertently destroyed itself, forcing an unforeseen mutation into second modernity / risk society. Forces are unleashed by first modernity that it cannot deal with, and which come to undermine it. These forces include: a capitalist economy that becomes ever more global in scope, undermining the power of national states to control their own financial situation and activities; capitalist production of goods, which leads to all sorts of problems of pollution and environmental degradation; and scientific innovations, such as genetic engineering of human, animal and plant life, the outcomes of which are very uncertain, and the morality of which becomes open to question. A condition of risk society is reached by the later twentieth century, and it is characterized by these factors: national governments struggle to deal with the various problems unleashed by the forces just mentioned; scientists and other experts disagree about the nature of the problems and how to deal with them; in the face of expert disagreement and apparent government impotence, the public come to be highly sceptical both about scientists and government officials, and their proposed solutions to problems; and attempted solutions to problems can often make matters worse, creating new problems that then have to be dealt with.

Thus risk society is one where radical uncertainty rules, and where ever more desperate attempts are made to try to control what may be uncontrollable. Such a situation affects all countries in the world, because the hazards unleashed by first modernity are global in scope, from the constant possibility of crisis and bust in the global capitalist economy, and an ever more unstable labour market, through to environmental crises that potentially affect everyone on the planet, such as global warming and the threat of nuclear catastrophe (Strydom, 2002). Under such a situation, social relations are radically reconfigured from the ways they were in first modernity. For example, the situation of being in the same job for life, that workers in the 1950s and 1960s in both capitalist West and Communist East would have expected, has disappeared under the ever more uncertain conditions of a globalized capitalism. For example, jobs in affluent core countries can be quickly relocated to semi-peripheral areas – e.g. the relocating of call centre jobs from the UK to India – with accompanying unsettling effects on the identities and outlooks of those workers who have lost their employment and are forced into low-paid, service sector 'McJobs' like working in fast-food restaurants (Beck, 2000). In world risk society, there is a constant unsettling of social relations and modes of being that seemed in first modernity to be fixed and secure.

Clearly a further important element in the recasting of social relations under globalizing conditions involves the widespread use of information technologies, both in the reproduction of existing sorts of relations and in the creation of novel forms of interaction. Much has been made of internet-based communications as making possible the increasingly transnational nature of social relations. For proponents of the internet's capacity to transform thoroughly the nature of the social, the information superhighway gives 'us all access to seemingly unlimited information, anytime and any place we care to use it', and thus allows the opening up of a whole series of new vistas for individuals in terms of what they know and with whom they interact (Gates, 1995: 184). A person connected to the internet can, for example, join chat-rooms involving people from potentially widely geographically dispersed locations, engaging in forms of (relatively) instantaneous communication with others that previously would have been impossible. The image of a fully 'wired world' conjures up pictures of people in all corners of the planet being able to engage in a whole series of different types of relations with each other, unconstrained by geographical locatedness and nationality (Hand and Sandywell, 2002).

Yet the question remains as to how thoroughly social relations have been and will be transformed by the spread of electronically based networks. One of the most influential accounts of the roles played by the internet in the contemporary world is the Spanish social theorist Manuel Castells' work on the 'network society'. Castells' ideas are part of the more general stream of 'post-industrial' thought (see Chapter 9) which claims that the economic structures of Western societies are no longer based fundamentally around production of commodities, but around the generation and dissemination of knowledge, especially through electronic means. However, Castells (2000: 10) notes that *all* societies are 'information societies', in that all require flows of information between their different parts in order for some sort of ongoing order to be possible at all (see Chapter 2). He differentiates this generic societal condition from what he calls the social order of 'informationalism', which has arisen only in the last few decades in the advanced capitalist societies. In the new 'Information Age', which replaces the 'Industrial Age' centred around the production and distribution of energy, 'human societies perform their activities in a technological paradigm constituted around microelectronics-based information/communication technologies', with activities centred around the creation and dissemination of various specialist knowledges, such as information about financial markets (2000: 5–6). In such a situation, 'information generation, processing and transmission become the fundamental sources of productivity and power' (1996: 21).

Castells argues that we are currently merely on the threshold of the revolution in human activities that the Information Age heralds. The social-structural expression of the Information Age is the 'network society'. For Castells, this mode of social organization now 'permeates most [nationally based] societies in the world, in various cultural and institutional manifestations' (2000: 5). Electronically based networks have come to replace bureaucracies as the main means of organizing social relations, as such networks are better at managing complexity (2000: 15). Electronic networks crucial in the network society include economic networks of trade and investment, political networks such as the 'network state' (which includes transnational political entities such as the European Union), and interpersonal networks enacted through email and networking websites.

Castells defines a 'network' in this way: (1) it has no 'centre'; (2) it is made up of a series of 'nodes', some of which are more important than others, but all are required for the network to operate; (3) the relative power of a node depends on how much information it processes; (4) networks only deal with information that is relevant to them; (5) 'Networks are open structures, able to expand without limits' (2000 [1996]: 501–2). Thus 'a network-based social structure is a highly dynamic, open system, susceptible to innovating without threatening its balance' (2000 [1996]: 501–2). Networked social relations are a 'dynamic, self-expanding form of human activity' which tends to transform 'all domains of social and economic life' (1998: 336–7). Moreover, each person is strongly affected by their positions within or in relation to different networks, including one's absence or exclusion from particular networks. As Castells puts it, 'presence or absence in the network and the dynamics of each network vis-à-vis others are critical sources of domination and change in our society' (1996: 469).

In part following Giddens, Castells sees networks as fundamentally restructuring the nature of time and space. Time becomes both highly compressed, as in the case of the split-second instantaneousness of electronic communication, and also 'desequenced', involving the blurring of past, present and future (2000: 13–14). Space is reorganized through the electronically mediated 'space of flows', which involves 'organizing the simultaneity of social practices without geographical contiguity' (2000: 14). Castells notes that electronic communication *is* geographically located to the extent that for people to engage in internet-based activities, there must be an infrastructure, involving computer hardware, internet service providers, etc. in place relatively near to their physical location. However, the space of flows itself is, in terms of the experiences it provokes and the functions it provides, very different from the 'space of places' where 'meaning, function and locality are closely interrelated' (2000: 14). Simultaneity in human relations has become profoundly decoupled from physical co-presence.

Castells' view of how thoroughly networked social relations have changed social relations has altered over time. At first he argued that it was mainly elite groups, especially those working within the institutions of the global capitalist economy, whose lives were structured within and through the space of flows, while the lives of non-elites still tended to be organized around and 'clustered in localities', where most social relations were characterized by physical vicinity (Castells and Ince, 2003: 56–7). The space of places, not that of electronic networks, was seen to be the locale where 'most people build their meaning[s] and live their lives' (Castells and Ince, 2003: 58). This suggested a world-wide divide between internet-using, 'cosmopolitan' elites on the one side, and internet-deprived, 'localized' masses on the other. While social relations for the one grouping are always potentially 'global', for the other they are still primarily 'local' and tied up with defensive forms of identity that are produced on the basis of feelings of exclusion from, and resentment towards, the networked elites.

While clearly there is some truth in this view (Bauman, 1998), it came to seem too simplistic, as it excluded the possibility of non-elite groups gaining access to electronically mediated networks altogether. Castells' later analysis asserts that 'people of all kinds, wishing to do all kinds of things, can occupy this space of flows and use it for their own purposes' (Castells and Ince, 2003). The creative use of the internet by certain 'anti-globalization' groups in the global South, most famously the Zapatistas in Mexico, testifies to non-elite intrusion into the space of flows (Appadurai, 1996). The space of flows can be enabling as well as disabling to those occupying non-elite social positions worldwide.

Globalization as Cultural Processes

Having looked at globalization as a series of transformations to social relations, we can now turn to examine the viewpoints of those who analyse the cultural aspects of globalization, and who regard globalization processes as being at least as much cultural in nature as they are economic, political or social.

Clearly one important aspect of cultural forms and forces is that they involve how particular groups of people think and feel about the world around them. One of the major cultural analysts of globalization is the British sociologist Roland Robertson (1992). He insists that globalization involves not just material changes as to how people live – that is, changes in economic, political and social circumstances – but also in how they think, both in general and about those circumstances (1992: 8). Globalization is defined by Robertson as 'the compression of the world and the intensification of consciousness of the world as a whole'. Concomitant with economic, political and social aspects of globalization, there is also a key cultural development, namely 'globality', which is comprised of forms of consciousness and ways of thinking which regard the whole earth as 'one place'.

Feelings of globality are dramatized in, for example, self-consciously 'global' affairs like the Olympic Games, media events televized around the globe such as Live Aid and other charity concerts, and the appropriately named soccer *World* Cup. For Robertson, such 'global' imaginings have come more and more to shape how we think, feel and respond to things in our lives. We come to see our own individual existences as being thoroughly connected to, and dependent on, events and affairs that encompass everyone and everything on the planet. This does not mean that everyone comes to think in exactly the same ways. Instead, globality is a situation whereby specific groups retain distinct – though complicated, overlapping and 'glocal' (see below) – viewpoints and identities. But all groups are compelled to frame their specific ways of thinking, especially thinking about themselves and who they are, vis-à-vis global frames of reference. They are compelled to see themselves as just one part of a much greater global whole, where that global whole is not a homogeneous mass, but a very complicated mixture of differing cultural dispositions and mentalities. So there are under conditions of globality multiple ways of thinking and acting; but they are all forced to frame themselves in relation to a world where everything is connected to everything else in an increasingly complex manner.

This situation means that, as Robertson (1992: 112) puts it, it is impossible to 'carry into the study of globalization the kind of view of culture that we inherit from the conventional analysis of the national society'. So just as some thinkers want to reject national societies, and the idea of 'society' in general, as the central focus of social theory, the same would apply to 'culture'. It is no longer adequate just to look at 'Canadian culture', 'Spanish culture' and so on. We must instead consider the ways in which 'the interconnectedness of the world, by way of interactions, exchanges and related developments, affect[s] . . . the organization of culture' (Hannerz, 1996: 7). We have to look at how culture is created, shaped, re-worked and contested within, across, beyond and above national borders (Hannerz, 1989).

A key notion for many analysts of cultural globalization is 'deterritorialization'. This refers to the ways in which global-level forces can diminish the significance of social and geographical location in the creation and experience of cultural phenomena (Featherstone, 1990), leading to 'the loss of the "natural" relation of culture to geographical and social territories' (Garcia-Canclini, 1995: 107). This involves examining the means by which specific cultural forms are 'lifted out' of their traditional 'anchoring' in particular locales, and transplanted and then transformed in places where they previously had not existed. Cultural forms and experiences are today no longer as rooted as they were in the places they happened to have originated in. The cultural possibilities on offer in a particular locale are no longer wholly or mostly 'traditional' to that locale. Cultural phenomena can be transplanted and take root in places many thousands of miles from where they originated. Think, for example, of the presence in many parts of the world of restaurants claiming to serve 'Italian' or 'Chinese' food: they indicate the radical re-transplanting of cultural forms across the world, those forms being constantly re-worked and reinvented as they travel and get embedded in new social and geographical contexts (Inglis and Gimlin, 2010).

The central dispute among analysts of the cultural dimensions of globalization concerns whether this domain primarily involves processes of 'cultural imperialism' or not. For Marxist and other radical critics, Western-based mass media companies are Trojan horses of capitalist and consumerist values, spreading ideas and encouraging ways of life which undermine 'local' cultures, in that these are 'battered out of existence by the indiscriminate dumping of large quantities of slick commercial media products, mainly from the United States' (Tunstall, 1977: 57). The primarily American Western mass media are on this view purveyors of 'cultural imperialism', involved in the imposition of the set of values of one country or region (the USA, the 'West') onto another country or region. The global exportation by Western media corporations of pop idols and film and television stars, push to the peripheries of national and local media cultures more indigenous media products that are made in the countries of transmission. Following Wallerstein's terms, it is certain 'core' countries, especially the US, which make most media products, and these dominate the cultural lives of people in the periphery and semi-periphery (Hannerz, 1989).

This situation of core countries dominating the rest of the world is alleged not just to apply to media programming but to consumer goods too (Klein, 2001). Brands globally recognizable today include those of American corporations such as Coca-Cola, Pepsi, Disney and Levis. Some Europe- and Japan-based brands, like Benetton, Motorola and Sony, are also globally present. As Beck (2000: 42) puts it, in 'the villages of Lower Bavaria, just as in Calcutta, Singapore or the "favelas" of Rio de Janeiro, people watch *Dallas* on TV, wear blue jeans and smoke Marlboro'. It is possible to view this collection of symbols, products and ideas as the constituent elements of a 'new world culture', the 'first universal culture ever' (Cvetkovich and Kellner, 1997: 7). As a consequence, 'the impressive varieties of the world's cultural systems are waning due to a process of "cultural synchronization" that is without historical precedent' (Hamelink, 1983: 3). Or as Seabrook (2004: 4) puts it, globalization (understood as global capitalism's spread and power) 'has declared war upon all other cultures . . . It imposes its own culture, which profoundly influences the lives of people everywhere'.

Radical critics' condemnations of cultural imperialism and global consumerism clearly identify certain real empirical trends. But they can be criticized for often being based upon 'superficial and anecdotal examples' rather than on in-depth analysis of particular contexts and situations (Schuerkens, 2003: 214). Entities such as 'Western culture' or 'American consumerism' are condemned as marginalizing or killing off 'local' cultures. But it is difficult actually to pin down what these actually 'are'. As Berger (2002: 15) puts it, 'a Hungarian, for instance, looking West for cultural inspiration, comes on free market ideology versus environmentalism, freedom of speech versus "politically correct" speech codes [and we might add, Christian fundamentalism], Hollywood machismo versus feminism, American junk food versus American health food, and so on. In other words, "the West" is hardly a homogeneous cultural entity.' So 'Western culture' is actually a contradictory constellation of ideas and values, its complexity and ambiguity preventing any simple, wholesale transportation of it from the West to anywhere else.

The cultural imperialism arguments also arguably fail to account for the possibility that media and consumer goods and images are received by people living in particular socio-cultural contexts. These everyday contexts cannot necessarily be conceptualized as having been completely shaped by such goods and images. Instead, the latter can be incorporated into the ongoing flow of everyday activities (Howes, 1996). As Hobsbawm (1998: 2) phrases this point, 'somewhere on the road between the globally uniform Coke-can and the roadside refreshment stand in Ukraine or Bangladesh, the supermarket in Athens or in Djakarta, globalization stops being uniform and adjusts to local differences, such as language, local culture or . . . local politics'. People respond to 'Western' media and branded goods in distinctive ways, shaped by the cultural contests within which they live, and these contexts have not necessarily been wholly colonized by 'Western' influences (During, 1997).

Cultural imperialism arguments are alleged by their critics to assume, rather than properly demonstrate, that cultural processes are wholly in tune with political and economic factors. It is presumed that *because* Western governments hold most of the political power in the world and *because* Western economic interests are dominant in the global capitalist economy, then it *must* be the case that 'the West' is dominant in cultural terms too. But this assumes too much, for it asserts a total congruence between economics, politics and culture, a congruence that has not yet come to pass (Appadurai, 1996).

It might be more sensible to say that, rather than being totally informed by the onslaught of 'global culture', many people's cultural experiences today can be seen as complex mixtures of the *more* (but never purely) 'local' and the *more* (but never totally) 'global' (Cvetkovich and Kellner, 1997). Sometimes the interpenetration of the 'local' and the 'global' can produce new forms of specifically 'local' culture, while at other times distinctive new combinations of local and global can be created.

This is the condition of 'glocalization', to use Robertson's (1992) phrase, where the more local and the more global facets of culture are complexly intertwined and constantly mutating to produce new forms. These new cultural combinations can be described as 'hybrid' or 'creole' cultural forms. Processes of hybridization and creolization involve the interweaving of hitherto separate – or relatively separate – cultural patterns, ideas, tastes, styles and attitudes (Werbner and Modood, 1997; Bhabha, 1994). Specific 'hybrid' products can emerge in local contexts, while more generic 'global culture' itself can be seen as a hybridized coming together of hitherto relatively discrete cultural traditions. An aesthetic of mixing and mingling, whereby, for example, Western traditions are fused with Asian and African influences, could be seen as the real nature of 'global culture', a rather different understanding of the latter term than one which emphasizes its purely Western and corporate consumerist roots (Pieterse, 1995).

However, this kind of analysis of cultural globalization has its own problems too. What sorts of cultural 'hybrids' are possible depends in large part upon the social relations in which particular groups of people are embedded and within which they act, and these relations always reflect and express power relations. Some analysis of cultural hybridization processes can be rather naïve, seeing them as purely positive expressions of alleged 'inter-cultural dialogues' (Pieterse, 2003). Such celebrations ignore

Marxists
cultural imperialism; global cultural homogenization (sameness)

Robertson
global consciousness; glocalization

Post-Colonial Scholars
cultural hybridization / creolization

Figure 12.4 Views of Cultural Globalization.

or downplay the unequal power relations in which hybrid products and processes are embedded, and which they may unintentionally express. On the other hand, as theorists of post-colonial cultural conditions might argue, certain hybrid cultural forms may involve situations where discourses associated with oppressed social groups enter into and challenge the discourses of the powerful, revealing and problematizing the power relations that made the hybridization possible and which shaped it in the first place (Bhabha, 1994: 162). Whatever may be the case, critics of the more simple variants of the cultural imperialism thesis are all agreed that cultural globalization involves more subtle and nuanced processes than merely the cultural domination of the 'rest' by the 'West'.

Conclusion

Globalization has become, in a relatively short space of time, one of the most important focal points for social theorizing. It is a crucial topic for social theoretical analysis because it encompasses – by its very nature – everything happening on and across our planet at the present time. Every single person's life today is fundamentally affected by globalization processes, sometimes for good, sometimes for ill. It is therefore crucial that thinkers engage deeply with the nature of globalization and the many problems, but also opportunities, it throws up. It is equally important that the ideas of social theorists about globalization issues are as widely disseminated as possible, because the more people understand the forces that increasingly shape and impinge upon every aspect of their existences, the more those forces may be brought under some sort of control. Regardless of the specific ways in which they define and analyse globalization, those using social theory have an important role to play in communicating to the widest possible audience both the nature of the problems people all across the planet face today, and what the ways of facing up to, and dealing effectively with, those problems will involve.

Further Reading

Bauman, Z. (2011) *Collateral Damage: Social Inequalities in a Global Age*. Cambridge: Polity.

Held, D. and McGrew, A. (2007) *Globalization Theory: Approaches and Controversies*. Cambridge: Polity.

Hirst, P., Thompson, G. and Bromley (2009) *Globalization in Question*, 3rd edn. Cambridge: Polity.

Jones, A. (2010) *Globalization: Key Thinkers*. Cambridge: Polity.

Martell, L. (2010) *The Sociology of Globalization*. Cambridge: Polity.

Conclusion: The Development of Social Theory in 13 Points

You may have just read particular chapters of this book before turning to this conclusion, or you may have read the whole book. Either way, it is difficult for a newcomer to the field of social theory to see how all the different theorists and theories fit together and relate to each other. How all the various ideas dealt with in this book relate to each other is an issue which only becomes really clear to anybody over a long period of time, once they have studied and thought about different strands of social theory in more depth.

Nonetheless, a brief sketch of the field of social theory as it has developed over the last 150 years or so, can be grasped through the following thirteen bullet-points:

- Classical social theory centrally draws upon Kant (ideas to do with the social and cultural construction of reality) and Hegel (ideas to do with the dialectical unfolding of social processes).
- Classical social theory develops these ideas in various ways: dialectical thinking is particularly promoted by Marx and Simmel in their own distinctive ways, while ideas of social construction are to be found variously in Marx, Weber and Durkheim.
- Classical social theory is particularly focused on what it sees as the destruction of older forms of community, and the rise of a new social order, 'modernity'.
- In modern social theory, the current phase of 'modernity' is interpreted variously as late modernity (e.g. Giddens), risk society (Beck) post-modernity (post-modernist theory) and globalized modernity (various types of globalization theory).
- Dialectical thinking inherited from classical social theory informs modern attempts to think about how social structures and individuals' forms of agency are intertwined and mutually constituting: major examples of a 'structuration' theory are provided by Elias' process sociology, Giddens and Bourdieu.

- Marxist thought since the death of Marx has developed in many different directions, with 'Western Marxism' particularly focused on issues of alienation, reification and the control of culture by dominant social groups, and 'critical theory' being fundamentally recast by Habermas in the direction of seeing language as the most important social phenomenon.
- Social evolutionary theory is promoted by classical thinkers like Spencer and Durkheim, and taken in new directions by functionalists like Parsons, neo-functionalists and systems theorists.
- Phenomenological thought attempted to reconstruct the 'lifeworlds' of particular individuals and groups, and developed the idea of 'practical consciousness', the semi-conscious ways of thinking people engage in most of the time. Micro-level forms of instruction were also closely studied by symbolic interactionists.
- Structuralism and post-structuralism launched radical deconstructions of the 'individual', seeing a person's 'subjectivity' as the product of social forms and forces. Post-structuralism is the main conceptual basis for post-modernism.
- Rational choice theories are aimed against what they see as accounts of social life which underplay the active role of the individual and their decision-making capacities; but these continue to have difficulties in conceiving of the 'social' aspects of human life.
- Feminist theory and political practice combined to mount a fundamental critique of the 'male-centred' nature of previous social theory, and developed new accounts of the social constitution of gender and sexuality.
- Many previously separate positions are synthesized in our own period by major theorists like Bourdieu (utilizing among other sources Weberianism, Marxism and phenomenology) and Giddens.
- If classical theory is mostly characterized by a combination of themes from Kant and Hegel, then modern theory involves new variations on these themes, plus in many cases the addition of phenomenology's focus on practical consciousness and the analysis of 'practices'. This can be seen in the work of many present-day theorists, from Bourdieu and Giddens to Habermas and Butler. To put the point rather too simply, modern social theory is in large part variations on Kant and Hegel, with some phenomenology added.

Needless to say, the above sketch is selective and vastly simplifies a complex reality. Yet it still captures many of the most central aspects of social theory, and how it has developed over time. As you read more about social theory, the thumb-nail sketch just offered should make more sense, and you will be able to pick out connections between different theories and theorists for yourself, including some of those mentioned above.

That leads us to a more general point. It is a strange thing, but a lot of what you learn during a university degree may only make complete sense some time – possibly years – after you have completed your studies. Some types of knowledge and ways of thinking take a long time to embed themselves fully in your mind. Particular social theories that may seem difficult to get your head around when you first encounter them, should make at least some sense by the time of the end of the course you encountered them within. You find yourself understanding enough of Weber or Parsons or Foucault or whoever, to be able to write an essay or paper on them, or to answer exam questions about their ideas. But it is entirely possible that you might feel you only really understand such theories – if you ever think about them again – a long time after the course has finished.

To really 'get' a particular theory or thinker is a long-term process. This is because true understanding is not about the surface-level knowledge needed to pass an exam, but is instead about particular ideas becoming part of your own mental landscape – becoming part of your own thinking – so that over time they start to seem natural and obvious to you. What once seemed weird, alien, off-putting and intimidating has over time become part of you, generally without you realizing this was what was going on. At its best, social theory is about ideas that you will remember and use to understand the world around you, long after your degree is finished.

When social theory has really done its job, it has succeeded in making you see the world in particular ways that you will never forget. It should be impossible to think about the institutions of policing, psychiatry and medicine ever again after reading Foucault, without regarding them in light of what he said about them. It should be impossible to look at anything to do with the education system, and not recall what Bourdieu said about its fundamentally class-based nature. It should be impossible to look at economic issues, to do with how people work and what they consume, and not understand these in light of what Marx and later Marxists have argued about them. And so on, for all the theories and theorists examined in this book.

The point is not that you have to agree with any particular thinker or theory. It is that, once you are aware of what social theory has said or can say about a particular issue or area of social life, you are mentally better equipped to understand that issue or area, and how it affects you and the people around you. Social theory's promise – which it generally lives up to – is to make those who read it, write about it and contribute to it, less naïve and more sophisticated and critical thinkers than they would have been if they had never encountered it. When social theory 'works', it sharpens up your thinking, and makes you more alive to the subtleties and nuances of human social life, as well as many of the processes that go on within it, both on the surface and in more hidden and tacit ways too. In essence, social theory has the capacity to make you more sensitive to what goes on around you, and that in turn opens up the possibility of finding new ways of understanding *yourself*, who you are and what place you hold in society (Thorpe, 2011).

All of that, though, takes time and perseverance on your part. This book has given you an overview of the terrain of social theory. But really to understand it, you have to stick with it, and to keep on reading and thinking about what you have read. Above all, you have to read the original writings of the thinkers we have covered. This is because it is only by engaging with these writings directly that you will really fully be able to make their thinking *your* thinking, allowing you to see the world through their eyes. The reason why that is worthwhile – and worth spending your time and energy on – is that the very best social theorists looked at the world in ways that no one can afford to ignore. Learn from them, and you will have done something very worthwhile.

So now it is over to you . . .

References

Abbott, P. and Wallace, C. (1999) *An Introduction to Sociology: Feminist Perspectives*. London: Routledge.

Abrams, P. (1982) *Historical Sociology*. Ithaca: Cornell University Press.

Adamson, W. L. (1981) *Hegemony and Revolution: A Study of Antonio Gramsci's Political and Cultural Theory*. Berkeley: University of California Press.

Adorno, T. W. (1990) *Negative Dialectics*. London: Routledge.

– (1996) *The Culture Industry: Selected Essays on Mass Culture*. London: Routledge.

Adorno, T. W. and Horkheimer, M. (1992 [1944]) *Dialectic of Enlightenment*. London: Verso.

Aho, K. (2005) 'The Missing Dialogue Between Heidegger and Merleau-Ponty: On the Importance of the *Zollikon Seminars*', *Body and Society*, 11(2): 1–23.

Albrow, M. (1990) 'Introduction' in M. Albrow and E. King (eds) *Globalization, Knowledge and Society*. London: Sage, pp. 3–16.

– (1996) *The Global Age*. Cambridge: Polity.

Alexander, J. C. (1983) *Theoretical Logic in Sociology, Vol. III. The Classical Attempt at Theoretical Synthesis: Max Weber*. London: Routledge.

– (1987) 'The Centrality of the Classics' in A. Giddens and J. Turner (eds) *Social Theory Today*. Cambridge: Polity, pp. 11–55.

– (1988) *Durkheimian Sociology: Cultural Studies*. Cambridge: Cambridge University Press.

– (1992) *Fin de Siecle Social Theory: Relativism, Reduction, and the Problem of Reason*. London: Verso.

– (2003) *The Meanings of Social Life: A Cultural Sociology*. Oxford: Oxford University Press.

Alexander, J. C. and Colomy, P. (1985) 'Toward Neofunctionalism', *Sociological Theory* 3(2): 11–23.

Almeder, R. (2007) 'Pragmatism and Philosophy of Science: A Critical Survey', *International Studies in the Philosophy of Science*, 21(2): 171–95.

Althusser, L. (1971) 'Ideology and Ideological State Apparatuses' in *Lenin and Philosophy and Other Essays*. London: New Left Books, pp. 121–76.

Althusser, L. and Balibar, E. (1998 [1965]) *Reading Capital*. London: Verso.

Andreski, S. (1972) *Social Sciences as Sorcery*. London: Andre Deutsch.

Appadurai, A. (1996) *Modernity at Large: Cultural Dimensions of Globalization*. Minneapolis: University of Minnesota Press.

Archer, M. (1990) 'Human Agency and Social Structure: A Critique of Giddens' in J. Clark, C. Modgil and S. Modgil (eds) *Anthony Giddens: Consensus and Controversy*. Brighton: Falmer, pp. 73–84.

Arthur, C. J. (1986) *Dialectics of Labour*. Oxford: Blackwell.

Askay, R. (1999) 'Heidegger, the Body, and the French Philosophers', *Continental Philosophy Review*, 32: 29–35.

Atkinson, P. and Housley, W. (2003) *Interactionism: An Essay in Sociological Amnesia*. London: Sage.

Atkinson, W. (2007) 'Anthony Giddens as Adversary of Class Analysis', *Sociology*, 41(3): 533–49.

Austin, J. L. (1962) *How to Do Things With Words*. Harvard: Harvard University Press.

Bagguley, P. (2003) 'Reflexivity Contra Structuration', *Canadian Journal of Sociology*, 28(2): 133–52.

Barbalet, J. (2007) 'Classical Pragmatism, Classical Sociology: William James, Religion and Emotion' in Baert, P. and Turner, B. S (eds) *Pragmatism and European Social Theory*. Oxford: Bardwell Press, pp. 17–45.

Barrett, M. (1980) *Women's Oppression Today: Problems in Marxist Feminist Analysis*. Verso Books.

Barthes, R. (1988) *The Semiotic Challenge*. Oxford: Blackwell.

– (1993 [1957]) *Mythologies*. London: Vintage.

Baudrillard, J. (1975) *The Mirror of Production*. St Louis: Telos Press.

– (1983a) *In the Shadow of the Silent Majorities or The End of the Social*. New York: Semiotext(e).

– (1983b) *Simulations*. New York: Semiotext(e).

– (1990a) *Fatal Strategies*. New York: Semiotext(e)/Pluto.

– (1990b) *Seduction*. London: Macmillan.

– (1995) *The Gulf War Did Not Take Place*. Bloomington: Indiana University Press.

– (1996a) *The Perfect Crime*. London: Verso.

– (1996b [1968]) *The System of Objects*. London: Verso.

Bauman, Z. (1989a) 'Hermeneutics and Modern Social Theory' in Held, David and Thompson, J. (eds) *Social Theory of Modern Societies: Anthony Giddens and His Critics*. Cambridge: Cambridge University Press.

– (1989b) *Modernity and the Holocaust*. Cambridge: Polity.

– (1998) *Globalization: The Human Consequences*. Cambridge: Polity.

Beauvoir, de S. (1997 [1949]) *The Second Sex*. London: Vintage.

Beck, U. (1992) *Risk Society: Towards a New Modernity*. London: Sage.

– (1999) *World Risk Society*. Cambridge: Polity.

– (2000) *What Is Globalization?*. Cambridge: Polity.

Becker, H. S. (1963) *Outsiders: Studies in the Sociology of Deviance*. New York: The Free Press.

Becker, H. S. and A. Pessin (2006) 'A Dialogue on the Ideas of World and Field,' *Sociological Forum*, 21: 275–86.

Becker, G. (1976) *The Economic Approach to Human Behaviour*. Chicago: University of Chicago Press.

Bell, D. (1976) *The Cultural Contradictions of Capitalism*. New York: Basic Books.

Bendix, R. (1967) 'Tradition and Modernity Reconsidered', *Comparative Studies in Society and History*, 9(3): 292–346.

Benhabib, S., Butler, J., Drucilla, C., Fraser, N. (1995) 'Feminism and Postmodernism: An Uneasy Alliance' in *Feminist Contentions: A Philosophical Exchange*. London: Routledge, pp. 1–16.

Bennett, J. (1966) *Kant's Analytic*. Cambridge: Cambridge University Press.

Berger, P. L. (2002) 'The Cultural Dynamics of Globalization' in Berger, P. L. and Huntington, S. (eds) *Many Globalizations*. Oxford: Oxford University Press, pp. 1–16.

Berger, P. L. and Luckmann, T. (1991 [1966]) *The Social Construction of Reality*. Harmondsworth: Penguin.

Berlin, I. (2000) *The Roots of Romanticism*. London: Pimlico.

Berman, M. (1983) *All That is Solid Melts Into Air*. London: Verso.

Bhabha, H. (1994) *The Place of Culture*. London: Routledge.

Blau, Peter (1964) *Exchange and Power in Social Life*. New York: Wiley.

Bloor, D. (1983) *Wittgenstein: A Social Theory of Knowledge*. London: Macmillan.

Bloor, D. (2002) *Wittgenstein, Rules and Institutions*. London: Routledge.

Blumer, H. (1969) *Symbolic Interactionism: Perspective and Method*. California: University of California Press.

Bohman, J. (2004) 'Expanding Dialogue: The Internet, the Public Sphere and Prospects for Transnational Democracy', *The Sociological Review*, Vol. 52 Issue Supplement, 131–55.

Bolton, S. and Boyd, C. (2003) 'Trolley Dolly or Skilled Emotional Manager? Moving on from Hochschild's Managed Heart', *Work, Employment and Society*, 17(2): 289–308.

Bourdieu, P. (1977) *Outline of a Theory of Practice*. Cambridge: Cambridge University Press.

– (1988) *Homo Academicus*. Cambridge: Polity.

– (1990) *The Logic of Practice*. Cambridge: Polity.

– (1991a) *Language and Symbolic Power*. Cambridge: Polity.

– (1991b) 'Genesis and Structure of the Religious Field', *Comparative Social Research*, 13(1): 1–44.

– (1992a) *Distinction: A Social Critique of the Judgement of Taste*. London: Routledge.

– (1992b) *The Logic of Practice*. Cambridge: Polity.

– (1993a) *The Field of Cultural Production*. Cambridge: Polity.

– (1993b) *Sociology in Question*. London: Sage.

– (1998a) *Acts of Resistance*. New York: The Free Press.

– (1998b) *Practical Reason*. Cambridge: Polity.

– (1998c) *The State Nobility*. Cambridge: Polity.

– (1999) *The Weight of the World*. Cambridge: Polity.

– (2000) *Pascalian Meditations*. Cambridge: Polity.

Bourdieu, P., Chamboredon, J.-C. and Passeron, J.-C. (1991) *The Craft of Sociology*. Berlin: de Gruyter.

Bourdieu, P. and Passeron, J.-C. (1990) *Reproduction in Education, Society and Culture*. London: Sage.

Bourdieu, P. and Wacquant. L. (1992) *An Invitation to Reflexive Sociology*. Cambridge: Polity.

Boyne, R. (1990) 'Culture and the World System', *Theory, Culture and Society*, 7(1): 57–62.

Brownmiller, S. (1975) *Against Our Will: Men, Women and Rape*. New York: Simon and Schuster.

Bruun, H. (2008) 'Objectivity, Value Spheres, and "Inherent Laws": On some Suggestive Isomorphisms between Weber, Bourdieu, and Luhmann', *Philosophy of the Social Sciences*, 38(1): 97–120.

Bryant, C. and Jary, D. (1991) 'Introduction: Coming to terms with Anthony Giddens' in Bryant, C. and Jary, D. (eds) *Giddens' Theory of Structuration: A Critical Appreciation*. London: Routledge, pp. 74–116.

Bulmer, M. (1984) *The Chicago School of Sociology: Institutionalization, Diversity, and the Rise of Sociological Research*. Chicago: University of Chicago Press.

Burke, P. (2005) *History and Social Theory*. 2nd edn, Cambridge: Polity.

Burkitt, I. (1991) *Social Selves: Theories of the Social Formation of Personality*. London: Sage.

Burns, T. (1992) *Erving Goffman*. London: Routledge.

Butler, J. (1989) *The Thinking Muse: Feminism and Modern French Philosophy*. Bloomington: Indiana University Press.

– (1990) *Gender Trouble: Feminism and the Subversion of Identity*. London: Routledge.

– (1993) *Bodies That Matter: On the Discursive Limits of Sex*. London: Routledge.

Calhoun, C., LiPuma, E. and Postone, M. (eds) (1993) *Bourdieu: Critical Perspectives*. Cambridge: Polity.

Calinescu, M. (1987) *Five Faces of Modernity: Modernism, Avant-garde, Decadence, Kitsch, Post-modernism*. Durham, NC: Duke University Press.

Callinicos, A. (1989a) 'Anthony Giddens: A Contemporary Critique', *Theory and Society*, 14: 133–66.

– (1989b) *Marxist Theory*. Oxford: Oxford University Press.

Camic, C. (1985) 'Review: The Return of the Functionalists', *Contemporary Sociology*, 15(5): 692–5.

Castells, M. (1996) *The Rise of the Network Society, The Information Age: Economy, Society and Culture,* Vol. I. Oxford: Blackwell.

– (1997) *The Power of Identity, The Information Age: Economy, Society and Culture,* Vol. II. Oxford: Blackwell.

– (1998) *End of Millennium, The Information Age: Economy, Society and Culture,* Vol. III. Oxford: Blackwell.

– (2000) 'Materials for an Exploratory Theory of the Network Society', *British Journal of Sociology,* 51(1): 5–24.

Castells, M. and Ince, M. (2003) *Conversations with Manuel Castells.* Cambridge: Polity.

Cavaletto, G. (2007) *Crossing the Psycho-Social Divide: Freud, Weber, Adorno and Elias.* Aldershot: Ashgate.

Certeau, de M. (1984) *The Practice of Everyday Life,* Vol. I. Berkeley: University of California Press.

Changfoot, N. (2009) 'The Second Sex's Continued Relevance for Equality and Difference Feminisms', *European Journal of Women's Studies,* 16(1): 11–31.

Charon, J. (2006) *Symbolic Interactionism: An Introduction, an Interpretation.* Englewood Cliffs: NJ Prentice-Hall.

Cixous, H. (1975) 'Sorties' in *New French Feminisms: An Anthology,* Marks, E. and de Courtivoron, I. (eds) New York: Pantheon Books, pp. 366–71.

– (1981) 'The Laugh of the Medusa' in *New French Feminisms.* Marks, E. and de Courtivoron, I. (eds) New York: Schocken Books.

Cohen, G. A. (1982) 'Reply to Elster on "Marxism, Functionalism and Game Theory"', *Theory and Society,* 11(4): 483–95.

– (1986 [1978]) 'Marxism and Functional Explanation' in Roemer, J. (ed.) *Analytical Marxism.* Cambridge: Cambridge University Press.

Cohen, I. J. (1987) 'Structuration Theory' in Giddens, A. and Turner, J. (eds) *Social Theory Today.* Cambridge: Polity, pp. 273–308.

– (1989) *Structuration Theory: Anthony Giddens and the Constitution of Social Life.* London: Macmillan.

Coleman, J. (1990) *Foundations of Social Theory.* Cambridge, MA: Belknap.

– (1993a) 'The Rational Reconstruction of Society', *American Sociological Review,* 58(1): 1–15.

– (1993b) 'The Impact of Gary Coleman's Work on Sociology', *Acta Sociologica,* 36: 169–78.

– (1994) 'A Rational Choice Perspective on Economic Sociology' in Smelser, N. and Swedberg, R. (eds) *The Handbook of Economic Sociology.* Princeton: Princeton University Press.

Collins, R. (1986) *Max Weber: A Skeleton Key.* London: Sage.

– (1988a) 'Theoretical Continuities in Goffman's Work' in Drew, P. and Wootton, A. (eds) *Erving Goffman: Exploring the Interaction Order.* Boston. Northeastern University Press, pp. 41–63.

– (1988b)*Theoretical Sociology.* San Diego: Harcourt Brace Jovanovich.

Cook, G. A. (1993) *George Herbert Mead: The Making of a Social Pragmatist.* Champaign, Indiana: University of Illinois Press.

Cook, K. S. and Whitmeyer, J. M. (1992) 'Two Approaches to Social Structure: Exchange Theory and Network Analysis', *Annual Review of Sociology,* 18: 109–27.

Cooley, C. H. (1998 [1908]) *On Self and Social Organization.* Chicago: University of Chicago Press.

Cornell, D. (1998) *At the Heart of Freedom: Feminism, Sex, and Equality.* Princeton: Princeton University Press.

Crespi, F. (1987) 'Social Action and the Ambivalence of Communication: A Critique of Habermas's Theory', *European Journal of Communication,* 2(4): 415–25.

Crossley, N. (1995) 'Merleau-Ponty, the Elusive Body and Carnal Sociology', *Body and Society,* 1(1): 43–63.

Culler, J. (1983) *Barthes.* Fontana: Glasgow.

Cvetkovich, A. and Kellner, D. (1997) 'Thinking Global and Local' in Cvetkovich, A. and Kellner, D. (eds) *Articulating the Global and the Local.* Boulder, Co: Westview.

Dahrendorf, Ralf (1959) *Class and Class Conflict in an Industrial Society.* London: Routledge.

da Silva, F. C. (2007) *G. H. Mead: A Critical Introduction.* Cambridge: Polity.

Davis, M. (1973) 'Georg Simmel and the Aesthetics of Social Reality', *Social Forces,* 51(1): 320–9.

– (1997) 'Georg Simmel and Erving Goffman: Legitimators of the Sociological Investigation of Human Experience', *Qualitative Sociology,* 23(3): 369–88.

Dawe, A. (1970) 'The Two Sociologies', *British Journal of Sociology,* 21(2): 207–18.

De Haan, W. and Vos, J. (2003) 'A Crying Shame: The Over-Rationalized Conception of Man in the Rational Choice Perspective', *Theoretical Criminology,* 7(1): 29–54.

Delamont, S. (2003) *Feminist Sociology.* London: Sage.

Denzin, N. K. (1970) *The Research Act: A Theoretical Introduction to Sociological Methods.* Chicago: Aldine.

– (1990) 'Reading Rational Choice Theory', *Rationality and Society,* 2: 172–89.

– (1992) *Symbolic Interactionism and Cultural Studies: The Politics of Interpretation.* Oxford: Blackwell.

Denzin, N. K. and Keller, C. (1981) '*Frame Analysis* Reconsidered', *Contemporary Sociology,* 10: 52–60.

Derrida, J. (1978) *Writing and Difference.* London: Routledge.

Dewey, J. (1958 [1929]) *Experience and Nature.* New York: Dover.

– (1963 [1931]) *Philosophy and Civilization.* New York: Capricorn Books.

Drew, P. and Wootton A. (1988) *Erving Goffman: Exploring the Interaction Order.* Cambridge: Polity.

Duncan, H. D. (1959) 'Simmel's Image of Society' in Wolff, K. H. (ed.) *Georg Simmel: A Collection of Essays with Translations*. Columbus: Ohio State University Press, pp. 100–18.

During, S. (1997) 'Popular Culture on a Global Scale: A Problem for Cultural Studies?', *Critical Inquiry*, 23(4): 808–34.

Durkheim, É. (1964 [1893]) *The Division of Labour in Society*. New York: Free Press.

– (1982 [1895]) *The Rules of Sociological Method*. New York: Free Press.

– (2001 [1912]) *The Elementary Forms of Religious Life*. New York: Oxford University Press.

Durkheim, É. and Mauss, M. (1969 [1903]) *Primitive Classification*. London: Cohen and West.

Eagleton, T. (1991) *Ideology: An Introduction*. London: Verso.

Eco, Umberto (1987 [1967]) 'Towards a Semiological Guerrilla Warfare' in *Travels in Hyper-Reality*. London: Picador.

Edles, L. and Appelrouth, S. (2007) *Classical and Contemporary Sociological Theory*. Thousand Oaks: Pine Forge.

Eisenstein, Z. (1979) *Capitalist Patriarchy and the Case for Socialist Feminism*. New York: Monthly Review Press.

Elias, N. (1970) *What is Sociology?* London: Hutchinson.

– (1985 [1982]) *The Loneliness of the Dying*. Oxford: Blackwell.

– (1994 [1939]) *The Civilizing Process: Sociogenetic and Psychogenetic Investigations*. Oxford: Blackwell.

– (1990) *The Germans: Power Struggles and the Development of Habitus in the Nineteenth and Twentieth Centuries*. Cambridge: Polity.

– (1991 [1939]) *The Society of Individuals*. Oxford: Blackwell.

Elias, N. and Dunning, E. (1986) *Quest for Excitement: Sport and Leisure in the Civilizing Process*. Oxford: Blackwell.

Eliasoph, N. (2005) 'Theorizing from the Neck Down: Why Social Research Must Understand the Body Acting in Real Space and Time and Why It's So Hard to Spell out What We Learn From This', *Qualitative Sociology* 28(2): 159–69.

Elliott, A. (2004) *Social Theory Since Freud*, London: Routledge.

Elster, J. (1982) 'The Case for Methodological Individualism', *Theory and Society*, 11(4): 453–82.

– (1985) *Making Sense of Marx*. Cambridge: Cambridge University Press.

– (1989) *The Cement of Society*. Cambridge: Cambridge University Press.

Emerson, R. M. (1972) 'Exchange Theory, Part I: A Psychological Basis for Social Exchange' in Berger, J., Zelditch, M., Jr and Anderson, B. (eds.) *Sociological Theories in Progress*, Vol. 2. Boston: Houghton Mifflin, 38–57.

Engels, F. (1968 [1890]) 'Letter to Bloch, September 21, 1890' in *Marx/Engels: Selected Works*. London: Lawrence and Wishart.

– (1978 [1884]) *The Origin of the Family, Private Property and the State*. Peking: Foreign Languages Press.

England, P. and Kilbourne, B. (1990) 'Feminist Critiques of the Separative Model of the Self', *Rationality and Society*, 2(2): 156–71.

Fallows, James (1996) 'Throwing Like a Girl', *The Atlantic Monthly*, August. http://www.theatlantic.com/issues/96aug/throw/throw.htm

Farganis, S. (1994) *Situating Feminism: From Thought to Action*. London: Sage.

Featherstone, M. (ed.) (1990) *Global Culture*. London: Sage.

– (1991) *Consumer Culture and Post-modernism*. London: Sage.

Fine, G. A. (1993) 'The Sad Demise, Mysterious Disappearance, and Glorious Triumph of Symbolic Interactionism', *Annual Review of Sociology*, 19: 61–87.

– (1996) *Kitchens: The Culture of Restaurant Work*. California: University of California Press.

– (2007) *Authors of the Storm: Meteorologists and the Culture of Prediction*. Chicago: University of Chicago Press.

Firestone, S. (1972) *The Dialectic of Sex: Case for Feminist Revolution*. New York: HarperCollins.

Fiske, J. (1989) *Understanding Popular Culture*. Boston: Unwin.

Flatham, R. (2000) 'Wittgenstein and the Social Sciences: Critical Reflections Concerning Peter Winch's Interpretations and Appropriations of Wittgenstein's Thought', *History of the Human Sciences*, 13(2): 1–15.

Foucault, M. (1977a [1975]) *Discipline and Punish*. Harmondsworth: Penguin.

– (1977b) 'Power and Sex', *Telos*, 32: 152–61.

– (1981) *The History of Sexuality*, Vol. I. Harmondsworth: Penguin.

– (1988) *Michel Foucault, Politics, Philosophy, Culture*. Kritzman, L. (ed.), New York: Routledge.

– (1991 [1971]) 'Nietzsche, Genealogy, History' in Rabinow, P. (ed.) *The Foucault Reader*. Harmondsworth: Penguin, pp. 76–100.

– (2001 [1966]) *The Order of Things: Archaeology of the Human Sciences*. London: Routledge.

– (2002 [1969]) *Archaeology of Knowledge*. London: Routledge.

Freud, S. (2002) *Civilization and its Discontents*. London: Routledge.

Friedman, D. and Hechter, M. (1988) 'The Contribution of Rational Choice Theory to Macrosociological Research', *Sociological Theory*, 6(2): 201–18.

Friedman, T. (1999) *The Lexus and the Olive Tree*. London: HarperCollins.

Frisby, D. (1993) 'Social Theory, the Metropolis and Expressionism' in Benson, T. O. (ed.) *Expressionist Utopias*. Los Angeles: LA County Museum of Art.

– (2002) *Georg Simmel*. London: Routledge.

Frisby, D. and Featherstone, M. (eds) (2006) *Simmel on Culture: Selected Writings*. London: Sage Publications.

Fromm, E. (1994) *Escape from Freedom*, New York: Holt.

Gadamer, G. H. (2006) 'Classical and Philosophical Hermeneutics', *Theory, Culture and Society*, 23(1): 29–56.

Garcia, L. (2008) 'On Paul Ricouer and the Translation Interpretation of Cultures', *Thesis Eleven*, 94: 72–87.

Garcia-Canclini, N. (1995) *Hybrid Cultures: Strategies for Entering and Leaving Modernity*. Minneapolis: University of Minnesota Press.

Garfinkel, H. (1967) *Studies in Ethnomethodology*. New Jersey: Prentice-Hall.

Garver, N. (1994) *This Complicated Form of Life: Essays on Wittgenstein*. Chicago: Open Court.

Gates, Bill (1995) *The Road Ahead*. New York: Viking.

Geertz, C. (1972) *The Interpretation of Cultures*. New York: Basic Books.

– (1983) *Local Knowledge: Further Essays in Interpretative Anthropology*. New York: Harper.

Giddens, A. (1971) *Capitalism and Modern Social Theory*. Cambridge: Cambridge University Press.

– (1976) *New Rules of Sociological Method*. London: Hutchinson.

– (1979) *Central Problems in Social Theory*. London: Macmillan.

– (1981) *A Contemporary Critique of Historical Materialism. Vol. 1: Power, Property and the State*. London: Palgrave Macmillan.

– (1984) *The Constitution of Society: Outline of the Theory of Structuration*. Cambridge: Polity.

– (1987) *Social Theory and Modern Sociology*. Stanford: Stanford University Press.

– (1988) 'Goffman as a Systematic Social Theorist' in Drew, P. and Wootton, A. (eds), *Erving Goffman: Exploring the Interaction Order*. Cambridge: Polity.

– (1990) *The Consequences of Modernity*. Cambridge: Polity.

– (1991) *Modernity and Self Identity: Self and Society in the Late Modern Age*. Cambridge: Polity.

– (1992) *The Transformation of Intimacy: Sexuality, Love and Eroticism in Modern Societies*. Cambridge: Polity.

– (1994a) 'Living in a Post-Traditional Society' in U. Beck, A. Giddens and S. Lash. *Reflexive Modernization: Politics, Tradition and Aesthetics in the Modern Order*. Cambridge: Polity, 56–109.

– (1994b) *Beyond Left and Right*. Cambridge: Polity.

– (2000) *The Third Way and its Critics*. Cambridge: Polity.

– (2002) *Runaway World: How Globalisation is Reshaping our Lives*. 2nd edn. London: Profile.

Giddens, A. and Pierson, C. (1998) *Conversations with Anthony Giddens: Making Sense of Modernity*. Cambridge: Polity.

Gilman, C. P. (2004 [1914]) *Social Ethics: Sociology and the Future of Society*. New York: Praeger.

Giulianotti, R. (1999) *Football: A Sociology of the Global Game*, Cambridge: Polity.

Glaser, B. and Strauss, A. L. (1967) *The Discovery of Grounded Theory*. Chicago: Aldine.

Goffman, E. (1959) *The Presentation of Self in Everyday Life*. Harmondsworth: Penguin.

– (1961) *Asylums*. Harmondsworth: Penguin.

– (1964) *Stigma*. Englewood Cliffs, NJ: Prentice-Hall.

– (1967) *Interaction Ritual: Essays on Face-to-Face Behaviour*. New York: Anchor.

– (1971) *Relations in Public: Microstudies of the Public Order*. New York: Basic Books.

– (1974) *Frame Analysis: An Essay on the Organization of Experience*. New York: Harper and Row.

– (1981) *Forms of Talk*. Oxford: Basil Blackwell.

– (1983) 'The Interaction Order', *American Sociological Review*, 48(1): 1–17.

Gottfried, H. (ed.) (1996) *Feminism and Change: Bridging Theory and Practice*. University of Illinois Press.

Gouldner, A. (1970) *The Coming Crisis of Western Sociology*. New York: Basic Books.

Gramsci, A. (1971) *Selections from the Prison Notebooks*. London: Lawrence and Wishart.

Gross, N. and Simmons, S. (2002) 'Intimacy as a Double-Edged Phenomenon? An Empirical Test of Giddens', *Social Forces*, 81(2): 531–55.

Grosz, E. (1994) *Volatile Bodies: Toward A Corporeal Feminism*. Bloomington: Indiana University Press.

Gurr, T. (1981) 'Historical Trends in Violent Crime', *Crime and Justice: An Annual Review of Research*, 3: 295–353.

Gutting, G. (ed.) (2005) *Continental Philosophy of Science*. Oxford: Blackwell.

Habermas, J. (1982) 'A Reply to My Critics' in Thompson, J. B. and Held, D. (eds) *Habermas: Critical Debates*. London: Macmillan.

– (1972) *Knowledge and Human Interests*. London: Heinemann.

– (1984) *The Theory of Communicative Action*, Vol. I. London: Heinemann.

– (1987) *The Theory of Communicative Action*, Vol. II. Cambridge: Polity.

– (1989 [1962]) *The Structural Transformation of the Public Sphere: An Inquiry into a category of Bourgeois Society*. Cambridge: Polity.

Halfpenny, P. (1992) *Positivism and Sociology*. London: Allen and Unwin.

Hall, S. (1993 [1980]) 'Encoding, Decoding' in During, S. (ed.) *The Cultural Studies Reader*. London: Routledge.

Halperin, D. (1995) *Saint Foucault: Towards A Gay Hagiography*. Oxford: Oxford University Press.

Hamelink C. J. (1983) *Cultural Autonomy in Global Communications*. New York: Longman.

Hand, M. and Sandywell, B. (2002) 'E-Topia as Cosmopolis or Citadel: On the Democratizing and De-democratizing Logics of the Internet, or, Toward a Critique of the New Technological Fetishism', *Theory, Culture and Society*, 19(1–2): 197–225.

Hannerz, U. (1989) 'Notes on the Global Ecumene', *Public Culture*, 1(2): 66–75.

– (1990) 'Cosmopolitans and Locals in World Culture' in Featherstone, M. et al. (eds) *Global Culture*. London: Sage.

– (1996) *Transnational Connections: Culture, People, Places.* London: Routledge.

Haraway, D. (1988) 'Situated Knowledges: The Science Question in Feminism and the Privilege of Partial Perspective', *Feminist Studies*, 14(3): 575–99.

– (1989) *Primate Visions: Gender, Race and Nature in the World of Modern Science.* New York: Routledge.

– (1991) 'A Cyborg Manifesto' in *Simians, Cyborgs and Women: The Reinvention of Nature.* New York: Routledge.

– (1997) *Modest-Witness @ Second-Millennium. FemaleMan Meets OncoMouse: Feminism and Technoscience.* New York: Routledge.

Harding, S. (1991) *Whose Science? Whose Knowledge? Thinking from Women's Lives.* Ithaca: Cornell University Press.

Hardt, M. and Negri, A. (2000) *Empire.* Cambridge, Mass.: Harvard University Press.

Harland, R. (2010) *Superstructuralism.* London: Routledge.

Harrington, A. (2000a) 'Objectivism in Hermeneutics? Gadamer, Habermas, Dilthey', *Philosophy of the Social Sciences*, 30(4): 491–507.

– (2000b) 'Alfred Schutz and the Objectifying Attitude', *Sociology*, 34(4): 727–40.

– (2001) 'Dilthey, Empathy and Verstehen A Contemporary Appraisal', *European Journal of Social Theory*, 4(3): 311–29.

Hartmann, H. (1979) 'The Unhappy Marriage of Marxism and Feminism: Towards a More Progressive Union', *Capital and Class*, 8, 1–33.

Harvey, D. (1989) *The Condition of Post-Modernity: An Inquiry into the Origins of Cultural Change.* Oxford: Blackwell.

Hassan, I. (1985) 'The Culture of Post-modernism', *Theory, Culture and Society*, 2(3).

Hawkes, T. (1997) *Structuralism and Semiotics.* London: Routledge.

Hawley, J. C. (ed.) (2001) *Post-Colonial Queer: Theoretical Intersections.* New York: State University of New York Press.

Hawthorn, G. (1976) *Enlightenment and Despair.* Cambridge: Cambridge University Press.

Heath, A. (1976) *Rational Choice and Social Exchange: A Critique of Exchange Theory.* Cambridge: Cambridge University Press.

Heckathorn, D. (1997) 'Overview: The Paradoxical Relationship between Sociology and Rational Choice', *The American Sociologist*, 28, 6–15.

Hedstrom, P. and Swedberg, R. (1996) 'Rational Choice, Empirical Research, and the Sociological Tradition', *European Sociological Review*, 12(2): 127–46.

Heelan, P. A. (1998) 'The Scope of Hermeneutics in Natural Science', *Studies in History of Philosophy and Science, Part A*, 29(2): 273–98.

Heeren, J. (1971) 'Alfred Schutz and the Sociology of Common-sense Knowledge' in Douglas, J. (ed.) *Understanding Everyday Life: Toward the Reconstruction of Sociological Knowledge.* London: Routledge, 45–56.

Hegel, G. W. F. (1979 [1807]) *Phenomenology of Spirit*. Oxford: Oxford University Press.

Heidegger, M. (1988 [1927]) *Being and Time*. Oxford: Blackwell.

– (1971 [1950]) 'The Thing' in *Poetry, Language, Thought*. New York: Harper and Row.

Held, D. (1980) *Introduction to Critical Theory*. Cambridge: Polity.

Held, D. et al. (eds) (1999) *Global Transformations: Politics, Economics and Culture*. Cambridge: Polity.

Held, D. and McGrew, A. (2000) *The Global Transformations Reader: An Introduction to the Globalization Debate*. Cambridge: Polity.

Held, D. and Thompson, J. B. (1989) *Social Theory of Modern Societies: Anthony Giddens and His Critics*. Cambridge: Cambridge University Press.

Hesmondhalgh, D. and Baker, S. (2008) 'Creative Work and Emotional Labour in the Television Industry', *Theory, Culture and Society*, 25(7–8): 97–118.

Hetcher, M. and Kanazawa, S. (1997) 'Sociological Rational Choice Theory', *Annual Review of Sociology*, 23: 191–214.

Hirst, P. and Thompson, G. (2000) *Globalization in Question: The International Economy and the Possibilities of Governance*. Cambridge: Polity.

Hobsbawm, E. (1998) 'The Nation and Globalization', *Constellations* 5(1): 1–9.

– (2011) *How to Change the World: Tales of Marx and Marxism*. London: Little, Brown.

Hochschild, A. (1983) *The Managed Heart: Commercialization of Human Feeling*. Berkeley: University of California Press.

Hodges, H. A. (1944) *Wilhelm Dilthey: An Introduction*. London: Routledge and Kegan Paul.

Hodgson, G. (1986) 'Behind Methodological Individualism', *Journal of Economics*, 10: 211–24.

Hollis, M. (1977) *Models of Man*. Cambridge: Cambridge University Press.

Holmwood, J. (1996) *Founding Sociology? Talcott Parsons and the Idea of General Theory*, London: Longman.

Holton, R. J. and Turner, B. S. (1986) *Talcott Parsons on Economy and Society*, London: Routledge.

Homans, G. C. (1961) *Social Behaviour: Its Elementary Forms*. New York: Harcourt, Brace.

– (1964) 'Bringing Men Back In', *American Sociological Review*, 29(5): 809–18.

– (1967) *The Nature of Social Science*. New York. Harcourt, Brace.

– (1974) *Social Behaviour: Its Elementary Forms*. New York: Harcourt Brace.

Honneth, Axel (1986) 'The Fragmented World of Symbolic Forms: Reflections On Pierre Bourdieu's Sociology of Culture', *Theory, Culture and Society*, 3(3): 55–67.

Horkheimer, M. (1972a) 'Art and Mass Culture' in *Critical Theory: Selected Essays*. New York: Herder and Herder.

– (1972b) 'Materialism and Metaphysics' in *Critical Theory: Selected Essays*, New York: Herder and Herder.

– (1972c) 'The Social Function of Philosophy' in *Critical Theory: Selected Essays*. New York: Herder and Herder.

Housley, W. and Atkinson, P. (2003) *Interactionism*. London: Sage.

Howes, D. (ed.) (1996) *Cross-Cultural Consumption: Global Markets, Local Realities*, London: Routledge, 1–18.

Howson, A. and Inglis, D. (2001) 'The Body in Sociology: Tensions Inside and Outside Sociological Thought', *The Sociological Review*, 49(3): 297–317.

Hughson, J., Inglis, D. and Free, M. (2004) *The Uses of Sport: A Critical Study*. London: Routledge.

Husserl, E. (1962 [1931]) *Ideas. A General Introduction to Pure Phenomenology*, London: Collier Macmillan.

Huyssen, Andreas (1984) 'Mapping the Post-Modern', *New German Critique*, No. 33, 5–52.

Inglis, D. (2001) *A Sociological History of Excretory Experience: Defecatory Manners and Toiletry Technologies*, Lewiston, NY: Mellen.

– (2010) 'The Death of History in British Sociology: Presentism, Intellectual Entrepreneurship and the Conundra of Historical Consciousness' in Burnett, J., Jeffers, S. and Thomas, G. (eds) *New Social Connections: Sociology's Subjects and Objects*. Basingstoke: Palgrave, pp. 105–24.

Inglis, D. and Gimlin, D (eds) (2010) *The Globalization of Food*. Oxford: Berg.

Inglis, D. and Robertson, R. (2008) 'The Elementary Forms of Globality: Durkheim and the Emergence and Nature of Global Life', *Journal of Classical Sociology*, 8(1): 5–25.

Inglis, D., Stockman, N. and Surridge, P. (2000) 'Bourdieu and Methodological Polytheism: Taking Sociology into the 21st Century' in Eldridge, J. et al. (eds) *For Sociology: Legacies and Prospects*. Durham: Sociology Press, 135–54.

Irigaray, L. (1985a) *Speculum of the Other Woman*. Ithaca, NY: Cornell University Press.

– (1985b) *This Sex Which Is Not One*. Ithaca, New York: Cornell University Press.

– (1987) 'Is the Subject of Science Sexed?' in *Hypatia*, 2(3): 65–88.

– (2004) *Luce Irigaray: Key Writings*. London: Continuum.

Jaggar, A. (1983) *Feminist Politics and Human Nature*. Totowa, NJ: Rowman and Littlefield.

Jamieson, L. (1999) 'Intimacy Transformed? A Critical Look At the Pure Relationship', *Sociology*, 33(3): 477–94.

James, W. (1890) *The Principles of Psychology*. Volume 1. New York: Henry Holt.

– (1897) *The Will to Believe and Other Essays in Popular Philosophy*. New York: Longmans, Green and Company.

– (1955 [1907]) *Pragmatism*. Cambridge: Harvard University Press.

– (1970 [1902]) *The Varieties of Religious Experience*. New York: Collier Books.

Jameson, F. (1972) *The Prison-House of Language: A Critical Account of Structuralism and Russian Formalism*. Princeton: Princeton University Press.

– (1991) *Post-Modernism: Or, the Cultural Logic of Late Capitalism*. London: Verso.

Jandy, E. C. (1969) *Charles Horton Cooley: His Life and His Social Theory*. Octagon Books: New York.

Jay, M. (1974) *The Dialectical Imagination*. London: Heinemann.

– (1984) *Marxism and Totality: The Adventures of a Concept from Lukacs to Habermas*. Cambridge: Polity.

Jencks, C. (1992) *The Post-Modernism Reader*. London: Academy Editions

Jenkins, R. (1982) 'Pierre Bourdieu and the Reproduction of Determinism', *Sociology* 16(2): 270–81.

Joas, H. (1985) *G. H. Mead: A Contemporary Re-examination of His Thought*. Cambridge: Polity.

Junker, B. (1960) *Fieldwork: An Introduction to the Social Sciences*. Chicago: Chicago University Press.

Kant, I. (1999 [1787]) *Critique of Pure Reason*. Cambridge: Cambridge University Press.

Kaspersen, L. B. and Gabriel, N. (2008) 'The Importance of Survival Units of Norbert Elias' Figurational Persepctive', *The Sociological Review*, 56(3): 370–87.

Keane, J. (2003) *Global Civil Society?*. Cambridge: Cambridge University Press.

Kellner, D. (1989) *Jean Baudrillard: From Marxism to Post-modernism and Beyond*. Cambridge: Polity.

Kilminster, R. (1991) 'Structuration Theory as a World-view' in Bryant, C. and Jary, D. (eds) *Anthony Giddens' Theory of Structuration: A Critical Appreciation*. London: Routledge, 74–116.

King, A. (2000) 'The Accidental Derogation of the Lay Actor: A Critique of Giddens' Concept of Structure', *Philosophy of the Social Sciences*, 30(3): 362–83.

– (2009) 'Overcoming Structure and Agency: Talcott Parsons, Ludwig Wittgenstein and the Theory of Social Action', *Journal of Classical Sociology*, 9(2): 260–88.

Klein, Naomi (2001) *No Logo*. London: Flamingo.

Klemm, D. (1983) *The Hermeneutical Theory of Paul Ricoeur: A Constructive Analysis*. Lewisburg: Bucknell University Press.

Kolakowski, L (2005) *Main Currents of Marxism: The Founders, the Golden Age, the Breakdown*. New York: W. W. Norton.

Korner, S. (1955) *Kant*. Harmondsworth: Penguin.

Kristeva, J. (1980) *Desire in Language: A Semiotic Approach to Literature and Art*. New York: Columbia University Press.

– (1997) *The Portable Kristeva*. New York: Columbia University Press.

– (1991) *Strangers to Ourselves*. London: Harvester Wheatsheaf.

Kurasawa, F. (2004) 'Alexander and the Cultural Refounding of American Sociology', *Thesis Eleven*, 79: 53–64.

Laclau, E. and Mouffe, C. (1985) *Hegemony and Socialist Strategy: Towards a Radical Democratic Politics*. Verso, London.

Lane, J. (2000) *Pierre Bourdieu: A Critical Introduction*. London: Pluto.

Lamiell, J. (1998) '"Nomothetic" and "Idiographic": Contrasting Windelband's Understanding with Contemporary Usage', *Theory and Psychology*, 8(1): 23–8.

Lasch, C. (1985) 'Historical Sociology and the Myth of Maturity: Norbert Elias' "Very Simple Formula"', *Theory and Society*, 14(5): 705–20.

Lash, S. (1990) *Sociology of Post-Modernism*. London: Routledge.

Lash, S. and Urry, J. (1987) *The End of Organized Capitalism*. Cambridge: Polity.

Lauretis, de T. (1991) 'Queer Theory: Lesbian and Gay Sexualities', *Differences*, 3(2): iii–xviii.

Layder, D. (1986) 'Social Reality as Figuration: A Critique of Elias' Conception of Sociological Analysis', *Sociology*, 20(3): 367–86.

– (1994) *Understanding Social Theory*. London: Sage.

Leach, E. (1966) 'Anthropological Aspects of Language: Animal Categories and Verbal Abuse' in Lenneberg, E. H. (ed.) *New Directions in the Study of Language*. Cambridge: MIT Press, pp. 23–63.

Le Corbusier (1986) *Towards a New Architecture*. New York: Dover.

Lehmann, J. M. (1994) *Durkheim and Women*. Lincoln: University of Nebraska Press.

Lehtinen, A. and Kuorikoski, J. (2007) 'Unrealistic Assumptions in Rational Choice Theory', *Philosophy of the Social Sciences*, 37(2): 115–37.

Lenin, V. I. (1977 [1916]) 'Imperialism, the Highest Stage of Capitalism' in *Selected Works*. Moscow: Progress Publishers.

Lévi-Strauss, C. (1986 [1963]) *Structural Anthropology*, Vol. I. Harmondsworth: Penguin.

Liebersohn, H. (1988) *Fate and Utopia in German Sociology, 1870–1923*. Cambridge, Mass.: MIT Press.

Lizardo, O. (2010) 'Beyond the Antinomies of Structure: Levi-Strauss, Giddens, Bourdieu and Sewell', *Theory and Society*, 39(6): 651–88.

– (2011) 'Pierre Bourdieu as a Post-Cultural Theorist', *Cultural Sociology*, 5(1).

Lockwood, D. (1964) 'Social Integration and System Integration' in Zollschan, G. K. and Hirsch, W. (eds) *Explorations in Social Change*. New York: Houghton and Mifflin.

Lofland, J. (1971) *Analyzing Social Settings: A Guide to Qualitative Observation and Analysis*. Belmont, CA: Wadsworth.

Lopreato, J. (1990) 'From Social Evolutionism to Biocultural Evolutionism', *Sociological Forum*, 5(2): 187–212.

Lovelock, J. (2000) *Gaia: A New Look at Life on Earth.* Oxford: Oxford University Press.

Luckmann, T. (1978) *Phenomenology and Sociology.* Harmondsworth: Penguin.

Luhmann, N. (1977) 'Differentiation of Society', *Canadian Journal of Sociology*, (1): 29–53.

– (1982) *The Differentiation of Society.* New York: Columbia University Press.

– (1986) 'The Autopoiesis of Social Systems' in Geyer, F. and van der Zouwen, J. (eds) *Sociocybernetic Paradoxes: Observation, Control and Evolution of Self-Steering Systems.* London: Sage, 171–92.

Luijpen, W. A. (1969) *Existential Phenomenology.* Pittsburgh: Duquesne University Press.

Lukacs, G. (1971 [1923]) *History and Class Consciousness.* London: Merlin.

Lyotard, J.-F. (1984) *The Post-modern Condition: A Report on the Condition of Knowledge.* Minneapolis: University of Minnesota Press.

McGuigan, J. (1992) *Cultural Populism.* London: Routledge.

McLellan, D. (2007) *Marxism After Marx*, Basingstoke: Palgrave.

McLennan, G. (2006) *Sociological Cultural Studies: Reflexivity and Positivity in the Human Sciences.* Basingstoke: Palgrave.

McNay, L. (1992) *Foucault and Feminism.* Cambridge: Polity.

Maier, J. B. (1984) 'Contribution to a Critique of Critical Theory' in Marcus, Judith and Tar, Zoltan (eds.), New Brunswick: Transaction Books.

Makkreel, R. A. (1975) *Dilthey: Philosopher of the Human Studies.* Princeton: Princeton University Press.

Mann, M (1986) *The Sources of Social Power,* Vol I. Cambridge: Cambridge University Press.

Manning, P. (1992) *Erving Goffman and Modern Sociology.* Cambridge: Polity.

Marcuse. H. (1991) *One-Dimensional Man: Studies in the Ideology of Advanced Industrial Society.* New York: Beacon Press.

– (1999) *Reason and Revolution: Hegel and the Rise of Social Theory.* New York: Humanity Books.

Mardorossian, C. M. (2002) 'Toward A New Feminist Theory of Rape', *Signs*, 27: 743–75.

Martin, B. and Szelenyi, I. (1987) 'Beyond Cultural Capital: Toward a Theory of Symbolic Domination' in Eyerman, R. et al. (eds) *Intellectuals, Universities and the State in Western Modern Societies.* Berkeley: University of California Press.

Martins, H. (1974) 'Time and Theory in Sociology' in Rex, J. (ed.) *Approaches to Sociology.* London: Routledge, 246–94.

Marx, K. (1977 [1859]) *A Contribution to the Critique of Political Economy.* Moscow: Progress Publishers.

– (1981 [1844]) *Economic and Philosophic Manuscripts of 1844.* London: Lawrence and Wishart.

– (1988 [1865]) *Capital, Vol. I.* Harmondsworth: Penguin.

– (1991 [1845–6)) *The German Ideology*. Arthur, C. J. (ed.), London: Lawrence and Wishart.

– (2000 [1852]) 'The Eighteenth Brumaire of Louis Bonaparte' in *Karl Marx: Selected Works*. McLellan, D. (ed.), Oxford: Oxford University Press.

Marx, K. and Engels, F. (1968 [1848]) 'Manifesto of the Communist Party' in *Marx-Engels Selected Works*. Moscow: Progress Publishers.

Mauss, M. (1973) 'Techniques of the Body', *Economy and Society*, 2: 70–88.

Mayer, T. (1994) *Analytical Marxism*. Thousand Oaks, CA: Sage.

Maynard, M. (1995) 'Beyond the "Big Three": The Development of Feminist Theory into the 1990s', *Women's History Review* 4(3): 259–81.

Mead, G. H. (1967) *Mind, Self and Society – From the Standpoint of A Behavioural Social Scientist*. Morris, W. (ed.) Chicago: Chicago University Press.

Medvedev, R. (1989) *Let History Judge: The Origins and Consequences of Stalinism* (Revised and expanded edition). New York: Columbia University Press.

Meltzer, B., Petras, J. and Reynolds, L. (1975) *Symbolic Interactionism: Genesis, Varieties and Criticisms*. London: Routledge and Kegan Paul.

Mennell, S. (1998) *Norbert Elias: An Introduction*. Dublin: University College Dublin Press.

– (2007) *The American Civilizing Process*. Cambridge: Polity.

– (2009) 'An Exceptional Civilizing Process', *Journal of Classical Sociology*, 9(1): 97–115.

Merleau-Ponty, M. (1965) *The Structure of Behaviour*. London: Methuen.

– (1996) *The Phenomenology of Perception*. London: Routledge.

Merton, R. K. (1949) *Social Theory and Social Structure*. New York: Free Press.

Mill, J. S. (1968 [1829]) *Essays on Some Unsettled Questions of Political Economy*. Clifton, NY: A. M. Kelley.

Millet, K. ([1970] 1977) *Sexual Politics*. Virago Press.

Mills, C. W. (1959) *The Sociological Imagination*. Oxford: Oxford University Press.

– (1966) *Sociology and Pragmatism: The Higher Learning in America*. New York: Oxford University Press.

Mitchell, J. (1966) 'Women: the Longest Revolution', *New Left Review*, No. 40: 11–37.

– (2000 [1974]) *Psychoanalysis and Feminism: A Radical Reassessment of Freudian Psychoanalysis*. New York: Penguin.

Moran, D. (2007) *Introduction to Phenomenology*. London: Routledge.

Mouzelis, N. (1995) *Sociological Theory: What Went Wrong?*. London: Routledge.

– (1974) 'Social and System Integration: Some Reflections on a Fundamental Distinction', *Sociology* 25: 395–409.

– (2007) 'Habitus and Reflexivity: Restructuring Bourdieu's Theory of Practice', *Sociological Research Online*, 12(6) http://www.socresonline.org.uk/12/6/9.html

Namaste, V. K. (2000) *Invisible Lives: The Erasure of Transsexual and Transgendered People*. Chicago: University of Chicago Press.

Nickel, T. (1992) 'Analytical Marxism: The Race for Respectability', *Critical Sociology*, 19(3): 81–106.

Nietzsche, F. (1977) *The Portable Nietzsche*. Harmondsworth: Penguin.

Oakes, G. (1984) *Georg Simmel: On Women, Sexuality and Love*. New Haven: Yale University Press.

– (1989) *Weber and Rickert: Concept Formation in the Cultural Sciences*. Cambridge, Mass.: MIT Press.

Oakley, A. (1972) *Sex, Gender and Society*. London: Maurice Temple Smith Ltd.

– (1974) *Housewife*. London: Allen Lane.

– (1976) *Women's Work: The Housewife, Past and Present*. New York: Random House.

Ohmae, K. (2000) *The End of the Nation State: The Rise of Regional Economies*. New York: Free Press.

Okin, S. (1989) *Justice, Gender and the Family*. Basic Books: New York.

O'Neill, J. (1972) *Sociology as a Skin-Trade*. London: Heinemann.

Osiander, A. (2001) 'Sovereignty, International Relations, and the Westphalian Myth', *International Organization*, 55: 251–87.

Oswin, N. (2008) 'Critical Geographies and the Uses of Sexuality: Deconstructing Queer Space', *Progress in Human Geography*, 32(1): 89–103.

Outhwaite, W. (1975) *Understanding Social Life: The Method called Verstehen*. London: Allen and Unwin.

Outhwaite, W. (2009) *Habermas: A Critical Introduction*, Cambridge: Polity.

– (2010) 'Canon Formation in Late 20th-Century British Sociology', *Sociology*, 43(6): 1029–45.

Pakulski, J. and Waters, M. (1996) 'The Reshaping and Dissolution of Social Class in Advanced Society', *Theory and Society*, 25(5): 667–91.

Palmer, E. (1969) *Hermeneutics: Interpretation Theory in Schleiermacher, Dilthey, Heidegger, and Gadamer*. Evanston: Northwestern University Press.

Papastergiadis, N. (2000) *The Turbulence of Migration*. Cambridge: Polity.

Parsons, Talcott (1937) *The Structure of Social Action*. New York: Free Press.

– (1951) *The Social System*. New York: Free Press.

– (1961) 'Introduction – Part Four – Culture and the Social System' in Parsons, T. et al. (eds) *Theories of Society*, Vol. II. Glencoe: Free Press.

– (1968) 'Cooley and the Problem of Internalization' in Reiss Jr, A. J. (ed.) *Cooley and Sociological Analysis*. Ann Arbor: University of Michigan Press, 48–67.

Parsons, T. and Bales, R. (1956) *Family, Socialization and Interaction Process*. London: Routledge and Kegan Paul.

Parsons, T. and Shils, E. A. (1951) *Towards a General Theory of Action*. Harvard: Harvard University Press.

Parsons, T., Platt, G. M. and Smelser, N. J. (1973) *The American University*. Cambridge: Harvard University Press.

Parsons, T. and Smelser, N. J. (1956) *Economy and Society: A Study in the Integration of Economic and Social Theory*. London, Routledge.

Pierce, C. S. (1955 [1868]) 'Some Consequences of Four Incapacities' in *Philosophical Writings of Pierce*. Buchler, J. (ed.). New York: Dover, 228–50.

Pieterse, J. N. (1995) 'Globalization as Hybridization' in M. Featherstone et al. (eds) *Global Modernities*. London: Sage.

– (2003) *Globalization and Culture: Global Mélange*. Lanham: Rowman and Littlefield.

Pressler, C. and Dasilva, F. (1996) *Sociology and Interpretation: From Weber to Habermas*. New York: SUNY Press.

Priest, Stephen (1998) *Merleau-Ponty*. London: Routledge.

Przeworski, A. (1985a) *Capitalism and Social Democracy*. Cambridge: Cambridge University Press.

– (1985b) 'Marxism and Rational Choice', *Politics and Society*, 14(4): 379–409.

Radcliffe-Brown, A. R. (1965) *Structure and Function in Primitive Society*. New York: The Free Press.

Readings, B. (1991) *Introducing Lyotard: Art and Politics*. London: Routledge.

Reay, D. (2004) ' "It's All Becoming a Habitus": Beyond the Habitual Use of Pierre Bourdieu's Concept of Habitus in Educational Research', *British Journal of Sociology of Education*, 25(4): 431–44.

Reckwitz, A. (2002) 'Toward A Theory of Social Practices', *European Journal of Social Theory*, 5(2): 243–63.

Rickman, H. P. (1979) *Wilhelm Dilthey: Pioneer of the Human Studies*. London: Paul Elek.

Ricoeur, P. (1981) *Hermeneutics and the Human Sciences: Essays on Language, Action and Interpretation*. Cambridge: Cambridge University Press.

– (1991) *A Ricoeur Reader: Reflection and Imagination*. New York: Harvester Wheatsheaf.

Rickman, H. P. (1988) *Dilthey Today*. New York: Greenwood.

Roberts, M. (1996) *Analytical Marxism: A Critique*. London: Verso.

Robertson, R. (1992) *Globalization: Social Theory and Global Culture*. London: Sage.

Roche, M. (1973) *Phenomenology, Language and the Social Sciences*. London: Routledge and Kegan Paul.

Rock, P. E. (1979) *The Making of Symbolic Interactionism*. London: Macmillan.

Roemer, J. (1982a) 'Methodological Individualism and Deductive Marxism', *Theory and Society*, 11(4): 513–20.

– (1982b) *A General Theory of Exploitation and Class*. Cambridge, Mass.: Harvard University Press.

– (1986) ' "Rational Choice" Marxism: Some Issues of Method and Substance' in Roemer, J. (ed.) *Analytical Marxism*. Cambridge: Cambridge University Press, 191–201.

Rowbotham, S. (1993) *Women in Movement: Feminism and Social Action*. London: Routledge.

Russell, B. (2000 [1945]) *History of Western Philosophy: And its Connection With Political and Social Circumstances From the Earliest Times to the Present Day.* London: Routledge.

Ryan, A. (1987) *J. S. Mill and Jeremy Bentham: Utilitarianism and Other Essays.* London: Penguin.

Sacks, H. (1972) *Lectures on Conversation.* Oxford: Blackwell.

Santoro, M. (2011) 'From Bourdieu to Cultural Sociology', *Cultural Sociology,* 5(1).

Sargent, L. (ed.) (1981) *Women and Revolution.* Boston: South End Press.

Sartre, J. P (2003 [1943]) *Being and Nothingness: An Essay on Phenomenological Ontology.* London: Routledge.

Saussure, F. (1959 [1906–11]) *Course in General Linguistics.* New York: Philosophical Library.

Savage, M. (2007) 'Changing Social Class Identities in Post-War Britain: Perspectives from Mass-Observation', *Sociological Research Online,* 12(3) http://www.socresonline.org.uk/12/3/6.html

Schatzki, T. R. (1997) 'Practices and Actions: A Wittgensteinian Critique of Bourdieu and Giddens', *Philosophy of the Social Sciences,* 27(3): 283–308.

Schatzman, L. and Strauss, A. L. (1973) *Field Research: Strategies for a Natural Sociology.* Englewood Cliffs, NJ: Prentice-Hall.

Schinkel, W. (2010) 'The Autopoiesis of the Artworld after the End of Art', *Cultural Sociology,* 4(2): 267–90.

Schmidt, J. (1985) *Maurice Merleau-Ponty: Between Phenomenology and Structuralism.* Basingstoke: Macmillan.

Schubert, H. J. (2006) 'The Foundation of Pragmatic Sociology: Charles Horton Cooley and George Herbert Mead', *Journal of Classical Sociology,* 6(1): 51–74.

Schuerkens, U. (2003) 'The Sociological and Anthropological Study of Globalization and Localization', *Current Sociology,* 51: 209–22.

Schutz, A. (1967) *The Phenomenology of the Social World.* Evanston: Northwestern University Press.

– (1971) *Collected Papers Vol 1: The Problem of Social Reality.* The Hague: Martinus Nijhoff.

Seabrook, J. (2004) *Consuming Cultures: Globalization and Local Lives.* London: New Internationalist.

Sewell, Jr, W. H. (2005) *Logics of History: Social Theory and Social Transformation.* Chicago: University of Chicago Press.

Shalin, D. (1986) 'Pragmatism and Social Interactionism', *American Sociological Review,* 51(1): 9–29.

Shalin, D. (1991) 'The Pragmatic Origins of Symbolic Interactionism and the Crisis of Classical Science', *Studies in Symbolic Interactionism,* 12: 223–51.

Silva, E. and A. Warde (eds) (2010) *Cultural Analysis and Bourdieu's Legacy: Settling Accounts and Developing Alternatives.* London: Routledge.

Simmel, G. (1923) 'Fragmente und Aufsatze aus dem Nachlass und Veroffentlichungen der letzten Jahre', Munich: Drei Masken Verlag.

– (1968) *Georg Simmel: The Conflict in Modern Culture and Other Essays*. Etzkorn, H. P. (ed.). New York: Teachers College Press.

– (1990 [1907]) *The Philosophy of Money*. London: Routledge.

– (1991) *Schopenhauer and Nietzsche*. Chicago: University of Illinois Press.

Simmel, G. (1997 [1911]) 'The Concept and the Tragedy of Culture' in *Simmel on Culture*, Frisby, D. and Featherstone, M. (eds). London: Sage, 55–74.

Simons, J. (1995) *Foucault and the Political*. London: Routledge.

Skeggs, B. (2004) 'The Re-branding of Class' in, F. Devine, M. Savage, J. Scott and R. Crompton (eds) (2004) *Rethinking Class: Culture, Identities, Lifestyle*. Basingstoke: Palgrave, 46–67.

Skinner, B. F. (1957) *Verbal Behaviour*. New York: Appleton-Century-Crofts.

– (1965 [1953]) *Science and Human Behaviour*. New York: Free Press.

Skinner, Q. (1969) 'Meaning and Understanding in the History of Ideas', *History and Theory*, 8: 3–53.

Sklair, L. (2004) *Globalization: Capitalism and its Alternatives*. Oxford: Oxford University Press.

Smart, B. (2002) *Michel Foucault*. London: Routledge.

Smelser, N. (1959) *Social Change in the Industrial Revolution: An Application of Theory to The British Cotton Industry*. Chicago: University of Chicago Press.

– (1990) 'Can Individualism Yield a Sociology?', *Contemporary Sociology*, 19(6): 778–83.

Smith, D. (1987) *The Everyday World as Problematic: A Feminist Sociology*. Toronto: University of Toronto Press.

– (1990a) *The Ideological Practice of Sociology: The Conceptual Practices of Power – A Feminist Sociology of Knowledge*. Toronto: University of Toronto Press.

– (1990b) *K is Mentally Ill: The Anatomy of a Factual Account, Texts, Facts and Femininity: Exploring the Relations of Ruling*. London: Routledge.

– (1997) 'Comment on Heckman's "Truth and Method": Feminist Standpoint Theory Revisited', *Signs*, 22(21): 392/7.

– (1999) *Telling the Truth After Post-Modernism, Writing the Social: Critique, Theory and Investigations*. Toronto: Toronto University Press.

– (2000) 'Schooling For Inequality', *Signs*, 25(4): 1147–51.

Smith, G. B. (2001) 'Gender Theory', *Encyclopaedia of European Social History*, Volume 1, Stearns, P. N. (ed.), New York: Scribner, 95–104.

Somers. M. (1996) 'Where is Sociology After the Historic Turn?' in McDonald, T. J. (ed.) *The Historic Turn in the Human Sciences*. Ann Arbor: Michigan State University Press, pp. 53–89.

Stark, W. (1961) 'Herbert Spencer's Three Sociologies', *American Sociological Review*, 26: 515–21.

Stavro, E. (1999) 'The Use and Abuse of Simone de Beauvoir: Re-Evaluating the French Poststructuralist Critique', *European Journal of Women's Studies*, 6: 263–80.

Straus, E. (1966) *Phenomenological Psychology*. New York: Basic Books, pp. 137–56.

Strauss, A. L. (1978) *Negotiations: Varieties, Contexts, Processes and Social Order*. San Francisco: Jossey-Bass.

Strydom, P. (2002) *Risk, Environment and Society*. Buckingham: Open University Press.

Stryker, S. (1980) *Symbolic Interactionism: A Social Structural Version*. Menlo Park: Benjamin Cummings.

Sturrock, J. (2002) *Structuralism*, 2nd edn. Oxford: Blackwell.

Sydie, R. A. (1987) *Natural Women, Cultured Men: A Feminist Perspective on Sociological Theory*. Milton Keynes: Open University Press.

Sztompka, P. (1993) *The Sociology of Social Change*. Oxford: Blackwell.

Therborn, G. (2010) *From Marxism to Post-Marxism*. London: Verso.

Thomas, W. I. and Znaniecki, F. (1984 [1918–1920]) *The Polish Peasant in Europe and America*. Urbana: University of Illinois Press.

Thorpe, C. (2011) 'The Dual-Edged Sword of Sociological Theory: Critically Thinking Sociological–Critical Theoretical Practice', *Distinktion: Scandinavian Journal of Social Theory*, 12(2): 215–28.

Tilly, C. (1997) 'James S. Coleman as a Guide to Social Research', *American Sociologist*, 28: 82–7.

Tomasi, L. (1998) *The Tradition of the Chicago School of Sociology*. Aldershot: Ashgate.

Tunstall, J. (1977) *The Media Are American*. London: Constable.

Turner, B. S. (1991) 'Neo-Functionalism and the "New Theoretical Movement": The Post-Parsonian Rapproachement between Germany and Britain' in Robertson, R. and Turner, B. S. (eds) *Talcott Parsons: Theorist of Modernity*. London: Sage, 234–49.

– (1996) *For Weber: Essays on the Sociology of Fate*. London: Sage.

Turner, J. H. (1986) 'Review: The Theory of Structuration', *American Journal of Sociology*, 91(4): 969–77.

Turner, J. H. and Maryanski, A. (2008) *On The Origin of Societies by Natural Selection*. Boulder, CO: Paradigm Press.

Turner, W. (2000) *A Genealogy of Queer Theory*. Philadelphia, PA: Temple University Press.

Urry, J. (2000a) 'Mobile Sociology', *British Journal of Sociology*, 51(1): 185–203.

– (2000b) *Sociology Beyond Societies*. London: Routledge.

– (2003) *Global Complexity*. Cambridge: Polity.

Van Assche, K. and Verschraegen, G. (2008) 'The Limits of Planning: Niklas Luhmann's Systems Theory and the Analysis of Planning and Planning Ambitions', *Planning Theory*, 7(3): 263–83.

Van Krieken, R. (1998) *Norbert Elias*. London: Routledge.

– (1998) 'What Does it Mean to be Civilized? Norbert Elias on the Germans and Modern Barbarism', *Communal/Plural*, 6(2): 225–33.

Venturi, R. (1966) *Complexity and Contradiction in Architecture*. New York: MOMA.

Venturi, R. et al. (1977 [1972]) *Learning from Las Vegas: The Forgotten Symbolism of Architectural Form*. Cambridge, MA: MIT Press.

Von Mises, L. (1949) *Human Action: A Treatise on Economics*. London: William Hodge.

Wacquant, L, (1989) 'Toward A Reflexive Sociology: A Workshop with Pierre Bourdieu', *Sociological Theory*, 7(1): 26–63.

– (2004) *Urban Outcasts: A Comparative Sociology of Advanced Marginality*. Cambridge: Polity.

Wajcman, J. (2004) *Technofeminism*. Cambridge: Polity.

Walby, S. (1990) *Theorizing Patriarchy*. Cambridge: Blackwell.

Wallerstein, I. (1974) *The Modern World-System I: Capitalist Agriculture and the Origins of the European World-Economy in the Sixteenth Century*. New York: Academic Press.

– (2004) *World-Systems Analysis: An Introduction*. Durham: Duke University Press.

Warnke, G. (1987) *Gadamer: Hermeneutics, Tradition and Reason*. Cambridge: Polity.

Waters, M. (1995) *Globalization*. London: Routledge.

Watson, K. (2005) 'Queer Theory', *Group Analysis*, 38(1): 67–81.

Weber, M. (1930) *The Protestant Ethic and the Spirit of Capitalism*. London: Methuen.

– (1978) *Max Weber: Selections in Translation*, Runciman, W. G. (ed.). Cambridge: Cambridge University Press.

– (1982) 'Class, Status, Party' in Gerth, H. H. and Mills, C. W. (eds) *From Max Weber*. London: Routledge.

Werbner, P. and Modood, T. (eds) (1997) *Debating Cultural Hybridity*. London: Zed.

Weingartner, R. H. (1959) 'Form and Content in Simmel's Philosophy of Life' in Wolff, K. H. (ed.) *Georg Simmel: A Collection of Essays*. Columbus: Ohio State University Press, pp. 33–60.

Wiggershaus, R. (1994) *The Frankfurt School*. Cambridge: Polity.

Williams, R. (1958) *Culture and Society 1780–1950*. London: Chatto.

Windelband, W. (1921) *An Introduction to Philosophy*. London: Unwin.

Wiley, N. (2006) 'Pragmatism and the Dialogical Self', *International Journal for Dialogical Science*, 1(1): 5–21.

Wirth, L. (1938) 'Urbanism as a Way of Life', *American Journal of Sociology*, 44(1): 1–24.

Wittgenstein, L. (2001 [1953]) *Philosophical Investigations*. Oxford: Blackwell.

Wolff, K. H. (ed.) (1959) *Georg Simmel: A Collection of Essays*. Columbus: Ohio State University Press.

Wood, E. M. (1989) 'Rational Choice Marxism: Is The Game Worth the Candle?', *New Left Review*, 177: 41–88.

Wrong, D. (1961) 'The Oversocialized Conception of Man in Modern Sociology', *American Sociological Review*, 26(2): 183–93.

Young, I. M. (1990) 'Throwing Like a Girl: A Phenomenology of Feminine Body Comportment, Motility and Spatiality' in *Throwing Like a Girl and Other Essays in Feminist Philosophy and Social Theory*, Bloomington: Indiana University Press.

Zafirovski, M. (1999) 'Unification of Sociological Theory by the Rational Choice Model: Conceiving the Relationship between Economics and Sociology', *Sociology*, 33(3): 495–514.

Zey, M. (1998) *Rational Choice Theory and Organisational Theory: A Critique*. London: Sage.

Žižek, S. (2006) *How To Read Lacan*. London: Granta.

Index